Security in 21st Century

21st Century Europe

General Editor: Helen Wallace

Drawing upon the latest research, this major series of concise thematically-organized texts provides state-of-the-art overviews of the key aspects of contemporary Europe from the Atlantic to the Urals for a broad student and serious general readership. Written by leading authorities in a lively and accessible style without assuming prior knowledge, each title is designed to synthesize and contribute to current knowledge and debate in its respective field.

PUBLISHED

Andrew Cottey: *Security in 21st Century Europe*
Christopher Lord and Erika Harris: *Democracy in the New Europe*
Colin Hay and Daniel Wincott: *The Political Economy of European Welfare Capitalism*

FORTHCOMING

Tom Casier and Sophie Vanhoonacker: *Europe and the World*
Klaus Goetz: *Governing 21st Century Europe*
Ben Rosamond: *Globalization and the European Union*
Anna Triandfyllidou: *What is Europe?*
Vivien Schmidt: *Political Economy of 21st Century Europe*

IN PREPARATION

Citizenship and Identity in 21st Century Europe
Society and Social Change in 21st Century Europe

21st Century Europe
Series Standing Order
ISBN 9780333960424 hardback
ISBN 9780333960431 paperback
(outside North America only)

You can receive future titles in this series as they are published. To place a standing order please contact your bookseller or, in the case of difficulty, write to us at the address below with your name and address, the title of the series and the ISBN quoted above.
Customer Services Department, Macmillan Distribution Ltd
Houndmills, Basingstoke, Hampshire RG21 6XS, England

Security in 21st Century Europe

Second Edition

Andrew Cottey

First published as *Security in the New Europe* in 2007
This edition 2013

Published by
PALGRAVE MACMILLAN

Palgrave Macmillan in the UK is an imprint of Macmillan Publishers Limited,
registered in England, company number 785998, of Houndmills, Basingstoke,
Hampshire RG21 6XS.

Palgrave Macmillan in the US is a division of St Martin's Press LLC,
175 Fifth Avenue, New York, NY 10010.

Palgrave Macmillan is the global academic imprint of the above companies
and has companies and representatives throughout the world.

Palgrave® and Macmillan® are registered trademarks in the United States,
the United Kingdom, Europe and other countries

ISBN 978-1-137-00646-2   hardback
ISBN 978-1-137-00645-5   paperback

This book is printed on paper suitable for recycling and made from fully
managed and sustained forest sources. Logging, pulping and manufacturing
processes are expected to conform to the environmental regulations of the
country of origin.

A catalogue record for this book is available from the British Library.

Library of Congress Cataloging-in-Publication Data
Cottey, Andrew.
Security in 21st century Europe / Andrew Cottey.—2nd ed.
p. cm.
ISBN 978–1–137–00645–5 (pbk.)—ISBN 978–1–137–00646–2
1. National security—Europe. 2. European Union—Military policy.
3. Europe—Military policy. I. Title.
UA646.C713 2013
355'.03304—dc23   2012024719

10   9   8   7   6   5   4   3   2   1
22 21 20 19 18 17 16 15 14 13

Printed and bound in China

This book is dedicated to my wife, Maeve, and my sons, Eoin, Oisin and Ultan, in the hope that the region of the world in which we live may continue to be stable and secure, and that we can help to bring at least some of that stability and security to less fortunate parts of the world.

Contents

List of Tables and Boxes

Tables

Boxes

List of Abbreviations

ABM	Anti-Ballistic Missile
ACP	African, Caribbean and Pacific
AFSJ	Area of Freedom, Security and Justice
AfT	Aid for Trade
ALTBMD	Active Layered Theatre Ballistic Missile Defence
AMM	Aceh Monitoring Mission
ARI	acute respiratory infections
ASEAN	Association of South East Asian Nations
AU	African Union
BRIC	Brazil, Russia, India and China
BTWC	Biological and Toxin Weapons Convention
CAP	Common Agricultural Policy
CBP	Customs and Border Protection
CBRN	chemical, biological, radiological and nuclear
CEPOL	European Police College
CESDP	Common European Security and Defence Policy
CFSP	Common Foreign and Security Policy
CIA	Central Intelligence Agency
CIS	Commonwealth of Independent States
COREPER	Committee of Permanent Representatives
CSCE	Conference on Security and Co-operation in Europe
CSDP	Common Security and Defence Policy
CSI	Container Security Initiative
CST/CSTO	Collective Security Treaty (Organization)
CTBT	Comprehensive Test Ban Treaty
CWC	Chemical Weapons Convention
DAC	(OECD) Development Assistance Committee
DRC	Democratic Republic of Congo
EaP	Eastern Partnership
EBA	Everything But Arms
EC	European Community
EDA	European Defence Agency
EDC	European Defence Community
EEAS	European External Action Service

EFSF	European Financial Stability Facility
EJN	European Judicial Network
EMP	Euro-Mediterranean Partnership
EMU	Economic and Monetary Union
ENP	European Neighbourhood Policy
EPC	European Political Co-operation
ESDI	European Security and Defence Identity
ESDP	European Security and Defence Policy
EU	European Union
EU BAM Moldova and Ukraine	EU Border Assistance Mission, Moldova and Ukraine
EU BAM Rafah	EU Border Assistance Mission, Rafah
EUFOR-Althea	EU Force Bosnia-Hercegovina/Operation Althea
EUFOR RD Congo	EU Force Democratic Republic of Congo
EUFOR TChad/ RCA	EU Force Chad/Central African Republic
EUJUST LEX	EU Integrated Rule of Law Mission for Iraq
EUJUST THEMIS	EU Rule of Law Mission to Georgia
EULEX	EU Rule of Law Mission in Kosovo
EUMC	EU Military Committee
EUMM Georgia	EU Monitoring Mission Georgia
EUMS	EU Military Staff
EUNAVFOR-Atalanta	EU Naval Force Somalia/Operation Atalanta
EUPM BiH	EU Police Mission Bosnia-Hercegovina
EUPAT	EU Police Advisory Team, Macedonia
EUPOL Afghanistan	EU Police Mission Afghanistan
EUPOL COPPS	EU Police Mission in Palestinian Territories
EUPOL KINSHASA	EU Police Mission in Kinshasa
EUPOL RD Congo	EU Police Mission Democratic Republic of Congo
EUSEC–DRC	EU Advisory and Assistance Mission for Security Reform in the DRC
EUSSR Guinea-Bissau	EU Mission in support for Security Sector Reform Guinea-Bissau

EUTM Somalia	EU Training Mission Somalia
FBI	Federal Bureau of Investigation
FIS	Islamic Salvation Front
FMCT	Fissile Material Cut-off Treaty
GATT	General Agreement on Tariffs and Trade
GDP	gross domestic product
GHG	greenhouse gas
GIA	Algerian Armed Islamic Group
GNI	gross national income
GNP	gross national product
GSP	Generalized System of Tariff Preferences
GUAM	Georgia, Ukraine, Azerbaijan and Moldova
IAEA	International Atomic Energy Agency
ICC	International Criminal Court
ICISS	International Commission on Intervention and State Sovereignty
IDP	internally displaced person
IFOR	Implementation Force, Bosnia-Hercegovina
IMU	Islamic Movement of Uzbekistan
INF	Intermediate Range Nuclear Forces
INTERFET	International Force for East Timor
ISAF	International Security Assistance Force, Afghanistan
JHA	Justice and Home Affairs
KFOR	Kosovo Force
LDC	least developed country
MAP	Membership Action Plan
MDG	Millennium Development Goals
MTCR	Missile Technology Control Regime
NATO	North Atlantic Treaty Organization
NIC	National Intelligence Council
NPT	Non-Proliferation Treaty
NRC	NATO–Russia Council
NSG	Nuclear Suppliers Group
ODA	overseas development aid
OSCE	Organization for Security and Co-operation in Europe
PAA	Phased Adaptive Approach
PCA	Partnership and Cooperation Agreement
PfP	Partnership for Peace
PJC	Permanent Joint Council

PNR	personal name records
PSC/COPS	Political and Security Committee
R2P	Responsibility to Protect
RABIT	Rapid Border Intervention Teams
RRT	Rapid Reaction Teams
SARS	severe acute respiratory syndrome
SCO	Shanghai Co-operation Organization
SDI	Strategic Defense Initiative
SFOR	Stabilization Force, Bosnia-Hercegovina
SIS	Schengen Information System
SPRING	Support for Partnership, Reform and Inclusive Growth
START	Strategic Arms Reduction Treaty
SWIFT	Society for Worldwide Interbank Financial Telecommunications
UfM	Union for the Mediterranean
UN	United Nations
UNFCCC	UN Framework Convention on Climate Change
UNMOT	UN Mission of Observers in Tajikistan
UNOMIG	UN Observer Mission in Georgia
UNPROFOR	UN Protection Force, Croatia/Bosnia-Hercegovina
UNSCR	United Nations Security Council Resolution
VIS	(Schengen) Visa Information System
WMD	weapon(s) of mass destruction
WTO	World Trade Organization

Foreword

The world of the early 21st century has become more complicated and more challenging than most of us could have imagined. Gone are the years of the tough binary contest between 'east' and 'west', a contest that was testing for both sides but one that with hindsight was relatively straightforward to characterize. In its place there is a confusing multipolar world, leaving the United States as a lonely superpower and an evolving reshaping of the global map in terms of shifting economic, political and security constellations. Moreover within many individual regions and countries deep processes of change seem to be at work with patterns that are hard to assess.

This context leaves Europeans with at least three different security problems. First, the definition of security has been extended to cover the range from the traditional military and defence issues to a whole spectrum of societal challenges. Second, Europe as such is much less important in global power terms than it used to be, and hence European governments and societies need to rethink their options and instruments in order to figure out what kind of provisions to make in order to enhance their security. In addition, it is hard to determine how far afield Europeans need to be engaged in order to contribute to efforts to create a safer world. Third, the geopolitical neighbourhood of Europe is one in which specific challenges continue to demand attention. All around the neighbourhood there are developments where the outcomes are uncertain. The Arab Spring has brought hopes of democratic transformation in previously authoritarian countries, yet the anchors for such a transformation are not so easy to find. The broader Middle Eastern region is plagued by serious security threats. South-eastern Europe still has unresolved problems about its development, albeit some encouraging progress is evident in parts, but only parts, of the western Balkans. Nor do we have a clear picture of the development of Russia as a global power and difficult neighbour.

Like its predecessor, *Security in the New Europe*, for which it is a very substantially revised and updated replacement, this volume not only provides a carefully crafted analysis of a complex subject but one which succeeds in illuminating on several levels. On the one hand, Andrew Cottey's assessment of the security challenges for Europe today, though nuanced and thoughtful, provides a straightforward account both accessible to the general reader and provocative for the student and specialist. On the other hand, he writes with empathy for the dilemmas facing policy-makers and citizens alike as they struggle to make sense of a confusing and unsettling world. This has been compounded by the global financial crisis that erupted in 2008 which brought turmoil to the eurozone and left Europeans with less political energy for dealing with other issues and with huge pressures on public spending, not least on defence and security budgets.

HELEN WALLACE

Preface

This book is a revised edition of a work first published by Palgrave Macmillan as *Security in the New Europe* (2007). It updates that earlier work, in particular addressing the implications of the 2008 global financial and economic crisis, the 2011 Arab Spring and the ongoing eurozone crisis of the early 2010s. The book is also the product of many years' interest in and research on European and global security. As such, I owe a debt of gratitude to the wider community of academics and policy-makers who have contributed to my thinking during that time. I would like to extend thanks to my colleagues in the Department of Government, University College Cork, for providing both intellectual stimulation and a supportive working environment. I wish particularly to thank series editor Helen Wallace and publisher Steven Kennedy for their support and for many helpful suggestions on the book's contents. I am grateful to Christiana Moos, visiting student at University College Cork in 2011, for helping in producing the tables for this book. The book also benefited from the comments of a number of colleagues, as well as anonymous reviewers, to whom I am grateful. The final contents are, of course, my own responsibility.

ANDREW COTTEY

Introduction

Since the mid-1980s three dramatic turning points have triggered major transformations in the international political order: the end of the Cold War in 1989, the 9/11 terrorist attacks in 2001 and the global financial and economic crisis in 2008. This book examines European security since the end of the Cold War, exploring the ways in which these three turning points have altered the European security agenda and the policy challenges facing states, societies and international security institutions, in particular the European Union (EU) and the North Atlantic Treaty Organization (NATO). From the late 1940s to the late 1980s, the European security agenda was defined by the Cold War division of the continent and the challenges of defence, deterrence and crisis management between East and West. The dramatic and unexpected collapse of the Eastern European communist regimes in 1989 brought this era to an end. Suddenly, governments faced the challenge of constructing a new post-Cold War European security and responding to violent conflict in post-communist Europe, in particular the wars in former Yugoslavia. A decade later the 9/11 terrorist attacks ushered in a second new era: globalized Islamic terrorism moved to the centre of the security agenda and the USA initiated two major wars – in Afghanistan and Iraq – the repercussions of which are still being felt. The Bush administration's 'war on terror', further, constituted a radical policy response to the threats posed by terrorism, the proliferation of weapons of mass destruction and so-called rogue states, emphasizing the unilateral assertion of American power and a willingness to use military force, including pre-emptively. Other states therefore faced the challenge of responding not only to globalized Islamic terrorism but also to what some described as a revolution in US foreign policy (Daalder and Lindsay, 2003). In 2008 a third turning point – the global financial and economic crisis – once again transformed the international political order: if the 1990s and the early 2000s had been an era of Western, especially US, domination, the 2008 financial and economic crisis suggested that that era had come to an end. Although the 2008 crisis was triggered by specific problems in the US economy, it was also intertwined with another longer-term trend: the rising economic power of major non-Western states, most prominently

1

China, but also other countries such as India and Brazil. What Fareed Zakaria terms 'the rise of the rest' constitutes a shift of world historic proportions and will fundamentally reshape the international economic, political and security order (Zakaria, 2009).

In this context, European states and the continent's two primary security institutions, the EU and NATO, have faced, and continue to face, a range of new security challenges. The end of the Cold War triggered a far-reaching debate over what kind of security order Europe needs – a debate which has resulted in major adaptations to both the EU and NATO since the early 1990s, but remains unresolved. The Yugoslav conflict of the 1990s was the first of a series of so-called new wars which raised large questions about military intervention as a tool of humanitarian goals and the viability of international nation-building operations – questions which subsequently resurfaced in Afghanistan, Iraq and Libya and will likely continue to face European states and the EU and NATO. In the wake of the 9/11 terrorist attacks on the USA, the March 2004 Madrid and July 2005 London bombings illustrated that Europe too was a target of globalized Islamic terrorism, raising major questions about how to tackle terrorism internationally and how to strike the appropriate balance between security and liberty domestically. The prospect that an increasing number of states may obtain nuclear, biological or chemical weapons has generated much debate about the extent of the threat posed by weapons of mass destruction (WMD), and what can and should be done to prevent their proliferation – a debate that has particular resonance for Europe because of its direct vulnerability to Iran should that country acquire nuclear weapons. Since the early 1990s, there has also been a growing recognition that non-military challenges – the global economic divide between rich and poor, climate change, dependence on external energy supplies, the spread of HIV/AIDs and other infectious diseases, mass migration and organized crime – may pose threats to the security and stability of states, including in Europe.

This book explores the nature of security in the new Europe of the early 21st century, and European responses to the new security agenda. It examines the changing character of security in contemporary Europe, the nature and extent of the threats posed by different security problems, and the policy challenges and dilemmas involved in responding to these problems. Its central argument is that European security has been reshaped fundamentally by the intersection between two developments: the development of a security community – a zone of peace where war is inconceivable – across much of Europe and the emergence of a set of new security challenges – in particular, new wars, proliferation and terrorism – beyond the borders of that security community.

Chapter 1 of this book examines the European security order of the early 21st century, arguing that the emergence of a security community in Western Europe since 1945 has fundamentally transformed the nature of European security. The term 'security community' is used here in the sense developed by Karl Deutsch, meaning a group of states between whom war and the use of force has become extremely unlikely, if not impossible (Deutsch *et al.*, 1969; Adler and Barnett, 1998). The Western European/North Atlantic security community has not only outlived the Cold War which helped to give birth to it but has also, since the 1990s, expanded to include the swathe of Central and Eastern European countries stretching from the Baltic to the Black Sea. The membership of the European security community is essentially the largely overlapping memberships of the EU and NATO, but while the EU and NATO may be central pillars of the European security community, that security community is not formally defined by or linked to either institution. Since the end of the Cold War, that security community is now the defining feature of the new European security landscape. Whereas the historic problem for European security was the risk of war – above all, great power war – within Europe, at the beginning of the 21st century the likelihood of such conflict is low, and the traditional pattern of balance of power politics and competing alliances has been replaced by the European security community (although, as is noted below and is returned to in the conclusion to this book, the ongoing crisis surrounding the euro in the early 2010s has raised fundamental questions about the future of the EU that could even call into question the continuity of the post-1945 European security community).

Chapter 2 examines the new global security agenda emerging beyond the borders of the European security community. It explores the threats posed by new wars, proliferation, terrorism and non-military security problems. Increasingly, European security is likely to revolve around the issue of how Europe responds to these global security challenges rather than the historic problem of war and peace within Europe. The chapter also examines the shifting global balance of economic and political power, in particular the rising power of the non-West and its implications for Europe: if in the past Europe – as part of the larger West – played a central role in shaping the international order and responses to international security problems, in future

Europe's and the West's ability to shape the international order will increasingly be constrained by the power, interests and priorities of the non-Western world.

Chapter 3 examines the transatlantic relationship, which has been at the heart of European security since the Second World War. It argues that, despite efforts to rejuvenate the transatlantic alliance and NATO's adoption of a variety of new roles, relations between Europe and America are now characterized by a continuing uneasy mix of co-operation, divergence and conflict. It concludes that the era when America and Europe were each other's default allies is coming to an end.

Parallel to this, the EU has since the end of the Cold War developed a growing security role. Chapter 4 examines the evolution of the EU as a foreign, security and defence policy actor, highlighting the Union's assumption – in the 1990s and 2000s – of increasing responsibility for security within Europe and, to some extent, also of a global role. The chapter concludes, however, by noting the way in which the crisis surrounding the euro in the early 2010s has called into question the future of the EU as a foreign policy actor, and even of the European integration project in its entirety.

Chapter 5 addresses Russia's position as the largest European power outside the European security community. It argues that Russia is not likely to become a full member of the European security community for the foreseeable future, and that Russia's relationship with that community is likely to continue to be characterized by an uneasy mix of co-operation and conflict. It also argues that both the security problems Russia faces and those it poses for others are likely to result from the unusual mix of great power strength and internal weakness that characterizes contemporary Russia.

The second half of the book – Chapters 6 to 9 – examines European perspectives on and responses to core aspects of the new global security agenda: the dilemmas of intervention in new wars; WMD proliferation; the new terrorism; and non-military security problems. These chapters show that European states and organizations, in particular the EU, are playing a growing role in addressing global security challenges beyond Europe, but also that they place a strong emphasis on multilateralism and soft power, in contrast to a US approach that emphasizes unilateralism and hard power. Europe's role in addressing the new global security agenda is, however, constrained by its limited hard power capacity, and by the politically fragmented nature of the EU as an international actor.

The book concludes by assessing the overall state of European security in the early 2010s. It highlights the way in which the consolidation of a security community across much of the continent has dramatically enhanced the security of Europe as a whole. Although there are important regional variations in security within Europe – the countries of the Balkans and the former Soviet Union, in particular, face much more serious security threats than the rest of Europe – the low likelihood of continent-wide great power war means that Europe and European citizens are more secure than they have been at any time in the continent's history. Furthermore, although problems such as terrorism and WMD proliferation pose serious threats to European states and their citizens, in terms of consequences these are not comparable to the Cold War threat of nuclear annihilation, nor to the historic danger of great power war in Europe. The conclusion also, however, highlights the significance of the rising power of the non-Western world and its implications for Europe and European security. Europe will increasingly live in a world in which it is (at least relatively) a declining force, where major non-Western powers are actors rather than objects and in which advancing European interests and addressing security challenges will require the building of shared interests and visions with non-Western states.

The conclusion to the book additionally discusses the way in which Europe appears, in 2011–12, to have entered a period of radical uncertainty, calling into question the future direction of European security and in particular of the EU. In the wake of the 2008 global financial crisis, steps were taken – in particular, economic stimulus plans by the major economies – that helped to avert a second great depression equivalent to that of the 1930s. By 2011–12, however, two interrelated concerns had emerged: first, a major debt crisis involving many of the eurozone countries and threatening to trigger the break-up of the euro, and second, the possibility that the global economy might still enter a 1930s-style depression. The conclusion discusses the range of possible scenarios that might emerge from this crisis and their likely implications for European security. Although some observers warn of the possibility of a return to Europe's war-prone past, I argue that, on balance, it is more likely that Europe's post-1945 security community will endure.

Chapter 1

Security in 21st Century Europe

This chapter explores the nature of security in early 21st century Europe. The first section examines what we mean by security, highlighting the contested nature of the concept, the difficulty of assessing threats to security, and the inherent security policy dilemmas commonly faced by governments. The rest of the chapter addresses the changing character of security in contemporary Europe. The central argument presented here, and one of the core theses of this book, is that the emergence of a security community, a zone of peace where war is inconceivable, has fundamentally transformed Europe. This security community emerged in Western Europe after the Second World War and has expanded to include much of Central and Eastern Europe since the end of the Cold War. Since the emergence of the modern nation-state system, the central problem of European security has been the risk of war, in particular of continent-wide great power war. The ever-present risk of war and the associated insecurity of states have also driven much of Europe's international politics, resulting in a system of balance of power politics and competing alliances. Although Cold War Europe differed from previous eras in important ways, the East–West conflict conformed to the historical pattern of a continent defined by balance of power politics, competing alliances and the risk of great power war. The end of the Cold War raised major questions about the prospects for war and peace in Europe, and the future direction of European security. Some argued that Europe was likely to return to its pre-Cold War pattern of a multipolar balance of power and that this would increase the danger of war on the continent (Mearsheimer, 1990). Instead, the Western European security community that emerged during the Cold War has outlasted the historical circumstances that gave rise to it, and is now the defining feature of the new European security landscape. The emergence and consolidation of this security community has dramatically reduced the likelihood of war in Europe and in so doing fundamentally transformed the nature of security in Europe. This chapter explores the nature and implications of this transformation. It concludes by analysing the prospects for the European security community in light of the global and European financial and economic crisis since 2008.

Security: a problematical concept

Analysis of security issues is inherently problematical, for a number of reasons. Although the term 'security' is widely used, it is broad and open-ended. The meaning of security is thus open to a variety of different interpretations and is often contested. In a general sense, security – being secure – implies the absence of threats or a lack of vulnerability. *Oxford Dictionaries*, for example, defines security as 'the state of being free from danger or threat ... the safety of a state or organization against criminal activity such as terrorism, theft, or espionage' (Oxford Dictionaries, 2011). Security is therefore a general term applicable to individuals or any social group and relating to a wide range of issues – from an individual's personal or psychological security, to a state's security against external attack, to humanity's security from global threats such as climate change. In international politics, however, security has come to have a narrower and more specific meaning centred on war and peace, and the protection of the territorial integrity and political independence of the nation-state from the threat or use of violent force. Writing during the Second World War, the American commentator Walter Lippman described security as the extent to which a nation is not in danger of having to sacrifice core values, if it wishes to avoid war, and is able, if challenged to maintain them, by victory in war (quoted in Wolfers, 1962, p. 150). This conception of security became widespread in international politics in the wake of the Second World War and in the context of the Cold War. What has come to be described as the traditional or narrow definition of security (Buzan *et al.*, 1998, p. 21) thus focuses on the military security of states, but has an important political dimension in that it also relates to the ability of states to maintain their freedom, independence and values (such as democracy).

Critics of the traditional definition of security argue that invasion, war and violent coercion are not the only potential threats to states' security or necessarily the most serious or pressing security problems. A wide range of non-military problems – dependence on foreign economic resources (such as oil or finance), environmental degradation, mass migration, transnational organized crime and pandemic diseases such as HIV/AIDS – may threaten the security of states and their citizens. Such critics argue for the broadening of the concept to include 'soft' security challenges or a range of non-military 'sectors' (Tuchman Mathews, 1989; Buzan *et al.*, 1998). The danger with this logic is that security may come to include virtually all international problems and in so doing arguably becomes so broad as to be meaningless (Walt, 1991). In the end, what constitutes security or a threat to security is subjective – it depends on *perceptions* of which communities, values and institutions matter, and the threats to those communities, values and institutions. Security therefore is not something that can be objectively defined or of which there is likely to be an agreed definition. The subjective nature of security points to another important issue: how and why do individuals or communities define some issues or problems (but not others) as security problems or threats? This process has been described as securitization and involves the definition of an issue as an existential threat requiring extraordinary or emergency measures above and beyond the bounds of normal day-to-day politics (Buzan *et al.*, 1998, pp. 23–6). Since the early 1990s, we have seen the securitization of a wide range of non-military issues including international economic relations, global environmental problems, mass migration, transnational organized crime and pandemic diseases (in particular HIV/AIDS), with governments and international organizations defining these problems as threats to security and seeking to mobilize action and resources on this basis. The nature and extent of the security threat posed by these problems and how states should respond to them, however, remain contentious. This issue is explored in more depth in the next chapter. European responses to this broader security agenda are returned to in Chapter 9.

A second problem with the concept of security revolves around the question of 'Whose security?' The traditional or narrow definition of security focuses on the nation-state as the 'referent object' (the entity facing threats and requiring protection) and is associated with the idea of national security. This state-centric focus, however, is problematical in two important ways. First, the focus on national security may in fact risk undermining security. Measures taken by one state to enhance its security risk provoking similar responses from other states, thus undermining the security of the first state and increasing the likelihood of war. This action–reaction dynamic is common in international politics and is referred to as the security dilemma, since states remain vulnerable if they do not take action to provide for their security but risk provoking damaging counter-actions if they act (Buzan, 1991a, pp. 294–327; Herz, 1950; Jervis, 1978). Critics have argued that the state-centric focus of national security needs to be replaced with a focus on co-operative approaches to the security of all states – variously termed collective security, international security, common security, co-operative security or a security regime (Jervis, 1982, 1985; Palme Commission, 1982; Buzan, 1991a, pp. 328–62; Carter *et al.*, 1992; Zartman and Kremenyuk, 1995). Second, drawing on classical liberal thinking, the state-centric concept of national security assumes that the state provides security for its citizens by maintaining order within its borders and protection against external threats. In many cases, however, states fail to provide for the security of their citizens and may even be the primary threat to their security. Through authoritarian rule, human rights abuses, and in extreme cases genocide, states often threaten the physical security, well-being and survival of their citizens. In multi-ethnic states, the state is often perceived as threatening by minority populations. Internally weak or failed states may be unable to provide the basic order necessary for security. Critics therefore argue that the state-centric concept of national security should be supplemented, or perhaps even replaced, by a focus on other referent objects such as the individual, society or humanity as a whole (Buzan, 1991a, pp. 35–56; Waever *et al.*, 1993; Buzan *et al.*, 1998, pp. 36–42 and 145–50; Commission on Human Security, 2003). From a European perspective, this debate on referent objects raises questions as to how far the traditional nation-state focus of European security is being, or should be, replaced by a focus on the security of the European Union, or alternatively the broader European continent.

Assessing threats to security is also inherently problematical (Buzan, 1991a, pp. 112–45). Threat assessment depends on information about the external world, yet such information is inevitably uncertain. Information about other states' military capabilities is rarely fully reliable, since all states are secretive about their armed forces and governments must rely on various forms of intelligence. Even if we have reasonably accurate knowledge of other states' military capabilities, however, assessing the significance and implications of these is often difficult. Assessing other actors' intentions is even more problematical, depending on inferences drawn from material capabilities, intelligence information on those intentions, past experiences and our own prejudices (Jervis, 1976). Furthermore, intentions are not static but may change over time and in response to changing external circumstances. In addition, others may try to deceive regarding their capabilities or intentions. Equally, our own assumptions and biases may give us a distorted view of the world. Given these problems, it is not surprising that history is replete with examples of threats that have been underestimated, exaggerated or misunderstood. While technological advances, in particular the development of reconnaissance satellites, may have significantly improved the information available to some states, the intelligence failures relating to Iraq's weapons of mass destruction (WMD) capabilities prior to the 2003 Iraq War show that the underlying problems of threat assessment remain (Butler Committee, 2004; Gormley, 2004; Commission on the Intelligence Capabilities of the United States Regarding Weapons of Mass Destruction, 2005; Hart and Simon, 2006). More broadly, assessment of the relative importance and urgency of different threats depends on a diverse range of factors including geographical location, political values and socio-economic circumstances. In a global context, therefore, states' threat assessments are bound to differ.

Security policy choices are equally problematical. Since policy decisions depend on threat assessments, they are deeply vulnerable to all the problems of threat assessment noted above. And policy decisions involve not only analysing others' capabilities and intentions, but also their likely reaction to our own actions: 'If we do X, how will they react? Are they more likely to do Y or Z?' The problem of assessing the likely reactions of others to our actions multiplies the uncertainty inherent in security policy decision-making, and makes the security dilemma referred to above one of the defining problems of international politics. Security policy-making is further complicated by the broader problem of unintended consequences. Blowback, where a state's foreign or security policy choices have major unintended negative consequences for that state, is a common phenomenon (Johnson, 2000). Few if any observers, for example, predicted that by arming Islamic guerrillas fighting the Soviet Union in Afghanistan in the 1980s the United States of America (USA) would help to fuel a global anti-American Islamic terrorist movement a decade later. The complexity and interconnectedness of the global political and economic system also means that it is vulnerable to 'system complexity effects', where a small action in one place can have indirect but major consequences elsewhere, or even on the system as a whole (Jervis, 1997).

Since actors also have other goals such as prosperity and freedom, security policy decision-making involves important trade-offs between competing goals. Analysts have argued that without survival the achievement of other goals is impossible, and that security – maintaining the survival of the state, society or community – is (or should be) the paramount goal. While states and other actors do sometimes face truly existential security crises, the choice between security and other goals is often not so absolute. Total security – complete invulnerability to a particular potential threat – is rarely, if ever, possible, so states and other actors normally have to live with a degree of insecurity. Security policy-making therefore often involves choices about the priority and resources to be allocated to security alongside other goals: what proportion of political, economic and other resources should be directed towards addressing a given security problem? What are the costs, both direct and indirect, in terms of opportunity costs, of responding to this security problem? Two forms of trade-off are particularly commonplace, between security and welfare, and between security and freedom. The security–welfare (or 'guns versus butter') trade-off involves decisions about the allocation of limited economic resources: expenditure on armed forces, police, border controls or other material security measures reduces funding available for health, education and other collective goods, and vice versa (Russett, 1982; Buzan, 1991a, pp. 272–4). Since armed forces are usually one of the largest components of state expenditure, debates on the security–welfare trade-off are commonplace. Such debates were ever-present in Europe during the Cold War. The end of the Cold War and the consequent reduction in, if not disappearance of, direct military threats to Western Europe reduced the salience of these 'guns versus butter' debates within Europe. The financial and economic crisis since 2008, however, has led European governments to further reduce defence expenditure – as part of more general budget cuts – leading observers such as NATO Secretary General Anders Fogh Rasmussen and US Secretary of Defense Robert Gates to warn that European states are seriously damaging their ability to contribute to peacekeeping or intervention operations and collective defence (Fogh Rasmussen, 2011; Gates, 2011b). The security–freedom trade-off relates to the danger that measures taken to enhance security may undermine the freedom and values on which democratic societies are based. Surveillance of potential domestic threats, arrest and detention without trial, limits on free speech, and other intrusions into people's privacy and constraints on their liberty are quite often justified by political leaders as responses to security threats. Such measures, however, threaten fundamental democratic principles that limit the arbitrary power of the state. They can also easily descend into witch-hunts, as occurred in the USA during the McCarthy era of the 1950s. European democracies have long experienced such dilemmas in relation to terrorist threats. In the wake of the

9/11 terrorist attacks, however, balancing freedom and security became a more acute problem.

Security is also open to abuse. Authoritarian regimes often justify repressive measures as being vital to the security of the state. Scapegoating, where leaders create or exaggerate external or internal threats in order to mobilize support, is commonplace in international politics and viewed by some analysts as an important cause of wars (Levy, 1989, pp. 92–8). Leaders may use the language of security to justify aggressive policies. State bureaucracies – defence and interior ministries, police and intelligence services – may develop institutional interest in particular security policies and the threats that underpin them. What governments and leaders do in the name of security should therefore not be taken at face value.

In summary, security is a deeply problematical concept. The problems identified here – the open-ended and disputed meaning of the term security, the question of whose security is being dealt with, the difficulty of assessing threats to security, the inherent security policy dilemmas faced by states, the trade-offs between security and other objectives, and the potential abuse of the concept – suggest that, for all its ubiquity, security is likely to remain a contested concept; that security poses some inherent dilemmas; and that security policies are likely to remain highly contentious.

The European security community

Historically, the defining problem of European security has been the danger of war, especially continent-wide war embracing Europe's major powers. As Kenneth Minogue (2000, p. 52) has put it, 'The history of Europe has largely been a story of war … preparing for war, waging war, or recovering from war.' Modern European history has been characterized by a series of continent-wide major wars: the Thirty Years' War in the early 17th century, the Seven Years' War in the mid-18th century, the Napoleonic wars at the beginning of the 19th century, and the First and Second World Wars and the Cold War in the 20th century. Even during periods of relative peace, lesser wars have been commonplace, while the risk of escalation to great power war has loomed in the background. Wars and the resort to violent force have generally resulted from two types of threat. Major powers have periodically posed what may be termed hegemonic threats, seeking to dominate the entire European continent – as in the cases of Napoleonic

France, Nazi Germany and arguably Soviet Russia. Aspiring hegemons have triggered wars either through their own efforts at aggrandizement or by provoking responses from other major powers trying to maintain the status quo. A second cause of war and resort to violent force may be termed revolutionary threats – that is, domestic political challenges to the status quo such as nationalist challenges to empires, democratic challenges to monarchies, and communism's challenge to capitalism. Such challenges have resulted in the violent overthrow of regimes (as with the revolutions of 1848 and 1917) or the use of force by rulers to suppress revolutionary movements. Often the two types of threat have been intertwined, with revolutionary domestic political change triggering both hegemonic ambitions and threats to the wider political status quo. Within this context, the dominant pattern of international relations in Europe has been balance of power politics: states have sought to advance their own interests and power and have balanced against potential hegemons, resulting in a shifting pattern of alliances reflecting changes in the distribution of power and/or domestic political regimes.

In security terms, the Europe of the early 21st century is radically different from its past, as the likelihood of war between Europe's major powers is lower than at any time in modern history. In contrast to the competing alliances of the past, Europe is dominated by a process of political, economic and security integration centred on the European Union (EU) and the North Atlantic Treaty Organization (NATO). The key development underpinning this has been the emergence of a security community, or what Singer and Wildavsky (1993) call a 'zone of peace'. This security community emerged in Western Europe during the Cold War, but has outlasted the end of the Cold War and subsequently expanded into Central and Eastern Europe. A security community is a group of states among whom conflicts are resolved by peaceful means, so there is a high expectation that this norm will be maintained and that war would therefore be extremely unlikely, if not inconceivable (Deutsch *et al.*, 1969; Adler and Barnett, 1998). In contrast to the historical pattern of conflict and war between Britain, France, Germany and the other states of Western Europe, an unprecedented period of peace has now developed between these countries.

Some observers suggest that Europe is characterized by the existence of two security communities, one transatlantic and based on NATO, and a second European and based on the EU. If a security community is understood as a group of states between whom war has become extremely unlikely if not inconceivable, however, it makes more sense to think in terms of a single European security community: the memberships of NATO and the EU, after all, largely overlap and it is this group of states – rather than a particular organization such as NATO or the EU – that constitutes the European security community. Alternatively, if there is a distinctive European security community it may be viewed as part of a larger transatlantic or Western security community which includes the USA and Canada (and in a larger Western version also Australia and Japan). In addition, although a security community may develop common policies towards neighbouring states or regions or indeed globally, the term as used here does not presume such a development. While the existence of a European security community may facilitate the development of common policies towards the rest of the world (whether in the context of the EU, NATO or more generally), therefore, it should not be assumed that the existence of a security community makes such a process inevitable or that it determines the extent or nature of policy co-ordination towards the outside world.

The emergence of this security community has fundamentally altered the nature of European security. In the past, European security was based on the possibility of war between Europe's major powers and the resulting balance of power politics, alliance building and military preparations. Today, European security is based increasingly on the assumption that primary security threats arise from outside the security community. And the development of this security community has gone hand-in-hand with the consolidation of democracy, unprecedented prosperity, and institutionalized co-operation and integration in both the EU and NATO. As a consequence, the existence of a security community in the western half of the continent is the defining feature of the new European security order, not only precluding war between its members but also acting as a dominant pole of attraction for most of the continent. This, furthermore, is a global rather than purely European phenomenon: the USA and other Western states (such as Canada, Australia, New Zealand and Japan) are part of a larger security community among the major industrialized democracies (Mueller, 1990; Buzan, 1991b; Jervis, 1991–2, 2002; Goldgeier and McFaul, 1992). The existence of this security community has fundamental implications for world politics.

Assessments of the origins of the Western European security community and of the prospects for peace in contemporary Europe depend in significant part on underlying assumptions about the nature of international politics. Realist theorists of international relations argue that the anarchic nature of the international system drives security competition among states, and issues of war and peace are determined by the balance of power (Morgenthau, 1985; Waltz, 1979). From this perspective, the Cold War confrontation and nuclear deterrence helped to keep the peace between East and West after 1945, while the existence of a unifying external threat (the Soviet Union), the support of a benign hegemonic power (the USA) and the division of Germany underpinned the development of peaceful co-operation in Western Europe (Gaddis, 1986; Kegley, 1991). Realists argued that, with the end of the Cold War, multiple centres of power would re-emerge, and an unstable multipolar balance of power and pattern of shifting alliances would be the result. Germany might be driven to develop nuclear weapons in order to provide for its own security, and the likelihood of war within Europe would increase significantly. In short, Europe might well return to the war-prone system that existed before 1945 (Mearsheimer, 1990).

In contrast, liberal theorists argue that security competition and war result not simply from the effects of international anarchy, but more from the aggressive ambitions of states and leaders and from the absence of mechanisms for managing relations between states. Liberals see common democratic values, close economic ties, free trade and international institutions as means of promoting peace between states (Keohane and Nye, 2001). From this perspective, while the Soviet threat, American hegemony and the division of Germany may have played an important role in facilitating the development of the Western European security community, that community is underpinned by other equally important factors. First, a high degree of interdependence – intensive international and transnational economic, political and societal ties – developed between the countries of Western Europe, increasing the costs of using force within the community and creating groups with an interest in the maintenance of peaceful co-operation. Second, Western Europe has developed an unprecedented network of international institutions based around the EU and NATO that provide mechanisms for the resolution of disputes and reinforce perceptions of common interest (Keohane *et al.*, 1993). Third, the democratic peace hypothesis suggests that common democratic values and the constraints imposed by democratic governance make war between democracies unlikely (Brown *et al.*, 1999; Russett, 1993). Bruce Russett and John Oneal (2001) argue that interdependence, international institutions and democracy form a reinforcing tripod underpinning the European and wider Western security community. Liberals therefore argued that the Western European security community would outlast the Cold War that helped to establish it (Van Evera, 1990–91; Jervis, 2002). To date, developments since the end of the Cold War have vindicated the liberal perspective. The security community that emerged after 1945 has remained deeply entrenched among the major Western powers, and as the second decade of the 21st century progresses, war appears to be very unlikely among its members.

The Western security community, further, not only survived the end of the Cold War but also expanded eastwards to include much of Central and Eastern Europe (Gambles, 1995). The collapse of communism and the end of the Cold War generated fears of a significantly increased likelihood of war and violent conflict in Central and Eastern Europe and the former Soviet Union (Nelson, 1991; Smith, 1991). The region was a potential tinderbox of unresolved disputes over borders and ethnic minorities. Difficult post-communist political and economic transitions might result in the emergence of demagogic nationalist and authoritarian regimes, exacerbating tensions with ethnic minorities and neighbouring states. Post-communist political and economic change might also generate new non-military security problems, such as mass migration and transnational organized crime. The problems of post-communist transition have led some to describe the region as a 'wild east' (Fishman, 2003; Swift, 2004), characterized by instability and violent conflict. Fears of an upsurge of conflict in post-communist Europe appeared to be confirmed by the onset of war in Yugoslavia 1991 and the subsequent conflicts in Bosnia in the mid-1990s and in Kosovo in 1999.

Viewing the security situation in Central and Eastern Europe through the lens of the Yugoslav conflict, however, provided a misleading perspective. The worst-case scenario of endemic instability across the region, with multiple Yugoslav-style conflicts, a widespread collapse of democracy and massive population movements, was avoided. Despite the Yugoslav conflict, setbacks to democracy in some states (such as Belarus) and conflicts in parts of the former Soviet Union, there has been progress towards democratic consolidation in Central and Eastern Europe, border and ethnic minority disputes have largely been managed without resort to violence and, while countries face serious economic and social challenges, these have not in most cases fundamentally destabilized states. The Western security community has also been a significant stabilizing influence in Central and Eastern Europe, providing a powerful impetus for reform and moderation within the region.

In the context of democratization and integration with Western institutions, Central and Eastern European states have made significant efforts to overcome historic disputes and develop new cooperative relationships (both bilaterally and multilaterally). Given the region's history, perhaps most significant has been the historic – but not always widely recognized – rapprochement between Germany and Poland. Since the early 1990s, Germany and Poland have developed a significant political, economic and military partnership (Cottey, 1995, pp. 40–2; Gardner Feldman, 1999). Although some tensions between the two countries resurfaced in the 2000s (for example, over relations with Russia, and over compensation for Germans expelled from Poland after the Second World War – see Associated Press, 2006), Poland is now a member of NATO and the EU alongside Germany and such tensions appear unlikely to lead to serious political (let alone military) conflict. War appears as unlikely today between Germany and Poland as it is between Germany and France – a remarkable development given the history of relations between the two countries. Elsewhere in the region, there have been significant improvements in historically conflictual relations between Hungary and its neighbours; Poland and its eastern neighbours; the Baltic States and Russia; and Romania, Bulgaria and their neighbours (Wohlfeld, 1997; Cottey, 1999b). New multilateral subregional co-operation frameworks such as the Visegrad Group (which brings together Poland, the Czech Republic, Slovakia and Hungary), the Council of Baltic Sea States and the Black Sea Economic Co-operation group have also been established (Cottey, 1999a). The Central and Eastern European states have also been institutionally and functionally integrated into the EU and NATO, a process that began with various co-operation arrangements established in the early and mid-1990s and culminated in full membership for a significant number of states in the late 1990s and 2000s. Overall, these developments suggest that the process of security community building based around democratic consolidation, interdependence and institutional integration that occurred in Western Europe after the Second World War has been repeated in postcommunist Central and Eastern Europe. This process has extended Western Europe's zone of peace into Central and Eastern Europe. As is discussed in more detail below, however, some major powers, in particular Russia and to some extent also Turkey, remain outside this zone of peace, as do some subregions of Europe, in particular the former Soviet Union.

Institutionalized security co-operation

A second defining feature of contemporary Europe is institutionalized security co-operation (Keohane *et al.*, 1993). Attempts at building co-operative security institutions are not new in European history, as the 19th-century Concert of Europe and the inter-war League of Nations illustrate. The extent and nature of institution building that has taken place since 1945, however, is radically different from that of previous eras. An unprecedented set of overlapping security institutions has been established, providing multiple frameworks in which states co-operate and co-ordinate their policies. Since 1949 NATO has provided a framework for military integration among its members and the co-ordination of policies towards external security challenges – the Soviet bloc during the Cold War, the new security problems of Central and Eastern Europe since the end of the Cold War, and more recently beyond Europe. The EU is a unique exercise in political and economic integration, driven – especially in its early years – by the implicit security goal of making war among its members impossible. Since the end of the Cold War, the EU has intensified efforts at building a common external foreign, security and defence policy, as well as enhancing internal security co-operation.

Beyond NATO and the EU, there are other less well-known European security institutions. The continent-wide Conference on Security and Co-operation in Europe (CSCE, renamed the Organization for Security and Co-operation in Europe – OSCE – in 1994) emerged as a framework for East–West détente during the 1970s, but has subsequently developed roles in promoting democracy and human rights, and in conflict prevention and post-conflict peace-building. The Council of Europe, which was initially a Western European organization but has now expanded to include most post-communist states, also plays a role in promoting democracy and human rights. The various subregional institutions noted above also address a variety of non-military security challenges, such as environmental problems and transnational crime. In short, European security at the beginning of the 21st century is deeply institutionalized: states co-operate with each other in a range of different institutions and across the spectrum of different security issues. In particular, the national security and defence policies of the members of the EU and NATO are increasingly co-ordinated and integrated into common policies towards external security challenges.

Some critics view these security institutions as a mask hiding more traditional calculations of state power and interest, and thus being of little substance. Realists may well be correct that the Soviet threat, US hegemony and the division of Germany made the establishment of NATO and the EU possible, but this does not necessarily mean that these institutions have no substance independent of these developments, or that they will not outlive the historical circumstances that gave rise to them. The existence and development of these institutions is in part a reflection of the emergence of the European security community: freed from the past risk of war with one another, the members of the security community now view external problems, rather than each other, as the primary threats to their security. Combined with the consolidation of common democratic values, this has facilitated the emergence of broad common security interests among the members of the European security community. In this context, it is hardly surprising that the countries of Western Europe, joined since the end of the Cold War by the new democracies of Central and Eastern Europe, have sought to conduct their national security policies through institutions such as the EU and NATO: these institutions provide a mechanism for countries to address common security challenges and to increase their leverage *vis-à-vis* those security challenges by acting collectively. The development of security institutions may also be a self-reinforcing process: membership of these institutions and the functional dynamics of co-operation reinforce perceptions of common interests and help to create the sense of common identity on which these institutions are in part based.

Enlargement and its consequences and limits

The third defining feature of the new Europe in security terms has been the eastward enlargement of 'Europe', not only in the sense of expanding the European security community or zone of peace, but also in terms of extending the membership of the EU and NATO. This has involved not only the extension of full membership to a swathe of Central and Eastern European states stretching from the Baltic to the Black Sea, but also the development of various partnership and co-operation arrangements with those states remaining outside the EU and/or NATO. The evolution of this enlargement process since the 1990s has resulted in the emergence of a Europe defined not only by an enlarged security community, EU and NATO, but also by a set of distinctive subregions with differing relations with the security

TABLE 1.1   *Regions of Europe and membership of European security organizations, 2012*

	EU	NATO	CoE	OSCE	CIS
North America					
Canada		X		X	
USA		X		X	
Western Europe (EU and/or NATO members)					
Austria	X		X	X	
Belgium	X	X	X	X	
Cyprus	X		X	X	
Denmark	X	X	X	X	
Finland	X		X	X	
France	X	X	X	X	
Germany	X	X	X	X	
Greece	X	X	X	X	
Iceland		X	X	X	
Ireland	X		X	X	
Italy	X	X	X	X	
Luxembourg	X	X	X	X	
Malta	X		X	X	
Netherlands	X	X	X	X	
Norway		X	X	X	
Portugal	X	X	X	X	
Spain	X	X	X	X	
Sweden	X		X	X	
UK	X	X	X	X	
Western Europe (non-EU and non-NATO members)					
Andorra			X	X	
Lichtenstein			X	X	
Monaco			X	X	
San Marino			X	X	
Switzerland			X	X	
Central and Eastern Europe (EU and/or NATO members)					
Bulgaria	X	X	X	X	
Czech Republic	X	X	X	X	
Estonia	X	X	X	X	

➜

community and differing prospects for eventual membership of that community and its institutions. Table 1.1 summarizes this emerging Europe. Contemporary Europe can thus be understood in terms of a set of concentric circles: Western Europe (where the majority of states are members of both the EU and NATO); Central and Eastern Europe (ten

→	EU	NATO	CoE	OSCE	CIS
Hungary	X	X	X	X	
Latvia	X	X	X	X	
Lithuania	X	X	X	X	
Poland	X	X	X	X	
Romania	X	X	X	X	
Slovakia	X	X	X	X	
Slovenia	X	X	X	X	
Western Balkans and Turkey					
Albania		X	X	X	
Bosnia and Herzegovina			X	X	
Croatia		X	X	X	
Macedonia			X	X	
Montenegro			X	X	
Serbia			X	X	
Turkey		X	X	X	
Western Former Soviet Union					
Belarus				X	X
Moldova			X	X	X
Ukraine			X	X	X
Russia			X	X	X
Caucasus					
Armenia			X	X	X
Azerbaijan			X	X	X
Georgia			X	X	X
Central Asia					
Kazakhstan				X	X
Kyrgyzstan				X	X
Tajikistan				X	X
Turkmenistan				X	X
Uzbekistan				X	X

Notes: EU = European Union; NATO = North Atlantic Treaty Organization; CoE = Council of Europe; OSCE = Organization for Security and Co-operation in Europe; CIS = Commonwealth of Independent States.

states, stretching from the Baltic Sea to the Black Sea, all of whom joined both the EU and NATO since the late 1990s); the Western Balkans (where Albania and Croatia joined NATO in 2009 and all states are effectively candidates for EU and NATO membership); the Western former Soviet republics that now lie between the enlarged

Western security community and Russia; Russia and Turkey, major powers that are in different ways outside the Western security community; and the Caucasus and Central Asia, on the geographical periphery of the new Europe.

The central drivers behind this enlargement process have been the desire of most of the states of post-communist Europe to integrate themselves with the West, in particular to join the EU and NATO, and the need for the West to find an adequate response to the political, economic and security challenges facing the region. Given their historic vulnerability to larger neighbours and the attractions of the Western security community, it is hardly surprising that many of the states of Central and Eastern Europe, the Balkans and the former Soviet Union have sought close ties with and membership of that community. Inclusion in the Western security community and its central institutions – the EU and NATO – makes a state part of the dominant force in contemporary Europe and gives it the capacity to contribute to and shape its policies towards the rest of Europe and the wider world. More concretely, NATO members gain the protection of the Alliance's Article V security guarantee – which commits members to provide all assistance to a fellow member if it is attacked – and the military infrastructure built up to support that commitment. EU membership provides states with the economic benefits associated with access to the Union's internal market and its redistributive economic policies, as well as its common foreign, security and defence policies. In the context of democratization, Central and Eastern European leaders viewed integration with the West as a return to the democratic Europe from which their countries had been separated artificially by the Soviet imposition of communism (Cottey, 1995).

Western governments were initially wary of extending full membership of the EU and NATO to post-communist states, fearing that these states had not made sufficient progress in democratization and economic reforms, that instability might be imported into the EU and NATO, and that both institutions might be weakened by taking in new members. With the new democracies of Central and Eastern Europe pressing for integration with the West, however, it was difficult to deny the principle that the Western security community and its institutions should be open to them. Integration with the EU and NATO, further, was one of the primary means by which the West might stabilize post-communist Europe: just as NATO and the EU had helped to bring peace, prosperity and stability to Western Europe after 1945, it was hoped that the same process might be repeated in the eastern half of the

TABLE 1.2 *NATO and EU enlargement 1990s–2000s*

	NATO	EU
1999	Czech Republic, Hungary, Poland	
2004	Bulgaria, Estonia, Latvia, Lithuania, Romania, Slovakia, Slovenia	Cyprus, Czech Republic, Estonia, Hungary, Latvia, Lithuania, Malta, Poland, Slovakia, Slovenia
2007		Bulgaria, Romania
2009	Albania, Croatia	

continent after 1989 (Allin, 1995). Against this background, the 1990s saw a gradual process of enlarging Europe through the development of new institutional arrangements (such as NATO's Partnership for Peace (PfP) and the EU's various association and partnership agreements with its eastern neighbours), functional integration, and eventually the extension of full membership of NATO and the EU to Central and Eastern European states (Croft *et al.*, 1999). After much debate about the timing and modalities of enlargement, and the relative merits of the candidate countries, between the late 1990s and the late 2000s the swathe of post-communist states stretching from the Baltic Sea in the north to the Black Sea in the south joined both the EU and NATO (see Table 1.2). Since most of these states have joined both the EU and NATO, the enlargement process has also strongly reinforced the essentially (though not completely) overlapping European memberships and borders of both organizations and their position as twin pillars of the European security community.

There is a strong argument that the processes of EU and NATO enlargement have been central to the stabilization of Central and Eastern Europe since the end of the Cold War (Grabbe, 2006; Cottey, 1999b). Both the EU and NATO made membership conditional on the consolidation of democracy, the normalization of relations with neighbouring states and progress in economic, administrative and military reforms. This conditionality provided a powerful impetus for states to undertake and entrench reforms. The EU and NATO also provided significant financial support and technical advice to support reforms. Additionally, the process of functional co-operation that began in the 1990s has helped to socialize the Central and Eastern European states towards the norms and standards of the EU and NATO. If there had not been a realistic prospect of EU and NATO membership, the material support both organizations provided and the experience of co-operation with them, Central and Eastern Europe's post-communist transition might well have been far more troubled than has been the case to date.

The enlargement of the EU and NATO has, however, also created new insider/outsider, inclusion/exclusion dynamics in European security, and given a new centrality to long-standing questions about the definition of Europe and where its borders lie. Such dynamics and debates are hardly new and their cutting edge has usually lain in the east and the south-east of the continent, where Europe meets Asia and the Middle East. The different histories, cultures and developmental paths of Central and Eastern Europe, the Balkans, Russia and Turkey compared to Western Europe have resulted in long-standing debates on the extent to which these countries and regions are European. For four decades after the Second World War, the Cold War division of Europe largely, though never completely, submerged these debates. The end of the Cold War re-opened them. The centrality of the European security community and its institutions – the EU and NATO – to the new Europe have made the question of whether or not one is a member of that community and its institutions, and the nature of one's relations with them, central foreign policy issues for all states. While membership of the European security community and its institutions confers major benefits, exclusion not only denies a state these benefits but also makes it vulnerable to the collective political, economic and military power of the community and a potential subject of its common external policies. For those European states remaining outside the Western security community and its institutions, whether by choice or by exclusion, the community and its institutions are thus potentially both highly attractive and highly threatening, and an inevitably looming presence. In broad geopolitical terms, the limits of the enlargement of the European security community and the nature of the relationships between that community and those states that remain outside it have become defining questions for the new Europe.

The processes of EU and NATO enlargement inevitably generated parallel dynamics of inclusion and exclusion, with fears of negative consequences for those states remaining outside and the possible emergence of new European dividing lines. Critics of NATO enlargement, in particular, argued that extending a military alliance into Central and Eastern Europe would be viewed as threatening by Moscow, provoke military counter-measures by Russia and in the worst case create a renewed Cold War-style military confrontation (Brown, 1995; Gaddis, 1998). Although less directly threatening in security terms, EU enlargement would involve the extension of the EU's common external trade tariffs, border controls and visa regimes to Central and Eastern European states, thereby disrupting economic, social and political ties with their own eastern and southern neighbours such as Ukraine and Russia. More broadly, the enlargement of the EU and NATO risked isolating those states remaining outside and undermining support in those countries for both domestic reforms and co-operation with the Western security community. In order to counter these dangers, NATO and the EU took a series of steps designed to avoid a new division of Europe, including strengthening institutional ties with these states, in particular Russia, and supporting the new NATO and EU members in building bilateral and subregional co-operation with their eastern and southern neighbours. Although the long-term impact of NATO and EU enlargement remains to be seen, worst-case scenarios of a new Cold War-style military confrontation and dramatic setbacks to reform in those states remaining outside NATO and the EU have been avoided.

The various regions and countries currently outside the European security community (see Table 1.1) are in quite different geostrategic and political situations and therefore face divergent foreign and security policy challenges and pose different challenges to NATO and the EU. The countries of the Western Balkans (the former Yugoslav states, plus Albania) are geographically proximate to the enlarged Western security community; became a de facto Western sphere of influence in the 1990s; are surrounded by the EU and NATO since the recent expansions of both organizations; have since the early 2000s all been recognized as potential candidates for EU and NATO membership; and are at various stages of the path towards that membership. The Yugoslav wars of the 1990s and the ongoing potential for violence, as illustrated by the outbreak of low-level violence in Kosovo in 2004, however, illustrate that the Western Balkans remains outside the Western security community inasmuch as war remains conceivable within the region. The region's prospects for membership of the EU and NATO are mixed (Krastev, 2011). Those states which are relatively stable and have made most progress with political and economic reforms are best placed to join NATO and the EU. Albania and Croatia joined NATO in 2009, but Macedonia's bid for NATO membership was held up by a dispute with Greece (which as a NATO member was able to veto Macedonia's membership bid). Croatia completed EU membership negotiations in 2010–11 and is expected to join the Union in 2013. Albania, Montenegro and Macedonia (assuming its bilateral disputes with Greece can be resolved) may join the EU at some point after 2013. Bosnia and Herzegovina's prospects for EU and NATO membership are severely constrained by the deep internal division of the country since the war of the 1990s between the (Muslim) Bosniak-Croat Federation and the Serbian Republika Srpska. Whether and how this division may be overcome is uncertain. Kosovo declared its independence from Serbia in 2008 and has been recognized as an independent state by the USA and a majority of EU members. Nevertheless, five EU member states (Spain, Romania, Slovakia, Greece and Cyprus) have not recognized Kosovo's independence. This problem, along with questions over authoritarianism and corruption, undermines Kosovo's prospects of EU and NATO membership. Serbia itself still lays claim to Kosovo and a resolution of the dispute over Kosovo's status is probably a pre-requisite for Serbian membership of the EU. Serbia may be less likely to join NATO because of antipathy towards the Alliance arising from its 1999 intervention in Kosovo. While the particular problems facing Bosnia and Herzegovina, Kosovo and Serbia may delay their possible membership of the EU and/or NATO, unless there is a return to large-scale violence the bigger picture seems likely to be one of gradual, and sometimes slow, integration of the Western Balkans into the EU, NATO and the European zone of peace.

Lying between Russia and the enlarged NATO and EU, the geostrategic situation of the countries of the Western former Soviet Union – Ukraine, Belarus and Moldova – differs radically from that of the Western Balkans and has led some to describe the region as the 'new Eastern Europe'. The domestic paths of these states further complicate their difficult geostrategic situation. Since the early 1990s, Ukraine has been pulled between Russia and the West, and between the legacy of communism and domestic reform. Ukraine's 2004 Orange Revolution – in which a crisis over presidential elections threatened the survival of democracy but eventually resulted in victory for the pro-Western reformer Viktor Yushchenko – appeared to open up the possibility of domestic reforms and strengthened ties with the West that might eventually put EU and NATO membership on the political agenda. After 2004, however, Ukraine faced continuing internal divisions over reform and in 2010 Yushchenko's main pro-Russian opponent, Viktor Yanukovich, was elected president. Ukraine, therefore, appears likely to remain pulled in competing directions. Belarus, under its maverick president, Alexander Lukashenko, remains an outpost of old-style communist authoritarianism and a close of ally of Russia, but observers fear that Lukashenko's eventual demise could trigger instability. Moldova's post-communist development has been largely defined by the unresolved conflict with the Russian-backed Transdnistria region in the country's east. There was violence here at the beginning of the 1990s and the region remains outside the control of the Moldovan government, with Russian military forces being deployed in the region despite a commitment by Moscow to withdraw those forces. The domestic and foreign policy problems facing Ukraine, Belarus or Moldova mean that they are not serious candidates for membership of the EU or NATO, certainly at least in the short to medium term. The ambiguous geostrategic status of the region is likely to pose ongoing dilemmas for the Western former Soviet states and be a source of potential conflict between the Western security community and Russia.

As major European powers in their own right, Russia and Turkey are the two most important outsiders in the new Europe. Both countries are characterized by tensions between a desire to join the European mainstream embodied in the Western security community and arguments that they have distinctive national identities that set them apart from the Western security community. The members of the Western security community also view Russia and Turkey ambiguously, trying to integrate them into that community through various partnership and co-operation arrangements but remaining wary of both states, and in particular of giving them full institutional membership of that community.

The positions of Russia and Turkey in relation to the European security community and the EU and NATO, however, differ in important ways. In the sense of being part of the zone of peace where war is all but inconceivable, Russia is not a full member of the Western security community. Although Russia's relations with the West have improved dramatically since the end of the Cold War, tensions have continued and at points during the Yugoslav conflict of the 1990s and the 2008 Georgia War could potentially have brought Russia and NATO into direct military confrontation. Although war between Russia and the West is unlikely at present, it is probably not entirely off the map of possibilities for decision-makers in Moscow or Western capitals. Russia, further, is a member of neither the EU nor NATO. Since the 1990s, both the EU and NATO have developed special partnership relationships with Russia, reflecting its status as a major European power. Although some observers have suggested that making Russia a member of NATO might be a way of bringing it into the Western security community and overcoming the insider/outsider dilemmas associated with NATO enlargement (Baker, 2002), neither Russia nor NATO or the EU appear to have any serious interest in pursuing Russia's full membership. Thus it appears likely that Russia will remain the major outsider beyond the European security community, and the extent to which Russia and that security community will be able to build a viable partnership short of full membership remains uncertain.

In contrast to Russia, Turkey was a Western ally throughout the Cold War and has been a member of NATO since 1952. Turkey, however, remained outside the EU and its predecessors, reflecting both European concerns about the absence of democracy in Turkey and Turkey's sense of having its own national identity separate from Europe. Turkey's relations with the larger European security community are also complicated by its relationship with Greece and the unresolved conflict over Cyprus. Greece and Turkey have a long history of conflict and came close to all-out war when Turkey invaded Cyprus in 1974. Although relations between Greece and Turkey have improved significantly since the late 1990s, war between the two states remains conceivable (as illustrated by disputes in the Aegean Sea that brought them to the verge of war in 1996). Despite being a long-standing member of NATO, therefore, Turkey's relationship with the European security community and the EU is thus characterized by an unusual mix of both insider and outsider, while the Greco-Turkish relationship also illustrates the limits of the security community as a zone of peace. As Turkey democratized in the 1990s and early 2000s, the prospects for Turkish membership of the EU improved, with formal membership negotiations starting 2004–05. At this point, with Istanbul initiating democratic and human rights reforms required by the EU, it appeared that Turkey might be moving towards membership of the Union. The EU, however, is divided over possible Turkish membership, with significant political forces wary of taking in a large, poor Muslim state straddling Europe and the Middle East. At the same time, Turkey has historically been ambiguous about EU membership. From the mid-2000s, further, Turkey also developed a new foreign policy, involving a greater role in the Middle East and increased independence from the USA and the EU (Ulgen, 2010). By the late 2000s and early 2010s, the combination of at best lukewarm EU support for Turkey and Turkish ambiguity over membership of the Union appeared to be making eventual Turkish membership less, rather than more, likely.

While Russia and Turkey are not (yet) fully integrated into the European zone of peace, neither country appears likely to pose the kind of hegemonic threat to European security that great powers have done in the past. Both countries have ambitions to (re-)establish themselves as major European powers, have disputes with many of their neighbours, and have intervened militarily in regions on their periphery (Russia in various parts of the former Soviet Union; Turkey in Cyprus and Iraq). In the Turkish case, while war between Turkey and some its neighbours (primarily Greece, but also conceivably Serbia and Bulgaria) remains possible, military conflict between Turkey and the larger Western or European security community seems extremely unlikely – partly because of Turkey's membership of NATO, but also because there are few, if any, sources of potential military conflict between Turkey and that security community. In the Russian case, despite some resentment of the dominance of the Western security community, Moscow does not appear to have serious ambitions to dominate Europe in the way that hegemonic powers have in the past. Even if this were to change, for the foreseeable future Russia lacks the material power to mount a hegemonic bid to dominate Europe. Although Russia's one million-strong armed forces are the largest in Europe, Russia does not realistically have the military capability to pose a hegemonic threat to European security, nor do its armed forces translate into significant political leverage over the rest of Europe. In economic terms, Russia's gross domestic product (GDP) is much less than those of the EU or the USA, and its defence expenditure is comparatively smaller. Russia also faces significant domestic political, economic and social challenges that further constrain its external ambitions. In short, while both Russia and Turkey are likely to remain security concerns for their weaker neighbours, neither is likely to pose a continent-wide threat to European security. The real questions for European security are how far they can be integrated into the Western security community, and whether they will be co-operative partners in dealing with security challenges such as proliferation, terrorism and conflicts beyond Europe.

Further to the east and south lie the former Soviet states of the Caucasus and Central Asia. Geography alone means that these states are more distant than other European states from the European security community and in part therefore less important to it. These countries' geostrategic location at the crossroads of Europe, Asia and the Middle East, and between a number of major powers (Russia and China, but also Turkey, Iran and India), and the existence of major oil and gas deposits within the region, however, mean that they are nevertheless of real significance for the European security community. Following the break-up of the Soviet Union, these states were integrated into European security structures through membership of OSCE, joining NATO's PfP initiative, the conclusion of Partnership and Co-operation Agreements (PCAs) with the EU, and in the case of the Caucasian states, membership of the Council of Europe. Geography, the existing challenges of enlargement, deference to Russian interests and the authoritarian character of most of the Caucasian and Central Asian regimes, however, has meant that these states have largely not been viewed as possible candidates for EU or NATO membership.

In the 1990s and early to mid-2000s, NATO and EU enlargement were dynamic and open-ended processes: both organizations committed themselves to enlargement in principle but the enlargement endgame – in terms of which countries would or would not become members, at what point and under what circumstances – was an open and often hotly debated issue. Eventually, both the EU and NATO undertook big enlargements taking in the swathe of Central and Eastern European states from the Baltic to the Black Sea. The EU and NATO also committed themselves to 'open door' policies regarding further enlargement, but the limits of the process were unclear. Since the mid- to late 2000s, however, those limits have become clearer. In the wake of the big enlargements of the early to mid-2000s, a period of 'enlargement fatigue' has followed, with NATO and especially the EU increasingly conscious of the costs and problems associated with enlargement and therefore wary of undertaking significant further enlargement. Factors behind this enlargement fatigue include arguments that some states had not made sufficient reforms before they were accepted into the EU or NATO, the fiscal transfers required by new members, concerns about a possible influx of migrants from the East and doubts about the stability of candidate countries.

The limits of enlargement have become particularly clear with regard to the former Soviet countries. The Rose and Orange Revolutions in Georgia and Ukraine in 2004 brought to power Western-oriented reformers in both countries, raising hopes of closer ties with the EU and NATO and eventual membership in both organizations. However, as was noted above, Ukraine's Orange Revolution did not prove to be the decisive event some hoped for and the country remains pulled between Russia and the West. The 2008 Georgia War only reinforced the reluctance of NATO and the EU to consider former Soviet countries as possible members. In the run-up to the 2008 war, the Bush administration in the USA pushed bids for Georgia and

Ukraine to be given NATO Membership Action Plans (MAPs), which would formally recognize them as candidates for NATO membership. Russia's decision to intervene in Georgia appears to have been designed to pre-empt possible NATO membership for Georgia and Ukraine (Asmus, 2010, pp. 111–40). In the wake of the war, NATO's members have stepped back from considering membership for Georgia and Ukraine (Bailes and Cottey, 2010, pp. 156–7). Although the Georgia War also led the EU to establish, in 2009, a new Eastern Partnership with the countries of the Western former Soviet Union and the Caucasus, in practice the substance of the Eastern Partnership has been limited and does not include any commitment to membership for these countries. The combination of the desire to avoid antagonizing Russia and doubts over stability and prospects for reform in the former Soviet countries has made both the EU and NATO reluctant to consider them as members. From the perspective of the early 2010s, it is clear that none of the former Soviet states is likely to join either the EU or NATO soon, if ever.

In the 1990s and 2000s the geopolitics of Europe's east were re-made by the twin enlargements of the EU and NATO. The prospect of membership, further, gave the EU and NATO great leverage over candidate countries, while the process of integrating states into the EU and NATO helped to reshape their national institutions and policies. With the limits of enlargement becoming clearer by the late 2000s and early 2010s, the challenge facing NATO and particularly the EU is the more difficult one of engaging their southern and eastern neighbours and attempting to promote reform in these countries without the powerful leverage provided by the prospect of membership. The challenges facing the EU's neighbourhood policy are discussed in more detail in Chapter 4.

Conclusion

This chapter has examined the nature of European security at the beginning of the 21st century. Its core argument, and the basis of this book, is that European security has been fundamentally transformed by the emergence of a security community in Europe. Historically, war has been a defining feature of the modern European state system. In this context, the behaviour of states has been shaped by the ever-present risk of war, and Europe's international politics have been driven by the realist logic of balance of power and competing alliances.

The emergence of a security community, a zone of peace within which war is inconceivable, in Western Europe since the Second World War has altered this pattern fundamentally. The Cold War to some extent obscured the significance of this development. The risk of a continent-wide East–West war suggested that the old logic of European security remained intact. The end of the Cold War has demonstrated the full depth and significance of the change in European security. In contrast to the predictions of realists, more than two decades after the end of the Cold War the Western security community remains intact. Furthermore, despite the Yugoslav conflict of the 1990s, that security community has expanded into much of Central and Eastern Europe. Russia and Turkey, however, are not full members of the European security community and their relationships with that community, and the West more generally, remain characterized by an uneasy mix of co-operation and conflict. In the Russian case in particular, war between Russia and the West cannot entirely be ruled out. Just as both Russia and Turkey are ambiguous about whether they are or want to be a full part of Europe or the West, the European security community is ambiguous and divided over whether Russia and Turkey are fully 'European', and whether it wishes to accept either as full members. Notwithstanding these problems, however, the realities of power – in particular the disproportionate imbalance of power between the European security community and Russia and Turkey – mean that neither power is likely to pose a hegemonic threat to European security.

Two further features relating to the existence of the security community also define the new Europe. First, Europe is characterized increasingly by institutionalized security co-operation, in particular in the contexts of the EU and NATO. The national security policies of the members of the security community are becoming integrated into common EU and/or NATO policies towards the rest of Europe and the world. While this process is not unproblematical, and the USA as the world's only superpower to some extent stands apart from it, there is a growing trend towards the convergence and integration of the foreign and security policies of the European members of the security community. Second, the security community and its core institutions, the EU and NATO, have enlarged eastwards, extending the zone of peace and relative stability to include much of Central and Eastern Europe. As has been noted, in the 1990s and early to mid-2000s enlargement was a dynamic and open-ended process; by the late 2000s and early 2010s, however, the limits of enlargement were becoming clear with the former Soviet countries likely to remain outside the EU and NATO.

The global and European economic crisis since 2008 has, to some extent, called these developments into question. In particular, as is discussed in more detail in Chapter 4 on the EU, there are new pressures to halt further European integration and possibly for the repatriation of powers from the EU level back to its member states. The economic problems facing some eurozone countries – in particular worsening recessions, growing budget deficits and loss of market confidence – have raised the prospect of some countries defaulting and being forced to withdraw from the euro or even of the euro disintegrating entirely and a return to national currencies. At a minimum, were such a development to occur, it would be a major setback for the EU and its political ambitions, including in the foreign policy area. In the worst case, were the collapse of the euro to trigger the unravelling of other elements of post-1945 European and Euro-Atlantic integration, such a development might even undermine the larger European security community discussed in this chapter, taking Europe back to the multipolar balance of power politics predicted by some realist theorists. The issue of alternative future scenarios for the development of European security is returned to in the concluding chapter of this book.

So long as the European security community – the zone of peace that has emerged in Europe since 1945 – remains intact, however, it is likely to be the defining feature of the European security landscape. The existence of this security community has a number of important implications. First, much of the old agenda of European security, revolving around the management of the balance of power, the role of alliances and military stability *within* Europe is simply no longer relevant. Second, to the extent that the risk of war within Europe has declined, the security agenda has shifted increasingly towards global issues, in particular conflicts elsewhere in the world and potential threats to Europe from challenges such as proliferation and terrorism. Third, the declining salience of traditional political-military security issues within Europe has pushed non-military problems such as economics, environmental degradation, migration and organized crime to the centre of the security agenda. In summary, the debate on European security is likely to revolve increasingly around the choices facing European states and institutions in relation to security problems outside Europe. At its root, this will be a debate not simply about specific policy choices but rather about what role European states and the EU as the primary expression of a collective European identity should play in relation to the rest of the world. The next chapter turns to the global challenges shaping the European security agenda of the early 21st century.

Chapter 2

The New Global Security Agenda

This chapter explores the emerging global security environment and agenda of the early 21st century. It argues that the international political order of the early 21st century is defined by a number of features: a broadly Western, liberal international order, but one challenged by a variety of countervailing forces; a historic shift in the balance of global power, driven by the rise of major non-Western powers such as China and India (a process accelerated by the global economic crisis since 2008); and the low likelihood of classical great power war. Within this context, the new global security agenda is defined by a number of more specific security challenges (United Nations, 2004; Brown, 2003):

- *New wars*: a shift in patterns of warfare from international wars to internal conflicts that nevertheless have significant regional and international repercussions.
- *Proliferation*: the prospect that a growing range of states, and potentially non-state actors, in particular terrorist groups, may obtain nuclear, biological or chemical weapons of mass destruction.
- *The new terrorism*: the emergence of radical Islamic terrorist groups, in particular al-Qaeda, engaged in a global struggle against the West, especially the USA, and willing to use terrorist violence on a scale not seen previously.
- *Non-military security threats*: an increasing recognition that non-military problems – poverty and economic instability, environmental change and degradation such as climate change, energy security, mass population movements, diseases such as HIV/AIDS, transnational crime and the protection of critical economic and technological infrastructures – may pose central challenges to human security and cannot be separated from the more traditional security problems of warfare and military security.

The rest of this chapter explores these dimensions of the new global security agenda in more detail. The chapter concludes by suggesting that while there is a loose consensus that the combination of new wars, proliferation, terrorism and non-military security threats constitute a new global security agenda, there is little international agreement on the priority and hierarchy that should be attached to different threats, and even less on how we should respond to these problems. The new global security agenda and the policy challenges it poses are therefore likely to remain highly controversial. The conclusion to this chapter also outlines briefly the implications of the new global security agenda for Europe. Subsequent chapters explore in more detail the challenges posed to Europe by the new global security agenda.

The new international (dis)order

The end of the Cold War in 1989 raised fundamental questions about what form of international order would replace the bipolar super-power conflict that had dominated international politics since the Second World War. Historically, the modern international system has been defined by multipolar balance of power politics between the great powers. Some speculated that the end of the Cold War would trigger a return to the type of politics that had existed before the Second World War, with the USA, Europe, Japan, Russia and China competing for power and influence, shifting alliances among these states, and an increasing risk of great power war. Rather than a return to past patterns, however, what emerged, or more accurately was consolidated, after the end of the Cold War was a Western-dominated international order. In material terms, the major Western centres of power – the USA, Europe and Japan, but also countries such as Australia and Canada – were the dominant forces in world politics. Economically, these countries provided the majority of the world's production, trade and investment. Militarily, these states had the greatest capacity to project military power beyond their borders. Ideologically, the period from the 1980s witnessed the global spread of liberal democracy, with democratization in much of Latin America, Central and Eastern Europe, Africa and parts of Asia. Paralleling this was a similar spread of market economics.

The Western-dominated post-Cold War international order could also be characterized in core–periphery terms: an order in which the West constituted the core of the international political and economic system, much of the rest of the world was defined by its relative lack of power and peripheral status, and the core–periphery relationship generated global tensions and conflict (Buzan, 1991b; Goldgeier and McFaul, 1992). The tensions generated by this Western-dominated international order can be seen in a number of areas. Despite the spread of democracy, a number of important states and regions – most importantly China and Middle Eastern states such as Saudi Arabia and Iran, but also countries such as Cuba, Myanmar (Burma) and North Korea – remain holdouts against the global spread of democracy. Similarly, while the Western world has become a 'zone of peace' in which war is extremely unlikely, many other parts of the world – in particular Africa and the Middle East, but also parts of Asia and South America – are 'zones of turmoil', where war, violent internal conflict and political and economic instability are commonplace (Singer and Wildavsky, 1993). The very dominance of Western states and values, further, provokes opposition to Western power, values and institutions, whether in the form of radical Islamic groups such as al-Qaeda; the resistance of Russian nationalists to the Westernization of their country; opposition to the 'imposition' of Western concepts of human rights in Asia; or North Korea's and Iran's attempts to develop nuclear weapons. Benjamin Barber thus describes the contemporary world order as 'Jihad versus McWorld', a 'collision between the forces of disintegral tribalism and reactionary fundamentalism ... and the forces of integrative modernization and aggressive economic and cultural globalization' (Barber, 2003, p. xii). Similarly, although Samuel Huntington's 'clash of civilizations' thesis posited a world divided between a number of distinct civilizational groups, Huntington (1993, p. 48) nevertheless concluded that 'the paramount axis of world politics will be relations between "the West and the Rest"'.

The tension between the Western-dominated international order and these countervailing tendencies has a number of dimensions. First, resistance to the dominant order sometimes takes a violent form, most obviously in the guise of Islamic terrorism but also in the context of national struggles (such as the Mexican Zapatista movement or Colombia's FARC) and sometimes through the action of so-called rogue states such as North Korea, Syria and Iran. Second, while stable established democracies may have low levels of internal violence and be unlikely to go to war with one another, the transitional process of democratization is usually prolonged, often produces instability both internally and internationally, and is vulnerable to setbacks. Democratization may thus trigger violent conflict within and between states, as in the former Yugoslavia, parts of what used to be the Soviet Union, and Iraq after 2003 (Mansfield and Snyder, 1995; Wimmer, 2003–4). 'Democratization' may also result in what Fareed Zakaria (1997, 2003) describes as 'illiberal democracies' – partial or stalled democratic transitions where leaders or governments are elected, but the weakness of other institutions means that there are no real alternatives to the dominant leader or party, and few constraints on executive power. Post-communist Russia provides a prime example of such a country. Third, the economic dimension of the Western-dominated international order also generates problems (Stiglitz, 2002). While the West has experienced unprecedented economic growth and prosperity since the Second World War, much of the rest of the world has suffered from poverty and economic underdevelopment. Similarly, while globalization, trade liberalization and market economic reforms have produced high economic growth rates in some countries since the 1980s, significant parts of the world – in particular, most of Africa and the Middle East – have not benefited from the new globalized economy. Market economic reforms and trade liberalization have created new classes of economic losers, as inefficient industries are put out of business. The liberalization of international financial markets has resulted in economic instability, and triggered major financial and economic crises in East Asia, Russia and Latin America in the late 1990s. These developments have generated widespread resentment of what are viewed as Western-imposed economic reforms, exacerbating more general anti-Western sentiment in much of the world. In short, what emerged after the end of the Cold War was a Western-dominated international order, yet the very existence of that Western-dominated international order generated the tensions driving new security challenges such as proliferation, terrorism and mass migration.

The rise of the rest

If in the 1990s and early 2000s the defining feature of international politics seemed to be the dominance of the West and of the United States in particular, from the perspective of the late 2000s and early 2010s the more important long-term trend appears to be the 'rise of the rest' (Zakaria, 2009) – the remarkable economic growth of major non-Western states, in particular but not only China and India, and the consequent reshaping of the balance of global economic and political power. In the 1990s some observers spoke of a 'unipolar moment', in which the USA would be the world's only truly great power (Krauthammer, 1990–1): the USA had emerged victorious from the Cold War, US/Western models of democracy and market economics were in the ascendant and the first Gulf War of 1990–91 and NATO's interventions in Bosnia in 1995 and Kosovo in 1999 reflected US military dominance. The American response to the 9/11 attacks reinforced the sense of American global dominance: the USA's ability to overthrow the Taliban in Afghanistan in late 2001 and remove Saddam Hussein from power in Iraq in 2003 highlighted America's overwhelming military power, while the Bush administration's policies were described by some as a foreign policy revolution based on the unilateral assertion of American power (Daalder and Lindsay, 2003). Observers spoke of America as an empire – a new Rome – reshaping the world (Freedland, 2002).

By the mid- to late 2000s, however, it was clear that sustained high economic growth rates in major non-Western countries were fundamentally altering the global balance of economic power, while the USA and the West seemed to be in decline. Since the 1990s, China, India and a significant number of other developing countries have experienced high economic growth rates (averaging somewhere between 5 and 10 per cent per annum). These growth rates are significantly higher than those among the developed Western states and have triggered a major shift in the balance of global economic, political and military power away from the old West and towards the non-West, especially Asia (Brown, 2000; Hoge, 2004; Mohan, 2006). The shift was highlighted in a 2003 Goldman Sachs research paper which popularized the term BRICs (Brazil, Russia, India and China): according to Goldman Sachs' projections the combined economies of the BRICs are likely to become larger (in real US$ terms) than those of the G6 largest developed economies (US, Japan, UK, Germany, France and Italy) by 2050, compared to the less than 15 per cent of G6 economies they equated to in the early 2000s, with China's economy becoming larger in real terms than that of the US by 2041 (Wilson and Purushothaman, 2003; see also O'Neil, 2001). Signalling the larger shift in economic power from the West to the rest, in 2005 the combined output of developed economies (measured at purchasing-power parity) accounted for the first time for more than half of world GDP (Woodall, 2006, p. 3). During the 2000s, further, the political impact of the shift began to become apparent. In the World Trade Organization (WTO), for example, which (along with its predecessor the General Agreement on Tariffs and Trade – GATT) had previously been dominated by the major Western powers, major developing powers such as China, India and Brazil were now exercising a decisive influence, including by resisting positions advanced by the Western powers. Similarly, in the United Nations Human Rights Council, established in 2005–06 to strengthen the UN's human rights role, non-Western states, led by countries such as China and Russia, were increasingly confident in resisting Western criticisms in relation to human rights.

Parallel to the rise of the rest, since the early 2000s there has been growing debate about the decline of the USA. After its initial successes in overthrowing the Taliban and Saddam Hussein, the USA faced growing insurgencies in Afghanistan and Iraq and was struggling to stabilize both countries. At the same time, the USA faced an increasing budget deficit, driven in part by the costs of the 'war on terror' but also by the ever-growing long-term costs of social security and healthcare within the United States. Then came the financial and economic crisis of 2008. The collapse or government rescue of major US financial institutions (such as the investment bank Lehman Brothers, the mortgage companies Freddie Mac and Fannie Mae and America's biggest insurance company AIG) was a massive systemic shock to US and wider Western economic and political confidence, pushed the USA and the world into the worst economic recession since the 1930s and dramatically symbolized the apparent decline of the world's dominant power. Furthermore, whereas the Western economies were amongst those hit worst by the economic crisis, the impact on China, India and other major developing countries was less severe. Observers began to discuss whether China would 'save the world', through its relative economic stability and a 4 trillion yuan ($586 billion) stimulus plan announced in November 2008 (Elegant, 2009; *The Economist,* 2008). The dramatic change in the global environment was summarized by a November 2008 US National Intelligence Council (NIC – the overarching body bringing together the USA's various intelligence agencies) report mapping likely global trends to 2025. The report argued that an unprecedented shift in relative wealth and economic power was under way, that a global multipolar system was emerging, and that while the USA would remain the single most powerful country it would have less power than it had enjoyed for many decades (National Intelligence Council, 2008). Table 2.1 summarizes this shifting balance of power.

The extent, likely future direction and impact of shifts in the global balance of power are all, however, contentious. If one considers the USA's position as the world's dominant power, some theorists argue

TABLE 2.1 *The shifting global balance of power*

Country/ Region	Territory (mn sq km)	Population (mn)			GDP (in constant 000 US$ bn)		
		1990	2000	2010	1990	2000	2010
USA	9.8	253	283	310	7,064	9,899	11,681
EU*	4.3	343	376	502	6,004	8,079	9,660
China	9.6	1 145	1 269	1 341	445	1,198	3,243
Russia**	17.1	148	147	143	386	260	414
Japan	0.4	122	126	127	4,150	4,667	5,064
Germany	0.4	79	82	82	1,543	1,900	2,071
UK	0.2	57	59	62	1,150	1,478	1,698
France	0.6	57	59	63	1,092	1,326	1,485
India	3.3	874	1 054	1 225	270	460	971
Brazil	8.5	150	174	195	502	645	916
South Africa	1.2	37	45	50	111	133	187

Notes: * European Union members (12 members in 1990, 15 members in 2000, 27 members in 2010); ** Soviet Union 1990, Russia 2000 and 2010.

Sources: territory – CIA World Factbook https://www.cia.gov/library/publications/the-world-factbook/index.html; population – United Nations (2010); GDP: World Bank world databank http://databank.worldbank.org/ddp/home.do;

that a number of factors inevitably work against prolonged hegemony. In the long term, changes in technology and modes of economic production result in differential economic growth rates, meaning that no country can permanently sustain the economic power that underpins a leading global role. Hegemony, it is argued, also results in imperial overstretch, as the costs of maintaining global power become unsustainable, forcing retrenchment or collapse (Kennedy, 1988). Realist international relations theorists additionally suggest that the existence of a hegemon inevitably provokes the emergence of either a rival challenger or a countervailing coalition (Layne, 1993). Developments since the early 2000s can be read as supporting these arguments. The problems and costs of trying to stabilize Iraq and Afghanistan, as well as fighting a multi-front global war against terrorism, can be seen as signs of imperial overstretch and have already forced US retrenchment. The broad international opposition to the 2003 Iraq War could be interpreted as the inevitable growth of international opposition to an overweening hegemon. Economically, further, the USA faces a series of major economic problems that pre-dated but were exacerbated by the economic crisis since 2008: a growing budget

Defence Expenditure (in constant 2009 US$ mn)			Armed Forces (personnel, 000s)			Nuclear Weapons (nuclear warheads)		
1990	2000	2010	1991–2	2000–1	2010–11	1990	2000	2010
502.7	375.9	687.1	2,117.9	1,371.5	1,564.0	21,211	10,615	<9,600
247.0	247.0	288.0	2,064.5	1,789.9	1,666.0			
17.2	32.1	114.3	3,030.0	2,820.0	2,285.0	430	400	240
232.5	26.0	52.6	3,988.0	1,004.1	1,046.0	33,417	10,201	<12,000
46.7	51.8	51.4	249.0	242.6	248.0			
69.3	49	46.8	469.0	332.8	251.0			
57.9	45.5	57.4	306.0	212.4	178.0	300	185	225
67.9	59.5	61.3	461.3	317.3	239.0	505	450	300
14.8	21.8	34.8	1,262.0	1,173.0	1,325.0		60	60–80
11.7	18.8	28.1	324.2	291.0	318.0			
5.1	2.7	3.7	77.4	70.0	62.0			

defence expenditure – Stockholm International Peace Research Institute (SIPRI) Military Expenditure Database http://milexdata.sipri.org/; armed forces – International Institute for Strategic Studies (1991, 2000, 2010a); nuclear weapons – Natural Resources Defense Council (2002) and Stockholm International Peace Research Institute (2010), table 8.1, World nuclear forces, January 2010.

deficit, estimated to be close to $1.5 trillion or 9.8 per cent of GDP in 2011 (Congressional Budget Office, 2011); rising costs for social security, healthcare and pensions; declining economic competiveness; and a long-term debt problem, with the USA's debt-to-GDP ratio set to rise, by some estimates, to 450 per cent by 2040 (Ferguson, 2010, p. 7). Some observers conclude that the USA faces an impending financial crisis that could severely undermine the country's economic power and standing, force it to radically cut military spending and produce a dramatic imperial collapse (Ferguson, 2010).

Predictions of imminent American decline should, however, be treated with caution (Strange, 1987). Observers at various points in the past – in the 1950s after the Korean War and in the 1970s and 1980s after the Vietnam War – predicted America's imminent decline. These predictions proved to be misplaced: although the Vietnam syndrome made the USA rather more reluctant to use military force, and its economic dominance was less than it had been in the years immediately after the Second World War, America nevertheless remained the dominant global power. Despite its current economic problems, further, the USA arguably has a number of long-term strengths that may enable it to maintain quite high economic growth rates in the medium term; a growing and relatively young population (compared to many of the other major powers that face declining and ageing populations); high levels of investment in education (especially higher education) and research and development; and an entrepreneurial economic culture (Joffe, 2009). In addition, although China, Russia, India, Japan and Europe to varying degrees express anti-American rhetoric and have sometimes co-operated with one another against the USA, America has generally acted with strategic restraint in its relations with the other major powers, avoiding threatening their survival or core interests and thereby averting the emergence of a coherent anti-hegemonic coalition (Ikenberry, 2001).

Despite its current problems, the USA remains the world's only complete global power; only the USA has the combination of global reach across the full spectrum of economic, military, political and 'soft' (cultural and ideational) power (Nye, 2002, pp. 1–40). No other state or group comes close to matching the USA across this spectrum of power. America's dominance is particularly marked in the military sphere, with the USA accounting for between 40 and 50 per cent of global defence spending. In 2009 US military expenditure totalled US$661 bn (43 per cent of total global military spending) compared to an estimated US$100 bn (6.6 per cent of the global total) for China, the next largest military spender (Perlo-Freeman *et al.*, 2010, p. 203). The USA is the only country capable of engaging in sustained large-scale warfare far from its national territory (as it did during the 1990–91 Gulf War, the 2003 Iraq War and in Afghanistan after 2001) and will remain so for at minimum some years to come. Short of a very dramatic economic collapse, the more likely scenario is that the USA will remain the world's most powerful state, but that its power will gradually decline *relative* to that of the other major powers and that its foreign policy influence and freedom of manoeuvre will be constrained by its economic problems and the legacies of the Iraq and Afghanistan wars.

If there are uncertainties about the decline in US power, there are similar uncertainties about the rising power of the non-West and likely implications of the non-West's increasing power. The underlying shift has been the result of sustained high economic growth rates (of up to 10 per cent of GDP per year), a process that emerged first in China in the 1980s but has spread to other major developing states (such as India and Brazil) since the 1990s. Projections of a continued shift in the global balance of power thus rest on the assumption of relatively high levels of economic growth in developing countries. This assumption is reasonable: developing countries are at relatively early stages in their economic development and economic history suggests that countries in earlier stages of development (as opposed to mature industrial or post-industrial economies) are able to sustain average high rates of economic growth for many decades. This process is described by some as the 'great convergence'. Modern global economic history was until recently defined by 'the great divergence': the dramatic gap in economic power and standards of living between the West and most of the non-Western world, resulting from the West's successful industrial development and consequent differential growth rates (Pomeranz, 2001). Whereas in 'the 19th and early 20th century ... the peoples of Western Europe and their more successful former colonies achieved a huge economic advantage over the rest of humanity. Now it is being reversed more quickly than it emerged ... [T]he great convergence is a world-transforming event' (Wolf, 2011). This process could be disrupted by various factors. Economic crises, poor economic policy choices or serious political disorder could derail economic growth in one or more major developing states. A global economic depression more severe than that which followed 2008 remains a real possibility and could halt economic growth in most countries. Nevertheless, the most likely medium-term outcome is that, as developing countries industrialize and open their economies to the world, this great convergence will continue.

The rise of China has generated particular debate. China is expected to overtake the USA as the world's single largest economy in the next few decades (exactly when depends on how one measures a country's economy and projections of economic growth). Some observers conclude that we will soon face a world in which China replaces the USA as the world's dominant power and will reshape the world in its interests and image. Martin Jacques, for example, suggests we are entering an era when China will 'rule the world' (Jacques, 2009). While China may well become the world's single largest power (especially in economic terms) and will have a central impact on global politics and security, suggestions that it will dominate the world are probably exaggerated. Even if China becomes the largest national economic power in the world, the combined economic and military power of the West (the USA, plus the EU and Japan, as well as countries such as Australia and Canada) will be significantly larger than that of China (Ikenberry, 2008, pp. 36–7). Additionally, India will remain a major power in its own right and one reluctant to be dominated by China (India's population is also projected to become both larger and younger than an ageing China, while India's economic growth rate may overtake that of China). China also faces major domestic challenges – providing an adequate standard of living for its enormous population, maintaining the stability of its economic and political systems, reforming health and education systems and developing its national infrastructure – that will likely constrain its global ambitions and could derail its economic growth (Hutton, 2007).

More generally, the extent to and pace at which the major non-Western powers will translate their new economic weight into political influence and military power and the implications of their rising power for the larger global order are unclear. China's and India's very large populations and territories, for example, may constrain their ability to convert economic growth into global political or military power. As was noted above, the gap in terms of military power between the USA and all other states also remains large: even if countries such as China and India continue to expand their military power, it will be some years, if ever, before they develop the kind of global military power projection capabilities currently possessed by the USA. The extent to which the rise of the rest represents a broader challenge to the liberal international order established since 1945 is also unclear. India, South Africa and Brazil are all democracies. These countries and China are increasingly market-orientated economies integrated into the world economy. All these countries are members of and have largely accepted the norms underpinning the primary international institutions created by the Western powers since the Second World War, such as the United Nations (UN) and the WTO. Central elements of the Western-dominated international order – democracy, capitalism and institutionalized international co-operation along broadly liberal lines – may therefore outlive the dominance of the old West that gave birth to them. Nevertheless, it is increasingly clear that in the multipolar order of the 21st century the West will no longer have the decisive voice that it once did in addressing global issues and that the major developing powers will have a central say in the new global politics.

The new wars

For much of the 20th century, the primary international security concern was the risk of 'total war' – great power war extending on a continent-wide or global scale (Aron, 1954). As was argued in Chapter 1, the emergence of a security community has radically reduced the likelihood of war among the major Western powers. Some analysts go further, arguing that we are witnessing 'the obsolescence of major war' (Mueller, 1990; see also Kaysen, 1990 and Mandelbaum, 1998–9). The decline of major war is attributed to a range of factors. The destructive power of nuclear weapons and the risk of all-out nuclear war has arguably changed the calculus of state behaviour among the major nuclear-armed powers: the destruction likely to be caused by a nuclear war – and the risk that any war among the major powers might escalate into nuclear war – mean that war is no longer a rational means of pursuing state objectives among nuclear weapon states. Even aside from the development of nuclear weapons, the increasing destructiveness of prolonged modern conventional warfare and the vulnerability of industrialized societies to such warfare may have reduced the likelihood of war among the major powers. At the same time, the experience of the 20th century – 'the century of total war' (Aron, 1954) – has resulted in important shifts in normative attitudes to war. Whereas in the 19th and early 20th centuries war was often viewed as a glorious, noble and virtuous activity that strengthened the individual and the nation, today war is widely viewed as an evil, usually justified only in order to prevent a greater evil. How far we should accept 'the obsolescence of major war' thesis remains contentious. War between the USA and China over Taiwan, or between Russia and the major Western powers on the fringes of the former Soviet Union, for example, is not beyond the bounds of possibility. Nevertheless, even these conflicts are probably less likely than great power war was a century ago. Even if such conflicts were to occur, the competing alliances that resulted in continent-wide and global escalation in 1914 and 1939 are not in place to the same degree today, suggesting that such conflicts might remain limited in scope rather than escalate to become a wider great power war.

Great power war is increasingly being replaced by the so-called new wars: internal conflicts within states but with significant regional and international dimensions – such as those that have occurred in the former Yugoslavia, Somalia, Rwanda, East Timor, Afghanistan, Colombia, the Caucasus, West Africa and Sudan since the 1990s (Duffield, 2001; Kaldor, 2001). Robert Kaplan (1994) described the new wars as harbingers of a 'coming anarchy' in which low-level violent conflict and state collapse would become the dominant features of global politics. While Kaplan's apocalyptic argument describes the reality in parts of the world (for example, West Africa, on which he drew in particular), it also exaggerates the extent and likely global impact of the new wars. Observers such as Kaplan suggest that there has been a dramatic upsurge in violent internal conflicts since the end of the Cold War. In fact, this is not the case. Between 1990 and 2009, the number of major armed conflicts (defined as conflicts involving more than 1,000 battle-related deaths a year) ongoing at any one time varied between a high of thirty-one in 1991 and a low of fourteen in 2007, with a trend towards a decreasing number of conflicts (Harbom and Wallensteen, 2006, 2010). While new conflicts emerged as a result of the end of the Cold War (in the former Yugoslavia and the Caucasus, for example), others came to an end (as in Central America and Southern Africa) (Wallensteen and Axell, 1993). According to a major survey published in 2005, the number of armed conflicts globally had declined by more than 40 per cent since the early 1990s, the number of armed secessionist conflicts stood at twenty-five in 2004 (the lowest number since the 1970s), and the number of genocides and politicides (attempts to wipe out political opposition groups) also declined significantly after the late 1980s (Human Security Centre, 2005). The vast majority of conflicts in the early years of the 21st century are internal. Indeed, the trend towards internal conflicts is not simply a post-Cold War phenomenon but can be traced back to at least 1945. The majority of wars since the Second World War have been internal conflicts, reflecting a pattern of recurrent internal conflict in parts of the Third World. The new wars of the 1990s and early 21st century are thus an extension of the types of conflict seen in much of the Third World since decolonization.

The new wars are defined by a number of distinct features. First, there has been a shift towards civilians as victims of wars, and a blurring of the boundary between soldiers and civilians. At the same time, there is a growing trend towards the forced displacement of people – 'ethnic cleansing' as it was termed in the Yugoslav conflict – as both a consequence and a means of war. Civilians are often also coerced into taking up arms, or have little alternative but to take up arms in self-defence, thus blurring the boundary between civilians and combatants. As a consequence, most new wars are also 'complex emergencies' or 'humanitarian crises' involving significant numbers of civilian deaths, mass population movements and associated problems of hunger and disease. Second, although not classical international conflicts, the new wars are increasingly regionalized, spreading into neighbouring countries and creating regional nexuses of conflict and instability: combatants, weapons and refugees cross state borders; neighbouring states and ethnic kin become involved; and illicit cross-border economic ties fuel the new wars. If the new wars are those of failed states, Wolff argues that the regional consequences and nature of these conflicts are such that we should think in terms of 'state failure regions' rather than of conflict contained within particular states (Wolff, 2011). The third feature of the new wars is their internationalization through the involvement of the wider international community: foreign troops are deployed as peacekeepers; governments and international organizations supply humanitarian aid and take on conflict resolution and peacebuilding tasks; and non-governmental organizations distribute aid and perform other functions, such as supporting democracy.

As was discussed in the introduction to this book and is returned to in the conclusion, the global financial and economic crisis since 2008 has raised major questions about the future not only of the European integration process but also of the larger European and Western security community. Nevertheless, that security community – in the sense of a 'zone of peace' where war between states is highly unlikely – remains intact and the worst-case scenario of a return to security competition and the risk of war between the major Western powers appears unlikely. Although war between the Western powers, in particular the USA, and China and Russia is more conceivable, even here there are powerful forces – in particular, the rising costs of extended war among industrialized states – working against such an outcome. Should such conflicts occur, for example between the USA and China over Taiwan, they are likely to be limited in duration and scope, in contrast to the total wars of the 20th century. While a number of regions could see more traditional inter-state wars – between Israel and its Arab neighbours, between India and Pakistan, and on the Korean peninsula – experience since 1945 suggests that such conflicts will remain reasonably rare. The most common form of conflict is likely to remain the internal but regionalized and internationalized wars the world has seen since the 1990s. While the numbers of such conflicts may be declining, the difficulty of preventing and resolving them suggests that their incidence is unlikely to subside very quickly. The existence of a core group of states (the Western security community), unlikely themselves to succumb to such conflicts, equally suggests, however, that apocalyptic predictions of a dramatic global upsurge in new wars are also misplaced.

Proliferation: the second nuclear age

For the first four decades of the nuclear age, the risk of all-out nuclear war between the USA and the Soviet Union was central to the global security agenda. The end of the Cold War has dramatically reduced the likelihood of such a conflict, but developments since the early 1990s have triggered increasing concern about the proliferation of nuclear, biological and chemical weapons to a growing range of states and possibly terrorist groups. After the 1990–91 Gulf War it was discovered that Iraq was much closer to developing nuclear weapons than had previously been thought, and might have been in a position to deploy a nuclear arsenal within a few years – a development that could have enabled it to succeed in its invasion and annexation of Kuwait and more broadly altered the balance of power within the Middle East. The break-up of the Soviet Union at the end of 1991 resulted in the dispersal of the superpower's nuclear weapons among its successor states and concern about 'nuclear leakage' – the possibility that nuclear weapons, materials or knowledge might be stolen or sold on the black market. In 1998, India and Pakistan went further, and tested nuclear weapons. Both states have since consolidated their status as nuclear weapon powers by expanding their nuclear arsenals and delivery systems. North Korea's and Iran's nuclear ambitions have also been a focus of ongoing international concern since the 1990s. North Korea tested nuclear devices in 2006 and 2009 and is believed to have sufficient plutonium for a small number of nuclear weapons, although the exact state of its nuclear arsenal is uncertain. Iran has been seeking to develop highly enriched uranium, which would give it the capacity to develop nuclear weapons. The fact that countries such as Iran, Iraq and North Korea had moved close to developing nuclear weapons despite being signatories of the Nuclear Non-Proliferation Treaty (NPT) and subject to International Atomic Energy Agency (IAEA) inspections of their nuclear facilities, raised serious doubts about the effectiveness of the NPT/IAEA regime in preventing proliferation. In addition, in 2004, a secret black market network in nuclear weapons technology linking Pakistan, Iran, Libya and North Korea was discovered (Traynor *et al.*, 2004). Finally, the September 2001 terrorist attacks on the USA and subsequent revelations of contacts between al-Qaeda and Taliban leaders and officials associated with Pakistan's nuclear weapons programme raised the possibility that terrorist groups might acquire nuclear weapons.

In combination, these developments suggest that the world may have reached a decisive turning point in nuclear proliferation: India, Pakistan and North Korea have joined the club of nuclear weapon states since the late 1990s, and Iran may follow suit. In this new strategic context, neighbouring states – Japan and South Korea in North East Asia, for example, and Saudi Arabia and Turkey in the Middle East – could also choose to develop nuclear weapons. Colin Gray (1999) has described such a development as the dawning of a 'second nuclear age', in which a much wider range of states will have the ability to threaten to use – or in extremis choose to use – nuclear weapons.

An additional dimension of the proliferation problem is the concern that a range of states or terrorist groups may have acquired chemical or biological weapons. Egypt, Iran, Iraq, Libya, North Korea and Syria are all believed to have (or in Iraq's and Libya's cases, have had) active chemical and biological weapons programmes. Although now often grouped together as weapons of mass destruction (WMD), the military threats and proliferation challenges posed by nuclear, chemical and biological weapons differ in important ways (Perkovich, 2004). Nuclear weapons have by far the greatest destructive potential – providing the capacity to destroy entire cities, large industrial or military facilities and large concentrations of armed forces, and kill many thousands, possibly millions, of people – but they require a large and complex infrastructure and are thus particularly difficult to develop. Chemical weapons are easier to develop, and can potentially kill hundreds or thousands of people, but are difficult to disperse over a large area and have hence been viewed more as tactical battlefield weapons or weapons capable of causing terror and disruption but unlikely to cause very large numbers – tens of thousands or more – of casualties. Biological weapons cannot cause the same physical destruction as nuclear weapons, but could if dispersed in populated areas – and because of the infectious nature of the diseases that might be involved – cause many thousands, possibly millions, of deaths. The global diffusion of biotechnology, the relative ease of developing biological weapons compared to nuclear weapons, their potential to cause death on a massive scale and the relatively small amounts of biological material required could make biological weapons the weapon of choice for weak states or terrorist groups, and have thus made them a particular proliferation concern (Chyba and Greninger, 2004). Some analysts, however, argue that the danger of true mass casualty use of biological weapons has been exaggerated (in particular, because of the difficulty of dispersing biological toxins over large areas) and that biological weapons are more likely to be used as more limited battlefield weapons or for terrorist attacks on a more limited scale (Dando, 2005).

The prospect of accelerating WMD proliferation raises major questions about what action can and should be taken to limit the spread of such weapons, and how to respond if proliferation cannot be prevented. An established non-proliferation infrastructure already exists in the form of the NPT, the IAEA, the biological and chemical weapons conventions (which ban the possession and use of these weapons), and related national and multilateral export controls. Developments since the 1990s, however, point to both the substantial limits of traditional approaches to non-proliferation and the difficulty of persuading determined states to abandon their WMD ambitions. Some, particularly in the USA, have argued that only more coercive approaches – diplomatic isolation, economic sanctions and ultimately the threat or use of military force – may persuade states such as Iraq, Iran and North Korea to abandon their WMD programmes. The 2003 Iraq War illustrated the controversies likely to surround this logic, and ongoing debates over how to respond to Iran's and North Korea's nuclear ambitions suggest that these issues will not go away. An alternative logic might suggest that only the more radical approach of moving towards a world free from nuclear weapons or centralized global control of such weapons might persuade states beyond the existing nuclear weapon powers not to develop WMD. This logic was implicit in US President Barack Obama's April 2009 endorsement of the objective of a nuclear weapon-free world, but – as is discussed further in Chapter 7 – this remains at best a distant prospect. Beyond this lies the question of how states should respond if proliferation cannot be prevented, for example by preparing to defend themselves against WMD attack (as the USA and NATO are now doing with their missile defence plans) or by supporting new nuclear powers to develop stabilizing rather than destabilizing nuclear forces and postures. The inadequacies of the existing non-proliferation regime and the difficulties inherent in the various alternatives to that regime suggest that proliferation will continue to generate controversial policy dilemmas.

The new terrorism

The 11 September 2001 attacks on the USA pushed terrorism to the top of the global security agenda. From a European perspective, terrorism is not a new phenomenon: European states have long experience of terrorism at the national level (the UK in Northern Ireland, Spain in the Basque country, terrorism by extreme left and extreme right groups in various countries) and European citizens and states were among the primary targets of Palestinian terrorism in the 1960s and 1970s. Nevertheless, the threat posed by what has been called the new terrorism is both fundamentally different in nature and significantly greater in magnitude than previous terrorist threats.

Although 9/11 dramatically symbolized the threat posed by the new terrorism, that threat had been emerging since the early 1990s (Simon and Benjamin, 2001–2; Burke, 2004). While other groups, such as the Aum Shinrikyo religious cult responsible for the 1995 nerve gas attack on the Tokyo underground, and far-right American terrorists, are sometimes seen as part of the phenomenon, the driving force of the new terrorism is the radical Islamism of al-Qaeda and associated groups. These groups were responsible for the first attempt to destroy the World Trade Center in New York in 1993, a 1995 attempt to destroy eleven jumbo jets over the Pacific, and the 1998 bombings of US embassies in East Africa, as well as a number of lesser terrorist incidents. The new terrorism differs from most past terrorism in a number of important ways. Much past terrorism was primarily national in that it took place within one country or was related to specific national goals, usually independent statehood or reunification with a neighbouring state. The new terrorism is driven by the assumption of an all-embracing global conflict between Islam and its enemies (the West in general and the USA and Israel in particular), and by a broad rejection of the current international order and its norms. Radical Islamic groups see conflicts in the Islamic world – in Palestine, Kashmir, Chechnya, Iraq and elsewhere – as part of this global struggle. The declared goal of al-Qaeda is to establish an Islamic Caliphate across the Muslim world, expelling foreign forces and overthrowing apostate local regimes in the process. Members of al-Qaeda and associated groups view themselves as being involved in a struggle against both the 'near enemy' (the current regimes in countries such as Saudi Arabia and the other Gulf states) and the 'far enemy' (the USA and other Western states). The new terrorism is also a global phenomenon in the sense that al-Qaeda and associated groups have proved themselves capable of initiating attacks in all parts of the world. The nature of Islamic terrorism as a global movement is, however, the subject of debate: up to and immediately after 9/11 some analysts described it as a relatively centralized movement, with the al-Qaeda leadership exercising a significant degree of political and operational control over groups elsewhere in the world. But after the overthrow of the Taliban and destruction of al-Qaeda's operating base in Afghanistan in late 2001, analysts suggest that Islamic terrorism as a global phenomenon had become increasingly decentralized and fragmented. The extent to which al-Qaeda leaders (based primarily in the Afghanistan–Pakistan border region) control or direct Islamic terrorist groups globally, or these groups are largely free-standing, remains the subject of debate. Whatever the case, it is clear that radical Islamic groups have been able to exploit conflicts and grievances in the Muslim world, and that a loose global movement using terrorism as one of its key modus operandi has emerged as a consequence. The term 'globalized Islamic terrorism' is used in this book to refer to this phenomenon. The new terrorism is also defined by an unrestrained attitude to the use of violence. In the past, most terrorists used violence in limited forms to bring attention to their cause, undermine political authorities or provoke repressive responses from their opponents. Thus, whereas past terrorists 'wanted a lot of people watching, not a lot of people dead', the new terrorists of al-Qaeda appear to have abandoned this logic and seek to maximize the death and destruction they cause (Jenkins, 2006, pp. 118–19). The new terrorism has thus also been described as 'catastrophic terrorism' because it threatens, in particular if terrorist groups obtain WMD, to inflict damage on a far greater scale than previous forms of terrorism (Carter and Perry, 1999, pp. 143–74).

In response to the 9/11 attacks, the Bush administration declared a 'war on terror', making this a central element of US foreign policy and – given America's predominant global role – world politics more generally. This has had a number of dimensions. Militarily, the USA intervened in Afghanistan in late 2001 to destroy al-Qaeda's bases in that country and overthrow the Taliban regime that had provided sanctuary for al-Qaeda. The USA also undertook a number of more limited military interventions against terrorist groups and targets, or provided military support to other governments for such operations, in places as diverse as the Philippines, Georgia, Yemen and Somalia. Politically and institutionally, the 'war on terror' resulted in a raft of international measures to counter terrorism. This included the establishment of a UN Counter-Terrorism Committee, intensified intelligence co-operation and new measures to tackle the financing of terrorism, as well as the provision of US economic and military aid to support allies' efforts against terrorism. The 'war on terror' also resulted in the emergence of a new homeland security agenda, with states taking a wide range of measures to strengthen border controls, provide for the physical security of vulnerable targets (such as nuclear power stations), intensify intelligence and law enforcement efforts directed against terrorist groups, and develop the capacity to respond to terrorist attacks should they occur. These steps have gone furthest in the USA, with the creation of the Department of Homeland Security, but other states have implemented similar measures. The new homeland security agenda has provoked renewed debate on the long-standing question of the appropriate balance between security and freedom, with critics arguing that some measures taken to counter terrorism risk undermining fundamental freedoms, democracy and the rule of law.

If the domestic dimensions of the Bush administration's response to 9/11 were controversial within the US, the international side of the 'war on terror' was even more so globally. The Bush administration linked the terrorist threat to the issues of WMD proliferation and 'rogue states' (in particular, the so-called 'axis of evil' of Iran, Iraq and North Korea), arguing that the risk of terrorists obtaining WMD from such states meant that the issues could not be separated and that these threats required fundamentally new policies. The result was the preventive war doctrine (announced in the Bush administration's 2002 National Security Strategy), the 2003 Iraq War, a major expansion of the practice of extraordinary rendition (whereby suspected terrorists are captured covertly in third countries by US intelligence or security agencies and secretly transferred out of those countries), the detention of prisoners from the 'war on terror' in a legal no man's land at the US military base in Guantanamo Bay, Cuba and the authorization of inter-rogation techniques previously viewed as torture (such as waterboard-ing). Critics argued that the Bush administration had dangerously conflated different security challenges, adopted an overly confronta-tional and militarized approach to counter-terrorism and in so doing alienated much of global opinion, especially in the Islamic world, while paying too little attention to addressing the root causes and grievances that give rise to terrorism (Record, 2003; Gordon, 2008). On coming to power in 2009 President Barack Obama sought to reverse significant elements of his predecessor's policies, dropping the term 'war on terror', withdrawing US forces from Iraq, closing down the network of Central Intelligence Agency (CIA) secret overseas prisons established during the Bush administration and barring the 'enhanced interroga-tion techniques' authorized by the Bush administration (Cole, 2011). Nevertheless, some observers argue that there remained substantial elements of continuity between the counter-terrorism policies of the

Bush and Obama administrations, in areas such as policy towards Afghanistan and Pakistan, the use of unmanned drone attacks and domestic wire-tapping (Lynch, 2010; McCrisken, 2011).

After 9/11 many observers suggested that the new terrorism and the 'war on terror' would define global politics in much the way that the 'Soviet threat' and the Cold War had shaped world politics from the late 1940s to the late 1980s. The Bush administration thus came to describe the post-9/11 struggle against terrorism as the 'long war' (US Department of Defense, 2006). By the early 2010s, however, this view seemed exaggerated: even for the USA terrorism is only one of a range of threats and although the US 'war on terror' had an enormous international impact in the 2000s it is unlikely to be the defining feature of global politics in coming decades. If 9/11 marked the beginning of the 'war on terror', the killing of Osama bin Laden by the USA in Pakistan almost a decade later in May 2011 symbolized the winding down of that conflict. Nevertheless, terrorism is unlikely to be eradicated entirely and historical experience indicates that terrorist conflicts are often prolonged, suggesting that terrorism, in particular globalized Islamic terrorism, will remain a significant element of the global security agenda.

Non-military security

As discussed in Chapter 1, security has traditionally been seen as relating to issues of war and military power. Since the 1980s, however, there has been a growing recognition that non-military problems also pose significant threats to the security of states, their citizens and in some cases, such as climate change, humanity as a whole (non-military security threats are sometimes described as 'soft' security problems). Since the early 1990s, governments and international organizations have increasingly come to accept the argument that non-military problems are central to the security agenda. The EU's first official security strategy document, adopted in December 2003, identified poverty, disease, dependence on transport, energy and information infrastructure, state failure and organized crime as security threats (European Union, 2003a). Similarly, the formal *National Security Strategy* documents of the Bush and Obama administrations identified problems such as disease pandemics and global health, natural disasters, climate change, food security and illicit trade (in drugs, weapons and people) as important parts of the global security agenda facing the USA (United States, 2002, 2006, 2010).

Arguments have also been advanced for the re-conceptualization of security as human security, with an emphasis on the full range of threats to the security and well-being of both human beings and communities, rather than the more traditional focus on the physical security and political independence of states. A number of governments, such as those of Japan and Canada, have formally supported the concept of human security. A UN-sponsored international Commission on Human Security (2003) argued that state security should be supplemented by the concept of human security focused on individuals and communities and aiming to provide not only protection from violent conflict but also basic economic security, healthcare and education for the populace. In 2004, a high-level panel established by UN Secretary-General Kofi Annan argued that poverty, infectious disease, environmental degradation and transnational organized crime should be viewed as central security challenges alongside warfare, WMD proliferation and terrorism (United Nations, 2004).

Although this wider interpretation of security is somewhat diffuse, a number of issues are generally seen as central to the emerging non-military, soft or human security agenda:

- *Economics*: there is growing recognition of the linkage between economics and security. The EU's 2003 security strategy document argued that:

  > In much of the developing world, poverty and disease cause untold suffering and give rise to pressing security concerns. Almost 3 billion people, half the world's population, live on less than 2 Euros a day. 45 million die every year of hunger and malnutrition ... In many cases, economic failure is linked to political problems and violent conflict. Security is a precondition of development. Conflict not only destroys infrastructure, including social infrastructure; it also encourages criminality, deters investment and makes normal economic activity impossible. A number of countries and regions are caught in a cycle of conflict, insecurity and poverty. (European Union, 2003a)

  The nature, meaning and challenges of economic security are, however, far from clear, with conceptions of economic security ranging from problems of dependence on external resources and/or markets, to the interconnected nature of globalized financial markets, and to the problems of underdevelopment and poverty in the Third World (Buzan, 1991a, pp. 230–69; United Nations, 2004, p. 26).

- *The environment*: there is a growing recognition that environmental change or degradation may pose security threats (Levy, 1995). Environmental degradation may pose a direct threat to human health, well-being and survival, as in cases of severe pollution or industrial accidents such as the 1984 accident at the Union Carbide plant in Bhopal, India, and the 1986 Chernobyl nuclear power station accident in Ukraine. Environmental change or degradation may also cause political instability and violent conflict, by intensifying competition for limited resources (Homer-Dixon, 1991, 1994). Competition for water resources has become part of the Israeli–Arab conflict, and some analysts predict an era of water wars in the Middle East (Gleick, 1993). The most important global environmental security issue, however, is climate change or global warming – the increasing temperature of the earth's atmosphere resulting in significant part from human economic activity. Climate change is likely to have a major impact on humanity in the coming decades, with rising sea levels submerging all or part of some countries, and major changes in weather patterns threatening the well-being and survival of many people and triggering wider economic, social and political changes. According to press reports, a suppressed report for the US Department of Defense argued that climate change may cause major violent conflicts and should be a central US national security concern (Townsend and Harris, 2004). Sir John Houghton (2003), former chief executive of the UK's Meteorological Office and co-chair of the scientific assessment working group of the Intergovernmental Panel on Climate Change (the primary international scientific body assessing climate change), described climate change as a 'weapon of mass destruction' that already kills more people than terrorism.
- *Energy security*: the issues of reliable access to key energy resources (in particular, oil and gas) and dependence on overseas energy supplies have re-emerged as central elements of the global security agenda post-9/11 (Harris, 2003; Kalicki and Goldwyn, 2005). This issue initially came to prominence in the 1970s after the first major oil crisis and the resulting global economic recession. Rapidly expanding global energy demand and the Middle East's position as both the epicentre of globalized Islamic terrorism and the region with the world's largest concentration of oil resources have, however, pushed the issue of energy security to the fore once more.

In parallel with this, Russia's emergence as a major global oil and gas supplier has allowed Moscow to regain some of its previous great power status, while further complicating its relations with the West. The consequences of European dependence on Russian gas in particular became clear in the mid- to late 2000s when Russia at various points cut off or reduced the supply of gas to Ukraine, through which the main gas pipelines from Russia to Central and Western Europe run, resulting in significant reductions of gas supply to a number of European countries (in particular in January 2009).

- *Mass population movements*: since the mid-1990s, mass population movements have increasingly been viewed as part of the security agenda (Weiner, 1995; Loescher and Milner, 2005). Wars, famines or environmental disasters cause short-term large-scale population movements, creating immediate humanitarian crises, but often also wider social, economic and political instability. Longer-term, large-scale population movements, driven primarily by people's desire to move from poorer parts of the world to richer ones, have also generated concerns about potential threats posed by migration.

- *Disease*: the global HIV/AIDS epidemic has made infectious diseases part of the new security agenda. An estimated 20 million people have died as a result of HIV/AIDS, a further 38 million are estimated to be infected with HIV, and China, India and Russia have high levels of HIV infection (UNAIDS, 2004). Other infectious diseases, in particular malaria, tuberculosis, acute respiratory infections (ARI), diarrhoeal infections and measles cause the deaths of nearly ten million people each year. HIV/AIDS and other infectious diseases also have wider socio-economic and political repercussions, weakening economies, exacerbating competition for limited resources and undermining states (Elbe, 2003). The 2003 SARS (severe acute respiratory syndrome) outbreak provided a warning of the possible emergence of new diseases (or new strains of existing diseases) that could potentially cause the deaths of many millions of people (Sample, 2003).

- *Crime*: over the last decade or so the scale of violent and/or organized crime has increased dramatically in a number of countries and regions (Goodson, 2003). In countries such as Colombia, Mexico and South Africa, for example, the threat of violent crime impinges on the daily lives of the entire population and threatens to destabilize the state, economy and democratic politics. Crime is also a notable feature of the new wars discussed above, with the economies of war zones becoming increasingly dependent on the illegal sale and trafficking of a wide range of goods. Organized criminality has also taken on a growing transnational dimension, with criminal groups, such as the Russian mafia, operating across state borders on a large scale. Additionally, transnational organized crime contributes to other security problems such as the illegal trafficking of arms and WMD materials.

• *Critical infrastructure protection and cyber security*: a further recent security concern is the protection of the key economic and technological infrastructure systems that underpin modern societies, including electricity grids, telecommunications systems, transport networks, water supply systems, and fire and rescue services (Lukasik *et al.*, 2003; Schmitt, 2005). The growing complexity of modern industrial and post-industrial societies has led to arguments that they are increasingly vulnerable to the disruption of such infrastructures, through direct physical attack (whether by states or terrorist groups) or by less direct means (such as poisoning of water supply systems or hacking into computer systems). The centrality of computer systems to critical infrastructures and the advent of the internet age have also led to growing concern about cyber security – the vulnerability of states, companies and economies to cyber-attack or cyber-terrorism, where computer viruses or hacking into computer systems can be used to disrupt critical infrastructures. Such attacks may be launched by states, terrorist groups, criminal organizations or 'lone wolf' individuals, but the origins of such attacks are difficult to trace or prove, with the consequence that definitively identifying who is responsible is almost impossible – in addition, states may employ criminal groups or individuals to do their cyber 'dirty work'. The issue came to the fore in 2007 when Estonia was the target of a large-scale cyber-attack that closed down the websites of government ministries, the parliament, banks, newspapers and broadcasters. Russia was widely believed to be behind the attack, although the Russian government denies the accusation. In response to the attack on Estonia, NATO has sought to develop a cyber defence policy involving enhanced co-operation amongst member states and strengthened cyber defences of NATO's central institutions. Although the extent to which nightmare scenarios – where societies might be thrown into chaos by cyber-attacks and the resulting disruption of critical infrastructures – are realistic is a matter for debate, cyber security and critical infrastructure protection are viewed by most governments as growing security problems.

While these non-military challenges are becoming an increasingly prominent part of the new global security agenda, the broadening of the concept of security is not without problems. The securitization of previously non-security issues risks producing exaggerated perceptions of the threats posed by such issues and/or overly confrontational or militarized policy responses (Buzan *et al.*, 1998, pp. 208–12; Krause and Williams, 1997).

Conclusion

This chapter has sought to review the contemporary global security environment and agenda. It has suggested the international political environment of the early 21st century – the context in which specific security challenges arise and are addressed – is defined by three inter-related elements: a Western liberal international order, which emerged after 1945 but is challenged by a variety of countervailing forces and trends; a shift of truly historic proportions in the global balance of power, underpinned by the growing economic power of major non-Western powers; and low likelihood of great power war, which has normally been viewed as *the* classical security problem. In this context, the classical security problem of inter-state war, and especially great power war, has been replaced by a set of new – and often inter-linked – security challenges: new internal wars that nevertheless have significant regional and international repercussions; the proliferation of WMD; globalized Islamic terrorism; and non-military security challenges.

While there is an emerging international consensus that these problems constitute a new global security agenda and need to be treated holistically (United Nations, 2004), the priority and hierarchy that should be attached to different threats and the appropriate response to them are deeply controversial. Differing geostrategic situations, political values and socio-economic positions inevitably produce differing assessments of threats and divergent policy responses. International responses to the new global security agenda reflect this basic reality. In the USA, the primary threats are usually seen as involving some combination of proliferation, terrorism, 'rogue states' and/or the rise of great power competitors. Yet, as the then UN Secretary-General Kofi Annan argued in 2003, 'for many around the globe, poverty, deprivation and civil war remain the highest priority' (United Nations, 2003, p. 3).

Similar divisions arise over responses to the new security agenda. The USA's enormous power gives it a greater capacity than other states to act independently and may create a natural inclination towards unilateral approaches to security problems. In contrast, weaker states lack a similar capacity to act unilaterally, are more vulnerable to unilateral action by others and may therefore be predisposed to multilateralism. While few states and peoples are inclined towards absolute pacifism, recent disputes over military intervention indicate that there is little international consensus as to when the use of military force may be necessary and legitimate. Although there is now much discussion about addressing the underlying root causes of security problems such as terrorism, there is little agreement on what this should involve in practice. In the context of globalized Islamic terrorism, for example, some argue that resolving the Israeli–Palestinian conflict is vital to address the deep resentment that gives rise to terrorism. Others argue that the absence of democracy in the Middle East underpins terrorism. In short, while there may be an emerging consensus that there is a new global security agenda, the priority that should be attached to different threats and what policies are necessary to address these threats are likely to remain highly controversial.

From a European perspective, the new global security agenda poses a number of challenges. First, while the likelihood of military conflict within Europe is low, the dangers of proliferation and terrorism suggest that the risk of violent attack from outside Europe is real – as the March 2004 and July 2005 terrorist attacks on Madrid and London made starkly clear. Second, even when security problems elsewhere in the world do not directly or immediately threaten Europe in a physical sense, they may nevertheless threaten European interests in indirect ways. New wars in other regions of the world may threaten European citizens and European economic interests. Instability, violent conflict and deep socio-economic problems in other parts of the world, especially those closer to Europe such as Africa and the Middle East, may have important long-term repercussions for Europe, by generating pressures for migration to Europe or fuelling problems such as transnational crime that may spill over into Europe. Put bluntly, it is difficult to avoid the consequences of living next door to poor, unstable and sometimes violent neighbours. Some global problems, such as climate change, will inevitably have important implications for Europe: in the early years of the 21st century, many more European citizens have died as a result of extreme weather conditions thought to be caused by climate change than have been killed by terrorism (World Health Organization, 2005). Third, even if global security problems do not have major implications for European interests, violence and suffering elsewhere in the world may create political pressure and arguably a moral duty to act. Given Europe's prosperity and relative security, European governments may face strong political pressure – from European citizens and from elsewhere in the world – to contribute to addressing the security problems of less privileged parts of the world. European states are already among the world's leading contributors to peacekeeping operations and economic development aid, but the scale of the new global security problems suggests that Europe may be called upon to do more in future.

European responses to the new global security agenda also relate to the wider issue of what role Europe (or perhaps more accurately *Europeans*, since Europe comes in many guises) can and should play in the world, and indeed of European identity and what it means to be European. A range of possible answers can be envisaged. An insular 'fortress Europe' would involve seeking to minimize vulnerability to the new security challenges by withdrawing inwards and strengthening Europe's borders. The other end of the spectrum would involve asserting Europe as an activist global force, seeking to make Europe a global superpower. Another alternative might involve emphasizing Europe's distinctive characteristics and comparative advantage by focusing on the application of soft power and non-military security challenges. Given Europe's close partnership with the USA ever since the Second World War and America's position as the world's leading power, these questions of Europe's role in the world inevitably also relate to its relationship with the USA: in responding to global security challenges, should Europe do so in close partnership with America, as a critical friend of America or as a counterweight or even competitor? The future of transatlantic relations is examined in more detail in the next chapter. The larger themes of Europe's global role and its relationship with the USA run throughout this book and will be returned to in the concluding chapter.

Finally, one should consider how the global economic crisis since 2008 has shaped, and may shape, the global security environment and agenda. To date, the economic crisis has accelerated but not fundamentally altered trends that pre-dated 2008. So far at least, despite what is generally viewed as the worst global recession since the 1930s, the post-2008 crisis has not had a major impact on relations between the great powers and in particular has not resulted in an increased like-lihood of great power war. In terms of global security, the primary impact of the post-2008 crisis has been to accelerate the shift in global economic and political power from the West to the non-Western world. Increasingly, therefore, as Europe responds to the new global security agenda it will do so in the context of a multipolar world where non-Western states are now major players. The full impact of the post-2008 economic crisis, however, remains to be seen and there is concern about the possibility of a yet worse economic depression to come. This possi-bility, and its potential impact on European and global security, is returned to in the conclusion to this book.

Chapter 3

The Transatlantic Relationship and NATO: The End of an Era?

Ever since the Second World War, the USA has played a central role in European security. After having come to Europe's rescue twice in less than half a century in the two World Wars, in the context of the Cold War the USA established a semi-permanent alliance with Europe, institutionalized in the form of the North Atlantic Treaty Organization (NATO) and a large US military presence deployed in Europe. For the four decades of the Cold War, NATO and the relationship with the USA were the bedrock of European security, at least for Western Europe. The end of the Cold War thus raised fundamental questions about whether NATO and the post-Second World War transatlantic relation would survive. Although the relationship with the USA has often been controversial and some in Europe advocate an EU foreign, security and defence policy based on independence from America, since the end of the Cold War there has been quite a strong consensus, in both Western Europe and the United States, in favour of maintaining transatlantic co-operation and NATO. When Europe attempted to deal on its own with the Yugoslav conflict in the early and mid-1990s, further, it conspicuously failed to do so, resulting in the USA assuming the lead in addressing the central European security challenge of the 1990s and NATO taking on the new task of intervention and peace-keeping on the European continent. The enlargement of NATO and the EU into Central and Eastern Europe in the late 1990s and 2000s also brought into both organizations a new group of members all of whom were broadly committed to maintaining NATO and continued close co-operation with the USA.

In the wake of the 9/11 terrorist attacks, the Bush administration's 'war on terror' and in particular the 2003 Iraq War triggered a crisis in transatlantic relations. Although some European governments – in particular those of the United Kingdom, Italy and Spain – supported the Bush administration, many European governments and the overwhelming balance of European public opinion strongly opposed central elements of the Bush administration's 'war on terror' and the Iraq War in particular. Early in 2003, hundreds of thousands of European citizens took to the streets of Berlin, Paris, London, Rome, Madrid and other European capitals to protest against the USA's plans for war in Iraq. The demonstrations were among the largest in the continent's history and seemed to symbolize a deepening rift between Europe and the USA. The crisis was widely seen as the worst in transatlantic relations since the US–European alliance had emerged in the Second World War (Peterson, 2004; Cox, 2005). The leading German political philosopher Jürgen Habermas argued that the demonstrations might 'go down in future history books as a signal for the birth of a European public' (Habermas, 2006, p. 40) – the point at which Europe defined its collective political consciousness independent of the USA. In retrospect, while the Bush administration's 'war on terror' and the Iraq War did provoke a major crisis in transatlantic relations, they did not generate the kind of fundamental rupture in the relationship which some predicted. Core elements of transatlantic relations – in economics and within NATO – were maintained, while, despite differences, new measures of US–EU counter-terrorism co-operation were agreed. Following the Iraq War, further, both the Bush administration and its European allies made efforts to re-establish relations. The election of Barack Obama in November 2008, further, brought to power a new American president committed to multilateralism and restoring US relations with its traditional allies in Europe.

This chapter examines transatlantic relations and NATO, exploring developments since the end of the Cold War and assessing the future prospects for the US–European relationship in light of competing theoretical perspectives and the wide range of factors bearing on that relationship. It suggests that the debate on the future of transatlantic relations is too often polarized between those who argue that we are witnessing a fundamental break in US–European relations and those who argue that a close US–European alliance can be maintained. Instead, a more complex and nuanced picture is emerging. The USA is gradually disengaging from Europe as its priorities shift to other regions of the world and the global challenges of terrorism and proliferation, but US disengagement from Europe is unlikely to be complete. NATO, further, has been adapted to a new era, taking on new tasks such as peacekeeping and partnerships with non-members, suggesting that it will remain an enduring and important element of Europe's security landscape. US–European relations at the beginning of the 21st century are thus characterized by important elements of co-operation, on issues ranging from mutual investment in each other's economies to counter-terrorism, but by equally significant differences in other areas, such as climate change. As will be explored in more detail in the next chapter, Europeans are also divided over relations with the USA, with some seeking to maintain a close alliance with America while others seek to establish the EU as a counterweight to it – suggesting that European policy towards America is likely to continue to be ambivalent. While the close alliance of the post-1945 era may be over, the most likely scenario for transatlantic relations remains one of important common interests but divergent perspectives on how those interests should be pursued, with a mixed pattern of co-operation in some areas, and differences – and occasional, but limited, competition – in others.

The post-Cold War era

The end of the Cold War raised fundamental questions about the post-Second World War alliance between the USA and Western Europe. In the absence of the unifying external threat posed by the Soviet Union, would the long-standing alliance between Europe and America survive? If, as mainstream opinion in both Europe and America argued, a continued alliance was desirable, what was the purpose of that alliance? The first Bush administration, which was in power as the Cold War ended from 1989 to 1992, sought to maintain the existing bases of the Euro-Atlantic alliance. In particular, it played a central role in the diplomacy surrounding German reunification in 1989–90, facilitating the negotiations that saw Germany unified and remaining a member of NATO and the EU on terms that the Soviet Union was willing to accept (Zelikow and Rice, 1995). The Bush administration also oversaw the first efforts to adapt NATO to a new era, resulting in a new strategic concept for the alliance adopted at its November 1991 Rome summit.

Nevertheless, the end of the Cold War triggered doubts about the future of the Euro-Atlantic alliance. In response to the fall of the communist regimes in Central and Eastern Europe and the withdrawal of Soviet troops from the region, the Bush administration initiated a substantial reduction in the US military presence in Europe. More significantly, when the Yugoslav war broke out in the summer of 1991, the Bush administration signalled that the management of the conflict should be primarily a European concern. Bush's Secretary of State, James Baker, infamously argued that the USA had 'no dog in that fight'

(Simms, 2002, p. 53). The new strategic concept adopted by NATO at the end of 1991 was to a significant extent still a backward-looking document, premised on the continued existence of a residual Soviet threat (NATO, 1991). Under the 1992 Maastricht Treaty, the new European Union – the successor to the European Community (EC) – was to have a Common Foreign and Security Policy (CFSP) 'covering all areas of foreign and security policy', 'including the eventual framing of a common defence policy, which might in time lead to a common defence' (European Union, 1992, Title V, Articles J1 and J4). The CFSP and a possible EU defence role raised the prospect of a more independent Europe, less in need of and less inclined to co-operate with the USA. The first year of the Clinton administration in 1993 saw continued tensions in transatlantic relations. In contrast to the foreign policy-oriented Atlanticist George Bush, during the 1992 presidential election campaign Bill Clinton had famously said 'it's the economy, stupid' and promised to 'focus like a laserbeam' on economic issues. Clinton's Secretary of State, Warren Christopher, also indicated that the new administration planned to pursue an 'Asia first' policy, emphasizing economic ties with the rapidly growing East (Cox, 1995, p. 75).

The Yugoslav conflict proved the most sensitive issue in transatlantic relations in the early to mid-1990s (Silber and Little, 1995; Simms, 2002). Reflecting more general disquiet in Washington, Clinton had criticized the Europeans for failing to take effective action against Serbia and the Bosnian Serbs. On coming to power, the Clinton administration proposed a policy of 'lift and strike': lifting sanctions and the arms embargo on the Bosnian government and using airstrikes against the Bosnian Serbs. The Europeans countered that such a policy would put their soldiers deployed on the ground as peacekeepers in danger and produce a level killing field rather than the level playing field Clinton desired. Warren Christopher's first visit to Europe as Secretary of State in 1993 resulted in acrimonious disputes over the 'lift and strike' policy and a humiliating back-down by the Clinton administration.

After these initial disputes, the Clinton administration sought to reassert America's role in European security affairs, and the 1990s witnessed a remarkable resurgence in transatlantic relations. Richard Holbrooke, one of the leading architects of the Clinton administration's European policy, argued that America was, and would remain, 'a European power' (Holbrooke, 1995). On all the key European security issues of the 1990s – the Yugoslav conflict, the transformation of

NATO, engagement with Central and Eastern Europe, and building a new relationship with Russia – the USA played a central role. On the Yugoslav conflict, the USA gradually gained support for a more robust policy, resulting in NATO's use of airstrikes against the Bosnian Serbs and the Bosnian peace agreement at the end of 1995 – symbolically agreed at a US military airbase in Dayton, Ohio. The USA was equally central in driving NATO's policy during the Kosovo air war of 1999, and the resulting peace agreement. The deployment of US forces as peacekeepers in Bosnia and Kosovo further reinforced America's commitment to European security. The USA also played the leading role in the transformation of NATO, initiating the Partnership for Peace (PfP) and then driving the policy of enlarging the Alliance into Central and Eastern Europe while at the same time trying to build a new co-operative relationship with Russia.

By the late 1990s, the USA had reasserted a central role in European security affairs, and American leadership had been largely welcomed by most European states – suggesting that transatlantic relations were in remarkably good health, given the concerns of the early 1990s. Beneath the surface, however, significant tensions and differences remained. The US Congress, which had come under Republican control in the 1994 Congressional elections, was unsympathetic to the multilateralism supported by most European governments, refusing to ratify and forcing the Clinton administration to back down on international agreements for a Comprehensive Test Ban Treaty (CTBT), the Kyoto Treaty on climate change and the establishment of the International Criminal Court (ICC). The Congress was also wary of the deployment of US forces on peacekeeping missions, constraining the Clinton administration's ability to act in the Balkans. And during the 1990s, broader American security thinking was shifting in important ways, in particular towards the new global security concerns of WMD proliferation and the 'new terrorism'. In the late 1990s, the Congressionally appointed bipartisan Hart-Rudman Commission had identified the growing vulnerability of the American homeland to terrorist and WMD attack as central threats to US security (US Commission on National Security in the 21st century, 1999), while the similarly established Rumsfeld Commission had argued that long-range ballistic missile proliferation posed a growing and potentially near-term threat to the USA (Commission to Assess the Ballistic Missile Threat to the United States, 1998).

From 9/11 to Obama and beyond

The accession to power of President George W. Bush in early 2001 and the Bush administration's response to the September 2001 terrorist attacks triggered a major crisis in transatlantic relations. Even before 9/11, Europeans had been wary of the Bush administration's likely policies: President Bush and his key foreign policy appointees (such as Vice-President Dick Cheney and Secretary of Defense Donald Rumsfeld) appeared to favour a more confrontational approach to other major powers such as Russia and China, were unsympathetic to US involvement in peacekeeping operations like the ongoing NATO missions in Bosnia and Kosovo and were strongly opposed to multilateral agreements which European governments supported (such as the CTBT, the ICC and Kyoto). One of the immediate impacts of 9/11 was to re-affirm transatlantic solidarity: *Le Monde* newspaper famously declared 'We are all Americans now' (Colombani, 2001); the NATO allies invoked the Article 5 security guarantee at the heart of the NATO treaty for the first time in the Alliance's history (NATO, 2001); and European states supported the US intervention in Afghanistan in late 2001.

The post-9/11 honeymoon in transatlantic relations, however, proved short-lived. The Bush administration's 'war on terror', which linked together terrorism, WMD proliferation and 'rogue states' and viewed military power as a central element in countering these threats, triggered major concerns in Europe about the strategic direction of US foreign policy. In his January 2002 State of the Union speech President Bush infamously referred to Iran, Iraq and North Korea as an 'axis of evil' and warned of the dangers of the 'world's most dangerous regimes' obtaining the 'world's most dangerous weapons' (Bush, 2002). The Bush administration's *National Security Strategy*, published in September 2002, made the concept of preventive war, the idea that one should strike potential threats first before they could develop, a centrepiece of US policy (United States, 2002) – a radical break with the dominant view that armed force should be used only in self-defence or in response to an ongoing conflict or humanitarian crisis. US foreign policy also became more unilateral, with a greater willingness to assert American power and to act with little concern for the views of long-standing allies – as reflected in Secretary of Defense Rumsfeld's dictum that 'The mission must determine the coalition, and the coalition must not determine the mission' (Department of Defense, 2002). In combination, these developments signalled a 'revolution' in

US foreign policy (Daalder and Lindsay, 2003), prompting deep European concerns about an increasingly unilateralist and militarized America with little concern for the views of its long-standing allies or wider international opinion.

Iraq became the lightning rod for diverging American and European perspectives on global security. During the 1990s there had been an uneasy transatlantic consensus on the containment of Saddam Hussein's Iraq through diplomatic isolation, economic sanctions and limited airstrikes by the USA and the UK. Even before 9/11 there was a significant political constituency on the US right favouring the use of force against Iraq; in the wake of 9/11, the Bush administration began to push for a policy of militarily imposed regime change in Iraq. The prospect of a US-led war in Iraq provoked a variety of concerns in Europe (Ortega, 2002; Gordon, 2002): whether the threat posed by Iraq and its WMD ambitions warranted military action; why the existing policy of containment needed to be abandoned; the possible dangers of the precedent set by a preventive war; the potential for destabilization in Iraq and the wider Middle East; and that focusing on Iraq would distract attention from what was widely viewed in Europe as the more important challenge of achieving an Israeli–Palestinian peace settlement.

The US determination to remove Saddam Hussein by force and European opposition to that policy triggered a dramatic crisis in transatlantic relations. As noted above, opposition to the Iraq War triggered massive protests in Europe in early 2003. In March 2003 France, Russia (permanent members of the UN Security Council, with the power to veto any Council resolution) and Germany (serving a two-year term as a non-permanent member of the Council) jointly announced that they would oppose any Security Council resolution authorizing the use of force (French Ministry of Foreign Affairs, 2003). Later that month, the USA chose to launch the war in Iraq without Security Council backing. Turkey, a long-standing US ally, refused to allow American forces to use its territory, forcing the USA to abandon plans for a two-front ground offensive from both south and north. Although Europe was itself divided over Iraq – with governments in Britain, Italy, Spain, Denmark, the Netherlands, Poland and the other Central and East European states supporting the USA – the crisis was nevertheless above all a transatlantic one. For the first time since the Second World War, two of America's major European allies were actively opposing the USA on the central security question of the day as the USA prepared to go to war, while European public opinion was overwhelmingly united against the USA. Although the USA succeeded in overthrowing the Saddam Hussein regime with relative ease in spring 2003, the subsequent confirmation that Iraq's WMD programmes were far less threatening than the USA had portrayed them to be, the prolonged instability and violence in Iraq after 2003, and the argument that the intervention in Iraq had exacerbated rather than ameliorated the problem of globalized Islamic terrorism largely reinforced European views that the US decision to go to war was a major strategic error.

Although arguably the most serious rift in transatlantic relations since the Second World War, the crisis over Iraq did not trigger a complete rupture in the relationship. Despite the differences over Iraq, other important elements of security co-operation continued. In particular, the USA and Europe not only maintained but actually deepened co-operation in relation to the wider problem of international terrorism – for example, in intelligence sharing and airline security (Rees, 2006). The EU's first formal security strategy document, developed and adopted in 2003, showed a significant degree of convergence with US security thinking, emphasizing the growing challenge posed by terrorism, proliferation and failed states and calling for a more robust response to these problems (European Union, 2003a). The differences over Iraq also did not significantly spill over into other areas of the transatlantic relationship such as mutual trade and investment, which were largely unaffected by the crisis. The second George W. Bush administration (2005–09), further, made efforts to repair the political damage done to transatlantic relations by the Iraq War and US–Europe relations stabilized during this period, with intensified efforts to co-operate on issues such as Afghanistan, Iran's nuclear programme and the Israeli–Palestinian conflict. Nevertheless, behind the scenes the legacy of the Iraq War and ongoing European concerns about American policy remained.

The election of President Barack Obama in November 2008 prompted hopes of a dramatic improvement in transatlantic relations (de Vasconcelos and Zaborowski, 2009). In contrast to the conservative, right-wing George W. Bush, Barack Obama's progressive political values were much closer to the European mainstream. On foreign and security policy, Obama was a multilateralist, whose positions on many issues – international law, arms control, climate change – seemed much closer to European views than those of his predecessor. When Obama visited Germany as a presidential candidate in July 2008 he was welcomed like a rock star by crowds numbering in the tens of thousands. On coming to power in 2009, the Obama administration committed to restoring relations with long-standing allies, including Europe, but also took other foreign policy initiatives which Europeans generally supported: a 'reset' designed to improve relations with Russia; a renewed commitment to pursue nuclear arms control; the offer of a 'hand of friendship' to Iran; a call for a 'new beginning' in America's relations with the Islamic world; and engagement with negotiations for a post-Kyoto agreement on climate change. Fairly rapidly, however, European 'Obamamania' began to wear off. Less than a year into Obama's presidency, one observer was discussing 'Europe's Obama fatigue' (Joyner, 2009). On many of the areas where Obama had seemed to promise change, in practice progress was much more difficult, either because of the intractability of the issues or because Obama faced domestic constraints (in particular because of opposition from his Republican opponents). In addition, whereas most, if not all, previous post-World War II US presidents had been instinctive Atlanticists who viewed Europe as important to America and the Europeans as America's natural allies, Obama seemed to come from a younger generation who simply attached less significance to Europe and saw America's core priorities as being in other regions of the world, in particular Asia and the Middle East. Indeed, Obama, who was born in Hawaii and lived for part of his childhood in Indonesia, described himself as 'America's first Pacific President' (Obama, 2009c). The declining importance of Europe was sharply brought home in February 2010 when the Obama administration informed the Europeans that the president would not be attending a planned US–EU summit in Spain in May because his schedule was 'full' (Peters *et al.*, 2010). Equally, the US foreign policy-making elite and the Obama administration were becoming disillusioned with the European allies: there had been hopes that the shifts in US policy under Obama would lead the Europeans to be more supportive of US policy elsewhere in the world. In Afghanistan, however, where the Obama administration expanded the US military presence as part of an effort to stabilize the country, most European allies provided only small numbers of additional troops themselves – reflecting scepticism about the wisdom of the operation. By 2011–12 attention was turning to the forthcoming November 2012 US presidential election. Republican candidates for the presidency promised a tougher approach to major powers like China and 'rogue states' such as Iran (Tisdall, 2012), suggesting that most Europeans would be happier with a second term for Obama. Nevertheless, the larger lesson of the transition from Bush to Obama seemed to be that while a Democratic president might improve the mood music of transatlantic relations, significant differences would remain regardless of who occupied the White House.

Behind the specific details of changing administrations in the USA and Europe are larger geostrategic shifts. With Europe relatively peaceful and stable, American priorities have shifted to the Middle East, where oil, Islamic terrorism and nuclear proliferation are central concerns for the USA, and to Asia, where the rise of China and the Asian market are key issues for the USA. In the 2000s the wars in Iraq and Afghanistan were the central preoccupations of US foreign policy. The last American troops were withdrawn from Iraq at the end of 2011 and the USA (and its NATO allies) planned to withdraw most forces from Afghanistan by 2014. In the context of the withdrawal from Iraq and Afghanistan, the Obama administration argued that the USA had reached a 'pivot point', at which it would re-orient US foreign policy towards Asia. According to Secretary of State Hillary Clinton 'in the 21st century, the world's strategic and economic center of gravity will be the Asia Pacific ... The 21st century will be America's Pacific century, a period of unprecedented outreach and partnership in this dynamic, complex, and consequential region' (Rodham Clinton, 2011).

The US strategic shift away from Europe has also been reflected in the American military presence in the region. In 1991 the USA still had just over 300,000 troops deployed in Western Europe; by 2000 this number had been reduced to 100,000, and by 2010 the number had been reduced to about 78,000. America's involvement in the NATO peacekeeping operations in Bosnia from 1995 and Kosovo from 1999 gave an additional dimension to the US military presence in Europe, with about 11,000 US troops deployed in the Balkans in 2000; but by 2010 this had been reduced to 800 troops in Kosovo (International Institute for Strategic Studies, 1991, 2000 and 2010a). In January 2012, further, the Obama administration published a new *Defense Strategic Guidance* document that reflected both the need to reduce defence spending in the context of ongoing budget deficit problems and the strategic pivot to Asia noted above. According to the document, the USA would 'of necessity rebalance toward the Asia-Pacific region ... In keeping with this evolving strategic landscape, our posture in Europe must also evolve' (Department of Defense, 2012, pp. 1–2). In the context of this defence review, the USA decided to reduce to two the four brigades currently deployed in Europe (three in Germany, one in Italy), a reduction of about 10,000 troops (Barnes, 2012). The new US

Defense Strategic Guidance and the decision to withdraw some forces from Europe prompted Britain's defence minister, Philip Hammond, to warn of the strategic uncertainties Europe faced in its relationship with Russia:

> If the US is going to see its focus drawn increasingly to the Asia Pacific region, how does it secure the backyard? How does it ensure that Russia is locked into a system of global governance and collaboration ... I am not sure we have an answer to that yet. That is going to be one of the big challenges: how that relationship is managed forward. (Quoted in Mannion, 2012)

While the US military presence in Europe is likely to be reduced, US disengagement from Europe is unlikely to be complete, certainly in the short to medium term. There is little pressure in the USA for the withdrawal of all American military forces from Europe or the abandonment of NATO, while American foreign policy-makers continue to view Europe as a region where the USA has significant interests. Nevertheless, the US re-orientation towards the Asia-Pacific and gradual US disengagement from Europe seem likely to continue, raising important questions about the management of security problems on the periphery of the European security community and the ability – or otherwise – of European states and the EU to take on this task.

NATO: transformation and uncertainty

The end of the Cold War and the disappearance of the 'Soviet threat' removed NATO's historic *raison d'être*. As François Heisbourg put it, the question was no longer simply what direction the Alliance should take but whether it could or should survive at all (Heisbourg, 1992). The mainstream view in both Europe and America was that NATO should be maintained, if only as an insurance policy against any residual Russian military threat, the emergence of an overly powerful Germany or a return to the conflicts of the first half of the 20th century. What roles NATO could or should play in the new Europe was less clear. At one end of the spectrum, some analysts argued for a minimalist NATO that would act as an insurance policy for worst-case scenarios but would not overstretch itself by taking on new tasks (Brown, 1999). Others argued that NATO's potential should be maximized by

giving the Alliance a central role in addressing the new security challenges in post-communist Europe and perhaps also globally (Hunter,
1999). The influential US Senator, Richard Lugar, argued that NATO
had to 'go out of area' – that is, take on new security tasks beyond the
defence of its members' territories – or risk going out of business
(Lugar, 1993).

NATO's transformation

Since the 1990s NATO has undergone a remarkable transformation
(Yost, 1998; Moore, 2007) – summarized in Table 3.1. NATO 1.0/1.1
was the Cold War alliance that was initially formed to defend Western
Europe (NATO 1.0) but from the late 1960s also took on the task of
political-military engagement and confidence building with the Soviet
bloc in the context of East–West détente (NATO 1.1). In the 1990s
NATO was radically re-defined as the Alliance took on new tasks in
post-communist Europe, in particular intervention and peacekeeping
in the Yugoslav conflict, the development of new partnership relationships with the post-communist states and enlargement of its
membership into Central and Eastern Europe (NATO 2.0). In the
aftermath of the 9/11 terrorist attacks, the Bush administration
sought to enlist NATO in its 'global war on terrorism'. This version of
the Alliance – NATO 2.1 or perhaps even NATO 3.0 – would have
involved NATO taking on a more central role in responding to terrorism, WMD proliferation and 'rogue states' and given the Alliance a
global remit. Although NATO did take on the task of peacekeeping in
Afghanistan, the European allies were sceptical of key elements of the
Bush administration's 'global war on terrorism' and wary of turning
NATO into a global policeman. NATO 2.1 was thus to some extent
stillborn. The 2008 Georgia War, further, prompted growing concern
about the possible military threat posed by Russia, leading to a
renewed emphasis on the Alliance's old roles of defence and deterrence *vis-à-vis* Russia. NATO's new strategic concept of 2010 (NATO
2.2) thus sought to strike a balance between the organization's role as
a defence alliance and its newer roles in addressing security challenges
beyond its borders (NATO, 2010a). In the twenty-odd years since the
end of the Cold War, NATO has thus undergone a remarkable transition from a defence alliance structured around the tasks of defence
and deterrence *vis-à-vis* the Soviet bloc to a radically different organization with a continuing defence role, but also heavily engaged in
peacekeeping/intervention operations, with a significantly expanded

membership, partnership arrangements with many non-members and a role in addressing new security challenges such as proliferation and cyber security.

NATO's new roles can be summarized as follows:

- *Peacekeeping/intervention*: during the Cold War, NATO's role was limited to defence and deterrence *vis-à-vis* the Soviet bloc and the Alliance did not engage in 'out of area' operations (NATO jargon for military operations beyond the territory of its members). Although initially reluctant to be drawn into the Yugoslav conflict, as the United Nations' and the European Union's peacemaking efforts in the Balkans failed, NATO eventually used air strikes to achieve peace settlements in Bosnia in 1995 and Kosovo in 1999, in both cases following this with the deployment of large peacekeeping forces on the ground. In the 2000s, this was followed by the deployment of an even larger force in Afghanistan as part of efforts to stabilize that country, leading NATO into its first real ground combat operation. By 2011–12, however, NATO was beginning a process of withdrawal from Afghanistan and the ultimate outcome of NATO's intervention in that country remained to be seen. In 2011 NATO once again used air strikes to halt an emerging conflict in Libya, resulting in the fall of the authoritarian Gaddafi regime. Although the Alliance's role in peacekeeping and intervention has been and remains controversial, NATO has at minimum demonstrated that where forceful military intervention may be necessary it is perhaps the only multilateral institution capable of providing the necessary institutional structure and military capability. (NATO's role in peacekeeping and intervention is examined in more detail in Chapter 6.)
- *Partnerships*: since the early 1990s NATO has established a series of partnership relations with non-members, which act as frameworks for political dialogue with these states, allow NATO to support military reforms in partner countries and facilitate partner states' armed forces in participating in NATO-led peacekeeping operations. The model for these partnerships was the Partnership for Peace (PfP), established in 1994, which has been joined by virtually all non-NATO European states (primarily now the former Soviet and Balkan states, plus the European neutral states). The PfP operates on the basis of flexible bilateral co-operation between NATO and each partner (determined primarily by the extent of the partner's interest in such co-operation), plus multilateral activities

TABLE 3.1 *NATO's evolution*

NATO Variant	Key document	Threat assessment	Geographical remit	Roles	Instruments
NATO 1.0 (1949–1966)	NATO Treaty 1949	'Soviet threat'	North Atlantic region	Defence and deterrence	Forward-deployed conventional forces and nuclear weapons
NATO 1.1 (1967–1989)	Harmel Report 1967	'Soviet threat' and risk of East–West conflict	North Atlantic region	Defence and deterrence, plus co-operation with the Soviet bloc	Forward-deployed conventional forces and nuclear weapons, plus political engagement and arms control
NATO 2.0 (1989–2001)	Strategic Concept 1999	Conflicts and instability in the Euro-Atlantic region	Euro-Atlantic region	Promotion of co-operation and stability in the Euro-Atlantic region	Partnership with non-members, enlargement of membership, peace keeping/intervention in conflicts (primarily former Yugoslavia)

NATO 2.1 (2001–2009)	Prague Summit Declaration 2002	Conflicts and instability in the Euro-Atlantic region, plus terrorism, WMD proliferation and failed states	Global	Promotion of co-operation and stability in the Euro-Atlantic region, plus prevention/ defence/deterrence *vis-à-vis* terrorism and proliferation, and stabilization of failed states	Partnership with non-members (globally), missile defence, preventive military action and peacekeeping/ intervention in failed states (primarily Afghanistan)
NATO 2.2 (2010–)	*Strategic Concept 2010*	Direct threats to NATO territory and members, plus consequences of instability beyond NATO's borders	Euro-Atlantic region, plus limited global role	Defence and deterrence, plus promotion of co-operation and stability in the Euro-Atlantic region (and globally)	Conventional forces, nuclear weapons and missile defences, plus partnerships with non-members, and peacekeeping

(such as military exercises) involving ad hoc combinations of NATO members and partners. In 1994 NATO also established a Mediterranean Dialogue with its North African neighbours and Israel, and in 2004 the Istanbul Co-operation Initiative as a framework for co-operation with the Persian Gulf states, with Bahrain, Kuwait, Qatar and the United Arab Emirates joining. The Mediterranean Dialogue and the Istanbul Co-operation Initiative have, however, been less successful than PfP, with limited substantive co-operation between NATO and its partners. NATO has also established partnership relations with a group of 'global partners', primarily Australia, Japan, New Zealand and South Korea, but also Afghanistan, Iraq and Pakistan. These states now have regular political dialogue with NATO, as well as in some cases participating in NATO-led peacekeeping operations. In addition to its partnerships with individual states, NATO has also established partnerships with a number of other international organizations, in particular the United Nations, the European Union and the African Union. These inter-organizational partnerships have focused primarily on peacekeeping, with NATO for example providing support to the African Union's peacekeeping operation in Darfur in the mid-2000s.

- *Enlargement*: a further controversial issue has been NATO enlargement. With the end of the Cold War, the post-communist Central and Eastern European states pressed for membership of NATO, both as part of their larger re-integration with the West and as a security guarantee against potential threats from Russia. Supporters argued that NATO membership could underpin democratization and reform in Central and Eastern Europe, just as it arguably had done in Western Europe after the Second World War (Allin, 1995; Asmus *et al.*, 1995). Critics argued that expanding NATO risked provoking a new confrontation with Russia and a new division of Europe (Brown, 1995; Gaddis, 1998). NATO sought to square this circle by extending membership to some states while offering enhanced co-operation to those remaining outside the Alliance, in particular Russia (Asmus, 2004). Poland, the Czech Republic and Hungary joined the Alliance in 1999, followed by Estonia, Latvia, Lithuania, Slovakia, Slovenia, Romania and Bulgaria in 2004, thereby extending NATO's membership across Central and Eastern Europe from the Baltic Sea to the Black Sea. Albania and Croatia joined NATO in 2009 and other Western Balkan states may follow suit in future. As was noted in Chapter 1, however, by the late 2000s/early 2010s the likely limits of NATO (and EU) enlargement were becoming clearer, with former Soviet states such as Ukraine and Georgia unlikely to join the Alliance (or the EU) for the foreseeable future. There has also been discussion of the possibility of extending NATO membership to countries outside Europe, such as Australia, Japan and Israel. Such a step might make NATO a key institutional expression of a global alliance of democracies. While some in the USA have supported this idea, there is little appetite amongst the European member states for such an explicitly 'global NATO' and the prospect of non-European states joining NATO is remote. While enlargement played an important role in NATO's transformation in the 1990s and 2000s, it seems likely to be less central to the Alliance's agenda in future.

- *NATO–Russia co-operation*: building a sustainable, peaceful relationship with NATO's former enemy, Russia, has been a major issue for the Alliance since the early 1990s. NATO has sought to do this by establishing institutionalized relations with Moscow (in particular via a NATO–Russia Founding Act signed in 1997 and a NATO–Russia Council established in 2002), as well as by engaging in practical co-operation with Russia (for example, through Russia's participation in NATO's peacekeeping operations in Bosnia and Kosovo). The NATO–Russia relationship, however, remains characterized by significant differences between the two partners and has sometimes been disrupted by serious disputes between them (in particular over the Kosovo War in 1999 and the Georgia War in 2008). Relations with Russia are likely therefore to be an ongoing and difficult challenge for NATO. (The NATO–Russia relationship is examined in more detail in Chapter 5.)

- *Proliferation*: since the 1990s, WMD proliferation has become an increasingly important part of NATO's agenda. In 2000 a WMD Centre was established within NATO's headquarters in Brussels to facilitate information exchange and co-operation amongst NATO members in relation to proliferation. NATO is working to enhance its members' chemical, biological, radiological and nuclear (CBRN) defence capabilities – that is, structures and forces designed to protect against attacks involving CBRN weapons or materials. NATO is also exploring how the concept of deterrence – and associated conventional and nuclear force structures – may be adapted to counter WMD threats (such as that potentially posed by a future nuclear-armed Iran). In addition, NATO is developing missile defences designed to protect against attack by missiles armed with WMD; initially, this involved defences designed to protect NATO forces deployed outside the Alliance's territory, but in 2010 the Alliance took the larger decision to develop defences to protect its member states' population and territory. (Proliferation is addressed in more detail in Chapter 7.)

- *Cyber security*: in 2007 Estonia experienced a major cyber-attack – widely believed to have been orchestrated from within Russia – which temporarily brought down the computer systems of Estonian government and economic institutions. In addition, the use of cyber-attacks against Georgia in the 2008 Georgia War highlighted the way in which offensive cyber action was likely to be a significant part of conventional wars in future. Although cyber security has been on NATO's agenda since the early 2000s, the Estonian and Georgian cases pushed the issue to the fore and resulted in the adoption of a formal NATO Cyber Defence Policy in July 2011. In this context, NATO has strengthened the cyber security of its headquarters in Brussels and its military command structure, intensified consultation and co-operation amongst member states on the issue, created Rapid Reaction Teams (RRTs) capable of being deployed at short notice to assist countries with cyber security and established a Co-operative Cyber Defence Centre of Excellence (based in Tallinn).

Reflecting NATO's ongoing adaptation to new security threats, a new Emerging Security Challenges Division was created within NATO's headquarters in Brussels in 2010, focusing in particular on terrorism, proliferation, cyber security and energy security. While NATO has taken a variety of steps designed to respond to such new or non-traditional security threats, the Alliance is, in practice, unlikely to be central in addressing these threats. Much counter-terrorism policy involves intelligence, internal security and policing issues that remain largely outside NATO's remit and where the EU and US–EU co-operation are more central (see Chapter 8). In relation to proliferation, global frameworks – such as the UN Security Council, the Nuclear Non-Proliferation Treaty (NPT) and the International Atomic Energy Agency (IAEA) – and specific regional negotiations – such as those involving Iran and North Korea – are likely to play a greater role than NATO (see Chapter 7). On energy security, core issues of energy policy are likely to be addressed at the national or EU level and, while hypothetically NATO could use military force to defend access to oil supplies, such action is more likely to be undertaken by the USA alone or by a US-led ad hoc coalition rather than though NATO.

NATO: continuing uncertainties

Despite NATO's remarkable transformation since the end of the Cold War, there has also been continuous uncertainty about NATO's future, with observers warning of a number of trends that threaten the unity, effectiveness and even survival of the Alliance. During this period, NATO experienced a number of major internal crises in relation to particular conflicts. In the early and mid-1990s deep divisions emerged between the USA and the European NATO members over the Bosnia conflict, with the USA effectively accusing the Europeans of appeasement and arguing for a more forceful approach and the Europeans responding that the USA had failed to understand the complexities of the conflict and, unlike the Europeans, was unwilling to put its own soldiers in harm's way on the ground. (These divisions were eventually overcome in 1994–95, when the USA took the lead in shaping a more forceful approach to the Bosnian conflict.) Over the 2003 Iraq War, two of NATO's leading members, France and Germany, not only sharply criticized American policy but also – for the first time in the Alliance's history – actively opposed that policy in the UN Security Council. In the run-up to the war, French, German and Belgian reluctance to prepare for the collective defence of fellow NATO member Turkey, lest such a step be seen as supporting US plans for war in Iraq, seemed to call the NATO security guarantee into question – triggering heated disputes and what the US ambassador to NATO called a 'near death experience' for the Alliance (Black, 2003). Although less severe than the crises over Bosnia and Iraq, Afghanistan and Libya also highlighted divisions within NATO. In Afghanistan, Germany, France and other European members were reluctant allies – contributing military forces but sceptical over what was a US-dominated operation and therefore limiting their military contributions, both in terms of troop numbers and by imposing national 'caveats' on the use of their forces. In relation to Libya in 2011, Germany and a number of other European allies were sceptical of NATO's intervention and did not contribute military forces to the operation.

A second problem for NATO has been defence spending and military capabilities. Since the end of the Cold War most NATO members have cut defence expenditure significantly, resulting in ongoing concerns about the Alliance's ability to maintain the capabilities necessary both for defence of NATO's territory and for intervention operations further afield. This problem also has a particular transatlantic dimension, both because the USA spends significantly more on defence (as a percentage of GDP) than most European NATO members and because of concerns that a European failure to invest in military high technology is producing a 'military gap', whereby European armed forces will no longer be capable of operating alongside their more advanced US counterparts. These concerns were exacerbated by the impact of 9/11, which resulted in a major increase in US defence expenditure but no comparable European increase. The global financial and economic crisis since 2008 has only added to these concerns, with all NATO members, but especially the European allies, significantly reducing defence expenditure. In 2011 then US Secretary of Defense Robert Gates argued that 'for all but a handful of allies, defense budgets – in absolute terms, as a share of economic output – have been chronically starved for adequate funding for a long time, with the shortfalls compounding on themselves each year', warning NATO's European members that they faced 'the very real possibility of collective military irrelevance' (Gates, 2011b).

An additional problem for NATO has been the EU's developing foreign, security and defence policy role (see Chapters 4 and 6). Some in the USA and in some European states, especially in the more Atlanticist countries such as the UK, view the EU's emerging role as a threat to NATO, fearing that the EU is seeking to supplant NATO. These fears have been reinforced by the reality that some European political leaders, in particular in France, view the EU as a counterweight to US political dominance in the transatlantic relation and to NATO. An additional concern is that the EU risks duplicating, at potentially significant financial cost, NATO's military planning and command and control structures. In practice, however, the EU's defence role remains limited: to date it has focused primarily on quite small-scale operations at the softer end of the spectrum of peacekeeping and intervention and has developed only a relatively small independent military planning and command and control capacity. Where larger-scale and more forceful military action has been undertaken, as in Bosnia, Kosovo, Afghanistan and Libya, NATO has remained the institutional vehicle of choice. Nevertheless, beneath the surface there remains an ongoing and unresolved debate about the appropriate balance between NATO and the EU.

These various problems have produced ongoing concerns about the durability of NATO, with politicians and analysts on both sides of the Atlantic warning on a fairly regular basis that NATO faces decline, irrelevance or even an end to its existence. It should be noted, however, that such warnings and predictions pre-date the end of the Cold War and have been a perennial feature of NATO's existence. Early crises such as the 1956 Suez War and the Vietnam War produced deep political divisions between NATO's members. Throughout its history, NATO has been characterized by debate over 'burden-sharing', with the USA consistently accusing its European allies of failing to contribute enough to collective defence. The European allies have often also balked at American dominance of NATO and been wary of specific US policies from Vietnam to Afghanistan. Despite these problems, NATO has endured. Furthermore, although some analysts predicted that the end of the Cold War and the disappearance of the 'Soviet threat' would result in NATO's demise, the Alliance has now outlived the Cold War by more than twenty years – half as long already as its Cold War existence. Furthermore, there remains a fairly strong political consensus in support of NATO: no member state's government has proposed winding up NATO; no member state has sought to withdraw from NATO; the Alliance's membership has expanded to include the Central and Eastern European states; and the attention of governments and policy-makers has focused on how best to reform and modernize the Alliance. These various factors suggest that, for all the warnings about NATO's decline or demise, the Alliance is likely to continue to exist (Thies, 2009). Nevertheless, NATO has changed in an important but more subtle way since the end of the Cold War. During the Cold War, NATO was *the* security institution of choice for its member states: the primary means for addressing the dominant security threat they faced. Since the end of the Cold War, NATO has become one of a number of institutional frameworks available to its member states for addressing the more diverse and complex range of security threats they now face, alongside the EU in particular, but also other institutions such as the United Nations, the Organization for Security and Co-operation in Europe (OSCE) and other regional and functional institutions. NATO will continue to exist and is likely to have continuing relevance for collective defence and where forceful military intervention is deemed necessary, but it is also unlikely to regain its earlier pre-eminence.

Interpreting transatlantic relations

How should we interpret the evolution of transatlantic relations since the end of the Cold War and September 2001, and what does this suggest about their future? Drawing on competing theoretical approaches, analysts suggest a variety of different conclusions. Realists and neo-realists argue that alliances are the products of common external threats or interests. From this perspective, the post-Second World War alliance between the USA and Europe was a product of the Soviet threat to Western Europe and the bipolar world dominated by the two superpowers. Such alliances, however, are not permanent and tend to disintegrate once the threat that gave rise to them ceases to exist (Walt, 1997). The disappearance of the Soviet Union was therefore bound to trigger the break-up of the post-war transatlantic alliance, as the unity imposed by a common external threat dissipated and European and American interests and threat perceptions diverged (Mearsheimer, 1990; Waltz, 1993).

An alternative realist perspective has been advanced by Robert Kagan (2002, 2003). Kagan argues that the dramatic differential in power, especially military power, between the USA and Europe, and the different historical experiences of the two are producing increasingly divergent approaches to global security. As the world's only super-power, the USA defines its security and interests in global terms. The USA's hegemonic power inclines it to act unilaterally and to view mili-tary force as a key tool of foreign policy. In contrast, Europe's relative weakness – its lack of military power compared to the USA, and the disunity resulting from Europe's decentralized power structure – leads it to support multilateral and non-military approaches to security problems. The post-war European experience of integration also leads Europe to view its post-modern 'paradise' as a model for world order. In contrast, the USA's experience as a global superpower leads it to view global politics primarily in terms of power. Kagan concludes that, while European and American leaders may seek to ameliorate the consequences of their differences, the underlying realities of power and history will produce increasingly divergent perspectives on global secu-rity challenges.

In contrast to these realist and neo-realist arguments, liberal and neo-liberal theorists argue that common democratic values, a shared identity and institutional ties will hold Europe and America together. For liberals, states' foreign policy choices are not simply a result of material factors (such as the balance of power or the existence of 'objective' external threats), but rather reflect states' values and political systems. From this perspective, the post-war transatlantic alliance reflected not simply the existence of a perceived external threat but also the common democratic and capitalist heritage of the USA and Europe. Despite the end of the Soviet threat, these common values will continue to provide a key basis for co-operation between the USA and Europe. As the two primary centres of democracy and capitalism in the world, they are therefore natural allies. Notwithstanding the recent transatlantic differences, the USA and Europe have much more in common with each other than they do with any other major centres of power or political forces (such as China, Russia or Islam). In concrete terms, the USA and Europe share a common interest in defending democracy against potential threats (such as globalized Islamic terrorism) and in maintaining the liberal international economic order on which capitalism rests. In the long run, common interests based on common values will reassert themselves (Nye, 2000).

A further variant of the liberal argument suggests that Europe and America share a common identity as the core of the West, forged not only by common values but also by a shared history and cultural heritage (Risse-Kappen, 1996; Sjursen, 2004). This common identity may facilitate continued transatlantic co-operation, since identity shapes states' perceptions of interests and threats. A third strand of liberalism focuses on the role of institutional ties in underpinning long-term co-operation, in particular NATO, but also the formal US–EU relationship established in the 1990s, as well as a multitude of lower-level diplomatic, military and economic ties between the USA and Europe. Here, it is argued that institutionalized ties between states help to maintain long-term co-operation, facilitate compromise, create bureaucratic interests in co-operation and reinforce a sense of common identity (Keohane and Martin, 1995). Together, liberals argue, the combination of shared values, a common identity and institutionalized ties generate a powerful imperative for continued close co-operation between the USA and Europe.

Where does the balance lie between these competing theoretical approaches? The realist argument that the perception of a common threat in the form of the Soviet Union played a central role in the establishment of the post-1945 transatlantic alliance is undoubtedly correct. The disappearance of that threat has removed a significant part of the glue that held the US–European alliance together. The different geostrategic positions of the USA and Europe and the disparity in power, especially military power, between the two has tended to produce different views of the world. The USA views the world from the perspective of a global superpower, with all the attendant risks and responsibilities that go with that status. Europeans tend to view the world from the perspective of a set of middle powers, more conscious of the limits of power and the value of multilateralism. While realists highlight the factors pulling Europe and America apart, the conclusion that these will inevitably produce a long-term split between the two probably stretches the argument too far.

Some weight should be given to the liberal view that common democratic values are likely to produce common perceptions of interests and threats. For all their differences, Europe and America, as noted earlier, still have much more in common with each other than they do with communist China, Islamic radicals or Russian nationalists. There is a strong case that Europe and America share a common long-term interest in maintaining a liberal international economic order, promoting democracy, preventing the emergence of potentially threatening hegemonic powers, countering international terrorism and containing WMD proliferation. At a minimum, shared democratic values provide an important basis for long-term co-operation. The liberal argument, however, also has shortcomings. While shared values may produce broadly similar world views, they do not necessarily result in more concrete common assessments of threats or how to respond to those threats. Since the 1990s, while there has been a broad transatlantic consensus that proliferation and terrorism are central security challenges, the nature and extent of the threats posed by these problems and how to respond to them have been much more contentious. In addition, while Europe and America share core democratic values, political sociologists have long pointed out that there are also important differences between the two (Lipset, 1990): the USA is more individualistic, more market-orientated and more religious, and Europe is more communitarian, more statist economically and more secular. Since the 1960s, further, American society and politics has shifted to the right, reinforcing the differences between the USA and Europe (Micklethwait and Wooldridge, 2004).

The liberal argument that institutional ties will help to maintain transatlantic co-operation also needs to be subjected to careful analysis. While it probably is the case that institutions can help to maintain co-operation that might dissipate in their absence, countervailing factors – such as changing external forces and changes in members' interests – may pull relationships in other directions. While institutions may have a degree of autonomous influence, their effectiveness as a means of maintaining co-operation nevertheless also depends to a significant degree on the willingness of member states to use them, suggesting that they require deliberate support from their members and may degrade over time if that support declines. Nevertheless, the survival and adaptation of NATO since the end of the Cold War suggests that institutions, once established, can have a significant impact in terms of maintaining co-operation amongst their members.

These different theoretical perspectives emphasize the primacy of a particular factor or set of factors – power for realists, values and institutions for liberals – and thus tend towards determinism. A more sophisticated analysis would suggest that the future of transatlantic relations is likely to be determined by the interaction between these factors, rather than any one of them alone. From this perspective, common democratic values are likely to produce important common general interests, but the very different geostrategic positions and power capacities of Europe and America are likely to produce different priorities and different approaches to addressing security challenges. There is thus a strong case that while the USA and Europe share important common interests, their strategic cultures – their broad approaches to foreign and security policy, in particular the use of force – are diverging in important ways. As the world's only superpower, the USA has an inherently global perspective, is used to wielding its hard power, has great capacity to act unilaterally, and balks at the constraints of multilateralism. In contrast, Europe – whether as the EU or as the many states that make up the continent – is often more concerned with developments in its immediate neighbourhood, has less capacity to utilize hard power or act unilaterally, and is more supportive of multilateral institutions. Robert Kagan has summed this up as the difference between a warlike Mars (the USA) and a pacifist Venus (Europe) (Kagan, 2002). Some critics have countered that the real division lies within the USA, between Martian Republicans and Venusian Democrats. While it is true that there are important foreign policy differences between Republicans and Democrats, and the latter's perspectives may generally be closer to those of much of Europe, there nevertheless remains a strong case that the centres of gravity in both domestic politics and foreign policy in the USA and Europe are quite different.

The different theoretical perspectives discussed here also give little space to agency – that is, the freedom of states and political leaders to make significant foreign policy choices, and the impact these choices may have on long-term developments. While states' foreign policies are constrained and shaped by long-term material and social forces, states nevertheless also retain the capacity for independent action and their choices may have an important impact on future patterns of relations. Agency may be particularly important during periods of major international flux: changed external circumstances enforce changes on states. The past two decades and current era – with all the changes triggered by the end of the Cold War, the 9/11 terrorist attacks and the 2008 global financial and economic crisis – can be viewed as just such a period of flux in transatlantic relations.

Against this background, James Steinberg (2003) has described the transatlantic relationship of the early 21st century as 'an elective partnership' – a relationship which both sides face strategic choices over whether, in what ways and at what cost, they wish to maintain. The USA faces the question of how far it continues to view the Europeans as valued partners, and to what extent it may be willing to compromise in order to maintain European support. In foreign policy terms, recent US presidential elections – those of 2004 and 2008, for example – have in part been debates about how far the USA should emphasize the unilateral exercise of American power and how far it should emphasize multilateralism and working with allies such as its partners in Europe, with Republicans generally favouring the former approach and Democrats the latter. In the 2000s and 2010s, the Bush administration epitomized the former approach and the Obama administration the latter, with the 2012 presidential election likely to produce a further round of this debate. The USA thus seems likely to remain pulled between different strategic approaches to relations with its allies, both in Europe and elsewhere.

Europeans also face strategic choices in their relations with America, in particular between seeking to maintain a close alliance with the USA and pursuing greater foreign and security policy autonomy. To the extent that the EU is emerging as an independent actor in its own right, it thus faces a choice between positioning itself as a partner and ally of the USA or acting as a counterweight to American power and policies. As will be explored in more detail in the next chapter, Europeans and the EU are divided on these questions. This intra-European divide is symbolized by the competing perspectives of Britain and France, with the former emphasizing a continued close alliance with the USA and seeking to influence US policy from within that relationship and the latter seeking to establish Europe as an autonomous force in its own right and influence the USA through the weight of its power. The divisions between and within European countries on relations with the

USA suggest that neither the British nor the French view is likely to win out completely. The most likely European strategic choice may therefore be one that combines elements of a continued alliance with the USA with greater European autonomy. Europeans, however, are likely to face important and ongoing choices as to where the balance should lie.

The transatlantic relation is thus shaped by contradictory dynamics on both sides of the Atlantic. For the USA, there are obvious advantages to unilateralism – in particular in terms of freedom of manoeuvre and being unencumbered by the constraints of working with allies – but there are also real benefits to working with its European allies, especially in terms of international legitimacy, political support and material assistance. For Europeans, there are arguments for asserting greater independence from the USA – because European interests arguably differ from those of America and because of the risks of being drawn into American policies over which Europe has little influence – but also arguments that Europe continues both to need the USA and to benefit from the US presence in Europe. These contradictory dynamics are likely to continue to shape the transatlantic relationship, suggesting that a dramatic rupture or complete erosion of the co-operation built up since the Second World War is unlikely but also that the relationship is likely to be characterized by periodic disputes and ongoing tensions.

Conclusion

The debate on the future prospects for transatlantic relations tends to be polarized between the view that European and American perspectives on global security are diverging and the transatlantic alliance is doomed, and an alternative perspective suggesting that shared democratic values, common interests and institutional ties will provide the basis for a continued long-term partnership. Realism and liberalism provide competing theoretical fuel for this debate. This chapter has suggested that a more subtle and nuanced assessment is needed. Europe and the USA share common democratic values and important broad interests, but European and American threat assessments, priorities and strategic cultures are also diverging in important ways. Since the end of the Cold War, US foreign policy priorities have shifted away from a Europe that is largely at peace – and therefore no longer a strategic 'problem' for the USA – and towards other regions, in particular Asia and the Middle East, and the new global security challenges of terrorism and proliferation. In this context, the USA has significantly reduced its military presence in Europe and Europe ranks lower in the hierarchy of American strategic priorities. At the same time, however, the USA has not completely abandoned Europe, nor does this seem likely: while American politicians and foreign policy-makers are often sceptical about the European contribution to addressing common security threats, there is nevertheless still a quite strong consensus in favour of NATO and of continued US engagement in Europe. Equally, the European side of the transatlantic relationship has changed significantly since the end of the Cold War: the establishment of the European Union, its Common Foreign and Security Policy (CFSP) and Common Security and Defence Policy (CSDP) – see the next chapter – have given greater strategic weight to Europe as a collective entity, in the form of the EU, and resulted in the EU playing a much greater role in its immediate neighbourhood and globally. In this context, the EU is sometimes a partner of the USA, sometimes an antagonist to the USA (at least on some specific policy issues such as climate change and the ICC) and sometimes acts independently of, but not in confrontation with, the USA (as in much of the EU's peacekeeping and crisis management activity). Some political leaders within Europe view the EU as a counterweight to the USA and see this as the defining feature of EU foreign policy. Most European states and politicians, however, view a continued US role in Europe as a major force for stability and security on the continent and the maintenance of a partnership with the USA as a central objective of national and EU foreign policy.

In this context, NATO remains the key institutional expression of transatlantic co-operation. NATO is based on a deeply entrenched political and legal commitment to the principle of collective defence and strongly institutionalized processes of political consultation and military co-operation amongst its members. Since the end of the Cold War, while retaining its initial function as a defence alliance, NATO has taken on new roles, in particular in the areas of peacekeeping/intervention and partnership with non-members, resulting in a major transformation of the Alliance. Although NATO has experienced periodic major disputes between its members, such as over the 2003 Iraq War, and there remain ongoing warnings of its decline or demise, NATO's member states remain strongly committed to maintaining the Alliance.

The outcome of these trends is a complex pattern of co-operation in some spheres of security, major policy divergences in other areas, and a set of transatlantic relationships – USA–EU, NATO, bilateral and within wider forums such as the United Nations – with a variety of different, overlapping, sometimes complementary and sometimes contradictory dynamics. This pattern does not suggest a complete breakdown in transatlantic relations or the emergence of an era of confrontation between the USA and Europe, but it does indicate that the post-1945 era in which Europe and America were each other's primary partners and default allies has indeed come to an end. For both the USA and Europe, the transatlantic relationship has become 'an elective partnership' – a partnership both sides have greater freedom to pursue (or not) than they did in the post-1945 era, and hence one more dependent on uncertain strategic choices.

Chapter 4

The EU and the Europeanization of European Security

In the 1990s and 2000s the European Union (EU) assumed an increasingly prominent role in European security affairs, as well as a growing but more limited role in responding to the new global security agenda. With a majority of member states also adopting a new single currency (the euro) and joining the new Schengen border-free zone, an increasingly integrated European Union with a growing role in the world seemed to be emerging. Under the Maastricht Treaty (provisionally agreed in 1991, signed in 1992 and entering into force in 1993), the EU's member states committed themselves to the establishment of a Common Foreign and Security Policy (CFSP) and co-operation in internal security or what the EU refers to as Justice and Home Affairs (JHA). During the 1990s, the CFSP was given substance through the development of a series of new policies and institutions directed towards the EU's immediate neighbours in Central and Eastern Europe, the Balkans, the former Soviet Union and the Mediterranean. Within this context, the EU in many ways assumed the central role in efforts to promote stability and security in the wider Europe. At the end of the 1990s, the EU also agreed to establish a common European defence policy, putting in place new political and military institutions for collective military operations. Since then the EU has launched its first, albeit modest, peacekeeping operations, primarily in the Balkans and Africa. Globally, the EU has for some decades played an important role in economic affairs, in particular in international trade negotiations and as a leading provider of development aid. Since the 1990s, however, the EU has also begun to develop a global political and security role, both in multilateral negotiations on issues such as climate change and through bilateral ties with other major powers.

While these developments might be viewed as pointing towards the development of the EU as an increasingly important foreign policy and security actor, the recent history of the CFSP has also been characterized by major failures and setbacks. In the early 1990s, EU member states were deeply divided over the 1990–91 Gulf War and the Yugoslav conflict, preventing the adoption of common policies in both cases (Salmon, 1992). The Union's inability to bring the bloodshed in the former Yugoslavia to an end, and eventual reliance on the USA and NATO to do so, exposed the gap between rhetoric and reality in EU foreign policy. A decade later, the acrimonious divisions within the EU over the 2003 Iraq War, in particular between the three largest members – Britain, France and Germany – suggested that the Union's ability to forge a truly common foreign and security policy remained, at best, limited.

Assessments of the EU's foreign and security policy vary significantly. Nearly four decades ago, François Duchêne (1972) described the EU's combination of economic power with relative political and military weakness as that of a 'civilian power'. Supporters of a common European foreign and security policy argue that the EU is gradually becoming a more complete power and is likely over time to assume an increasingly prominent foreign and security policy role – in particular within Europe, but also globally. Others argue that the EU is a distinctive and perhaps *sui generis* power: more than a traditional international organization yet not a centralized nation-state; a power which, because of its internal make-up and in contrast to past great powers, emphasizes norms, co-operation and soft power in its external behaviour (Manners, 2002). Critics argue that the continuing resilience of the nation-states that constitute the EU, and the often divergent foreign policy perspectives of those states, pose insuperable obstacles to a meaningful common foreign and security policy (Gordon, 1997–8).

Developments since the late 2000s have called into question not only the EU's emerging foreign policy but also the entire project of European integration. The global financial and economic crisis of 2008 hit European economies hard, significantly diminishing Europe's and the EU's economic and political standing relative to the rising powers of the non-Western world. By 2010–11, further, a new economic crisis revolving around very high levels of debt in many European states was threatening to trigger a second major recession and possibly the break-up of the euro. The future of the EU was more uncertain than it had been at any time in recent decades and perhaps even since the European project was launched after the Second World War. This chapter explores the EU's efforts to establish a common foreign and security policy, and the Union's emerging role in European and global security. The conclusion assesses the prospects for the EU's foreign and security policy in light of the economic crisis of the early 2010s.

Towards a common foreign and security policy?

The establishment of a common European foreign and security policy has been an ambition of supporters of European integration ever since the process was initiated after the Second World War. Following the establishment of the European Coal and Steel Community in 1951, France, West Germany, Italy, the Netherlands, Belgium and Luxembourg negotiated a European Defence Community (EDC) agreement, which would have established a supranational European military. Concerns over national sovereignty and the rearmament of Germany so soon after the Second World War, however, led the French National Assembly to vote against the ratification of the EDC Treaty and the project collapsed (Duke, 2000, pp. 12–41). The failure of the EDC consolidated NATO's position as the primary European security institution, while the European integration process took an essentially economic direction. The idea of a European foreign policy re-emerged in the early 1970s and the European Political Co-operation (EPC) process was established, based around regular meetings of European foreign ministers and efforts to co-ordinate European foreign policies on an inter-governmental basis (Duke, 2000, pp. 42–81). Although EPC gave the then European Community (EC) greater weight in international affairs, NATO and the transatlantic relationship with the USA remained the bedrock of security for Western Europe during the Cold War.

The end of the Cold War generated new momentum behind the idea of a European foreign and security policy (Keukeleire and MacNaughtan, 2008). The reunification of Germany in 1989–90 resulted in pressure for closer European integration in order to tie Germany into European structures. As was noted in the previous chapter, the disappearance of the Soviet threat reduced Europe's dependence on the USA for its security, and resulted in a partial US disengagement from Europe. The emergence of new security challenges on Europe's periphery, in particular the Yugoslav conflict, suggested that the EC needed a greater capacity to shape events beyond its borders. The result was the Maastricht Treaty, negotiated in 1990–91 and coming into force in 1993, under which the EC became the European Union, the framework for Economic and Monetary Union (EMU, which subsequently resulted in the introduction of the euro) was put in place, the CFSP was established, and JHA co-operation became a central component of the Union. In some ways, the CFSP established under the Maastricht Treaty did not differ greatly from

EPC, remaining based on inter-governmental co-operation and consensus decision-making. The political commitment to the CFSP was, however, significantly stronger than to EPC, with member states agreeing to 'define and implement a common foreign and security policy ... covering all aspects of foreign and security policy' (European Union, 1992, Title V, Art. J.1). The new geostrategic context of the post-Cold War era also meant that the prospects for the implementation of a common foreign and security policy were significantly enhanced.

After the Maastricht Treaty was concluded it was quickly recognized that the EU's efforts to establish a European foreign policy were inhibited by a number of major shortcomings. These included: the division between the political CFSP component of EU foreign policy (governed largely by inter-governmental co-operation between the member states) and the economic components such as trade and development policy (governed by different arrangements, where the European Commission played a central role); institutional divisions between the member states, the Council Secretariat (which provides the institutional support for the Council of Ministers) and the European Commission; the rotating presidency of the EU, which led member states to push national priorities during their six-months' presidency terms but often resulted in little follow-up or consistency; the lack of leadership and representation for the EU in the foreign policy area; and the absence of military capacity to back up the EU's political ambitions. Addressing these problems was a central issue in subsequent EU treaty negotiations in the 1990s and 2000s. The Amsterdam Treaty, signed in 1997 and coming into force in 1999, established the post of High Representative for the CFSP, which was held by Javier Solana, a former Spanish Foreign Minister and former NATO Secretary General, from 1999 to 2009. The Nice Treaty, provisionally agreed in 2000, signed in 2001 and coming into force in 2003, established a Common European Security and Defence Policy, giving the EU for the first time the capacity for collective military action (this is discussed in more detail below). The Lisbon Treaty, signed in December 2007 and entering into force in December 2009, combined the post of High Representative (now renamed High Representative of the Union for Foreign Affairs and Security Policy) with that of a Vice-President of the European Commission, and established a new European External Action Service (EEAS), bringing together the previous foreign policy roles of the European Commission and the Council Secretariat (plus staff seconded from national foreign ministries).

Despite the various reforms introduced by the Amsterdam, Nice and Lisbon Treaties, however, the central basis of most EU foreign policy activity remains inter-governmental co-operation, with decisions made by the EU's member states largely on the basis of consensus. This process operates through a series of core EU institutions: the European Council (approximately six-monthly meetings of heads of state and government); the Foreign Affairs Council (monthly meetings of foreign ministers, known up to the Lisbon Treaty as the General Affairs and External Relations Council); the Committee of Permanent Representatives (COREPER – national ambassadors to the EU, based in Brussels); the Political and Security Committee (PSC, also known by its French acronym COPS, established by the Nice Treaty and composed of ambassadorial-level representatives responsible for security and defence policy); and a variety of working groups, again composed of national representatives, responsible for specific policy areas.

The Lisbon Treaty was supposed to address the EU's institutional shortcomings in relation to foreign policy, but has only gone some of the way towards doing so (European Policy Centre/Egmont/Centre for European Policy Studies, 2010). Even the terminology of the Lisbon Treaty represented backtracking from more ambitious hopes: a proposed EU foreign minister was downgraded to the position of High Representative, while a proposed EU foreign ministry became the EEAS. Although the new EEAS now brings together core parts of the Council Secretariat and the European Commission responsible for foreign policy (plus staff from national foreign ministries), major policy areas (including trade, enlargement and neighbourhood policy, and development policy) remain under the control of the Commission and outside the EEAS. In terms of external representation, the High Representative must also vie with the President of the European Commission, as well as the now semi-permanent President of the European Council (a new post created by the Lisbon Treaty and elected for a two-and-a-half-year term, once renewable). The implementation of the foreign policy components of the Lisbon Treaty, furthermore, got off to an unimpressive start. The election of the first President of the European Council and the new High Representative in late 2009 involved much horse-trading between EU member states, with the low-profile former Belgian prime minister Herman van Rompuy eventually being appointed as first President of the European Council and the even less well-known British politician Baroness Catherine Ashton appointed as High Representative (Barber, 2010). Compared to her predecessor Javier Solana, Baroness Ashton lacked both political stature and foreign policy experience. Certainly, those who hoped that political heavyweights would be appointed to either or both posts were disappointed. The first steps in establishing the EEAS were also inauspicious, with member states scrapping over senior posts within the EEAS and the Commission transferring the international aspects of climate change and energy policy out of the soon-to-be-closed Directorate-General for External Relations in order to ensure that they remained under its control rather than that of the EEAS (Barber, 2010, pp. 63–4; Menon, 2011, pp. 78–9). The combining of the post of foreign policy High Representative with that of a Commission Vice-President and the creation of the EEAS may eventually produce greater coherence in EU foreign policy, but they are unlikely to produce the dramatic breakthrough that some hoped for.

Even after the Lisbon Treaty, the EU foreign policy-making process remains essentially inter-governmental and consensus-based and this reality fundamentally shapes and constrains the EU's ambitions in this area. In essence, the EU foreign policy depends on the Union's member states, especially its largest members, sharing common foreign and security policy objectives and priorities. The difficulty of developing a truly common foreign and security policy becomes clear when one considers the diversity of the EU member states' national foreign and security policy traditions and priorities: two former great powers, Britain a close ally of the USA and France with its Gaullist emphasis on independence from the USA; Germany, a semi-pacifist civilian power since 1945; northern European members, whose immediate foreign policy priorities include Russia and the Baltic Sea region; southern European members, whose immediate foreign policy priorities include the Mediterranean and North Africa; a majority of states who are also NATO members, but four neutral or non-aligned states (Austria, Finland, Ireland and Sweden); and twelve recent members who have joined the EU since 2004 (ten post-communist Central and Eastern European states, plus Cyprus and Malta). Welding the divergent foreign and security policies of twenty-seven – and in the future potentially more – member states into a single common EU policy is an inherently challenging task. As developments since the early 1990s have illustrated, distinctive national foreign and security policies remain deeply entrenched.

At the beginning of the 1990s, the first Gulf War and the Yugoslav conflict cruelly exposed the EU's limitations as a foreign policy actor (Salmon, 1992). In the first Gulf War, the UK strongly supported the

US-led military action; France also contributed military forces to the US-led coalition, but pursued a semi-independent diplomatic line; and Germany refused to contribute military forces but provided significant economic aid to the USA, while the other EU members were similarly divided. In the Yugoslav conflict, Germany advocated the early recognition of Slovenian and Croatian independence and the use of military force, but the UK and France opposed diplomatic recognition of Slovenia and Croatia or military action. In both cases a meaningful common EU position was impossible. A decade later, the 2003 Iraq War exposed similar divisions, with the UK again supporting the US-led war, and France and Germany opposing military action. These divisions were mirrored across the EU, with countries such as Spain, Italy and Poland supporting the US-led war, and others such as Sweden, Belgium and Austria opposed to it. Eight years later in 2011, EU members were once again divided over intervention in Libya, with the UK and France leading the push for intervention, but Germany (at this time a non-permanent member of the UN Security Council) abstaining in the Security Council vote authorizing military action and refusing to participate in the subsequent military operation (Jones, 2011, pp. 53–5) and only ten of the twenty-one EU member states that are also NATO members participating in the NATO operation (International Institute for Strategic Studies, 2011a).

Some have argued that enlargement of the EU, from fifteen to twenty-seven member states since 2004 and possible future expansion to include the Western Balkan states and Turkey, may significantly complicate the Union's efforts to develop a common foreign policy. For many in the French elite in particular, the strongly Atlanticist leanings of the post-communist Central and Eastern European states risked undermining the EU's ability to develop an autonomous foreign and security policy. These fears were reinforced in the run-up to the Iraq War in early 2003, when the leaders of Poland, the Czech Republic and Hungary joined the UK, Spain, Italy, Denmark and Portugal in signing the 'Letter of the Eight' calling for unity with the USA (Aznar *et al.*, 2003), and ten other Central and Eastern European states (the 'Vilnius Ten') signed an open letter supporting the USA (Vilnius Group, 2003). The French president, Jacques Chirac, responded by accusing the Central and Eastern European states of being 'not very well behaved' and having 'missed a great opportunity to shut up' (Lungescu, 2003). Although enlargement may have added to the EU's difficulties in developing a common foreign policy, however, it is far from clear that it has had, or will have, a major impact. The EU's new members shadowed the CFSP from the early 1990s, adopting the vast majority of common EU foreign policy positions without any problem long before they became EU members. Over the Iraq War, the EU's fundamental problem was not the complicated process of achieving consensus among a larger group of members, but rather the absence of agreement among its three largest members – the UK, France and Germany. Although other EU members may be uncomfortable with a foreign policy dominated by the 'big three', consensus among the UK, France and Germany is a prerequisite for common EU action. When such consensus exists, other member states are more often than not likely to accommodate themselves to that consensus – even in an enlarged Union.

While it is clear that developing a common EU foreign policy is difficult, some argue that the creation of institutions directed towards that goal and the process of co-operation will in the longer term facilitate foreign policy convergence among the Union's member states (Manners and Whitman, 2000; Tonra, 2001). This logic reflects neo-liberal institutionalist theories of international relations which argue that institutions help to create and sustain co-operation among states (Keohane and Martin, 1995). There is some evidence to support this thesis in relation to EU foreign policy: with regard to a variety of countries, policy issues and international organizations, the EU has gradually built up and maintained common positions, often involving compromise between the divergent views of member states. The EU may also have a capacity for learning from its failures: after their initial divisions over the Yugoslav conflict, for example, EU member states appear to have realized the importance of maintaining a common front and since the mid-1990s the Union has maintained quite a high degree of unity in its policy towards the Balkans. In the wake of the deep divisions over the Iraq War, in December 2003 EU members reached agreement on a formal European Security Strategy – an exercise designed deliberately to overcome the splits over Iraq and re-affirm common core EU interests and goals (European Union, 2003a). While this evidence suggests that there may be some validity to the neo-liberal institutionalist argument, building a common foreign policy nevertheless remains at best a slow and halting process. The experience of the Iraq War indicates that, while there may be gradual progress towards a common EU foreign policy, national foreign policy differences remain deeply entrenched and are likely to re-emerge in crisis situations involving controversial issues such as the use of force.

Euro-Atlanticism versus Euro-Gaullism

One of the central foreign policy divisions within the EU is over relations with the USA – what Timothy Garton Ash (2005, p. 58) describes as the clash between Euro-Atlanticism and Euro-Gaullism. Euro-Atlanticism envisages the EU as one half of a united Euro-Atlantic community and a close partner of the USA, influencing America through co-operative engagement and sharing the burden of addressing common security challenges. Euro-Gaullism – named, of course, after the former French president, Charles de Gaulle – envisages the EU as an independent force in world politics and a counterbalance to America's overweening power. Euro-Atlanticism and Euro-Gaullism present two radically different strategic visions of the EU's place in the world and its relationship with the USA. The debate between these two strategic visions has been ongoing since 1945, but intensified with the end of the Cold War in 1989–90 and became even more prominent post-9/11 and in the context of the Iraq War.

Euro-Atlanticists argue that partnership with the USA is vital to addressing shared security challenges, and that the best way to influence (and sometimes restrain) the USA is from inside such a partnership. However, Euro-Gaullists are of the view that Europe needs to assert distinctive European interest and values, that the USA can only be influenced by an independent and powerful Europe, and that the EU must be the vehicle for achieving both goals. Britain has been the leading advocate of Euro-Atlanticism, based on a history of close co-operation with the USA in the two World Wars and the Cold War, and uniquely close military and intelligence ties. France has been the leading proponent of Euro-Gaullism, based on a tradition of foreign policy independence from the USA. Germany – West Germany after 1945 and the reunited Germany since 1990 – has generally sought to chart a middle course, combining an alliance with the USA with a strong commitment to European integration. Given the British and French positions, this makes Germany the swing country in determining the balance of opinion within Europe. Other EU member states have been similarly divided: Denmark and Portugal have generally been on the Euro-Atlanticist side of this debate; Belgium and Luxembourg have sided with the Euro-Gaullists; and the Netherlands, Italy, Spain and Greece have often followed the German model of seeking to balance the two approaches. Although not members of NATO, the neutral/non-aligned EU states (Austria, Finland, Ireland and Sweden) have supported the development of an EU foreign policy but also value co-operation with the USA. The new Central and Eastern European EU members, grateful for US support during the Cold War and still wary of Russia, are generally committed Euro-Atlanticists.

The divisions within Europe over relations with the USA occur not only between countries but also within them. In general, parties and leaders from the right of the political spectrum are closer to the Euro-Atlanticist position, while those from the left are more inclined towards Euro-Gaullism. Changes of government can therefore result in significant shifts in national positions – the right-wing government of the Spanish prime minister, Jose Maria Aznar, was strongly supportive of the US war in Iraq, whereas the left-wing government of Jose Luis Rodriguez Zapatero, elected after the March 2004 Madrid bombings, withdrew Spanish troops from Iraq. European public opinion has also been divided along similar lines. Although European views of the USA have shifted back and forth since 1945, the overall balance of political forces, both between states and within them, has been such that there has never been a decisive consensus in support of either the Euro-Atlanticist or the Euro-Gaullist position.

The debate between Euro-Atlanticism and Euro-Gaullism is also shaped by America's foreign policy choices. In the 1990s, Europeans were generally comfortable with the Clinton administration's liberal internationalist foreign policy leanings and, after initial divisions, welcomed the USA's willingness to engage in the Balkans. After 2000, Europeans were wary of the Bush administration's more nationalist, unilateralist and militarist approach to foreign policy. In particular, the US 'war on terror' and the Iraq War prompted a significant shift in European opinion towards Euro-Gaullism and the articulation of a distinctive European approach to foreign and security policy, based on multilateralism and soft power. The advent of the Obama administration in 2009 resulted in more positive European views of the USA and hopes of renewed transatlantic co-operation, but since then disillusionment has set in on both sides of the Atlantic (Volker, 2010). Future changes of administration in Washington, DC or other shifts in US policy will doubtless tilt the continuing European debate between Euro-Atlanticism and Euro-Gaullism.

Some observers have argued for a middle way between Euro-Atlanticism and Euro-Gaullism (Garton Ash, 2005; Howorth, 2003–4). Since neither Euro-Alanticism nor Euro-Gaullism can command a decisive majority within Europe, such observers argue that the best way both to unite Europe and to influence America is around a policy of constructive but critical partnership with the USA. Such an approach would require a historic compromise between Britain and France, with both countries moderating their traditional policies in order to facilitate a common European policy. While the logic of this argument may be sound, the entrenched nature of national foreign policies is likely to make the development of such a policy difficult, and continued European divisions over relations with the USA are probably more likely than a historic compromise between Euro-Atlanticism and Euro-Gaullism.

Neighbourhood politics

Relations with countries and regions neighbouring the EU have been central to the Union's foreign and security policy since the early 1990s (Dannreuther, 2004; Bretherton and Vogler, 2006, pp. 137–61). The EU has put in place a set of policies towards the countries of Central and Eastern Europe, the Balkans, the former Soviet Union and the Mediterranean designed to build long-term co-operation with these regions. Implicitly, the EU's objective is to forestall or contain potential security problems arising from challenges such as violent conflict within these states, nationalist and fundamentalist political ideologies, socio-economic discontent and mass migration. The EU's policies have had a number of dimensions. Institutionally, they have been based on a combination of 'bilateral' ties with individual states, and region-wide (for example, Mediterranean or Balkan) co-operation. Politically, the EU has sought to promote an agenda of good governance, democratization and respect for human rights. Economically, it has provided aid to its various partners while also seeking to promote mutual free trade. The Union has also promoted practical functional co-operation in areas such as environmental protection and transport infrastructure, providing funding to support joint activities in these areas.

In the 1990s and 2000s, enlargement was at the centre of the EU's neighbourhood policy. After the collapse of communism, the leaders of Central and Eastern Europe's new democracies viewed integration with and membership of the EU as being vital to consolidating democracy, underpinning market economic reforms and securing their independence from Russia. The EU was initially cautious about enlargement, but in 1993 agreed that full membership would be open to these states provided they established stable democracies and functioning market economies, were able to cope with the competitive pressures of the Union's internal market and could meet the obligations of

EU membership in terms of the Union's existing rules and laws (the *acquis communautaire*) – the so-called Copenhagen criteria (named after the location of the 1993 EU summit where they were agreed) (European Union, 1993). Throughout the 1990s, the EU used a combination of political dialogue, economic aid and technical assistance to help the Central and Eastern European states to entrench democracy, reform governmental and administrative structures, undertake difficult market economic reforms and prepare for membership of the Union (Mayhew, 1998). A key element of this process was conditionality: since membership depended on meeting the conditions laid down by the Union, the EU had substantial leverage over the Central European states. As discussed in Chapter 1, this process culminated in 2004 with eight Central European states (the Czech Republic, Estonia, Hungary, Latvia, Lithuania, Poland, Slovakia and Slovenia), plus Cyprus and Malta, joining the Union as full members, followed by Bulgaria and Romania in 2007. This eastward enlargement of the Union has been widely viewed as a success story: a powerful example of the ability of the EU to use the magnetic attraction of membership to promote stability and security. Enlargement and the conditionality associated with it were thus one of the key foreign policy instruments of the Union.

From the late 1990s, the EU sought to implement a similar policy towards the Western Balkans (Lehne, 2004). The EU became the main donor of economic aid to the former Yugoslav republics and Albania, introduced 'bilateral' Stabilization and Association Agreements with these states, agreed in principle that full membership of the Union was open to them and sponsored regional co-operation, in particular through the Stability Pact for South Eastern Europe, which brought together the countries of the region. As was discussed in Chapter 1, it is likely that most or all of the Western Balkan countries will gradually be brought into the EU over the next decade or so. Nevertheless, the region continues to pose significant challenges for the EU. In particular, the continued internal division of Bosnia between its constituent Muslim-Croat and Serbian components and the status of Kosovo (which declared its independence from Serbia in 2008 and was recognized by some EU members but not by others or by Serbia and much of the wider international community) represent major unresolved problems. The extent to which the EU is able to use the leverage associated with potential membership to resolve these conflicts will be a major test of the stabilizing effect of enlargement.

Beyond those countries which have joined the Union or are candidates for membership, the EU has put in place a set of policies designed

to promote co-operation with and encourage reform in its other neighbours in the former Soviet Union and the Mediterranean. These policies include bilateral co-operation agreements with other states,
financial and technical assistance programmes, regional arrangements
(such as the Euro-Mediterranean Partnership/Union for the
Mediterranean and the Eastern Partnership with some of the former
Soviet states) and an overarching framework known as the European
Neighbourhood Policy (ENP). The ENP, established in 2004, was a
recognition that in the context of enlargement into Central and Eastern
Europe, the EU needed to do more to strengthen co-operation with and
provide support to those neighbouring states likely to remain outside
the Union (European Commission, 2004). The ENP covers the EU's
Mediterranean partners (Algeria, Egypt, Israel, Jordan, Lebanon,
Libya, Morocco, the Palestinian Authority, Syria and Tunisia) and the
western (Belarus, Moldova and Ukraine) and Caucasian (Armenia,
Azerbaijan and Georgia) former Soviet states. The ENP involves the
negotiation of ENP Action Plans between the EU and individual partners, designed to set concrete reform goals for the partner states, and
EU financial and technical assistance to help achieve these goals. A
number of other neighbouring countries and regions are not included
in the ENP: Turkey, because it is a formal candidate for EU membership and therefore has a distinctive bilateral relationship with the
Union; Russia, because of its distinctive status as a great power in its
own right (the EU's relationship with Russia is discussed in Chapter 5);
and the Central Asian former Soviet states, because of their greater
geographic and political distance from Europe.

In the former Soviet Union, the EU concluded 'bilateral' Partnership
and Co-operation Agreements (PCAs) with the former Soviet republics
in the 1990s and began providing economic and technical assistance to
them. In contrast to Central and Eastern Europe and the Western
Balkans, however, the former Soviet republics were not viewed as
potential candidates for EU membership. As a consequence, the scale
of EU political and economic engagement with the former Soviet states
has been significantly less than in Central and Eastern Europe and the
Western Balkans. The 2008 Georgia War led the EU to conclude that
it needed to do more to support the non-Russian former Soviet states
and in May 2009 a new Eastern Partnership (EaP) was launched with
the six states of the western former Soviet Union and the Caucasus.
The EaP involves periodic high-level meetings between the EU and the
six EaP partners, the negotiation of new Association Agreements
(including commitments to free trade), programmes to support the

development of administrative capacity in the partner states, 'mobility and security pacts' to facilitate easier travel to the EU from these states and increased EU funding to the EaP states (Council of the European Union, 2009). Since 2009, however, it has become clear that the substance and impact of the EaP is likely to be limited (Bobinski, 2011). The slow pace of political and economic reform in most of the EaP states, and its complete absence in others such as Belarus, further limits the prospects for the EaP.

To the south, in 1995 the EU established the Euro-Mediterranean Partnership (EMP) or Barcelona Process (after the city in which it was launched). The EMP was a broad framework for dialogue and co-operation between the EU and the countries on the southern and eastern shores of the Mediterranean (Algeria, Egypt, Israel, Jordan, Lebanon, Libya, Morocco, Syria, Tunisia and the Palestinian Authority). The aims of the EMP were to foster economic co-operation, including trade liberalization, facilitate practical co-operation (in areas such as environmental protection) and act as a framework for political dialogue (in particular, in relation to human rights). The EU also has bilateral political and economic relations with its Mediterranean partners, and a variety of aid programmes to support co-operation. The future of the EU's Mediterranean policy was thrown into the air by a 2007–08 proposal from French president Nicolas Sarkozy for a Mediterranean Union modelled on the EU. The European Commission, Germany and other EU member states were wary of the proposal because only Mediterranean states would be involved (thereby excluding the rest of the EU), it appeared unrealistically ambitious and it might duplicate the Barcelona Process. After some negotiation a more modest Union for the Mediterranean (UfM) was launched in July 2008, involving all EU states and their Mediterranean neighbours and integrating the existing *acquis* of the Barcelona Process. Like the Barcelona Process, however, the UfM was constrained by the unresolved Arab–Israeli conflict (which led to the cancellation of planned summits in 2009 and 2010 when the Arab states refused to attend), as well as the authoritarian character of most of the North African and Middle Eastern regimes. By 2011 observers were describing the UfM as having 'atrophied as a largely failed exercise in relaunching the Union's multilateral policy towards the Mediterranean basin' (Whitman and Juncos, 2011, p. 199). How far the Arab Spring will enable the EU to play a more proactive role in the Mediterranean remains to be seen (see Box 4.1).

By the late 2000s the limitations of the EU's neighbourhood policy were becoming increasingly clear. Whereas in the 1990s and early to

Box 4.1   The EU and the Arab Spring

The Arab Spring was a strategic shock which the EU, like the rest of the world, had not expected and was not prepared for. Although the EU had sought to encourage political and economic reform in the southern Mediterranean through the Barcelona Process, this did not play any significant role in the origins of the Arab Spring. Indeed, European governments and the USA had long faced the dilemma of having often problematic relations with the Middle Eastern and North African states but fearing that political change might bring to power radical Islamic groups with strongly anti-Western views (as occurred in Iran after its 1979 revolution).

As the dramatic events of 2011 unfolded, there was a strong sense of European (and US) leaders struggling to keep up with developments and to come to terms with the winds of change sweeping the region. In the key country of Egypt, Western governments were initially slow to back democracy protestors or press President Hosni Mubarak to step down. As it became clear that fundamental change was under way in Tunisia, Egypt and Libya and might occur in other countries also, however, the EU began to put in place new policies. In March 2011 the European Commission and EU foreign policy High Representative Catherine Ashton jointly proposed a new Partnership for Democracy and Shared Prosperity with the South Mediterranean, under which the EU would provide increased assistance to those countries undergoing democratic transitions (European Commission/High Representative of the Union for Foreign Affairs and Security Policy, 2011a). In September 2011 the EU launched a new SPRING (Support for Partnership, Reform and Inclusive Growth) programme to support democratic transformation, institution building and economic growth, with €350 million allocated for 2011 and 2012 (European Commission, 2011b). Nevertheless, critics argued that the EU (and US) response to the Arab Spring did not match the historic scale of these events – or the significance of the chance to extend democracy to a major part of the Arabic and Islamic world.

In some ways the EU should be well-suited to supporting the consolidation of democratic reforms in those countries where authoritarian regimes have been overthrown: gradual processes of institution building and technical assistance are a central part of the EU's modus operandi; the EU, further, has substantial experience of supporting just such reform in post-communist Europe since the 1990s. Nevertheless, the EU faces dilemmas in supporting democratization in North Africa and the Middle East. A large-scale, high-profile programme of support for change might be viewed as the most appropriate response to the Arab Spring – and a political signal that the EU supports democracy over the false stability of authoritarianism. Given Europe's history of imperialism in the region, however, publics and elites might be wary of European intervention and such a high-profile approach could backfire. The extent to which the EU can use its influence to promote democracy in North Africa and the Middle East thus remains to be seen.

mid-2000s the EU had been able to use the process of enlargement and the carrots and sticks associated with the prospect of EU membership to help promote reform and stability in Central and Eastern Europe, with the prospects for further enlargement circumscribed the EU's leverage over those countries unlikely to join the Union was much more limited. Many of the EU's neighbouring states were ruled by authoritarian regimes (most of the southern Mediterranean up to the Arab Spring and Belarus, Armenia, Azerbaijan and the Central Asian states in the former Soviet Union), where leaders were far more interested in regime survival than co-operation with the EU. Even in the important case of Ukraine, which has swung between reform and retrenchment since gaining independence in 1991, the EU's ability to encourage political and economic reform has proven limited. In addition, the various conflicts in the region – in Israel–Palestine, Cyprus, Georgia and Moldova – have proven intractable, with the EU able to exercise at most limited influence over them. Against this background, in 2010–11 the EU undertook a strategic review of the ENP. The review concluded that 'there is room for improvement on all sides of the relationship. ... EU support to political reform in neighbouring countries has met with limited results. ... A new approach is needed to strengthen the partnership between the EU and the countries and societies of the neighbourhood' (European Commission/High Representative of the Union for Foreign Affairs and Security Policy, 2011b, p. 1). The review proposed greater support to those countries engaged in building democracy, more support for sustainable economic and social development, strengthening the EaP and the UfM and improving the relevant EU mechanisms and instruments. The review could not, however, address the underlying problem of the limits of the EU's influence over its neighbours. The result may be a more modest neighbourhood policy than earlier visions of the EU as the central actor in promoting reform and stability in its neighbourhood.

A global role?

Since the 1960s, the EU has played a major global economic role. This has a number of dimensions: the negotiation of preferential trade relations with former European colonies (the so-called ACP (African, Caribbean and Pacific) countries); the adoption of common EU policies within the World Trade Organization (WTO) and its predecessor, the General Agreement on Tariffs and Trade (GATT), which made the

EU a key force in these negotiations; and the EU and its members' roles as suppliers of economic development aid, where they have for some decades been the largest aid providers. These policies have made the EU a leading global economic player for some decades (the security dimension and implications of the EU's global economic role, in particular in the areas of aid and trade, are examined in Chapter 9).

Since the 1990s, the EU has developed a growing but still limited political and security role beyond Europe. It has, in particular, placed a strong emphasis on the development and strengthening of multilateral international institutions. As the Union's 2003 *European Security Strategy* put it:

> In a world of global threats, global markets and global media, our security and prosperity increasingly depend on an effective multilateral system. The development of a stronger international society, well functioning international institutions and a rule-based international order is our objective. (European Union, 2003a)

The EU's emerging global political and security role has a number of dimensions:

- *'Bilateral' relations*: the EU has sought to develop 'bilateral' relations with a growing range of partners, in particular major powers such as China, India and Japan. While these relations were initially primarily economic, they have since the 1990s been expanded to include regular political dialogue on wide range of global, regional and bilateral issues, including both generic security issues (such as proliferation) and specific conflicts and crises. These relationships have thus been re-christened as 'strategic partnerships' (Grevi and de Vasconcelos, 2008; Renard, 2011).
- *Inter-regional co-operation*: the EU has a growing set of inter-regional relationships with other organizations, including in particular the Association of South East Asian Nations (ASEAN), the African Union (AU) and the Latin American MERCOSUR/ MERCOSUL (Mercado Común del Sur/Mercado Comum do Sul, generally known as MERCOSUR or the Southern Common Market). While these relations again have a strong economic basis, they have also developed an increasing political and security dimension.
- *Global institutions*: the EU has sought to support global institutions such as the United Nations (UN), the international financial

institutions (the World Bank and International Monetary Fund) and global arms control regimes (such as the Nuclear Non-Proliferation Treaty and the Biological and Chemical Weapons Conventions), through the adoption of common negotiating positions within these frameworks and the provision of political, technical and financial support for specific activities. Since the early 1990s, the EU has often played a central role in shaping debates within the UN and other global institutions.

- *Conflict prevention and crisis management*: the EU has also engaged in and supported international conflict prevention and crisis management efforts (European Union, 2001a). In Africa, in particular, the EU has sought since the 1990s to make conflict prevention and resolution a central element of its policies towards that continent. The EU has also supported conflict prevention and management initiatives undertaken by the UN, regional organizations or ad hoc coalitions of states. As is discussed further below and examined in more detail in Chapter 6, in the context of its common defence policy the EU has, since the early 2000s, undertaken over twenty civilian and military crisis management operations, many outside Europe and in particular in Africa.

Taken together, these developments suggest that the EU is likely to develop a growing global dimension to its emerging foreign policy. Nevertheless, the EU also faces serious constraints on its ability to shape and respond to the global security agenda. The general problem of co-ordinating foreign policy among the EU's member states impinges significantly on the EU's global role. While the EU has been supportive of efforts to strengthen and reform the UN, for example, divergent positions on Security Council reform (in particular Germany's demand for a permanent seat on the Council, and Italy's opposition to this) have precluded the adoption of a common EU approach on UN reform. Similarly, the fact that Britain and France are nuclear weapon states and the other EU member states are not has inhibited efforts to develop common positions on nuclear non-proliferation.

While the EU is an economic superpower, it has struggled to translate its economic might into comparable political power. The EU's role in the Middle East highlights this reality. Ever since EPC was established in the 1970s, the EU has sought to play a role in resolving the Israeli–Palestinian conflict; yet throughout this period the USA has been the key external power broker. Although the EU has been part of

the international Quartet (alongside the USA, Russia and the UN) facilitating Israeli–Palestinian peace negotiations since the 1990s, the USA
has nevertheless remained the dominant external actor. While the EU is
a major trading partner of Israel and the largest provider of economic
aid to the Palestinian Authority, it has been unable to use this latent
economic power to exercise a decisive influence on the conflict. The
USA's and the EU's respective roles in the Israeli–Palestinian conflict
highlight the contrast between America's combination of a single
centralized foreign policy and global political, economic and military
power and the EU's decentralized foreign policy, global economic
power but more limited political weight and military capacity.
Although the EU may well develop an increasing global role, the
Union's global impact is likely to remain limited by differences between
its member states and its inability to convert its economic weight into
political influence.

Nevertheless, in some areas of global security – broadly conceived –
the EU may play a leading role. The 1997 Kyoto agreement on climate
change and the International Criminal Court (ICC), established in
1998, illustrate this dynamic. In both cases, international negotiations
began in the mid-1990s among a wide group of states, but the USA,
which had initially supported the processes, gradually disengaged and
then refused to sign the resulting treaties. In each case, the EU acted as
the key driver behind the international negotiations and was central to
subsequent efforts to ratify and implement the agreements. The effectiveness of both the Kyoto agreement and the ICC has, of course, been
open to question. Nevertheless, they suggest that in at least some areas
the EU may act as a key driver behind multilateral efforts to address
global security challenges. How far the range of global issues in which
the EU plays a leading role will expand remains to be seen.

The military dimension: peacekeeping and beyond?

In 1999, EU leaders reached an historic agreement that the Union
should develop a Common Security and Defence Policy (CSDP),
declaring that 'the Union must have the capacity for autonomous
action, backed up by credible military forces, the means to decide to
use them, and a readiness to do so' (European Union, 1999). Given the
EU's essentially non-military character up to this point, the decision to
give the Union a military role was a major strategic shift in its character as an international actor (Howorth, 2007; Biscop and Coelmont,

2011). The decision reflected a growing awareness that the EU might need the capacity to respond to crises with military means, and concern about Europe's continuing military dependence on the USA – both factors having been sharply illustrated by the Kosovo War in the spring of 1999.

The political commitment to give the EU a military role was backed by decisions to develop new military force structures and new political institutions for the conduct of EU military operations. The EU established the 'Helsinki Headline Goal' of being able by 2003 to deploy a force of 50,000 to 60,000 troops (approximately one military corps or fifteen brigades), which should be available within sixty days (but include more rapidly deployable elements), sustainable for a year and militarily self-sustaining (in terms of command, control and intelligence, logistics, and air and naval forces). The EU also established new institutions for the management and conduct of military operations: the PSC/COPS discussed above, plus an EU Military Committee (EUMC) composed of Military Representatives of the EU members, to provide military advice and recommendations to the PSC, and an EU Military Staff (EUMS) to plan and manage military operations. In 2003, the EU undertook its first military mission, deploying a small force of approximately 400 soldiers to support the implementation of a peace agreement in Macedonia. Since then the EU has undertaken over twenty military or civilian operations in the context of its CSDP, in particular in the Balkans and Africa (Gross and Juncos, 2010) (the EU's role in peacekeeping and intervention is examined in more detail in Chapter 6). In 2004 the EU added two further elements to its emerging common defence policy: a commitment to establish eleven high-readiness battle groups of 1,500 troops capable of deployment at very short notice and a European Defence Agency (EDA) to co-ordinate military procurement amongst member states. At the end of the 2000s the Lisbon Treaty introduced further elements to the EU's common defence policy, in particular a mutual defence clause committing member states to come to each other's defence in the event of an attack (although moderated by caveats relating to the concerns of the neutral member states) and the concept of 'permanent structured cooperation', which allows for a core of member states to proceed with closer defence co-operation (although it remains to be seen whether and how this may be used).

The establishment of the CSDP was a significant strategic step, giving the Union for the first time the capacity to undertake collective military operations and initiating an ongoing process of defence

---

Box 4.2   The EU, defence and the CSDP: terminological confusion;
political confusion

The debate on the EU's defence role and the CSDP has been surrounded
by considerable terminological and political confusion. When the EU
first agreed to develop defence co-operation in 1999–2000 the policy
was referred to as the Common European Security and Defence Policy
(CESDP). By the mid-2000s the EU was using the term European
Security and Defence Policy (ESDP). By the late 2000s and the Lisbon
Treaty the EU had adopted the term Common Security and Defence
Policy (CSDP). In addition, in the 1990s the term European Security and
Defence Identity (ESDI) was used, particularly within NATO, to
describe European defence co-operation. The EU now appears to have
settled on Common Security and Defence Policy (CSDP) as its agreed
terminology.

The confusion over European defence co-operation and the CSDP,
however, is more than just terminological and reflects a number of important political issues. To the lay person, the use of the term 'defence' might
be thought to imply that the EU plays a role in or has taken responsibility
for the military defence of the territory, airspace and territorial waters of
the Union and its member states. This is not, however, the case. Defence of
the territory, airspace and territorial waters of EU member states remains
a national and NATO responsibility, with NATO planning for collective
territorial defence and managing air defence for its member states (which
is the majority of EU member states except for the neutral/non-aligned EU
states). The EU therefore plays no role in planning for the defence of the
territory, airspace and territorial waters of the Union and its member
states – in significant part because most EU member states (which are also,

→

co-operation amongst EU member states. The CSDP has, however,
been surrounded by considerable confusion over its meaning and
substance – see Box 4.2. Furthermore, the CSDP remains constrained
by a number of significant factors. First, like the broader EU foreign
and security policy of which it is part, the CSDP is essentially inter-
governmental in character, based on co-operation among the Union's
member states and largely consensus decision-making. The basis for
the CSDP is thus still twenty-seven national militaries, rather than an
integrated single European military. Compared to a military superpower such as the USA with a single defence policy and military, the
EU's CSDP inevitably involves enormous inefficiencies and duplication
amongst member states. Second, European defence spending has been
falling fairly significantly since the 1990s, with the consequence that
the resources available for the development and maintenance of mili-

→

of course, NATO members) prefer to leave this task to the 'tried and trusted' NATO. Under the 2007 Lisbon Treaty, EU member states did agree a mutual defence clause committing them to provide assistance to one another in the event of an external attack. Nevertheless, responsibility for territorial defence remains in national and NATO hands.

The development of a common security and defence policy might also be thought to imply the development of supranational EU armed forces – an EU military – alongside or replacing national armed forces. Such perceptions may have been reinforced by some observers' descriptions of the initial CSDP decisions taken in 1999–2000 as involving the creation of a 'European rapid reaction force' (Brown, 2001). In fact, the CSDP does not involve the creation of supranational European armed forces or a single EU military. Rather, it involves the development of political and military institutions for the management of EU military operations, with military forces being provided by the member states on a voluntary basis and remaining ultimately subject to national control. The CSDP also involves a capabilities development process designed to enhance member states' military capabilities, but again defence spending, weapons procurement and related decisions remain under national, rather than EU, control. As is examined in more detail in Chapter 6, in the context of the CSDP the EU has undertaken a variety of peacekeeping, crisis management and post-conflict operations/missions. Most of these operations/missions, however, have been civilian in character, involving the deployment of diplomatic and police personnel, as well as support for justice and security sector reform in the states concerned. As a consequence, much of what the EU does under its Common Security and Defence Policy is actually non-military in character.

tary power projection capabilities are limited (Giegerich, 2008). This problem has only been exacerbated by the global and European financial and economic crisis since 2008. It is no coincidence that the initial Helsinki Headline Goal of being able to deploy a force of 50,000 to 60,000 troops has been quietly dropped. Indeed, frustration with the slow development of EU defence co-operation was one factor behind the conclusion by the UK and France of a bilateral Defence and Security Co-operation Treaty in November 2010. Third, although the EU has undertaken a significant number of operations in the context of the CSDP since the early 2000s, these have all been relatively small in size, have been at the softer end of the spectrum of crisis management operations and have not yet involved large-scale war fighting or combat operations (see Chapter 6). When the UK and France pressed for military intervention in Libya in 2011 it was striking that they turned to NATO, rather than the EU, as the institutional framework for that intervention – reflecting both the need for US involvement and the view that only NATO (and not the EU) was capable of providing the necessary command and control structures. In short, while the EU's role in peacekeeping, nation-building and crisis management grew significantly in the 2000s and may expand further in future, the Union remains very far from becoming a military superpower comparable to the USA.

Internal security: Justice and Home Affairs co-operation

Since the 1990s Justice and Home Affairs (JHA) has become an increasingly central part of the EU: this involves co-operation in relation to a wide range of internal security issues such as crime, terrorism, police, legal and judicial systems, asylum seekers and refugees, visa policies and border controls (Monar, 2010). Historically, such internal security challenges have been viewed as the prerogative of the nation-state, yet the EU has developed a rapidly expanding role in JHA. There are two drivers behind this development. First, the process of European integration, in particular the removal of internal border controls between most EU member states under the Schengen Agreement, has driven the demand for common controls over the Union's external borders and collective responses to issues such as immigration, asylum and crime. Second, the changed international security environment has led to increasing concern about the Union's vulnerability to transnational security threats such as organized crime and terrorism.

EU co-operation in JHA can be traced back to 1975 when the Trevi Group was established as a loose framework to facilitate co-operation to deal with cross-border terrorism. Similar groups were then established to address judicial co-operation, customs, immigration and organized crime. Under the 1985 Schengen Agreement, five core members of the EU (France, Germany, the Netherlands, Belgium and Luxembourg) agreed to remove internal border controls between themselves, generating a need for new common external border controls and a system for their management. The majority of the other EU members gradually joined the Schengen regime, as did non-EU members Norway and Iceland. The Central and Eastern European states that have joined the EU since 2004 are also being integrated into the Schengen system. Britain and Ireland have, however, opted out of Schengen and retain their national border controls.

The Maastricht Treaty established JHA as one of the three pillars of the EU (alongside the CFSP and the primarily economic European Community). The Maastricht Treaty also identified nine JHA areas of 'common interest': asylum policy; border controls; immigration policy; drug trafficking; international fraud; judicial co-operation; customs co-operation; police co-operation against terrorism; and police co-operation in relation to organized crime (European Union, 1992, Art. K.1). Under the Amsterdam Treaty EU JHA co-operation was re-christened the Area of Freedom, Security and Justice (AFSJ), embodying the idea that the EU is based on providing an area of free movement and common justice for its citizens combined with common policies to ensure security against threats such as crime, terrorism and illegal immigration (European Union, 1997, Art. K.1). The term JHA is, however, often still used to describe EU co-operation in this area. Detailed agendas for EU JHA co-operation have been laid out in a series of policy documents: the Tampere Programme (1999–2004), the Hague Programme (2005–10) and the Stockholm Programme (2010–14). Continuing concern relating to internal security threats also resulted in the adoption of a formal EU Internal Security Strategy (entitled *Towards a European Security Model*) in 2010 (Council of the European Union, 2010). This was followed by a European Commission document on the implementation of the strategy, which identified five strategic objectives: disrupting international criminal networks; preventing terrorism and addressing radicalization and recruitment; raising levels of security for citizens and businesses in cyberspace; strengthening security through border management; and increasing Europe's resilience towards crises and disasters (European Commission, 2010). Box 4.3 summarizes the main areas of EU JHA co-operation. The EU's responses to two particular JHA-related security challenges – terrorism and immigration – are examined in more detail in Chapters 8 and 9.

As Box 4.3 shows, EU JHA co-operation is now very wide-ranging, with many areas that were traditionally the sole preserve of the nation-state becoming to varying degrees Europeanized. Although both member states and the EU collectively have significantly strengthened policies in relation to the spectrum of internal security threats since the 1990s, these issues remain a major concern for governments and publics. In significant part, this reflects the intractable nature of these challenges: problems such as organized crime, illegal immigration and terrorism are ones that societies can combat but not entirely defeat and therefore have to live with to a certain degree. The increasingly transnational nature of these challenges, however, poses a particular

---

Box 4.3   EU Justice and Home Affairs (JHA) co-operation

- *Schengen Agreement*: removal of internal border controls among the majority of EU member states; concomitant commitment to harmonize external border controls and develop a common visa policy.
- *Asylum*: EU members are committed to developing a common asylum policy, based on common asylum procedures.
- *Immigration*: EU members are committed to developing a common immigration policy; an Action Plan on Illegal Immigration was adopted in 2002.
- *Terrorism*: an Action Plan on Combating Terrorism was adopted in September 2001 and has been expanded substantially since then; an EU Counter-Terrorism Co-ordinator was appointed in March 2004.
- *Police co-operation*: Europol, established under the 1992 Maastricht Treaty, facilitates police and intelligence co-operation within the EU, in particular in relation to organized crime; a European Police Chiefs Task Force, which first met in 2000, also facilitates co-operation among national police authorities; a European Police College (CEPOL), also established in 2000, undertakes training of national police personnel in support of European police co-operation.
- *Customs co-operation*: EU member states are committed to co-operation in relation to customs, in particular in relation to illegal goods; co-operation includes a Customs Information System and arrangements for mutual customs assistance.
- *Organized crime and drugs*: responding to organized crime and the illegal drugs trade are priorities for EU JHA cooperation; in 2004, the EU adopted a Drugs Strategy and a Drugs Action Plan.

→

---

problem for the EU. In the context of an EU involving economic integration, the free movement of goods, services and people and the dismantling of national borders, there is an intrinsic logic to addressing these challenges at the EU level and transferring powers to EU institutions. At the same time, however, there remains resistance in many member states to surrendering control over policy areas that have traditionally been viewed as important parts of national sovereignty and statehood. One prominent illustration of this occurred in 2011, when in the context of the granting by the Italian government of residence permits to 22,000 unauthorized migrants from Tunisia (themselves fleeing the political turbulence in North Africa) France temporarily reintroduced border checks with Italy, prompting a bilateral diplomatic row between the states and a wider debate on the future of the Schengen free movement zone (Carrera *et al.*, 2011) (migration is examined in more detail in Chapter 9). The current EU

- *Criminal justice*: the EU has sought to facilitate co-operation between national judicial systems and the approximation of national legislation; a European Judicial Network (EJN) of national contact points was put in place in 1998, and Eurojust – a central team of magistrates, prosecutors, judges and legal experts to support co-operation – was established in 2001; a Convention on Mutual Assistance in Criminal Matters was concluded in 2000; and a Framework Decision on a European Arrest Warrant – providing for the issuing of arrest warrants on an EU-wide basis – was agreed in 2002.
- *Border protection*: in 2004 the EU established Frontex (formally the European Agency for the Management of Operational Cooperation at the External Borders of the Member States of the EU), which provides support to member states in protecting external borders and engages in some collective border management activities, in particular through Rapid Border Intervention Teams (RABIT) of multinational EU forces for deployment in exceptional circumstances (the first such deployment was to the Greco-Turkish border in 2010).
- *External relations*: the ongoing development of JHA co-operation within the EU has also resulted in the development of EU co-operation with other states and their police and judicial authorities, in particular the USA.

Source: Data from European Commission, Directorate-General for Home Affairs website, http://ec.europa.eu/dgs/home-affairs/index.html (accessed 13 November 2011).

JHA co-operation system is a hybrid between elements of integrated common EU policies, inter-governmental co-operation and other policy areas that remain essentially under national control. In terms of the future, the EU faces competing pressures for, on the one hand, the development of more integrated JHA policies and, on the other hand, the maintenance of national control over important policy areas or even the repatriation of some powers to the member states. This debate, in turn, reflects and feeds into the larger political debate on the future of the Union.

Conclusion

From the early 1990s to the mid-2000s, the EU assumed an increasingly prominent role in responding to security challenges within

Europe and to some extent globally. Supporters contended that the EU was emerging as a powerful foreign and security policy actor, even a new superpower. Critics pointed to the gap between rhetoric and reality in EU foreign policy, arguing that there were fundamental obstacles that would prevent the EU from developing a true common foreign and security policy and severely limit the Union's international impact. The reality was and is a more complex and mixed picture. The EU's member states have made major progress in co-ordinating their national foreign and security policies since the early 1990s, in particular with regard to the Union's immediate neighbourhood, but also in relation to third countries, other regions and global issues. The EU's economic and political weight and its multifaceted relations with third countries, furthermore, give it substantial power and influence, particularly in the wider Europe. While there remain important foreign policy differences between the Union's member states and periodic major breakdowns in co-operation (as over the 2003 Iraq War), the larger trend has been towards the Europeanization of foreign and security policy within the EU. The arrangements for foreign and security policy co-operation put in place since the early 1990s, further, have provided quite a strong institutional basis for this development, in particular by maintaining bureaucratic momentum for co-operation.

The nature of foreign and security policy co-operation within the Union, however, significantly shapes and constrains the EU as an international actor. The inter-governmental, consensus nature of EU foreign and security policy-making means that the Union is particularly dependent on processes of consensus building and internal bargaining among its member states. As a consequence, it is hardly surprising that the EU has not proved well-suited to international crisis management requiring rapid decision-making on controversial issues of diplomacy and force – as with the Yugoslav conflict in the 1990s. In contrast, the Union has proved to be far better suited to the longer-term strategic challenge of developing political, economic and security relations with other states and regions. Indeed, to the extent that the new security agenda involves a range of complex, multifaceted political, economic and social issues it may be argued that the EU is particularly well-suited to responding to these challenges.

Since the mid-2000s and in particular since the global financial and economic crisis of 2008, however, the EU has entered a period of major political and economic crisis which has called into question the trend towards an increasing EU foreign and security policy role. The rejection of the proposed EU Constitutional Treaty by the French and Dutch

---

Box 4.4 The European debt crisis and the future of the euro

By the late 2000s a number of European countries faced major debt problems. Within the seventeen-member eurozone, Greece, Ireland and Portugal were forced to seek large bailouts from the International Monetary Fund and the EU, with fears that Spain, Italy and even France might be forced to follow suit. The crisis threatened to trigger a second Europe-wide and global recession following that of 2008, called into question the future of the euro and severely damaged Europe and the EU's credibility as an economic and political actor. The debt crisis threatened the euro in a number of ways: economic collapse in one eurozone state could easily spill over into others; the creditor states within the eurozone (above all Germany) faced a choice between bailing out debtor states or potentially forcing their expulsion from the euro; debtor states faced the choice of seeking bailouts (and accepting the harsh austerity conditions attached to such assistance) or potentially withdrawing from the euro; and, as the crisis played out, financial markets were becoming increasingly sceptical about the value and future of the euro. In 2010–12 EU member states put in place policies designed to address the crisis, in particular a European Financial Stability Facility (EFSF, providing financial assistance to states facing debt problems) and a Fiscal Compact or Fiscal Stability Treaty (formally, the Treaty on Stability, Co-ordination and Governance in the Economic and Monetary Union, signed in January 2012), designed to prevent signatories developing excessive levels of debt and with national budgets to be monitored by the EU. Most observers argued that the crisis was only likely to be resolved by the EU providing much larger-scale financial support to countries facing budget crises combined with some form of fiscal union amongst the eurozone states involving much greater oversight and control of national budgets (as envisaged in the January 2012 Fiscal Compact) (Begg, 2011; Nicoll, 2011; Nottebaum, 2011). At the beginning of 2012, the outcome of the crisis remained deeply uncertain, with a number of eurozone countries, in particular Greece but also Portugal, Ireland, Spain and Italy, as well as non-eurozone EU members such as Hungary, facing severe recessions and budgetary crises. In one scenario, some countries might leave or be forced to leave the euro, potentially triggering the complete collapse of the euro (Belke, 2011). Alternatively, the majority of eurozone countries might agree to greater fiscal union, significantly deepening the process of economic and political integration amongst them (Begg 2011; Nicoll, 2011; Nottebaum 2011).

---

publics in referenda in 2005 was a significant setback for European integration, in particular because it appeared to reflect a more general, Europe-wide disillusionment with the EU and the idea of European integration. The European project was further damaged by the initial Irish rejection of the Lisbon Treaty in a June 2008 referendum. When the

Lisbon Treaty eventually entered into force in December 2009, after a second Irish referendum in October 2009 had produced a 'yes' vote, it seemed to be limping across the finish line. The 2008 global crisis hit European economies particularly hard, limiting the political capital and economic resources available for wider EU foreign policy ambitions and in addition suggesting that Europe was a declining global force compared to the rising non-Western powers which were less severely affected by the crisis. In 2010–11, further, Europe was engulfed by a debt crisis that called into question the future of the euro and many observers viewed as the most severe crisis in the history of the EU (see Box 4.4).

The outcome of the euro crisis is likely to have major implications for the entire European project, including the EU's foreign and security policy. A break-up of the euro would be a major setback for the EU as a whole, spilling over, even if only indirectly, into the area of foreign and security policy. Movement towards fiscal union within the euro-zone would be a significant further step in European economic and political integration, but would raise the prospect of a two-tier EU divided between an inner core euro group and those states remaining outside. Britain, Denmark and Sweden, who all chose in the 1990s and 2000s to remain outside the euro, would presumably remain outside the euro. The Central and Eastern European EU members would face difficult choices about whether to pursue membership of the inner core Europe. There might also be tensions between the maintenance of a common foreign and security policy at the level of all EU member states and the idea of the inner core proceeding with deeper integration also in the area of foreign and security policy. Whatever the specific outcome of the euro crisis, the likelihood is that it will leave the EU and its members economically weakened and preoccupied with internal European issues for some years, limiting their appetite and capacity for wider foreign policy activism.

Chapter 5

Russia: Insider/Outsider in European Security

The end of the Cold War, the disintegration of the Soviet Union and the collapse of communism in 1989–91 raised major questions about Russia's place in the world and its relations with the rest of Europe, the West more broadly, and its neighbours in the former Soviet Union. For the forty years or so since the onset of the Cold War, and arguably the seventy-odd years since the 1917 revolution, the Soviet Union/Russia had been the defining external security threat for the West. For the Soviet Union, the combination of ideology and geopolitics made confrontation with the West, especially the USA, the defining feature of its foreign relations. With the demise of the Soviet Union, some observers in both Moscow and Western capitals hoped for the development of a close partnership between Russia and the West, and even that a democratic Russia might become a full part of the West. Within Russia, however, others argued that their country had a distinctive Eurasian identity and specific national interests of its own, and must re-assert its independence from the West and its influence in the former Soviet Union. In the West, some argued that Russia was still far from a democracy, that Russian and Western interests were likely to collide, and that, in the worst case, the collapse of communism might produce a hyper-nationalist 'Weimar Russia'. In the former Soviet Union, decades and in many cases centuries of close integration between Russia and the other former Soviet republics, plus a history of violent conflict, suggested that dismantling the Soviet empire was likely to be a prolonged, difficult and sometimes bloody process.

This chapter examines the evolution of Russian foreign policy since the collapse of communism, and explores Russia's place in the new European security order of the early 21st century. It highlights the way in which post-Cold War Russo-Western relations have been characterized by an uneasy mix of co-operation and confrontation. The consolidation of an authoritarian regime in the 2000s, under the leadership of Vladimir Putin – Russia's president from 1999 to 2008, prime minister from 2008 to 2012 and re-elected as president in March 2012 – however, consolidated Russia's place as an outsider in the European security order dominated by the NATO/EU security community. This chapter also examines Russia's efforts to re-establish a sphere of influence in the former Soviet Union, but concludes that Moscow's ability to achieve this goal remains limited, and countries such as the Baltic States, Georgia, Moldova and Ukraine are likely to continue to resist Russian hegemonism. The chapter also explores the Janus-faced nature of Russian power: Russia retains many of the characteristics of a major power but is also a weak state facing major challenges, including an unbalanced economy, population decline, a dysfunctional governmental system, widespread crime and serious public health problems. Russia's impact on the European and global security environment is likely to remain defined by this unusual mix of strength and weakness.

Russia: post-communism and foreign policy

Since 1991, Russia has gone through a period of dramatic turbulence and transition. In 1991 a failed coup by hard-liners within the Soviet Communist Party and the military against reformist Soviet president Mikhail Gorbachev triggered the disintegration of the Soviet Union, with its fifteen constituent republics becoming independent states. In 1993 violent confrontation between reformist Russian president Boris Yeltsin and his communist and nationalist political opponents was resolved in Yeltsin's favour when the military sided with the president – allowing Yeltsin to consolidate his power. Although Yeltsin introduced market economic reforms, his presidency became associated with political disorder and economic decline, with Yeltsin's rule becoming increasingly maverick and a dramatic financial and economic collapse in 1998. Yeltsin was replaced as president by Vladimir Putin in 1999 and in the 2000s Putin re-established political order and oversaw a return to economic growth (based on gas and oil exports), but consolidated an increasingly authoritarian regime.

The relationship between domestic politics and foreign policy in Russia is complex. During the 1990s, the Russian foreign policy debate was often characterized as one between Westernizers and Eurasians, the former advocating integration with the West and the latter emphasizing Russia's distinctive place as a Eurasian power. Alexei Arbatov described the Russian foreign policy spectrum in terms of four groups: a pro-Western group, whose central goal was to integrate Russia politically and economically into the West; moderate liberals, who, while supporting democracy and market-orientated economics, argued for a more pragmatic approach based on Russian national interests; centrists and moderate conservatives, who emphasized the restoration of Russian influence in the former Soviet Union and the development of ties with states such as China, India and Iran; and neo-communists and nationalists supporting the re-establishment of the Russian empire and a strongly anti-Western foreign policy (Arbatov, 1993, pp. 8–14; see also De Nevers, 1994, pp. 23–39).

At the beginning of the 1990s, President Boris Yeltsin, his foreign minister, Andrei Kozyrev, and key economic reformers (such as Prime Minister Yegor Gaidar) pursued a strongly pro-Western foreign policy, winding down the Cold War military confrontation with the West and seeking Western financial support for market economic reforms. Yeltsin's market economic reforms and pro-Western foreign policy, however, provoked opposition, which coalesced in the Russian Duma (parliament). Tensions between President Yeltsin and his opponents came to a head in September 1993: Yeltsin dissolved the Duma, Duma deputies responded by taking up arms, pro-parliamentary mobs took to the streets and Russia appeared to be on the verge of civil war or state collapse. The Russian military, however, supported Yeltsin and shelled the Duma, forcing the deputies to surrender and restoring order. Duma elections in December 1993, however, produced strong support for Yeltsin's communist and nationalist opponents (including the neo-fascist Liberal Democratic Party, led by the extremist Vladimir Zhirinovsky – viewed by some as a potential Russian Adolf Hitler).

The rise of opposition to Yeltsin raised fears of a possible red-brown communist–nationalist coalition, while the severe economic dislocation associated with market reforms generated concern about a potential 'Weimar Russia' that might collapse into extreme nationalism, as Germany had in the 1930s. In the event, these worst-case scenarios did not come to pass, and Yeltsin won the presidential elections in 1996. In the face of domestic criticism and disillusionment with Western support, Yeltsin's early pro-Western foreign policy was significantly modified and a greater emphasis was placed on the re-establishment of influence in the former Soviet Union. In 1998, however, the Asian financial crisis of the previous year spread to Russia, with a massive exodus of foreign capital triggering a 30 per cent devaluation of the rouble in August 1998, a collapse of the banking system and a 4.6 per cent decline in gross domestic product (GDP) by the end of the year.

The 1998 financial collapse symbolized the increasing weakness of post-communist Russia.

In the 2000s, the chaos and disorder of the Yeltsin era was replaced by a period of relative stability but creeping authoritarianism under Vladimir Putin. Putin succeeded Yeltsin when the latter resigned at the end of 1999 (Putin was at that point prime minister and the Russian constitution mandated that the prime minister become president in such circumstances) and then won presidential elections in 2000 and 2004. The Russian constitution limits presidents to serving not more than two consecutive terms; Putin therefore stepped down as president in 2008, with his chosen successor Dmitry Medvedev elected president in March 2008. Putin, however, was appointed prime minister by Medvedev and it was widely recognized that Putin remained the real power within Russia. The Russian political system under Putin became one of authoritarian 'managed democracy' (Anderson, 2007; Beer, 2009). Russia retained the formal institutions of democracy, in particular an elected presidency and parliament, but real power remained in the hands of Putin and the central elite associated with him – a group known as the *siloviki* (from the Russian for those commanding force or power) and composed of senior figures from the security and intelligence services and military (Bremmer and Charap, 2006–07). The central aims of the *siloviki* were to restore domestic order within Russia and re-establish the country as a great power. Putin and the elite controlled the appointment of the government and powerful regional governors, and key state institutions such as the military and the security services. The Duma was dominated by the pro-Putin United Russia party and became neutered as a source of opposition or criticism. The media was largely controlled by the state and became a mouthpiece for the Putin elite. Opposition was permitted, but the legal system and the police were used to intimidate and silence critics.

The political system which emerged in the 2000s was underpinned by a remarkable economic recovery following Russia's 1998 financial and economic collapse – a recovery, however, based almost entirely on gas and oil exports. Russia has the largest gas reserves in the world and the eighth largest oil reserves. Rising global demand for oil and gas, rapidly increasing oil and gas prices and the restoration of Russian oil and gas production after their decline in the 1990s produced annual GDP growth rates of 4–7 per cent between 2000 and 2006 (almost all of this growth being accounted for by revenues from gas and oil exports). This economic recovery improved the situation of the

Russian people significantly, caused a dramatic increase in the financial resources available to the Russian state, and allowed Russia to pay off the majority of its foreign debt. The combination of economic growth and the restoration of political stability made Vladimir Putin a genuinely popular leader, with consistently high poll ratings. Economic recovery also allowed Russia to regain part of its lost international power and prestige, with observers describing it as one of a number of new 'energy superpowers' (Hill, 2002, 2004).

In terms of foreign policy, Russia under Putin initially shifted between a Eurasian and a Western-orientated foreign policy, but from the mid-2000s followed an increasingly assertive policy, seeking to re-establish Russia as a great power independent of the West. National security strategy and military doctrine documents adopted in 2000 were based on the assumption of a confrontation between a US-led West and Russia. In response to the 9/11 terrorist attacks, however, Putin adopted a significantly more pro-Western foreign policy, supporting US intervention in Afghanistan, including by acquiescing to the deployment of US troops in the Central Asian former Soviet republics and supplying arms to America's Afghan allies the Northern Alliance (Antonenko, 2001). Putin's turn towards the West appeared to reflect a genuine belief that Russia and the West faced a common enemy in Islamic terrorism (with Russia's war in Chechnya one front in this confrontation), but also a more pragmatic assessment of 9/11 as an opportunity for Russia to build political capital with the West and in particular the USA. After 2001, however, Russia gradually returned to a foreign policy emphasizing the re-establishment of Russia as a great power, support for a multipolar (as opposed to US/Western-dominated) world order and the re-assertion of Russian influence in the former Soviet Union. As part of its support for a multipolar world and efforts to counter US influence, Russia has also strengthened political, economic and military ties with a variety of non-Western states (including China, India, Middle Eastern states and Venezuela). Russia's willingness to confront the West and re-assert influence in the former Soviet space was brought sharply into focus by the 2008 Georgia War (the war and its impact on Russo-Western relations are examined in more detail below). These general directions of Russian foreign and security policy were re-affirmed in new official documents adopted in 2008–10: *Foreign Policy Concept* (July 2008), *National Security Strategy* (May 2009) and *Military Doctrine* (February 2010) (President of Russia, 2008, 2009; de Haas and Schroder, 2009; Giles, 2010).

Until the early 2010s, it was often assumed that the Putin era would continue relatively undisturbed. In September 2011 President Medvedev proposed that Putin stand for president again, an offer Putin accepted, and it was widely expected that Putin would win presidential elections in March 2012 without significant opposition. In late 2011, however, parliamentary elections triggered unexpected protests against Putin and his regime. The pro-Putin United Russia party won the elections with 46 per cent of the official vote, but this was significantly down on its 64 per cent in previous elections in 2007 and only achieved by massive vote-rigging and ballot stuffing (United Russia received 99.5 per cent of votes in some regions and voter turn-out appeared to exceed 140 per cent in others). The fraudulent elections triggered protests involving tens of thousands of people on the streets of Moscow. The opposition reflected more general discontent with the political system – captured in a popular blogger's description of United Russia as 'the party of crooks and thieves' (*The Economist* 2011b, 2011c). Putin won the presidential elections in March 2012, with 64 per cent of the vote, but critics argued that there had been no real presidential electoral competition, with Putin and his allies using their control of state institutions and the media to ensure the outcome. The protests of late 2011, which re-emerged after the March 2012 presidential election, however, suggested that cracks had suddenly appeared in an apparently invulnerable regime. The protests reflected deeper problems with the regime: the concentration of power in the hands of an unaccountable elite almost inevitably resulted in massive corruption, with the elite using its power to advance its own economic interests; economically, corruption and an unaccountable political system were undermining the prospects for the longer-term development of an advanced economy not dependent on gas and oil exports. It remains to be seen how Russia's domestic politics will evolve. Putin faces a choice between liberalizing the system (which might ultimately threaten the power of Putin and the elite surrounding him) or using greater repression to hold on to power. Some observers have warned that Putin might also seek external or internal scapegoats to distract public attention from the problems associated with the regime (*The Economist*, 2011c). Were Putin to hold another two presidential terms until 2024, he would have ruled Russia for nearly a quarter of a century – longer than the 18 years Leonid Brezhnev had led the Soviet Union and close to Joseph Stalin's 31-year domination of the Soviet system. The possible foreign policy implications of Russia's changing domestic politics are returned to at the end of this chapter.

Russia and the West: a troubled partnership

The post-Cold War relationship between Russia and the West has been characterized by an uneasy mix of co-operation and confrontation. As was noted above, following the collapse of Soviet communism there were hopes of a new strategic partnership between Russia and the West, but these were quickly dashed as tensions emerged, in particular over the Yugoslav conflict and NATO's enlargement. This pattern of initial hope of a fundamental breakthrough in relations followed by disillusionment as differences re-emerged was also repeated after the events of 9/11. Russian–Western relations reached a new low in 2008 with the Georgia War (see Box 5.1). Russia's intervention in Georgia suggested a new willingness on Moscow's part to use military force to re-assert its influence in the former Soviet space, leading some observers to predict the emergence of a new Cold War with the West (Lucas, 2008). The Georgia War, however, has not been followed by further Russian military interventions in the region and both Russia and the West quickly sought to re-build relations – suggesting that neither side had the appetite for prolonged confrontation. When the Obama administration came to power in 2009, further, one of its first major foreign policy initiatives was to pursue a 're-set' in relations with

---

Box 5.1   The Georgia War 2008

In August 2008 Russia and Georgia fought a five-day war, with Russian forces entering Georgia, rapidly defeating the Georgian military and taking control of the secessionist regions of South Ossetia and Abkhazia. The background to the war was Georgia's efforts to break out of Russia's sphere of influence, in particular its bid for full membership of NATO, and an increasingly personalized struggle between Georgia's pro-Western president Mikhail Saakashvili and Russian prime minister Vladimir Putin. Russia justified the intervention as necessary to prevent attacks and a potential genocide against Georgia's South Ossetian minority. Most Western observers viewed the war as a clear-cut case of international aggression by Russia designed to bring a recalcitrant neighbour into line. The war was ended when the EU (in particular French president Nicolas Sarkozy, because France was holding the rotating EU Presidency at this point) brokered a cease-fire, but it ended essentially on Russian terms, with Russia in control of South Ossetia and Abkhazia and Georgia's aspirations of NATO membership in tatters. Russia subsequently recognized South Ossetia and Abkhazia as independent states, but the rest of the international community has not done so.

Russia, the centre-piece of which was the 2010 New START (Strategic Arms Reduction Treaty) nuclear arms control agreement reducing Russian and US nuclear arsenals.

A variety of factors explain the mixed pattern of relations between Russia and the West since the end of the Cold War and suggest that it is likely to continue into the future. The demise of communism in the Soviet Union removed what had been the key ideological source of tension between Russia and the West since 1917. The withdrawal of Soviet forces from Central and Eastern Europe and the break-up of the Soviet Union ended the geostrategic military threat that the Soviet Union had posed to the West since 1945. In order to reform and modernize its economy, Russia needs Western aid, trade and investment. During the 1990s, the West – individual Western states, Western banks and the International Monetary Fund (IMF) – helped to underpin Russian economic reforms by supplying aid, loans and debt relief, and Russia became to a significant degree dependent on Western economic support. Russia and the West also arguably share basic common interests in addressing key elements of the new global security agenda, such as globalized Islamic terrorism and WMD proliferation.

There are, however, countervailing pressures that generate tensions between Russia and the West. Many in Russia, and especially in the Russian security and military elite, still view the West as a threat. NATO's enlargement into Central and Eastern Europe, its intervention in the former Yugoslavia and the expansion of US influence in the Caucasus and Central Asia have fed into historic Russian fears of encirclement. More broadly, Russia has opposed the Western- and especially US-dominated post-Cold War global order, instead advocating a multipolar world in which Russia will be one of the poles. Similarly, Russia's residual great power status and uncertainty about its longterm future direction makes other European states wary of Moscow. More immediately, Russia's efforts to maintain its sphere of influence in the former Soviet Union (see below) have generated tensions not only with the former Soviet republics but also with other European states and the USA. Russia's drift into authoritarianism under Vladimir Putin also generated tensions with the West. In addition, Russia's engagement in the arms and nuclear technology trade has been criticized by the West, especially in the case of Iran, where Russia is a key supplier of the nuclear technology that underpins Tehran's reputed efforts to develop nuclear weapons.

More broadly, if the Western security community discussed in Chapter 1 is the defining feature of contemporary Europe, Russia is not a member of that community. Russia's drift towards authoritarianism means that it does not fully share the core democratic values on which that security community is based. Russia is not a member of that community's key institutions, the EU and NATO, nor does it share the high level of economic interdependence that marks that community. Although unlikely, armed conflict between Russia and the West cannot be ruled out. It is not impossible that Russia could yet become a full member of the Western security community, but such a development would require major domestic political change – a shift towards a more substantive democracy – within Russia. Indeed, since the late 1990s, Russia has been moving further away from, not closer to, the Western security community.

Given this balance of factors, it is hardly surprising that the Russian–Western relationship is pulled in contradictory directions. The global balance of power discussed in Chapter 2, however, means that the relationship between Russia and the West (or even between Russia and the EU) is hardly one of equals. Regardless of the EU's dependence on Russian energy supplies, in terms of broad economic, political and military power, the West remains the dominant partner. Thus, while Russia poses a potential (and in some cases real) threat to its weaker and smaller neighbours, it lacks the power to pose a major strategic threat to the rest of Europe as a whole for the foreseeable future. Renewed military confrontation with the West would also be extremely costly for Russia. For these reasons, while continued tensions between Russia and the West appear to be likely over a range of issues, a full-blown political-military confrontation akin to the Cold War seems unlikely.

Russia and NATO

Since the end of the Cold War, NATO and Russia have sought, but often struggled, to build a new, co-operative relationship. NATO–Russia ties have gradually been institutionalized (Weitz, 2005, pp. 59–73): Russia joined NATO's Partnership for Peace (PfP) in 1994; a NATO–Russia Founding Act on Mutual Relations, Co-operation and Security was signed in 1997, at which point a NATO–Russia Permanent Joint Council (PJC) was established; and in 2002 a new NATO–Russia Council (NRC) replaced the PJC. As a consequence, there is now regular political and military dialogue between NATO and Russia.

Despite these efforts to institutionalize co-operation, NATO–Russia relations remain troubled by a number of factors. The Russian leadership, in particular the military, continue to view NATO as a serious potential, and perhaps actual, threat to Russia's security. According to Russia's 2009 *National Security Strategy* document, 'A determining aspect of relations with NATO remains the fact that plans to extend the alliance's military infrastructure to Russia's borders, and attempts to endow NATO with global functions that go counter to norms of international law, are unacceptable to Russia' (President of Russia, 2009, para. 17). In particular, Russia has strongly opposed NATO's eastward enlargement into its former sphere of influence. At various points in the 1990s and early 2000s, Russian political and military leaders warned of the emergence of a new 'Cold Peace' between Russia and NATO, and threatened counter-measures in response to the Alliance's enlargement into Central and Eastern Europe. In practice, Russia was unable to prevent NATO's enlargement into Central and Eastern Europe and chose to learn to live with the new reality. NATO's possible enlargement into the former Soviet space, however, is an even more neuralgic issue for Moscow. The desire to prevent Georgia and other former Soviet states, such as Ukraine, from joining NATO was one of the key drivers behind Russia's intervention in Georgia in 2008 (Asmus, 2010, pp. 111–40). Since 2008, NATO has effectively mothballed plans for possible enlargement to include former Soviet states such as Georgia and Ukraine, largely removing the issue as a major source of tension with Russia.

Intervention in the Yugoslav conflict proved a particular bone of contention between NATO and Russia throughout the 1990s. NATO's intervention was viewed in Moscow as an encroachment into a former Russian sphere of influence, directed against Russia's Slavic kin, the Serbs, and setting a potential precedent for NATO intervention closer to Russia (or even in Russia itself) (Kremenyuk, 2002). In the complex peacemaking efforts in the former Yugoslavia, Russia generally backed the Serbs, while Western sympathies lay primarily with the Bosnian Muslims, Croats and other non-Serb groups. NATO–Russia relations reached a post-Cold War nadir during NATO's 1999 intervention in Kosovo, when Russia formally broke off relations with NATO and rushed 200 paratroopers from its peacekeeping force in Bosnia to deploy ahead of NATO forces at the airport in Kosovo's capital, Pristina, prompting the commander of NATO forces on the ground, the British General Sir Michael Jackson, to warn of a possible 'Third World War' (quoted in Tran, 1999). In both Bosnia in 1995 and Kosovo in 1999, however, Russia was eventually persuaded to contribute forces to the NATO-led peacekeeping operations.

The 2008 Georgia War also provoked a crisis in NATO–Russia relations, with NATO formally severing relations with Russia. While
NATO criticized Russia's intervention in Georgia, however, the
Alliance's members were not willing to risk a direct confrontation with
Russia by responding militarily. After the war ended, further, NATO
quickly re-established relations with Russia and initiated efforts to build
a more durable partnership (Bailes and Cottey, 2010, pp. 154–9).

Although NATO and Russia share certain common security interests, in particular in countering terrorism and proliferation, the relationship between the two is likely to remain a fractious one marred by
periodic crises. Russia's leaders, especially its security and military
elite, continue to view NATO as a threat – a perception reinforced by
NATO's eastward enlargement and its interventions in the Balkans,
Afghanistan and Libya. NATO remains wary of Russian efforts to re-
establish a sphere of influence in the former Soviet space and some
Alliance members, such as the Baltic States and Poland, still view
Russia as a potential military threat to their security. NATO's decision
in November 2010 to develop Alliance-wide missile defences was an
additional source of tension with Moscow: although NATO argues
that such defences are designed only to defend against limited missile
threats (in particular that potentially posed by Iran), Russia fears that
missile defences might be expanded to negate its own nuclear deterrent
and has threatened to take counter-measures.

Russia and the EU

Like NATO, the EU has sought to develop an institutionalized partnership with Russia (European External Action Service, nd). A
Partnership and Co-operation Agreement (PCA) between the EU and
Russia was signed in 1994, coming into force in 1997. The PCA
provides the framework for regular political dialogue with Russia, as
well as for economic and trade relations. Since the mid-1990s, the
EU–Russia relationship has expanded to include regular summits of
leaders (twice-yearly since 2000), regular meetings of officials on a
wide range of issues, meetings between the European Parliament and
the Russian Parliament and (since 2005) six-monthly consultations on
human rights. The EU has also provided financial and technical assistance to Russia (in particular to support safety of nuclear facilities and
promote cross-border co-operation in northern Europe where the EU
has its only direct borders with Russia) – amounting to about three
billion euros since 1991. In 2003, further, the EU and Russia agreed to

create four 'common spaces' – in economics and the environment, freedom, security and justice, external security, and research and education
– as a focus for co-operation.

Although Russia and the EU have developed a quite strongly institutionalized relationship and theoretically now engage in extensive co-operation, in reality the relationship is a problematic one. This can be gauged
from the titles of reports and articles on the relationship by the late 2000s:
'EU–Russia Relations: Towards a Way Out of Depression' (Gomart,
2008), 'EU–Russia Relations: Unfortunate Continuity' (Moshes, 2009)
and 'EU–Russia Relations: Reset or Stagnation?' (Bovt, 2009). EU–Russia
relations are undermined by a number of problems. Despite regular meetings of leaders and officials and the four 'common spaces', in practice
substantive co-operation between the EU and Russia is limited. Although
the trade relationship between Russia and the EU is quite significant, this
reflects primarily Russian gas and oil exports to EU member states rather
than a deeper or more balanced economic relationship. The continuing
predominance of the gas and oil sectors in the Russian economy and the
absence of wider economic development has meant that the EU's ability to
engage with or support Russia's economic development has been limited.
There is also a major political values gap between the EU and Russia: as a
union of democratic states the EU has been critical of Russia's slide to
authoritarianism (as well as many specific human rights issues) since the
1990s; Moscow, in contrast, has been wary of EU interference in Russia's
internal affairs. More broadly, there are major differences of culture and
strategic outlook between the EU and Russia. As Daniel Gros of the
Brussels think tank, the Centre for European Policy Studies, put it, 'The
EU is really a large bureaucratic machine whereas Russia works on the
basis of power politics so there are often difficulties in the relationship
between them' (quoted in Smyth, 2006).

The EU is not perceived by Russia to be a military threat, and
Moscow has been much less concerned about the EU's eastward
enlargement or the Union's emerging defence role than it has about
NATO's post-Cold War evolution. As a consequence, Russia's relationship with the EU has not been as problematic as that with NATO.
Nevertheless, there are certain international and security tensions
between Russia and the EU. Russia is wary of the EU's development of
relations with the other former Soviet states. When the EU launched
its Eastern Partnership with the western and Caucasian former Soviet
states in 2008–09, Russia viewed this as an attempt to counter its influence in the region. Although the EU is reluctant to be drawn into a
zero-sum competition for influence with Russia in the former Soviet

space, this may to some extent be unavoidable. So far this competition has been a limited one, but should EU membership for some of the former Soviet states move closer to political reality (something which is not the case at the moment), this competition for influence could escalate. An additional problem from the EU perspective has been Russia's 'energy diplomacy': Russia's use of interruptions of gas supplies to bring political and economic pressure to bear on neighbouring states (including Central and Eastern European EU member states, as well former Soviet states), its efforts to maintain a monopoly of gas and oil pipelines in the former Soviet region and its efforts to buy into European energy supply and distribution companies all suggest that for the EU Russia is hardly a reliable energy partner. While EU member states have little choice but to continue to rely on Russian oil and especially gas exports, the relationship is likely to remain a problematic one. The EU–Russia relationship is also complicated by Russia's tendency to use 'divide and rule' tactics in its relations with the Union: although the EU's aggregate economic, political and military power is much greater than that of Russia, EU member states are often divided over issues such as relations with the former Soviet states and energy diplomacy, allowing Russia to exploit these differences and limiting the EU's influence over Russia (Leonard and Popescu, 2007).

The problematic nature of the EU–Russia relationship is reflected in the fact that since the ten-year term of the EU–Russia Partnership and Co-operation Agreement expired in 2007 the two have not yet been able to conclude a new agreement (relying instead on the existing PCA being renewed on an annual basis until such time as it can be replaced by a new agreement). In 2009–10, an emerging debate within Russia on 'modernization' – with President Medvedev appearing to favour economic reform and political liberalization – resulted in the establishment of an EU–Russia Partnership for Modernization (EU-Russia Centre, 2010). There were hopes within the EU that if the Russian leadership was serious about economic modernization and recognized that this would require both a more broadly based economy and political liberalization there might be an opportunity to develop a more substantive EU–Russia partnership. By 2011, however, the initial hopes surrounding Russia's modernization agenda had dissipated and the EU–Russia Partnership for Modernization appeared stillborn. The development of a real EU–Russia partnership will likely depend on deeper political and economic change within Russia.

Russia and the former Soviet Union: the 'near abroad'?

In many ways, Russia's relations with the other former Soviet republics are the classical problems of withdrawal from empire: the imperial power's reluctance to lose its empire, the weakness of newly emergent post-colonial states, the continued significance of economic ties developed under the empire, and the potential for violent conflict over borders and ethnic minorities. In the former Soviet case, however, these problems are compounded by geography: proximity means that Russia and the other former Soviet republics are destined to be neighbours.

Historically, there was never a clear dividing line between the Russian state and the Russian empire: 'Until at least the late nineteenth century, Russia was defined not as the land of the Russians but as the territory of the Russian Empire-State' (Melvin, 1995, p. 7), a pattern upon which the Soviet Union built after 1917. Russia has thus struggled to come to terms with the loss of much of its empire-state. According to Eugene B. Rumer, no Russian foreign policy interest 'has been articulated more frequently, clearly, or with greater consistency throughout the post-Soviet period than the consolidation of a Russian sphere of influence among the former countries of the Soviet Union' (Rumer, 2007, 25). This is re-affirmed in the 2008 *Foreign Policy Concept* and 2009 *National Security Strategy* noted above (President of Russia, 2008, section IV; President of Russia, 2009, para. 13). Relations between Russia and the other former Soviet states have been further complicated by the Russian diaspora in the region – the approximately 25 million ethnic Russians left outside Russia by the break-up of the Soviet Union. The largest of these Russian minorities were in Ukraine (8 million), Kazakhstan (4.5 million), Belarus (1.2 million), Latvia (700,000), Uzbekistan (650,000) and Kyrgyzstan (600,000). Russia has set itself up as the defender of the rights of these Russian minorities, but has also used the issue of Russian minority rights to assert influence over the other former Soviet republics. Russian concerns about encirclement and the penetration of other powers into the region have reinforced a consensus in Moscow in favour of maintaining a sphere of influence in the former Soviet Union.

The initial vehicle for Russian efforts to maintain a sphere of influence was the Commonwealth of Independent States (CIS), established at the end of 1991. Many of the other former Soviet republics, in particular Ukraine, viewed the CIS as little more than a vehicle for a civilized divorce from the Soviet Union, and while it continues to exist more than two decades after its creation, the CIS has become a largely paper institution. Russia has also sought to build alliances with those states supportive of its dominant role in the region (such as Armenia, Belarus and Kazakhstan), while putting pressure on others (such as Georgia, Moldova and Ukraine), which have pursued greater independence from it. During the early 1990s, Russia intervened militarily in conflicts in Moldova, Georgia and Tajikistan, both as a means of maintaining influence in the region and in order to put pressure on these states to accede to Russian demands. A Collective Security Treaty (CST), incorporating a mutual defence guarantee similar to that on which NATO is based, was signed by a number of CIS states in 1992–93. Ukraine, Moldova and Turkmenistan, however, stayed outside the CST, and Azerbaijan, Georgia and Uzbekistan withdrew from it in 1999 (although Uzbekistan rejoined in 2006). The CST was upgraded to the status of an organization (the CSTO) in 2002–03 and at the time of writing includes Russia, Armenia, Belarus, Kazakhstan, Kyrgyzstan, Tajikistan and Uzbekistan. The former Soviet Union is thus characterized by a patchwork of security arrangements, including the CSTO, bilateral military co-operation arrangements between Russia and various former Soviet states, and multilateral military exercises among varying combinations of states (Willerton and Cockerham, 2003, pp. 193–6).

The attitudes of the other former Soviet states towards Russia have varied significantly. Belarus, which lacks a strong sense of national identity independent of Russia, has been Moscow's most loyal ally in the former Soviet space. Armenia has maintained a strategic alliance with Russia to counter its historical enemies, Azerbaijan and Turkey. The Central Asian states have largely sought to maintain close relations with Russia, with the partial exception of Uzbekistan, which has been torn between asserting itself as a power in its own right within Central Asia and maintaining an alliance with Russia. The Baltic States – Estonia, Latvia and Lithuania – refused to join the CIS in 1991, succeeded in consolidating their independence from Russia after this, and joined NATO and the EU in 2004, effectively moving out of what is conceived of as the former Soviet space. Azerbaijan, Georgia, Moldova and Ukraine have also sought to distance themselves from Russia. Since the late 1990s, the GUAM (Georgia, Ukraine, Azerbaijan and Moldova) group have co-operated in efforts to counter-balance Russia, but GUAM remains at best a weak framework for co-operation.

Relations with Russia are linked to domestic politics within the former Soviet states, with internal divisions between those supporting close ties with Russia and those seeking greater independence from Moscow. These divisions also relate to democracy, with authoritarian regimes generally supporting close ties with Russia, and their liberal opponents seeking closer ties with the West. In November 2003, Georgia's Rose Revolution brought to power a new leadership committed to democratization and closer ties with the West. A year later, Ukraine's Orange Revolution followed a similar pattern, and in 2005 Kyrgyzstan's Tulip Revolution saw the overthrow of that country's authoritarian post-communist regime. This series of 'colour revolutions' seemed to hint at a wave of political change that might see the overthrow of authoritarian post-communist rulers in most of the post-Soviet space, and alter its geopolitics in the process. Developments since these revolutions have shown, however, that even under new leadership these countries face major challenges in reforming their political systems and economies. Fear of similar revolutions has also led other states to clamp down on dissent, as in Uzbekistan in May 2005, when security forces opened fire on protestors in the city of Andijan, killing many of them.

Since the early 1990s, a variety of factors – the need to respond to conflicts within the region, access to its oil and gas resources, the rise of Islamic movements, opposition to Russian neo-imperialism, and concerns about democracy and human rights – have drawn other external actors, in particular the USA, the EU, China, Turkey and Iran, into the former Soviet space. Some argue that a new great game is emerging in the former Soviet Union, with the major powers competing for influence, just as Russia and Britain did in Central Asia in the 19th century. In practice, however, the USA and European states have been very cautious in engaging in the region, reflecting both the limited nature of their interests there, and a desire not to antagonize Russia. China and Iran, further, have largely co-operated with Russia in the former Soviet space rather than opposing it. In particular, the Shanghai Co-operation Organization (SCO), established in 2001, brings together Russia, China and four Central Asian states (Kazakhstan, Kyrgyzstan, Tajikistan and Uzbekistan). The Shanghai co-operation process began in the late 1990s with the conclusion of arms reduction and military confidence-building agreements, and the SCO now brings its members together on a regular basis, with a focus on security concerns relating to Islamic movements and terrorism. The SCO is also to some extent a counterweight to Western, and in particular US, influence in the region.

Two decades after the break-up of the Soviet Union, the former Soviet space remains a strategic no man's land. Russia is still by far the most important international actor in the region, yet it has not been able to fully re-establish a sphere of influence and its pursuit of regional integration via vehicles such as the CIS and the CSTO has made little progress. Other external actors have been drawn into the former Soviet space, but in practice have limited interests in the region and are wary of antagonizing Russia. By the mid- to late 2000s, further, it was increasingly clear that EU and NATO membership were unlikely to be extended to former Soviet states any time soon – a dynamic reinforced by the 2008 Georgia War. The Georgia War generated fears of a wider Russian effort to re-assert influence by forceful means, especially as it was accompanied by a Russian declaration of a zone of 'privileged interests' in the former Soviet Union. As was noted above, however, this has not occurred and Russia has been cautious in its relations with the former Soviet states since 2008. In October 2011, in the context of his bid for re-election as Russian president in March 2012, Prime Minister Vladimir Putin called for the creation of a new 'Eurasian Union' (Clover and Gorst, 2011). The Eurasian Union would be based on an existing customs union between Russia, Belarus and Kazakhstan, be open to other former Soviet states and pursue deeper integration over time. Given the failure of other former Soviet integration schemes since the early 1990s, there were good reasons to be sceptical about the prospects for Putin's proposed Eurasian Union. In particular, while some former Soviet states may support such a Eurasian Union, others, most importantly Ukraine, remain wary of Russian proposals for integration, especially if they might threaten their independence.

The security problems of Russian weakness

With the break-up of the Soviet Union, Moscow lost half of its population, 40 per cent of its gross national product (GNP), and a quarter of the territory it once controlled. In absolute GNP terms, Russia fell from third in the world in 1987 to fifteenth by the mid-1990s, behind India, Australia, the Netherlands and South Korea and just ahead of Mexico, Switzerland and Argentina (Graham, 1999, p. 3). The 1998 economic collapse further exacerbated Russia's decline and internal weaknesses. Thomas Graham, Jr., a former US diplomat who served in the American embassy in Moscow, warned of the possibility of 'a world without Russia' (Graham, 1999). As Russia's economy recovered in the 2000s and the country came to be described as an 'energy superpower', discussions of Russian weakness dissipated. Rather than going away, however, the underlying problems which Russia faces were only hidden by the country's gas- and oil-fuelled economic growth and in some cases were exacerbated by the political-economic system which emerged in the 2000s. In various ways, these problems of weakness pose security challenges both for Russia and for neighbouring states and the wider Europe.

- *The economy*: the collapse of communism and the transition to a market economy resulted in a major recession within Russia. Russia's GDP contracted by an estimated 40 per cent between 1991 and 1998. The 1998 financial crisis further exacerbated the situation. Many Russians were impoverished, while much of the Soviet-era welfare system was dismantled or downgraded. As was noted earlier, Russia's economic recovery in the 2000s was driven almost entirely by gas and oil exports. Reliance on gas and oil exports and the corruption associated with the Putin-era political-economic system, further, severely inhibited the development of other sectors of the economy. Absent the development of a much more broadly based industrial/post-industrial economy, Russia is unlikely to possess the basic economic requirements of great power status into the mid-21st century, and the experience of other oil/gas-exporting developing economies – such as Saudi Arabia, Nigeria or Venezuela – hardly provides a viable alternative model for an aspiring great power.
- *Demographic decline*: Russia faces a major problem of demographic decline: its population fell from 149 million in 1992 to 143 million in 2003; Russian fertility rates are below the replacement level of 2.1 children per woman of reproductive age, and mortality rates are high compared to many other states; if current trends continue, Russia's population is expected to decline by over 30 per cent over the next fifty years (World Bank, 2005, p. 3). In 2006 Prime Minister Putin described Russia's declining population as 'the most acute problem facing our country today' (Eberstadt, 2011). Russia's demographic decline is likely to cause or exacerbate a number of problems. The proportion of the Russian population of working age will decline, inhibiting the prospects for economic development. Demographic decline will reduce the numbers of men of conscription age and increase the proportion of the state budget that has to be allocated to health care and social problems. Demographic decline also raises the prospect that parts of the

Russian Federation, especially in the Far East, may become depopulated. The Russian Far East already faces significant economic and population penetration from China – a trend that is likely to grow and which some observers fear could even trigger Chinese territorial claims against Russia.

- *Governance*: Russia faces major governance problems. As was noted above, although the Putin-era system which emerged in the 2000s stabilized Russia after the political and economic disorder of the Yeltsin period, that system was based on control of the state and the economy by an unaccountable elite and had corruption built into it. At the same time, in the wake of the wars in Chechnya in the 1990s and early 2000s, ongoing low-level violence in the North Caucasus and the inability of the Russian government to stabilize the situation there threatens to turn southern Russia into a semi-permanent arc of instability (Dunlop and Menon, 2006). In various ways, therefore, the development of effectively functioning state institutions, which have legitimacy in the eyes of the Russian population, constitutes a major challenge.

- *Health*: although the Soviet Union's health situation had begun to worsen from the 1970s, the sudden transition to a market economy in the 1990s resulted in a dramatic deterioration in the health of the population, and Russia is now one of the few countries in the world where life expectancy is falling. Problems include high rates of death from non-communicable diseases such as heart disease; the return of communicable diseases such as tuberculosis and diphtheria; widespread alcoholism; a high suicide rate; and high levels of traffic and work-related accidents (World Bank, 2005). According to Nicholas Eberstadt (1999, p. 4), 'Russia's heath profile no longer remotely resembles that of a developed country; in fact, it is worse in a variety of respects than those of many Third World countries'. Russia's health problems also exacerbate its existing economic, demographic and governance crises.

- *Crime*: crime has become a pervasive feature of post-Soviet Russia. The collapse of communism resulted in a dramatic upsurge in crime in Russia, and the emergence of powerful organized criminal groups. By the mid-1990s there were an estimated 5,700 criminal gangs in Russia, with a total of more than 100,000 members (International Institute for Strategic Studies, 1995, p. 25). Violent crime poses a direct threat to the security of Russian citizens: Russia's homicide rate increased rapidly during the 1990s and is now one of the highest in the world; almost 30,000 Russians died as a result of homicide in 1999 (World Bank, 2005, p. 10). Despite the relative stabilization of Russian politics in the 2000s, further, rates of crime, including violent crime, remained high, with one observer describe the situation as 'out of control' (Goble, 2008).

- *Environment*: the Soviet Union's industrial, agricultural and military development from the 1930s through to its collapse was undertaken with almost no regard for the protection of the environment, and consequently caused major environmental problems. Russia and the former Soviet republics will face the legacy of these problems for many decades. Various Russian cities and regions constitute dangerous environmental hotspots which continue to pose serious threats to the health and lives of local people.

- *Military weakness*: with the break-up of the Soviet Union, the Russian military lost many of its bases, large numbers of front-line troops, and much of its latest weaponry. Defence spending declined dramatically in the 1990s, with the consequence that funds for re-organization and modernization were severely constrained. Many professional soldiers left the military, draft dodging was widespread, training was limited and much equipment was barely maintained. The operational effectiveness of the Russian military was seriously undermined, and the armed force became increasingly 'de-professionalized' (Herspring, 2002). Regional commanders hired out soldiers as labourers in order to raise funds, and elements within the military were widely believed to be involved in corruption and criminality. The practice of *dedovshchina* – hazing, where senior military personnel beat and brutalize their juniors – became all-pervasive. Economic recovery in the 2000s allowed increased funding to be directed towards the military and some problems were addressed. Nevertheless, observers suggest that the Russian military remains a weak and outdated force, rather than one at the cutting edge of modern military technology and organization (Eberstadt, 2011).

Overall, Russia is an uneasy and complex mix of a great power and a weak state. Russia retains important elements of international power: a large territorial and population base (notwithstanding the latter's decline); an important geostrategic location at the heart of the Eurasian landmass; a large military and a substantial military-industrial base; a large nuclear arsenal; and permanent membership of the UN Security Council and the associated veto over Security Council decisions. Economic recovery in the 2000s, further, allowed Russia to re-establish some of its lost power and prestige. Nevertheless, as an economic power Russia remains fundamentally unbalanced due to its heavy dependence on gas and oil exports, while it faces major problems in terms of demographic decline, governance, health and crime. For the average Russian citizen many of these problems pose much greater threats to their day-to-day security than possible conflict with NATO, the USA and the West. Russia's weakness also poses security threats to neighbouring states. The European Commission's 2002–06 *Country Strategy Paper* for Russia argued that ' "soft" security threats from Russia are a serious concern for the EU and require continued engagement – nuclear safety, the fight against crime, including drug trafficking and illegal immigration, the spread of disease and environmental pollution' (European Commission, 2001, p. 3). The extent to which Russian weakness poses major security challenges for Europe as a whole, however, is less clear. Other former Soviet states are primarily vulnerable to Russia because of their *own* internal weakness, which is often even more severe than Russia's. Elsewhere, neighbouring states are vulnerable to transnational security problems emerging from Russia (as in the case of northern European concerns about disused nuclear reactors from submarines based in Russia's far north), but the potential for Russia's weakness to cause more widespread destabilization or security threats, especially on a European-wide scale, is limited.

Conclusion

The end of the Cold War and the break-up of the Soviet Union opened up major questions about Russia's place in Europe and the wider world. Following the domestic turbulence of the 1990s, in the 2000s Russia's political and economic situation stabilized and an authoritarian pseudo-democratic system was established under Vladimir Putin. Yet, as the protests against fraudulent parliamentary elections in December 2011 suggested, the apparent stability of Russia's Putin-era political order may be fragile.

At the beginning of the 1990s there were hopes in both Moscow and the West that Russia might become a strategic partner of the West, even a full member of the Western security community. As this chapter has shown, however, the post-Cold War Russo-Western relationship has been defined by an ambiguous mix of co-operation, competition and periodic crises. Russia itself is pulled between the West and its distinctive Eurasian geostrategic identity and interests. From a Western perspective, Russia's drift towards authoritarianism and key elements of its foreign policy preclude it from being viewed as a fully reliable partner, let alone a full member of the Western security community. Both Russia and the West have important interests in maintaining a reasonably co-operative relationship, but real differences remain – over democracy and human rights, the future of the former Soviet space, and on global security issues such as peacekeeping and proliferation. The uneasy relationship between Russia and the West is therefore likely to continue for the foreseeable future.

In the former Soviet space, Russia has sought to maintain a dominant role. Russia's residual power, the support of some former Soviet states, the weakness of others and the caution or reluctance of external powers to intervene in the region has allowed Moscow to maintain a leading role there. While other actors – the USA, the EU, China, Turkey and Iran – have gradually expanded their engagement in the region since the early 1990s, they have generally been cautious in doing so, both because of the limited nature of their interests in the region and for fear of antagonizing Russia. While there are elements of competition between these powers in the former Soviet space, there are also important elements of strategic restraint and co-operation – suggesting that images of a new great game being played out in the former Soviet Union are exaggerated. Furthermore, by the late 2000s and especially in the wake of the 2008 Georgia War, it was clear that none of the former Soviet states was likely to join NATO or the EU for the foreseeable future. In these circumstances, the former Soviet space is likely to remain in a situation of strategic ambiguity, caught between Russia's efforts to maintain its dominant role in the region and the reluctance or inability of other external powers to assert a more powerful role.

Despite its (re-)emergence as an 'energy superpower' in the 2000s, Russia also remains characterized by major internal weaknesses – economic and governance problems, demographic decline, public health problems, pervasive criminality, environmental degradation and a decaying military – which will not be addressed easily. These problems pose significant threats to the security of Russian citizens and to some extent to the long-term stability of the Russian state. Russia is thus likely to be characterized by an unusual mix of great power strength and internal weakness.

With the unexpected protests against the parliamentary elections in December 2011, Russian politics appeared to have entered a new era of unpredictability. Although Vladimir Putin was re-elected as president in March 2012, some analysts compared Putin's Russia to the

Brezhnev-era stagnation which preceded the break-up of the Soviet Union: an apparently stable order based on a combination of authoritarianism and oil and gas wealth, but an essentially dysfunctional and unviable long-term system (Buhler, 2011). The Putin leadership might attempt to liberalize the system, but this could threaten its own power or trigger demands for more radical change (in the same way that Soviet president Mikhail Gorbachev's reforms had in the late 1980s). Alternatively, it might use greater repression to maintain the existing system, presumably further undermining Russia's relations with the West. A combination of co-option of parts of society and repression might allow the system to continue, as had arguably been the case in the 2000s. Alternatively, wider protests might trigger the collapse of the system or violent confrontation between the regime and its opponents. The new element of unpredictability in Russian politics might also extend into foreign policy. Facing domestic problems, the Russian leadership might seek to use nationalism and external scapegoats to maintain domestic support. The 2008 Georgia War was a sharp reminder of the potential for unexpected crises in the former Soviet space, which might drag in the West and/or neighbouring states. In this way, Russia's domestic politics could easily generate new tensions with both the West and its former Soviet neighbours. Nevertheless, while Russia will remain a significant European and second-order international power, the scale of the shift in the balance of power that took place with the end of the Cold War and the break-up of the Soviet Union suggests that is unlikely ever to regain its superpower status or to pose a hegemomic threat to the rest of Europe.

Chapter 6

The New Wars and the New Interventionism

From the Yugoslav conflict of the 1990s, through the US-led wars in Iraq and Afghanistan in the 2000s, to NATO's intervention in Libya in 2011, military intervention has been one of the most controversial security issues of the contemporary era. The patterns of military intervention that have emerged since the 1990s, both in Europe and globally, reflect the new strategic environment explored in Chapters 1 and 2. The emergence of a security community has made war unlikely in much of Europe, while direct military threats to that security community are limited. Beyond the Western security community, however, a variety of factors have contributed to the prevalence of civil wars and failed states (the so-called new wars), while major regional wars remain real possibilities in places such as the Middle East, India-Pakistan and the Korean peninsula, and a major war drawing in great powers, in particular the USA, China and Japan, remains conceivable in East Asia. In this new strategic environment, European states are most likely to use military force not to defend their national territory or in a major European war, but rather to intervene in new wars on Europe's periphery or beyond, or in the context of major conflicts elsewhere in the world.

The new interventionism

The period since the end of the Cold War has witnessed major changes in patterns of international military intervention. Military intervention, of course, is hardly a new feature of international politics: states have intervened militarily in regions beyond their borders and in the internal affairs of other states since at least ancient Greek times. During the Cold War, the two superpowers and their allies intervened militarily to protect allies, uphold client regimes and extend their influence, as well as in various proxy wars. In parallel with this, United Nations

(UN) peacekeeping emerged as a very different form of military intervention, with UN forces deployed to monitor and reinforce cease-fires, rather than in combat operations. With the end of the Cold War, the pattern of competitive intervention by the two superpowers came to an end, but in the 1990s the new wars and the humanitarian crises associated with them resulted in a new generation of 'humanitarian interventions'. In Iraqi Kurdistan in 1991, in Somalia in 1992–94, in Bosnia in 1992–95, in Haiti in 1994, in Kosovo in 1999, in East Timor in 1999–2000 and in Sierra Leone in 2000, various combinations of states and international organizations intervened militarily in order to bring an end to or alleviate large-scale human suffering (Wheeler, 2000; Weiss, 2005). The defining features of these interventions were the humanitarian crises that generated them, the fact that they involved intervention in the *internal* affairs of the states concerned (often without the consent of those states' governments) and the use of military force to bring an end to violence or secure other humanitarian objectives such as the delivery of food aid or the return of refugees or internally displaced persons. Humanitarian intervention was not entirely new in international politics, but until the 1990s such interventions had been rare – the exception rather than the norm. Although the intervening states in most cases also had more self-interested reasons for taking action, the initiation of a relatively large number of interventions in which humanitarian concerns arguably played a central part suggested that a new norm and practice of humanitarian military intervention was emerging.

Europe was a crucible of the emerging practice of humanitarian intervention: as discussed in more detail below, the Yugoslav conflict was one of the key test cases that drove the demand for more forceful intervention in humanitarian crises. European states also played a significant role in humanitarian interventions elsewhere in the world – the UK and France in Iraqi Kurdistan in 1991, and the UK in Sierra Leone in 2000 – with European states also making contributions to interventions in Somalia, Haiti and East Timor. By the end of the 1990s, the majority of European states – in particular, the Western, Central and Eastern European states constituting the security community that is the core of contemporary Europe – had broadly adopted the concept of humanitarian intervention and, as also discussed below, NATO and the EU were being re-orientated towards this new mission.

The concept and practice of humanitarian intervention, however, remained highly controversial. Humanitarian intervention runs contrary to the basic principles of state sovereignty and non-intervention in states' internal affairs on which the modern international system has been based. State sovereignty and non-intervention are viewed as providing the basis for an international order founded on the mutual recognition of states and a defence against egregious interventions: in the absence of these principles, states might have *carte blanche* to intervene in other states' affairs. Under the Charter of the United Nations, states agree to 'refrain in their international relations from the threat or use of force against the territorial integrity or political independence of any state' and are only permitted to use force in self-defence or if authorized by the UN Security Council (which has 'primary responsibility for the maintenance of international peace and security') (United Nations, 1945, Arts 2, 51 and 24). Furthermore, the UN Charter states that 'nothing contained in the present Charter shall authorize the United Nations to intervene in matters which are essentially within the domestic jurisdiction of any state' (United Nations, 1945, Art. 2). While some of the humanitarian interventions of the 1990s were authorized explicitly by the UN Security Council, others, such as NATO's 1999 intervention in Kosovo, were not, or were undertaken on the basis of broad (and contentious) interpretations of pre-existing Security Council resolutions. The legal basis for the emerging practice of humanitarian intervention was thus ambiguous.

The humanitarian interventions of the 1990s were also controversial for other reasons. Many governments, especially in the non-Western world, feared an erosion of the principle of state sovereignty that might result in more widespread interventions in the future, especially if the requirement for UN Security Council authorization was abandoned. Russia and China, for example, feared that the precedent of humanitarian intervention might be turned against them in Chechnya and Tibet. Critics also argued that apparent humanitarian concern was, or might in future be, simply a cover for more self-interested strategic or economic motivations hidden behind humanitarian rhetoric. Some argued that the military instrument was ill-suited to the humanitarian goals of protecting people and providing them with food and shelter – an argument to some extent vindicated by the US-led intervention in Somalia in 1992–94, which escalated from the initial humanitarian goal of facilitating the delivery of food aid to a fighting war between US forces and Somali factions and ended with the USA withdrawing its forces. Critics could also point to the lack of consistency in the emerging practice of humanitarian intervention: while the major Western powers were willing to intervene in circumstances where humanitarian goals coincided with other interests, other equally deserving cases saw no intervention – most starkly the 1994 Rwandan genocide, when the international community stood by as an estimated one million people were slaughtered in the space of a few weeks.

In parallel with the debate on humanitarian intervention, new types of peacekeeping and post-conflict peacebuilding missions also emerged. From the 1980s onwards, the UN undertook a series of major new peacekeeping missions in countries such as Cambodia, El Salvador and Mozambique. In contrast to traditional UN peacekeeping missions, these operations involved not just the monitoring of cease-fires but also a much wider set of tasks in support of peace processes (including mediating political settlements, facilitating elections, demobilizing combatants, monitoring human rights, helping to rebuild political and governmental institutions, and economic reconstruction). Many of the humanitarian interventions of the 1990s also resulted in similar follow-on missions designed to promote longer-term stability. These complex, multifaceted missions became referred to as post-conflict peacebuilding, state-building or nation-building operations, and often combine peacebuilding with elements of enforcement (usually under a mandate from the UN Security Council that includes authorization to use military force). These operations also involve complex interaction between a variety of international organizations (the UN, regional organizations such as NATO and the EU, and economic institutions such as the IMF and the World Bank), as well as between the military and civilian components of external intervention. Most of the major interventions of recent years – NATO's interventions in Bosnia and Kosovo in the 1990s; most recent UN operations, such as those in Liberia, Democratic Republic of Congo, Haiti and elsewhere; NATO's operation in Afghanistan; and even, to some extent, the US-led operation in Iraq after 2003 – fall into this broad category of post-conflict peacebuilding or state/nation-building. In recognition of the growing challenge posed by these operations, in 2005–06 the UN established an inter-governmental Peacebuilding Commission to integrate efforts at post-conflict peacebuilding, supported by a Peacebuilding Fund and a peacebuilding office within the UN Secretariat (United Nations, 2005, paras 97–105).

The terrorist attacks of 9/11 significantly altered these emerging patterns of intervention, triggering the US-led interventions in Afghanistan and Iraq and raising major questions of principle over the Bush administration's 'preventive war' doctrine. In response to the attacks of 9/11, the USA, joined by a coalition of allies, intervened in

Afghanistan in late 2001 to overthrow the Taliban regime (which had been hosting al-Qaeda's presence in the country), destroy al-Qaeda's operating base in the country, and kill or capture al-Qaeda leaders and fighters. On a smaller scale, the USA also supported the governments of other states, such as the Philippines and Georgia, in taking military action against Islamic 'terrorists'. In January 2007, US air forces intervened in Somalia, attacking Islamic militant groups believed to include those responsible for the bombing of the US embassies in East Africa in 1998.

The new US policy was enshrined in the Bush administration's September 2002 *National Security Strategy*, which controversially placed a strong emphasis on the need for pre-emptive military action against terrorist groups, WMD proliferation and 'rogue states' (United States, 2002, pp. 14–15). Pre-emptive military action is not new in international politics, and the USA and other states have long maintained the right to take pre-emptive action in the face of imminent attack. The elevation of pre-emption to a central place in US doctrine, and the extension of the concept to 'taking anticipatory action to defend ourselves, even if uncertainty remains as to the time and place of the enemy's attack' (United States, 2002, p. 15), however, marked a radical break with past policy, implying that pre-emptive military action might become to some extent the norm rather than the exception. Against this background, Iraq became the test case for the new doctrine of pre-emption, with the need to prevent Iraq from developing WMD, and to deal once and for all with the threat posed by Saddam Hussein's regime, providing the rationale for the Iraq War in 2003. Furthermore, in the immediate wake of the overthrow of Saddam Hussein's regime, supporters of the pre-emptive war doctrine argued that Iran, North Korea and Syria might be the next targets for such action. The Bush administration's second *National Security Strategy*, published in March 2006, reaffirmed the central place of pre-emption in US policy (United States, 2006, p. 23).

The new US doctrine of pre-emption was controversial and problematic for a number of reasons. At its root, the doctrine provoked fears that the USA was aggregating to itself the right to attack and invade any state that it deemed to be a threat. Such fears were compounded by the strongly unilateralist inclinations of the Bush administration and its willingness to intervene in Iraq without UN Security Council authorization and in the face of massive global opposition. Although the US doctrine used the language of self-defence and pre-emption, it amounted to a radical extension of the concept of self-defence, and critics argued that it risked becoming an open-ended call for preventive wars against potential threats. In addition, there were fears that the US adoption of the pre-emptive war doctrine and its implementation in Iraq could be used as a precedent by other states, risking descent into a wider generation of pre-emptive or preventive wars.

Although European states supported the US intervention in Afghanistan in late 2001 and contributed military forces to the subsequent NATO-led operation in that country, European governments and publics were generally wary of the Bush administration's preventive war doctrine. European governments were deeply divided over the Iraq War and European publics were almost universally (with the partial exception of the UK) opposed to the war. EU member states were also divided on the issue of pre-emptive military action during the drafting of the EU's *European Security Strategy* in 2003. The final version of the *European Security Strategy* stated that 'Our traditional concept of self-defence – up to and including the Cold War – was based on the threat of invasion. With new threats, the first line of defence will often be abroad ... we should be ready to act before a crisis occurs. Conflict prevention and threat prevention cannot start too early' (European Union, 2003a) – reflecting divisions within the Union on pre-emptive military action but also a preference for non-military preventive action. As will be discussed in Chapter 7, European governments also generally appear wary of possible pre-emptive military action to prevent Iran from developing nuclear weapons.

9/11 also seemed to trigger a retreat from humanitarian military intervention: whereas in the 1990s Western governments were willing to intervene for primarily humanitarian reasons, the US-led wars in Afghanistan and Iraq were justified as responses to major threats to Western interests in the form of terrorism and WMD proliferation. With counter-terrorism, counter-proliferation and 'rogue states' their new priorities, Western governments became reluctant to intervene in purely humanitarian crises. This was most obvious in the case of the Darfur conflict in western Sudan in the early to mid-2000s, where large-scale loss of life and attacks on civilians provided an obvious case for humanitarian intervention, but Western states were reluctant to take action. By the mid-2000s, some observers were declaring the death of the doctrine of humanitarian intervention (Weiss, 2004; MacFarlane *et al.*, 2004).

During the mid- and late 2000s, the USA and its allies became increasingly bogged down in Iraq and Afghanistan: they faced prolonged insurgencies in these countries; large numbers of troops were tied down fighting these insurgencies; the costs of these interventions were high, in terms of lives lost and funding the operations; and, in both cases, decisive victory seemed unlikely. The more widespread application of the preventive war doctrine also appeared unlikely: the number of situations where preventive war might be relevant was small, while one of the lessons from Iraq and Afghanistan was that the costs of post-conflict peacebuilding following preventive interventions were both high and difficult to avoid. Some analysts suggested there would be an 'Iraq syndrome' like that which had followed the Vietnam War: an increasing reluctance on the part of the USA to use military force, especially to put large numbers of troops on the ground in conflict situations, unless very clear national interests were involved (Mueller, 2005).

The shift to the Obama administration reflected this changing logic. Barack Obama had been one of the few US Senators to oppose the Iraq War when it was launched in 2003. During the 2008 presidential election, his campaign pledges included a commitment to withdraw all US forces from Iraq. Obama set about implementing this commitment when he assumed power in 2009: in February 2009 he announced that all US combat forces would be withdrawn by the end of August 2010. Negotiations continued with the Iraqi government over a possible longer-term US military presence, but these broke down in October 2011 and all US military forces were withdrawn from Iraq by the end of 2011. The Obama administration's *National Security Strategy*, published in May 2010, also quietly dropped the Bush administration's preventive war doctrine (United States, 2010). Obama, however, was not a pacifist. While he opposed the Iraq War, Obama supported the intervention in Afghanistan, arguing that this was where the real threat to America lay. In order to better pursue the war in Afghanistan, Obama announced increases in the numbers of US troops deployed in the country of 17,000 in February 2009 and another 30,000 in December 2009, taking total US forces in Afghanistan to about 100,000 personnel (Bailes and Cottey, 2010, pp. 151–3). There were limits, however, to the Obama administration's commitment to Afghanistan: there was much debate within the administration over the risks and costs of different possible strategies in Afghanistan, with President Obama reportedly stating that he was not willing to engage in a trillion dollar nation-building campaign in Afghanistan (Woodward, 2010, p. 251). The surge in troops announced in 2009 was thus also combined with a commitment to begin withdrawing US forces in 2011. Obama's foreign policy was described by some observers as one of realism: he might be willing to use force, but he was also acutely conscious of the limits and costs of such use of force. Obama's approach to intervention was neatly summarized by two presidential speeches. In his December 2009 speech accepting the Nobel Peace Prize, Obama made the case for the concept of just wars, arguing that in an imperfect world the use of force is sometimes necessary to prevent greater evils (Obama, 2009d). In June 2011, announcing initial troop withdrawals from Afghanistan, Obama argued that in light of the financial and economic crisis facing the USA and the country's domestic problems it was time for America to focus on nation-building at home rather than overseas (Obama, 2011). These two speeches reflected a larger tension facing not only the USA, but also European states, NATO and the EU: the tension between the demand to 'do something' in the face of conflicts and humanitarian crises and increasing awareness of the costs and risks of intervention in an era of economic austerity. How this tension plays out will have a major bearing on patterns of intervention in coming years.

Doctrinally, debates on intervention have also been shaped by another development: the emergence of the concept of the responsibility to protect (R2P). In response to the controversies surrounding the humanitarian interventions of the 1990s, supporters of such interventions sought to develop political, legal and ethical principles that might provide a basis for international consensus on the issue. In particular, the International Commission on Intervention and State Sovereignty (ICISS) developed the concept of R2P, which argued that governments have a responsibility to protect their citizens, and that when governments fail or are unable to uphold this duty and massive death or human suffering ensues, the international community has not only a right but also a duty to intervene (ICISS, 2001). While the ICISS's report – published at the end of 2001 – was initially overshadowed by the impact of 9/11, the US intervention in Afghanistan and the Iraq War, international support for R2P has grown since then. In September 2005, the World Summit of UN Heads of State and Government, called to reach decisions on the future direction of the United Nations, formally adopted the concept of R2P, emphasizing that the international community has 'the responsibility ... to help protect populations from genocide, war crimes, ethnic cleansing and crimes against humanity', and declaring a willingness 'to take collective action ... should peaceful means be inadequate and national authorities manifestly fail to protect their populations' (United Nations, 2005, para. 139). The

UN's adoption of R2P was a remarkable break with the principle of state sovereignty and indicated at least a degree of international consensus on the issue. Analysts, however, pointed out that many UN member states remained resistant to R2P and that the international community had yet to really put the idea into practice (Bellamy, 2010). The Arab Spring of 2011 altered this situation. In response to escalating violence in Libya, Libyan government attacks on its political opponents and the risk of massacres by government forces if they attacked the country's second city Benghazi and other cities and towns under rebel control, in March 2011 the UN Security Council passed a resolution specifically referring to R2P and authorizing the use of military force to protect civilians (United Nations Security Council, 2011). On this basis, NATO launched an air campaign designed to prevent attacks by the Libyan government on rebel-held cities and towns, but also with the implicit (but unstated) aim of bringing down the regime of Colonel Muammar Gaddafi. The Libyan case suggested that earlier predictions of the demise of humanitarian intervention were exaggerated and that the concept of R2P was perhaps beginning to become established as an international norm – although critics argued that the circumstances surrounding the Libyan intervention were exceptional and could point to the failure to intervene in Syria in late 2011 and early 2012 as evidence of continued inconsistency in relation to humanitarian intervention and R2P.

The experience of the last twenty years suggests that conflicts on the periphery of the European security community and beyond are likely to continue to generate situations where European governments feel compelled by interests, moral concerns or combinations of the two to intervene militarily. Such interventions, however, are costly and risky, with no guarantee of success. European states, NATO and the EU are likely to face continuing challenges in balancing these competing imperatives.

Intervention within Europe

The Balkans

On 25 and 26 June 1991, Yugoslav federal police and customs officers, supported by 2,000 Yugoslav army troops, moved to take control of land border crossings and the main airport in the secessionist republic of Slovenia, which had declared its independence on 25 June. On 27

June, Slovenian forces shot down a Yugoslav army helicopter, killing its pilot and a mechanic (Silber and Little, 1995, pp. 169–74). Europe had entered the era of the new wars. For the next decade, European governments, NATO, the EU and the UN struggled with the dilemmas of whether and how to intervene in the wars in the former Yugoslavia, approximately 100,000 people were killed, 3.7 million became refugees or were internally displaced within their countries and the term 'ethnic cleansing' entered the lexicon.

European governments were initially reluctant to intervene in the Yugoslav conflict: fearing the consequences of the country's disintegration, they sought to hold together the Yugoslav federation, composed of six republics: Bosnia, Croatia, Macedonia, Montenegro, Serbia and Slovenia, plus two autonomous regions of Serbia, Kosovo and Vojvodina. In the autumn of 1991, however, the war spread to Croatia, and in 1992 to Bosnia, where fighting broke out between the Muslim, Serbian and Croatian populations. From this point onwards, there was growing debate about whether to intervene forcefully to end the bloodshed. European governments were, however, wary of being drawn into a complex internal conflict, while the USA viewed the conflict as one that the Europeans should take the lead in managing. A UN peacekeeping force (the UN Protection Force, or UNPROFOR), composed primarily of troops from European countries, was deployed in Croatia and Bosnia. UNPROFOR's mandate, however, was limited to peacekeeping and it was not armed or organized to use force. As the war continued, the UN was increasingly humiliated, with UN Security Council-declared 'safe areas' subject to attacks and UN peacekeepers held hostage. In July 1995, Bosnian Serb forces overran the so-called 'safe area' of Srebrenica, which was in theory being protected by Dutch UN peacekeepers, and massacred 7,000 unarmed Muslim men who had been sheltering there – the largest war crime in Europe since the Second World War.

The failures of the UN and European states led the USA to take on the leading role in responding to the Yugoslav conflict. The USA persuaded its European allies to support the use of force against the Bosnian Serbs, widely viewed as the primary aggressors in the Bosnian conflict. In August–September 1995, following Bosnian Serb attacks on the Bosnian capital, Sarajevo, NATO launched Operation Deliberate Force, a campaign of sustained airstrikes against Bosnian Serb forces, backed up by artillery fire from a UK–French–Dutch Rapid Reaction Force, now part of UNPROFOR. Combined with Croatian and Muslim ground offensives, Operation Deliberate Force compelled the Bosnian Serbs to withdraw from territory they had taken earlier in the war, and brought them to the negotiating table. A cease-fire was agreed in October 1995, and in November a peace agreement was signed at a US Air Force base in Dayton, Ohio. An almost 60,000-strong NATO force – the Implementation Force (IFOR), subsequently renamed the Stabilization Force (SFOR) – was deployed. Unlike UNPROFOR, IFOR/SFOR was mandated and equipped to use force to implement the Dayton agreement if necessary (Daalder, 1999).

Three years later, in 1998–99 fighting broke out in Kosovo between the region's predominantly Albanian population and Serbian police and military forces. Recalling their earlier failures in Bosnia, Western leaders determined to act decisively. The USA and European governments sought to broker a settlement between the Kosovar Albanians and the Serb authorities, but warned the Serbs that if they did not accept such a settlement NATO would initiate airstrikes against Serbia. The Serbs rejected the outcome of negotiations at Rambouillet, near Paris, in February–March 1999, and on 24 March NATO launched Operation Allied Force, a campaign of sustained airstrikes against Serbia. NATO's leaders expected that the Serbs would back down quickly, as they had in Bosnia, but they responded by initiating a large-scale offensive against Kosovo's Albanian population, triggering a massive refugee crisis as 1.5 million Kosovar Albanians fled the Serb attack. NATO's airstrikes continued throughout April and May, amid growing concern that the Alliance might be forced to mount a ground invasion of Kosovo or risk defeat. In June, however, Serbian leader Slobodan Milosevic capitulated, agreeing to withdraw Serbian military and police forces and to the deployment of a NATO peacekeeping force. Like I/SFOR in Bosnia, NATO's 55,000-strong Kosovo Force (KFOR) was mandated and equipped to use force if necessary (Judah, 2000; Daalder and O'Hanlon, 2000). Two years later, in 2001, amid tensions between Macedonians and Albanians in Macedonia, a much smaller NATO force was deployed to support a peace agreement and to help to disarm Albanian guerrillas.

A number of conclusions may be drawn from the international community's interventions in the Balkans in the 1990s. First, the region became a de facto Western sphere of influence: although Western powers were initially reluctant to intervene in the former Yugoslavia, major Western European states, the USA, NATO and the EU nevertheless emerged as the central external brokers in the region. Second, efforts to end the war in Bosnia in the first half of the 1990s highlighted the limits of diplomacy and peacekeeping in the face of intransigent parties to a conflict, resulting in the subsequent adoption of more forceful approaches. Third, the centrality of the USA and NATO in ending the wars in Bosnia and Kosovo illustrated Europe's dependence on American political leadership and military capacity.

Since the early 2000s the Balkans has been at peace, at least in the sense of the absence of armed conflict. There are residual risks of conflict within the region: Bosnia remains internally divided between the two 'entities'– the Muslim-Croat Federation and the Serbian Republika Srpska – that have made up the country since the end of the war in 1995, while Kosovo, which formally declared its independence from Serbia in 2008, remains unrecognized by the Serbian government in Belgrade. If these situations were to escalate, new demands for military intervention could arise. The more likely scenario, however, is gradual but slow (and in some cases glacial) progress in overcoming underlying conflicts. In these circumstances, NATO and the EU are winding down their peacekeeping operations in the region, while gradually integrating the Balkan states into both organizations. As was noted in Chapter 3, one feature of this process is a transfer of responsibility for the Balkans from the USA and NATO to the EU, with the EU taking over the peacekeeping mission in Bosnia in 2004 and perhaps that in Kosovo in coming years.

The former Soviet Union

A very different pattern of intervention emerged in the former Soviet Union in the 1990s. In the context of conflicts triggered by the break-up of the Soviet Union, Russia intervened militarily in a number of other former Soviet republics, in particular Georgia, Moldova and Tajikistan – see Table 6.1. While Russia's interventions were partly motivated by the wish to end or contain conflicts, they were also driven by the desire to consolidate Russian influence in the region and to put pressure on states, such as Georgia and Moldova, which Moscow feared were moving out of its orbit. In general, other external powers were reluctant to intervene in these conflicts on a significant scale. A number of small UN and Organization for Security and Co-operation in Europe (OSCE) peacekeeping or political missions were, however, deployed to monitor cease-fires and promote political settlements. In 1994 war broke out in Chechnya in Russia's North Caucasus, and Russia used military force against Chechen separatists. A cease-fire was agreed in 1996, leaving Chechnya de facto outside Russian control. In 1999, Russia launched a new military offensive to regain

TABLE 6.1 *Intervention in conflicts in the former Soviet space*

Country/Region	Conflict	Russian involvement	Other external involvement
Nagorno-Karabakh, Armenia-Azerbaijan	1988–94 conflict in region of Nagorno Karabakh between secessionist Armenians and Azeris; cease-fire since 1994; region remains under control of Karabakh Armenians	Russian backing for Armenia and Karabakh Armenians; over 3,000 Russian troops deployed in Armenia since 1990s	OSCE 'Minsk Group' has sought to mediate a political settlement
South Ossetia, Georgia	1990–92 violence between South Ossetians and Georgians; cease-fire 1992–2008; 2008 war between South Ossetia/Russia and Georgia; cease-fire since 2008	Russian–Georgian–Ossetian peacekeeping force 1992–2008 (approx. 500 Russian troops deployed in South Ossetia); approx. 3,500 Russia troops deployed in South Ossetia since 2008	1992–2008 OSCE Mission to Georgia (approx. 100 personnel), monitored joint peacekeeping force and sought to promote negotitions; EU Monitoring Mission since 2008 (see below)
Abkhazia, Georgia	1992–94 violence between Abkhaz nationalists and Georgian government forces; cease-fire 1994–2008; 2008 war between Abkhazia/Russia and Georgia; cease-fire since 2008	Russian military support for Abkhazia 1992–94; Russian peace keeping force 1992–2008 (approx. 1,600 Russian troops deployed in Abkhazia); approx. 3,500 Russian troops deployed in Abkhazia since 2008	UN Observer Mission in Georgia (UNOMIG) monitored cease-fire 1993–2009 (approx. 500 military and civilian personnel); EU Monitoring Mission since 2008 (see below)
Transdniestria, Moldova	Violence between Transdniestrian secessionists and Moldovans in 1991–92; cease-fire since 1992; Transdniestria quasi-state established	Russian 14th army backed Transdniestrian separatist forces in 1991–92; approx. 1,500 Russian troops deployed in Moldova since 1990s	OSCE has sought to broker a political settlement and a Russian withdrawal; civilian OSCE Mission to Moldova 1993–
Tajikistan	1992–94 civil war between competing regional and political factions	1992– Russia-led peacekeeping force backed Tajik government and brought war to an end; Russian	UN Mission of Observers in Tajikistan (UNMOT) monitored cease-fire 1994–2000 (80 military

Region	Conflict	Russian involvement	International involvement
		forces also deployed for border protection purposes; approx. 5,000 Russian troops deployed in Tajikistan as of early 2010s	obersvers); UN Tajikistan Office of Peacebuilding 2000–
Ferghana Valley, Uzbekistan–Kyrgyzstan–Tajikistan	The Ferghana Valley is divided between Uzbekistan, Kyrgyzstan and Tajikistan; ongoing tensions between the three ethnic groups, as well as Islamic groups; various violent incidents since 1989	Russian support for Uzbek, Kyrgyz and Tajik governments against Islamic groups	OSCE diplomatic efforts to moderate tensions in the Ferghana Valley
Chechnya/North Caucasus, Russia	1994–96 and 1999–2000 war between Chechen separatists/Islamists and Russian government forces; terrorist attacks by Chechen forces in Chechnya and elsewhere in Russia since 1990s; terrorism and low-level violence has also spread to other parts of North Caucasus (Dagestan and Ingushetia) since 1990s	Suppression of Chechen separatists by Russian military	1995–2002 OSCE Assistance Group to Chechnya (6 personnel) monitors situation
Georgia War	August 2008 Russian intervention in Georgian regions of South Ossetia and Abkhazia	Russian support for South Ossetian and Abkhazian independence from Georgia; approx. 7,000 Russian troops in South Ossetia and Abkhazia since 2008	EU Monitoring Mission (EUMM – 200 civilian personnel) since 2008; EUMM monitors ceasefire and promotes political reconciliation
Kyrgyzstan	April–June 2010 violence between Kyrgyz and Uzbek ethnic groups; estimated 2,000 killed and 100,000 displaced	Russian diplomatic support for Kyrgyz government	OSCE training of Kyrgyz police since 2010

Sources: Data from Baev (1999); Weisbrode (2001); IISS (2006); UN Department of Peacekeeping Operations website:http://www.un.org/Depts/dpko/dpko/; Organization for Security and Co-operation in Europe, OSCE Field Operations: http://www.osce.org/about/ 13510.html; and EU Monitoring Mission (EUMM) in Georgia website: http://www.eumm.eu/en/.

control of Chechnya, which it largely succeeded in doing by the year 2000. Low-level violence has, however, continued since then, also spreading to neighbouring parts of the North Caucasus. The Russian military intervention involved extensive use of airstrikes and artillery, destroying much of the Chechen capital Grozny and resulting in thousands of deaths. The Russian military was also accused of committing war crimes in Chechnya. Western critics argued that the Russian intervention in Chechnya bore little resemblance to the peacekeeping operations and humanitarian interventions that had been undertaken elsewhere in the world since the early 1990s.

At the end of the 2000s, two different conflicts in the former Soviet region highlighted important realities about the willingness and ability of different actors to intervene in the region: the Georgia War of 2008 (see Chapter 5) and a conflict between different ethnic groups in Kyrgyzstan. At the time, the 2008 Georgia War appeared to signal a new era of Russian willingness to re-assert is influence in the former Soviet space, including by military means if necessary (Asmus, 2010). There were fears of similar interventions elsewhere in the region, for example in the Ukrainian province of Crimea. The Georgia War, however, has not been followed by similar interventions elsewhere in the region. In retrospect, the Georgian War appears more the result of very particular circumstances surrounding Georgia and the Russo-Georgian relationship, as well as of Russian concerns about the prospect of NATO's enlargement into the region (Hassner, 2010). The Georgia War also involved significant political costs for Russia in terms of relations with other states, not only in the West but also in the former Soviet region and countries such as China, which, to varying degrees, viewed the war as an aggressive act and a dangerous precedent for support of secessionist minorities. Since the Georgia War, further, Russia has invested significant diplomatic capital in trying to re-establish its credentials as a responsible power within the region, for example through efforts to broker a peace agreement on the long-running dispute between Armenia and Azerbaijan over Nagorno-Karabakh (International Institute for Strategic Studies, 2011b). Ironically, therefore, the larger implication of the Georgian War may be that while Russia is more willing than any other state to intervene militarily in the former Soviet region the circumstances in which it is actually likely to do so are quite limited.

In summer 2010 violence broke out in the Central Asian state of Kyrgyzstan, with fighting between Kyrgyz and Uzbeks in the southern city of Osh resulting in somewhere between 200 and 2,000 deaths and 400,000 people (mainly Uzbeks) being displaced, mostly across the border to Uzbekistan. There was an obvious case for the deployment of some form of peacekeeping force and the situation might have provided an opportunity for one of the former Soviet regional organizations – such as the Collective Security Treaty Organization (CSTO) or the Shanghai Co-operation Organization (SCO) (see Chapter 5) – to assert a leading role. Despite calls from the Kyrgyz government for exactly such a peacekeeping force, however, all of the outside powers (including Russia) were reluctant to support or provide troops for such a force. In the event a very small and limited OSCE police training mission was deployed. The conclusion one could draw was that the main relevant powers – Russia, the USA, the EU and China – are both wary of being drawn into complex internal conflicts in the former Soviet space and do not believe that their direct interests in the region are sufficient to warrant the costs and risks of such interventions (Melvin, 2010).

Europe and global interventions

In the post-1945 era, European states intervened militarily outside Europe in three different – although sometimes interrelated – contexts. First, European states engaged in neo-imperial interventions in attempts to defeat nationalist movements and retain control of or influence over their empires and colonies (for example, France in Indochina (1945–54), Britain in Kenya (1952–56), France in Algeria (1954–62), and the Anglo-French (and Israeli) 1956 Suez War). As the European empires gained independence and the decline of European power became clearer, however, European military forces were gradually withdrawn from Africa, Asia and the Middle East, and European interventions of this type began to wane. Second, European states deployed forces outside Europe in the context of the Cold War. In the 1950s, Belgium, Denmark, France, Greece, Italy, Luxembourg, the Netherlands, Norway, Sweden, Turkey and the UK deployed forces alongside the USA in the Korean War. During the Cold War, however, the priority for Western European governments was to defend Western Europe against the Soviet Union, and European states generally played a declining part in Cold War conflicts beyond Europe, with the USA taking the leading role. European states did not participate in the Vietnam War in the 1960s and 1970s. Third, European states contributed to the new model of UN peacekeeping that emerged after 1945. In particular, the Nordic countries (Denmark, Finland, Norway and Sweden) and some of the other European neutral states (Austria and Ireland) established reputations for contributing to UN peacekeeping operations. The overall picture from 1945 until the end of the Cold War in 1989, however, was one of declining European military involvement outside Europe.

The new generation of humanitarian interventions, nation-building operations and counter-terrorism missions since the end of the Cold War have generated a new debate on the extent to and ways in which Europe – in its various guises – should and can play a significant military role beyond Europe. In the first Gulf War in 1990–91, following the Iraqi invasion of Kuwait, the UK contributed 42,000 troops to the US-led coalition, and France 20,000, while quite a large group of European states (Czechoslovakia, Denmark, Greece, Hungary, Italy, the Netherlands, Norway, Poland, Portugal, Spain and Turkey) contributed small numbers of troops, mainly in non-combat roles. The USA, however, contributed the overwhelming majority of the forces, more than half a million military personnel, and the conflict symbolized – the UK and France aside – European reluctance and inability to deploy military forces outside Europe.

European states did, however, play a role in the humanitarian interventions and expansion of UN peacekeeping of the 1990s. The UK and France contributed to the enforcement of a no-fly zone and the establishment of safe havens in Iraqi Kurdistan in 1991 following the end of the Gulf War, and a number of other European states also contributed ground forces. The Netherlands contributed an infantry battalion to the UN peacekeeping operation in Cambodia in 1992–93. Belgium, France and Italy contributed infantry battalions to the US-led force that intervened in Somalia in 1992–93. France, Germany, Ireland, Italy, Norway, Portugal and the UK contributed forces to the International Force East Timor (INTERFET) operation in 1999–2000. In most cases, however, European forces were deployed only as part of larger missions, led by either the USA or the UN. France's intervention in Rwanda in 1994 – Operation Turquoise, which involved the deployment of 2,500 French troops to establish protected areas – and the UK's intervention in Sierra Leone in 2000 – Operation Palliser, involving the deployment of 1,100 troops to support the Sierra Leone government against rebels and help to stabilize the country – were exceptions in which European states played the central role. After 9/11, European countries played a significant role in the US-led interventions in Afghanistan and Iraq. In 2006, European countries agreed to provide the core of the expanded UN peacekeeping mission in Lebanon following the Israeli–Lebanese war, with Italy contributing 3,000 troops, France 2,000, Spain 1,000 and a number of other states smaller numbers (Pirozzi, 2006). The UK and France provided a major part (alongside the USA) of the air and naval forces for NATO's intervention in Libya in 2011, with other European NATO members making smaller military contributions.

Developments since the early 1990s suggest a number of conclusions about European involvement in peacekeeping and intervention operations beyond Europe. Although European contributions to such operations have increased since the early 1990s, European military involvement beyond Europe remains relatively limited in scale. European states, further, have in general deployed forces either as part of US-led operations in which the USA remains the dominant partner, or as part of UN operations to which European states have been some of a number of contributors (rather than the leading partners). The extent to which European states will move beyond this and establish a more distinctively European contribution to peacekeeping and intervention, and what the nature of that contribution should and will be, probably depends on the evolution of NATO and the EU as frameworks for collective military intervention, to which this chapter turns next.

NATO and the EU: global peacekeepers?

NATO

As discussed in Chapter 3, NATO has since the early 1990s undergone a transition from a collective defence alliance based on the defence of its members' territory to a security organization addressing security challenges beyond its members' borders. Peacekeeping and intervention have been central to this transformation. In the 1990s, NATO took on the tasks of peacekeeping and peacemaking in the Balkans. Since 9/11, it has taken on these tasks beyond Europe, most prominently in Afghanistan and Libya but also in various smaller-scale and less prominent missions. NATO's peacekeeping and intervention activities to date are summarized in Table 6.2.

In the 2000s and early 2010s Afghanistan and Libya were the main tests of NATO's role as a peacekeeper. In Afghanistan NATO has struggled to combine a counter-terrorism operation designed to defeat al-Qaeda and the Taliban with a nation-building operation designed to build up a viable Afghan state and win the 'hearts and minds' of the Afghan people. After the initial defeat of the Taliban regime in late 2001, the Bush administration was reluctant to engage in a large-scale

TABLE 6.2 *NATO peacekeeping and crisis management operations*

Operation	Country/Region	Date	Mission/Role	Force size
Operation Maritime Monitor/Sharp Guard	Adriatic Sea	1992–96	Enforcement of economic sanctions and arms embargo against former Yugoslavia	Naval forces
Operation Deny Flight	Bosnia and Herzegovina	1993–95	Enforcement of no-fly zone and close air support for UN peacekeeping force	Air forces
Operation Deliberate Force	Bosnia and Herzegovina	August–September 1995	Airstrikes and artillery attacks against Bosnian Serb targets to coerce acceptance of a peace agreement	Air and ground forces
Implementation Force (IFOR)/ Stabilization Force (SFOR) Operation	Bosnia and Herzegovina	1995–2004	Support and enforce Dayton peace agreement	60,000 troops
Operation Allied Force	Kosovo/Serbia–Montenegro	March–June 1999	Airstrikes to halt Serbian attacks on Kosovar Albanians and coerce acceptance of deployment of a NATO ground force	Air and naval forces
Kosovo Force (KFOR)	Kosovo	1999–	Enforce cease-fire and withdrawal of Serbian military and police forces; support maintenance of peace	55,000 troops
Operations Essential Harvest, Amber Fox and Allied Harmony	Macedonia	2001–03	Disarm Albanian guerrilla groups; protect and support international monitors	3,500 troops
Operation Eagle Assist	United States	October 2001– May 2002	Help protect US airspace post-9/11	Surveillance aircraft

Operation Active Endeavour	Mediterranean Sea	2001–	Monitor and escort vessels for counter-terrorism purposes	Naval forces
Operation Display Deterrence	Turkey	February–April 2003	Deter Iraqi attacks on Turkey	Surveillance aircraft and missile defences
International Security Assistance Force (ISAF)	Afghanistan	2003–	Assist Afghan government in exercising its authority; help create conditions for stabilization and reconstruction	130,000 troops
Distinguished Games	Greece	August–September 2004	Maritime and airspace surveillance during Olympics	Naval and air forces
Pakistan Earthquake Relief Operation	Pakistan	October 2005–February 2006	Deliver relief supplies	1,200 troops; air forces
NATO Assistance to the African Union (AU) in Darfur	Darfur, Sudan	2005–07	Provide support to AU peacekeeping mission	Air forces (transport of AU troops)
NATO Training Mission in Iraq	Iraq	2005–	Train Iraqi armed forces and security personnel	Training inside and outside Iraq
Operations Allied Provider, Allied Protector and Ocean Shield	Seas off the Horn of Africa	2008–	Provide protection to civilian vessels and deter/counter piracy	Naval forces
Operation Unified Protector	Libya	March–October 2011	Protect civilians and enforce no-fly zone and arms embargo	Air forces

Source: Data from NATO website: http://www.nato.int/.

nation-building operation in Afghanistan, with the result that two parallel military operations were established in late 2001: a primarily US counter-terrorism operation and a separate nation-building operation (the International Security Assistance Force (ISAF), mandated by the UN Security Council and with European NATO members providing the majority of its forces). In August 2003, NATO assumed command and control of the ISAF, which had up to that point been operating under ad hoc command arrangements. The first-stage ISAF had only 5,000 troops and its mandate was limited to the Afghan capital Kabul and the surrounding region. In the face of escalating violence from Taliban insurgents, from the mid-2000s the ISAF operation was gradually extended to cover the entire country, expanded in size and integrated with the previously separate US counter-terrorism operation. By late 2011 NATO had 130,000 troops under its command in Afghanistan, with the USA contributing 90,000 of these, the UK 9,500, Germany 5,000, France 4,000, Italy 4,000, and other NATO members smaller numbers (NATO, 2011a).

In Afghanistan NATO found itself engaged in a protracted and difficult ground war: in contrast to its earlier peacekeeping operations in Bosnia and Kosovo, there was no viable peace settlement and NATO forces were involved in intense combat operations against insurgents. In this context, NATO faced a number of major dilemmas: how far and at what cost it was possible to defeat the Taliban and al-Qaeda militarily; how far it was possible to build an effectively functioning nation-state in a country with deep ethnic/tribal divisions and little history of a strong state; whether to negotiate with the Taliban as part of efforts to establish a new political settlement in the country; and the problem that intensified military operations against the Taliban and al-Qaeda were causing significant numbers of civilian casualties and thereby undermining the goal of winning the 'hearts and minds' of the Afghan people. As was noted above, in 2009 the Obama administration announced significant increases in US troop numbers in Afghanistan in an effort to stabilize the country. By 2010–11, however, it was clear that NATO was beginning to look for the exit door in Afghanistan, with most NATO troops due to be withdrawn by 2014 and a focus on handing over responsibility for the country's security to the Afghan military and police. The exact circumstances of NATO's withdrawal remained to be seen, but it appeared that the best the Alliance could hope for was an 'ambiguous victory'. NATO's experience in Afghanistan therefore seems likely to make the Alliance's members wary of engaging in large-scale nation-building exercises, especially if this involves putting significant numbers of troops on the ground in situations of ongoing conflict.

In Libya in 2011, as it had in Bosnia in 1995 and in Kosovo in 1999, NATO used airstrikes to bring an end to attacks on civilians and as part of an effort to coerce a political settlement. NATO succeeded in preventing further major attacks by the Gaddafi regime and in autumn 2011 rebel forces, backed by NATO, gained control of Libya. Although NATO's intervention in Libya could be viewed as a success story, NATO and the international community still faced the challenge of supporting the establishment of an effectively functioning (and hopefully democratic) nation-state in a country marred by the legacy of its previous dictatorial regime.

NATO's interventions in the Balkans, Afghanistan and Libya suggested a number of conclusions about the Alliance's role as a peace-keeper. First, NATO remains an American-led alliance: US political leadership and military capability were central to NATO's Balkan, Afghan and Libyan interventions and in the absence of active US engagement NATO is unlikely to act. Second, as the Alliance's second military powers, Britain and France are also central to NATO and the Alliance is similarly unlikely to act without their involvement. Third, there remains significant wariness amongst NATO's members about both specific operations and extending the Alliance's peacekeeping role more generally: leaders and publics in many NATO countries, for example, were sceptical about the cases for intervention in both Afghanistan and Libya. Fourth, despite being (at least notionally) 'the strongest military alliance in the world', NATO is constrained by the limits of its member states' military capabilities: in most of its operations NATO's member states have struggled to provide the required military forces. NATO, therefore, is unlikely to become a 'global policeman'. Nevertheless, there are likely to remain some situations, in particular when 'high-end' combat operations and a rapid response are called for, where NATO is viewed by its members as the best available framework for collective military intervention.

The European Union

As discussed in Chapter 4, the development of a military role since the late 1990s has been a major strategic shift for the EU. Since 2003, the EU has given substance to its ambitions in this area by undertaking quite a large number of peacekeeping and crisis management operations (a total of 25 between 2003 and late 2011) – see Tables 6.3 and 6.4. A

TABLE 6.3 *EU military peacekeeping and crisis management operations*

Operation	Country	Date	Mission/Role	Force size
Operation Concordia	Former Yugoslav Republic of Macedonia	Mar–Dec 2003	Provide security to support peace agreement	357 military personnel
Operation Artemis	Democratic Republic of Congo	June–Sept 2003	Provide stability and security in an area experiencing ongoing fighting, prior to deployment of larger UN peacekeeping force	2,000 military personnel
Operation EUFOR – Althea	Bosnia	Dec 2004–	Ensure compliance with peace agreement and support peace process	7,000 military personnel
Operation EUFOR RD Congo	Democratic Republic of Congo (plus Gabon)	July–November 2006	Support UN peacekeeping force during elections	2,000 military personnel (including 'over the horizon' forces in Gabon)

EUFOR TChad/RCA	Chad/Central African Republic	Jan 2008–March 2009	Protect civilians and facilitate delivery of humanitarian aid	3,700 military personnel
EUNAVFOR Somalia/ Operation Atalanta	Somalia/Horn of Africa (naval operation)	December 2008–	Deter, prevent and end piracy	6–12 naval vessels; 2–4 maritime patrol and reconnaissance aircraft; 2,000 military personnel
EU Training Mission (EUTM) Somalia	Somalia/Uganda	April 2010–	Train Somalian security forces	141 military personnel
EUFOR Libya	Libya	April 2011–	Movement/evacuation of displaced persons and support of humanitarian agencies	Force not actually deployed

Sources: Data from Lindstrom (2004); and *EU Operations* website: http://www.consilium.europa.eu/eeas/security-defence/eu-operations. aspx?lang=en.

TABLE 6.4 *EU civilian/police/mixed crisis management operations*

Operation	Country	Date	Mission/Role	Force size
EU Police Mission (EUPM) BiH	Bosnia-Herzegovina	Jan 2003–	Support development of police	472 police; 57 civilians
Operation Proxima	Former Yugoslav Republic of Macedonia	Dec 2003– Dec 2005	Support development of police	200 police
EU Rule of Law Mission to Georgia (EUJUST THEMIS)	Georgia	July 2004– July 2005	Support development and reform of criminal justice system	10 civilians, plus local staff
EU Police Mission in Kinshasa (DRC) – (EUPOL KINSHASA)	Democratic Republic of Congo	April 2005– June 2007	Support development of Congolese police	30 police/civilians
EU Advisory and Assistance Mission for Security Reform in the DRC (EUSEC–DRC)	Democratic Republic of Congo	June 2005–	Advise and assist on security sector reform	50 civilian/police/ military
EU Integrated Rule of Law Mission for Iraq (EUJUST LEX)	Iraq	July 2005–	Training of judiciary, police and penitentiary staff	Training takes place in the EU and in the region; EU liaison office in Baghdad
EU Support to AMIS	Sudan (Darfur)	July 2005– December 2007	Advice, assistance, equipment, training and transport for AU Mission in Sudan	30 police, 15 military
Aceh Monitoring Mission (AMM) – EU jointly with Norway, Switzerland and Association of South East Asian Nation (ASEAN) states (Brunei, Malaysia, Philippines, Singapore and Thailand)	Indonesia (Aceh)	September 2005– December 2006	Monitor and support implementation of peace agreement	226 civilians (130 from EU, Norway, Switzerland, 96 from ASEAN states)

Mission	Location	Date	Mandate	Personnel
EU Border Assistance Mission (BAM) Rafah	Palestinian Territories (Gaza–Rafah border crossing point)	November 2005–	Monitor border crossing point and support development of Palestinian border control capacity	70 civilian personnel
EU Border Assistance Mission (BAM) to Moldova and Ukraine	Moldova and Ukraine	Dec 2005–	Support development of Moldovan and Ukrainian border control capacity	69 civilian experts
EU Police Advisory Team (EUPAT)	Macedonia	Dec 2005–June 2006	Support development of Macedonian police	30 police advisers
EU Police Mission in Palestinian Territories (EUPOL COPPS)	Palestinian Territories	June 2006–	Support development of Palestinian police	33 civilian personnel
EU Police Mission (EUPOL) Afghanistan	Afghanistan	June 2007–	Support development and reform of Afghan police	510 police/civilians
EUPOL RD Congo	Democratic Republic of Congo	July 2007–	Support security sector reform	57 civilians
EU Rule of Law Mission in Kosovo (EULEX)	Kosovo	February 2008–	Support Kosovo authorities in relation to law enforcement	2,850 civilians
EU Mission in support for Security Sector Reform (EUSSR) Guinea-Bissau	Guinea-Bissau	June 2008–September 2010	Support for security sector reform	24 civilians
EU Monitoring Mission (EUMM) Georgia	Georgia	October 2008–	Monitoring and support for peace agreement	300 civilians

Sources: Data from Lindstrom (2004), and *EU Operations* website: http://www.consilium.europa.eu/eeas/security-defence/eu-operations.aspx?lang=en.

number of features of the EU's operations to date are notable (Gross and Juncos, 2010). First, although framed within the context of the EU's Common Security and Defence Policy, the majority of EU crisis management missions (16 of the 25 missions up to late 2011) have actually been civilian, in particular in the areas of policing, security sector reform and justice/rule of law – suggesting that the EU is developing a specialized role in this area. Second, where the EU has undertaken military operations (in cases such as Macedonia, Bosnia, the Democratic Republic of Congo (DRC) and Chad/Central Africa Republican (CAR)), these have been relatively small-scale in size, the largest being the 7,000-strong peacekeeping operation in Bosnia, and have focused primarily on post-conflict peacekeeping, stabilization and nation-building. Although the mandates of these operations have included enforcement and forces have sometimes (in the DRC and Chad/CAR, in particular) been deployed in situations of low-level violence, the EU has yet to undertake an operation involving large-scale air operations (comparable to NATO's interventions in Bosnia, Kosovo and Libya), large-scale ground operations (comparable to the NATO operation in Afghanistan) or even large-scale post-conflict peacekeeping (comparable to the NATO operations in Bosnia from 1995 and Kosovo from 1999). An additional feature of some of the EU's operations, in particular those in the DRC and Chad/CAR, is that the Union has quite rapidly deployed relatively small forces (of approximately a few thousand troops) to stabilize a situation ahead of the deployment of a larger UN force (which takes longer to organize and mobilize). In terms of the use of military force the conclusion is clear: to date, the EU has developed a niche role in relatively small-scale operations primarily involving post-conflict peacekeeping, stabilization and nation-building and largely steering clear of war-fighting. It remains to be seen whether the EU will cross the rubicon of significantly larger operations and in particular substantial ground or air combat operations, but at minimum it can be said that many EU member states and the Union collectively remain wary of taking this step.

The EU's crisis management operations to date have also had a particular geographic focus, with six of the 25 to late 2011 being in the Balkans and eleven in Africa. This suggests that the EU is taking on particular responsibility for regions in its immediate neighbourhood, especially in situations where the USA does not take the lead. Although the EU has also undertaken small-scale missions in the former Soviet Union, the Palestinian territories, the Aceh region of Indonesia, Iraq and Afghanistan, it seems unlikely that the EU will dramatically expand its crisis management role in regions far from the European continent.

In the military sphere, the EU faces a number of significant limitations. Although the Union's member states collectively possess large armed forces, their ability to deploy these forces overseas for peacekeeping or other intervention operations is generally quite limited. In most cases, only small percentages of European states' armed forces are capable of participating in peacekeeping or intervention operations. The EU and its members also lack the key capabilities necessary for rapid deployment, such as strategic air and sea transport. The development of the EU's defence role since the late 1990s has been designed to address these shortcomings. Initial plans centred around the development of a 50,000–60,000-strong reaction force. In 2004, the EU adopted a further goal of developing battle groups of around 1,500 troops to be deployable within fifteen days, with two battlegroups to be available at any one time. The EU also agreed in 2004 to develop strategic lift co-ordination, a European airlift command, and the availability of an aircraft carrier by 2008, as well as a European Defence Agency (EDA) to facilitate armaments and procurement co-operation (European Union, 2004a). Unless and until the EU's members prove willing to take the radical step of developing truly supranational armed forces, which might enable the Union to achieve significant economies of scale and enhance its collective military capability, the EU will remain dependent on its member states for peacekeeping and intervention operations. While EU member states are enhancing their armed forces' ability to contribute to peacekeeping and intervention operations, this is proving to be a slow process and the experience since the late 1990s suggests that the EU's Common Security and Defence Policy (CSDP) will have at best a limited impact in accelerating the restructuring of armed forces for such operations (Forster, 2006, pp. 139–45, 210–14).

Conclusion

This chapter has explored European responses to the new wars and the new interventionism. In terms of patterns of intervention, a number of trends can be identified. Within Europe, two distinct geostrategic spheres emerged in the 1990s, with very different patterns of intervention. The Balkans was the subject of major military interventions by the leading Western powers and institutions, and in effect became a Western sphere of influence. The failure of European and UN efforts to end the Yugoslav wars in the early 1990s, further, led the USA and NATO to assume the central role in peacemaking in the region. Since the end of the Yugoslav wars, however, responsibility for post-conflict peacebuilding is gradually being transferred to the EU. Assuming that violence does not break out again, this trend is likely to continue. Renewed violence in the region would, however, raise once again the questions of whether Europe, in particular the EU, can halt such bloodshed, and, if not, whether the USA remains willing, or would be forced, to step into the breach. In the former Soviet region, Russia intervened in a number of conflicts in the 1990s as part of its larger strategy of maintaining a dominant role in the region, while other states and international institutions were reluctant to intervene on a significant scale or to challenge Russia. Although the 2008 Georgia War triggered fears of similar Russian interventions elsewhere in the former Soviet Union, Russia's willingness to intervene militarily in the region has in practice remained limited. Serious violence or instability in one or more of the former Soviet states would, however, raise renewed questions about how Russia and the wider international community should and would respond, and the extent to which the region will remain a Russian sphere of influence.

Beyond Europe, European states have contributed to a widening range of military operations, but these have usually been as part of either US-led interventions or UN peacekeeping operations. While there have been a number of essentially unilateral national interventions – France in Rwanda in 1994 and the UK in Sierra Leone in 2000 – these have been the exception rather than the norm. The expanding roles of NATO and the EU also suggest that collective Euro-Atlantic and European approaches to intervention beyond Europe are beginning to emerge. The limited scale and nature of NATO and EU engagement beyond Europe to date, however, indicate that this is likely to be a slow development. The very great difficulties the USA and its allies faced in attempting to stabilize Iraq after 2003 and Afghanistan after 2001, further, are likely to make both the USA and European states, as well as NATO and the EU, reluctant to engage in large-scale ground wars in future. As US Secretary of Defense Robert M. Gates put it in 2011, 'any future defense secretary who advises the president to again send a big American land army into Asia or into the Middle East or Africa should "have his head examined," as General MacArthuer so delicately put it ... [T]he odds of repeating another Afghanistan or Iraq

– invading, pacifying, and administering a large third world country may be low' (Gates, 2011a). Reluctance to engage in major ground force interventions, however, does not mean that the USA and European states will be unwilling to intervene per se. Conflicts and consequent demands for intervention are likely to continue to arise in unpredictable ways. At the beginning of 2011, few, if any, predicted that within a few months NATO would find itself involved in a major military intervention in North Africa. By late 2011, there were growing demands for intervention in Syria – where an estimated 4,000 people had been killed as a result of government repression of opposition protests (Bakri, 2011; Rachman, 2011).

The debates on intervention since the early 1990s also highlight significant differences between European and US approaches to intervention, but also between various European states. European states have tended to place a strong emphasis on multilateralism and legitimization by international law and/or international organization, whereas the USA has been more wary of being constrained by multilateral institutions. In terms of military doctrine and culture, the USA places a strong emphasis on high-end war-fighting operations, whereas European states place a greater emphasis on mid-range peacekeeping and/or peace enforcement. There is also, however, a significant gap between the United Kingdom and France, which have strong traditions of the use of military force, and many other European states, most importantly Germany, which are wary of the use of force. Thus, while European states, especially in the framework of the EU, often place a greater emphasis on state-building, post-conflict peacebuilding and non-military aspects of intervention, they are also willing to pursue more forceful interventions.

The European contribution to international intervention will also be constrained by the realities of military capacity. Lord George Robertson, NATO Secretary General from 1999 to 2004 and British Defence Secretary before that, repeatedly highlighted the point that the European NATO members had over 1 million regular soldiers and 1 million reserves, yet struggled to deploy 50,000 troops on peacekeeping and intervention operations (Robertson, 2003). O'Hanlon and Singer (2004, p. 84) estimate that whereas the USA has approximately 400,000 troops that could be deployed beyond its borders within 1–3 months and sustained for a year, the rest of NATO's members can muster only 84,000 such troops. Both nationally and collectively within NATO and the EU, European states have been expanding their capacity to contribute to peacekeeping and intervention operations since the early 1990s, but this process is proceeding only slowly (Giegerich, 2008). It may also be argued that a more general decline in bellicosity in Europe since the Second World War has made European governments and publics reluctant to invest heavily in defence or intervene militarily elsewhere in the world. Critics, especially in the USA, argue that this has made Europe increasingly incapable of dealing with the new security threats of the post-Cold War and post-9/11 era. To the extent that European bellicosity has declined, however, this may have contributed in an important way to the emergence of the European and wider Western security community discussed in Chapter 1. Given the costs and risks of any large-scale military intervention, further, a cautious attitude to military intervention may be no bad thing – a lesson the USA has arguably learned at high cost in Iraq and Afghanistan.

Chapter 7

Proliferation

Since the early 1990s, the threat posed by the proliferation of weapons of mass destruction (WMD) has moved to the centre of the global security agenda. As discussed in Chapter 2, the increasing prominence of proliferation reflects two factors. First, the end of the Cold War dramatically reduced the risk of nuclear war between the USA and Russia, effectively bringing the first part of the nuclear age to an end. Second, India's and Pakistan's 1998 nuclear weapons tests, the 2003 Iraq War and the controversy surrounding Iraq's WMD programmes, North Korea's 2006 and 2009 nuclear tests, Iran's ongoing efforts to develop nuclear weapons, and fears, following 9/11, that terrorist groups might obtain WMD, suggested that the world was on the verge of a major new wave of proliferation. This might in particular expand the number of nuclear weapon states significantly, and place nuclear or other WMD in the hands of terrorists.

From the 1960s through to the early 1990s, an international non-proliferation regime was put in place, based around a series of multilateral arms agreements – in particular, the Nuclear Non-Proliferation Treaty (NPT), the Biological and Toxin Weapons Convention (BTWC) and the Chemical Weapons Convention (CWC) – and controls on the export of WMD-related technologies. The emerging wave of proliferation since the 1990s has, however, highlighted the limitations of existing non-proliferation arrangements. Beginning in the 1990s, but accelerating under the Bush administration after 9/11, US non-proliferation policy shifted away from the traditional instruments of arms control, export controls and diplomacy and towards political, economic and military coercion (Andréani, 1999–2000; Perkovich, 2003). The USA became increasingly sceptical towards multilateral arms control: in 1999 the US Senate rejected the Comprehensive Test Ban Treaty (CTBT) and the Bush administration effectively torpedoed a verification protocol for the BTWC and brought the 2005 NPT Review Conference to the point of collapse. The Bush administration's 2002 pre-emptive war doctrine, the 2003 Iraq War and discussion of the possible use of force against Iran and North Korea suggested the emergence of a radical new approach to non-proliferation based on coercive diplomacy and the use of force. When it came to power in 2009 the Obama administration sought to re-emphasize US support for arms control and multilateralism and articulated the long-term vision of a nuclear weapon-free world. Nevertheless, progress in arms control and disarmament has been slow and more coercive approaches to proliferation remain on the agenda, including the possible use of force, in particular against Iran.

This chapter examines European responses to the WMD proliferation threat and in particular addresses the question of how far there is a distinctive European approach to non-proliferation and the problems associated with such an approach. As this chapter will show, European governments, while concerned by the proliferation threat, do not view it with the same sense of urgency as does the USA, and remain strongly committed to traditional multilateral non-proliferation policies and are wary of the more coercive approaches advocated by some in the USA. Nevertheless, in the wake of the 2003 Iraq War, the EU in particular sought to develop a more proactive role in non-proliferation, adopting a formal *EU Strategy Against Proliferation of Weapons of Mass Destruction* at the end of 2003 (European Union, 2003b) and taking the lead, via the Union's three largest members – the UK, France and Germany – in international diplomatic efforts to persuade Iran not to develop nuclear weapons. The difficulties the EU has faced in using its 'soft power' to influence Iran, and the possibility, perhaps even likelihood, that Iran will go on to develop nuclear weapons, however, indicate the serious challenges facing European non-proliferation policy.

Assessing the proliferation threat: European perspectives

European governments generally accept that WMD proliferation is a major security problem. The EU's 2003 *European Security Strategy* argues that proliferation 'is potentially the greatest threat to our security' (European Union, 2003a). Similarly, a 2008 official EU policy statement on proliferation stated that WMD 'constitute one of the greatest security challenges which Europeans may ever face' and that the Union 'must accord the highest priority to protecting European citizens and our friends and allies against the existing and growing risk presented by the proliferation of such weapon' (Council of the European Union, 2008b, p. 3). In reality, however, the nature, extent and implications of the threat posed by WMD proliferation are controversial. Assessing the threat posed by WMD proliferation is deeply problematical because it depends on intelligence information (which may be unreliable, partial or politically biased) but also because it depends on strategic assessments of the consequences of proliferation, which are inevitably political. Bearing in mind these caveats, Table 7.1 summarizes the 2012 state of play in terms of WMD proliferation beyond the five established nuclear weapon states (the USA, Russia, China, the UK and France), indicating states that are believed to have nuclear, chemical and/or biological weapons or research programmes, as well as details of the missile systems these states are believed to possess or have under development. Beyond the states listed in Table 7.1, which have been the primary focus of proliferation concern, there is a larger group of states that do not have WMD programmes as such but have actual or planned civilian nuclear programmes which might in future give them the capacity to develop nuclear weapons. These include industrialized Western states such as Germany, Japan and Sweden, but also states such as Saudi Arabia, the United Arab Emirates, South Korea, Taiwan, Venezuela, Brazil, Argentina and South Africa (the latter three having had nuclear weapons programmes in the past but abandoned them in the 1980s or 1990s).

From a broad European perspective, the current proliferation landscape poses a number of threats (Krause, 1996; Muller, 2003):

- *Direct attack*: in the worst case, European states might be the subject of WMD attack by states outside Europe. In the short to medium term, the only states that might develop WMD and missiles capable of attacking much of Europe are in the Middle East, in particular Iran. Even if Iran and/or other Middle Eastern states develop WMD and missiles capable of reaching much of Europe, the costs of undertaking such attacks (including the possibility of conventional or nuclear retaliation by the USA, the UK or France) probably make such attacks unlikely. Nevertheless, a radical regime – for example, if an Islamic revolution brought to power al-Qaeda-style forces in Saudi Arabia – might be willing to threaten to use, or even in fact use, nuclear weapons against European states in a bid to persuade them to withdraw military forces from the Middle East or cease support for Israel. While a direct WMD attack on Europe (or the threat of such an attack) is probably unlikely in the short to medium term, and perhaps also in the longer term, if proliferation widens in the Middle East such a scenario cannot be entirely ruled out.

TABLE 7.1 WMD proliferation: the state of play, 2012

State	Nuclear weapons	Biological weapons	Chemical weapons	Missiles (current)	Missiles (development)
Egypt	–	RP	W	SR (550km)	–
India	W	–	D	MR (3,000km)	LR (5,500km)
Iran	RP	RP	W	MR (1,300–2,000km)	MR/IR (2,000–4,000km)
Israel	W	W	W	MR (1,500km)	MR/IR/LR (3,000–6,000km)
Libya	–	–	D	SR (300km)	–
Pakistan	W	–	–	MR (1,300km)	MR (3,000km)
North Korea	W?	W	W	MR (1,300km)	IR/LR (3,500–5,500km)
Syria	–	RP	W	SR (500km)	SR (700km)

Notes:

Weapons: W = known or suspected weapons or weaponizable agents; RP = known or suspected research programme; D = declared chemical weapons or weapons programme scheduled for destruction in accordance with the terms of the Chemical Weapons Convention.

Missiles: SR = short-range (<1,000km); MR = medium-range (1,000–3,000km); IR = intermediate-range (3,000–5,500km); LR = long-range (5,500km+).

Sources: Data from Carnegie Endowment for International Peace (2009); Arms Control Association (2007).

- *Threats to European armed forces on 'out-of-area' missions*: in a second set of scenarios, European armed forces deployed outside Europe might be the subject of WMD attacks by either states or terrorists, or be threatened with such attacks, in order to deter military action. After the 1990–91 Gulf War many observers concluded that the lesson was 'don't take on the USA unless you have nuclear weapons', a lesson reinforced by the 2003 Iraq War and which is probably a factor behind North Korea's and Iran's pursuit of nuclear weapons. The development of nuclear weapons by Iran and/or North Korea would thus have a potentially very significant impact in terms of deterring US/Western military action against these countries. Indeed, North Korea's ability to threaten massive conventional and possibly nuclear retaliation against South Korea and US forces based there may already preclude US military action against Pyongyang. The use or threatened use of WMD against European forces deployed outside Europe is probably one of the more likely threats if proliferation proceeds.
- *Chemical and biological weapons*: as was noted in Chapter 2, although the term 'weapons of mass destruction' is now widely used, there are important differences between nuclear, chemical and biological weapons (Perkovich, 2004). The destructive power of nuclear weapons gives them unparalleled capacity to destroy large population centres or concentrations of military forces and to kill many thousands (or even millions) of people, making them by far the most serious proliferation concern. Chemical and biological agents, in contrast, are difficult to disperse over large areas, and are more likely to be used for limited battlefield purposes or smaller-scale terrorist attacks.
- *Eroding the WMD taboo*: since the use of nuclear weapons by the USA against Japan in 1945, a powerful taboo against the use of WMD, and in particular nuclear weapons, has emerged, but proliferation increases the long-term risk of the use of such weapons. The 'successful' use of WMD by one or more states – in the sense of allowing that state to achieve its strategic objectives or end a conflict on better terms than might otherwise have been the case – might create significant incentives for other states to acquire WMD and consider their use. Even if European states were not affected directly in the first place, erosion of the WMD taboo, and in particular of the international proscription of the use of nuclear weapons, would create a significantly more dangerous international security environment in general, and increase the risk of

European states becoming the subject of WMD attack at some point in the future.

- *WMD terrorism*: the 9/11 terrorist attacks generated significant debate about the prospect of terrorist groups obtaining and using WMD. As is discussed in Chapter 8, after 9/11 Europe became one of the main 'fields of *jihad*' for Islamic terrorists, suggesting that, were terrorists to obtain WMD, Europe might be one of their most likely targets. The likelihood and extent of the threat posed by WMD terrorism is, however, controversial. Some, especially in the USA, argue that WMD terrorism, in particular nuclear or biological terrorism, is a very real possibility and would give terrorists the potential to kill, or threaten to kill, millions of people. Senator Richard Lugar, former chair of the US Senate Foreign Relations Committee, has argued that 'for the foreseeable future, the United States and other nations will face an existential threat from the intersection of terrorism and weapons of mass destruction' (Lugar, 2005, p. 3). Others argue that there are very serious technical obstacles to true mass casualty terrorism, and that the most likely forms of WMD terrorism are small-scale chemical, biological or radiological attacks such as the 1995 Aum Shinrikyo nerve gas attack on the Tokyo underground and the distribution of anthrax spores in the USA after 9/11(Frost, 2005; Ruppe, 2005).

Assessments of the threat posed by proliferation also depend to a significant degree on political and strategic context. As the world's only superpower, deeply engaged in all regions of the world, and in particular in the regions of most immediate proliferation concern – the Middle East and North East Asia – the USA is the most likely target of WMD attack and would have its policy options most constrained by the further proliferation of WMD. In contrast, despite the fact that Europe is closer to the Middle East and thus more exposed to direct WMD attack from that region, Europeans have not in general viewed the proliferation threat in as immediate or dramatic terms as it is viewed in the USA. Leading German non-proliferation expert, Harald Muller, for example, argued in 2003 that, while proliferation is a 'distinct danger' that is 'increasing incrementally', it 'does not yet pose an immediate threat to the European Union' (Muller, 2003, p. 97). Similarly, Schmitt, noting that the number of states actively pursuing WMD is limited (essentially to Iran and North Korea in the case of nuclear weapons), concluded that there are 'good reasons to believe that the threat of WMD proliferation is manageable' (Schmitt, 2003, p. 90). Andréani concludes that there is 'considerable asymmetry in the way the issue is characterized on both sides of the Atlantic', reflecting the fact that 'Europe is geographically more exposed than the USA, but strategically considerably less so' (Andréani, 1999–2000, pp. 56–7). The debate surrounding how to respond to Iran's efforts to develop nuclear weapons illustrates these differences: whereas many in the USA view the prospect of a nuclear-armed Iran as serious enough to warrant the use of force (Allison, 2006), much European opinion does not view a nuclear-armed Iran as a fundamental threat and argues that the costs of using of force against Iran outweigh the risks of its developing nuclear weapons (Grgic, 2004; Woollacott, 2005). European governments may have become more concerned by the threat posed by proliferation since the early 2000s. A 2008 update of the EU's 2003 *European Security Strategy* argued that the risk posed by proliferation had 'increased in the last five years', noting in particular that 'the Iranian nuclear programme has significantly advanced, representing a danger for stability in the region and for the whole non-proliferation system' (European Union, 2008b, pp. 3, 1). Nevertheless, it remains the case that Europe is, in general, less concerned by proliferation than the USA.

From a European perspective, in the short to medium term the proliferation threat may be more limited than the sometimes lurid public debate suggests, essentially to the development of nuclear weapons by North Korea and Iran, and the risk of small-scale chemical or biological weapons attacks by terrorists. Two important caveats should, however, be attached to this assessment. First, although the likelihood of true mass casualty terrorism – involving nuclear or biological weapons – is difficult to assess, the possibility of such attacks should not be excluded and it is a threat of a fundamentally different magnitude from that of more limited, small-scale WMD terrorism. Second, while the Iranian and/or North Korean development of nuclear weapons may in itself constitute only a limited threat, if it triggers further proliferation in the Middle East and Asia, a more general breakdown of the non-proliferation regime and, in the worst case, the use of nuclear weapons by one or more states, it will pose a major long-term threat to European and global security.

Arms control

Multilateral arms control has been at the heart of the traditional approach to non-proliferation developed since the Second World War.

In general, this has involved two types of arms control regimes: global arms control regimes prohibiting or limiting the possession of entire classes of weapons (the NPT, the BTWC and the CWC); and multilateral export/technology control regimes under which suppliers of the relevant weapons systems and technologies agree common rules constraining the supply of weapons and technologies to other states (the Nuclear Suppliers Group – NSG; the Zangger Committee, which like the NSG seeks to control the export of nuclear materials and technologies; and the Missile Technology Control Regime – MTCR). In general, European states have been strong supporters of these regimes. The EU's December 2003 *European Strategy Against Proliferation of Weapons of Mass Destruction* affirmed the 'conviction that a multilateralist approach to security, including disarmament and non-proliferation, provides the best way to maintain international order and hence our commitment to uphold, implement and strengthen the multilateral disarmament and non-proliferation treaties and agreements' (European Union, 2003b). Virtually all European states (EU members, the Balkan states, and Russia and the other former Soviet states) are members of the main multilateral non-proliferation agreements (the only real exceptions are the technology control regimes of which some Balkan and former Soviet states are not members, largely because they are not potential suppliers of the technologies concerned). France and Spain were not initially signatories of the NPT, criticizing the discriminatory basis of the treaty, but Spain joined in 1987 and France in 1992.

Since the early 1990s, European states have supported, and to varying degrees led, international efforts to strengthen the various multilateral arms control and non-proliferation agreements. The NPT, which entered into force in 1970, reached the point of a twenty-five-year special review conference in 1995, at which the treaty was extended indefinitely. At the 2000 NPT review conference (the NPT is also subject to regular five-yearly review conferences) signatories endorsed a thirteen-point programme for nuclear arms control and disarmament. During the 1990s, the International Atomic Energy Agency – IAEA, the body charged with verifying states' compliance with the NPT – established a strengthened system of 'safeguards' for monitoring states' nuclear facilities and activities. The CWC was signed in 1993 and came into force in 1997. The CTBT was signed in 1996, but has not yet come into force (because not all relevant states have ratified the treaty). European states have also supported negotiations to agree a Fissile Material Cut-off Treaty (FMCT), which would ban the further production of the fissile material required for nuclear weapons, and a verification protocol for the BTWC, but both sets of negotiations have been stalled since the late 1990s. The negotiations related to these various agreements have been one of the main areas in which the EU has, beginning in the 1980s but especially since the 1990s, sought to develop common policies and assert a collective influence. In addition, since the 1990s the EU has provided a wide range of financial and technical assistance measures to support the development and implementation of multilateral non-proliferation and arms control agreements and policies (see Table 7.2).

European states and institutions, however, face significant obstacles in advancing the multilateral arms control approach to proliferation. The verification mechanisms associated with these arms control regimes are imperfect (as illustrated by Iran's, Iraq's, Libya's and North Korea's progress towards developing nuclear weapons in the 1980s and 1990s despite being signatories of the NPT and subject to IAEA inspections), and strengthening these verification mechanisms has proved difficult. The NPT, BTWC and CWC contain no sanctions or enforcement measures for dealing with states that might violate their commitments not to develop nuclear, biological or chemical weapons under these treaties; and the NPT permits states to withdraw from the treaty (which North Korea did in 2003 and Iran may do in future) and then lawfully develop nuclear weapons. The network of international technology and materials control regimes contains significant holes in terms of the range of technologies and materials covered, and the states that are not members or do not fully enforce its provisions: China has in the past helped Pakistan and North Korea to develop nuclear weapons or missiles; Russia has supplied Iran with civilian nuclear technology; and North Korea and Pakistan have been involved in helping other states to develop nuclear weapons and/or missiles.

Even more fundamentally, there is an undeniable double standard at the heart of the existing non-proliferation regime: while the NPT commits the majority of the world's states not to develop nuclear weapons, it formally recognizes the status of the five established nuclear weapon states. Although the NPT commits the nuclear weapon states 'to pursue negotiations in good faith on effective measures relating to cessation of the nuclear arms race at an early date and to nuclear disarmament', relatively little progress has been made in this direction since the NPT came into force in 1970. This double standard has led India, Pakistan and Israel to reject the NPT, made many states reluctant to agree tough action against states that attempt to develop nuclear weapons, such as Iran, Iraq and North Korea, and more generally

TABLE 7.2   *EU support for multilateral non-proliferation agreements and policies*

Institution/Treaty/Policy	EU actions
United Nations Security Council Resolution (UNSCR) 1540, April 2004 (under UNSCR 1540 UN member states must report to the 1540 committee on national measures taken to comply with, implement and support arms control and non-proliferation agreements)	Engagement with and support to third countries in relation to compliance with UNSCR 1540: • Co-sponsorship of regional seminars on UNSCR 1540 in Asia-Pacific, Africa, Latin America, the Caribbean the Arab region
International Atomic Energy Agency (IAEA)	Financial support for IAEA projects to: • Strengthen physical protection of nuclear materials in countries such as Egypt, Kazakhstan and Libya • Provide legislative assistance for the implementation of state's obligations under IAEA safeguards agreements (e.g., in Angola, Turkey, Ukraine and Uzbekistan)
Comprehensive Test Ban Treaty (CTBT)	Support to the Preparatory Commission of the CTBT Organization for projects on. • Capacity building in CTBT signatory states • Improving knowledge of noble gas measurements (relevant for the detection of nuclear explosions) • Development of on-site inspection system • Assisting African states in relation to future implementation of the CTBT monitoring and verification system →

undermined efforts to establish a truly universal non-proliferation regime. Since the UK, France and Russia are three of the five established nuclear weapon states, this double standard has a significant European dimension: although the UK, France and Russia have reduced their nuclear arsenals since the 1990s, none appears likely to

→

Institution/Treaty/Policy	EU actions
Chemical Weapons Convention (CWC)	Support for: • Regional workshops and bilateral visits/programmes • Expert visits to countries to support their national implementation of the CWC • Training and equipment for relevant laboratories • Fora and workshops with the chemicals industry
Biological and Toxin Weapons Convention (BTWC)	Support for: • Regional workshops on the BTWC • National implementation of the BTWC in third countries • Laboratory bio-security and bio-safety
G8 Global Partnership (established in 2002 by the G8 – the Group of Seven industrialized democracies (Britain, Canada, France, Germany, Italy, Japan and the USA), plus Russia – to help ensure secure control over materials, technologies and expertise from the WMD arsenal of the former Soviet Union)	Support for activities in Russia: • Construction of chemical weapons destruction facilities • Improving storage conditions for spent reactor fuel and radioactive waste from nuclear submarines • Safe transport, storage and disposal of plutonium • International Science and Technology Centre (which re-trains and provides employment for scientists and engineers)
Export controls	Support to third countries in developing and implementing export control systems, e.g., China, Ukraine, United Arab Emirates

Source: Data from Council of the European Union General Secretariat (2008a).

abandon their status as a nuclear weapon state. The UK's and France's status as nuclear weapon states also constrains the EU's approach to non-proliferation: while the majority of EU members would support substantial further measures towards nuclear disarmament, the UK and France have been wary of such steps and the EU's position within the NPT negotiations has sometimes been a lowest common denominator dictated by the UK and France. In the 2000s European efforts to support multilateral arms control were also undermined by the increasing opposition of the USA under the Bush administration to such approaches: while European states, and especially the EU, supported the CTBT, a verification protocol for the BTWC and the thirteen-point arms control and disarmament programme agreed at the 2000 NPT Review Conference, US opposition stymied progress in all these areas. With the coming to power of the Obama administration in 2009 US non-proliferation policy moved back towards European multilateralism; nevertheless, there remain important areas of difference, such as the CTBT which the US Senate remains reluctant to ratify and which is unlikely to enter into force unless and until this step is taken.

In 2000 Camille Grand argued that, with the USA increasingly antipathetic to arms control, China committed to modernizing its nuclear arsenal, and Russia determined to maintain the vestiges of its nuclear superpower status, other 'countries, including the Europeans in the first instance, are becoming the main and practically sole defenders of the logic of non-proliferation', and that the EU should play a central role in promoting a multilateral, arms control-based approach to proliferation (Grand, 2000, pp. 3–5). While the EU has taken significant steps in this direction since the early 1990s, the inherent problems of arms control, the UK's and France's status as nuclear weapon states and US scepticism towards multilateral arms control are likely to impose significant constraints on the EU's ability to assert leadership in this area.

Dealing with tough cases: diplomacy, sanctions and the use of force

Since the early 1990s there has been ongoing debate over how best to respond to proliferation's 'tough cases': the small number of states that appear determined to develop WMD, and in particular nuclear weapons. In the 1990s the primary states in this category were Iraq, Iran, Libya and North Korea. With Libya abandoning its nuclear programme and Saddam Hussein removed from power in Iraq, Iran and North Korea are now the primary concerns, in particular from a Western perspective. India and Pakistan are also countries of particular proliferation concern, although both countries have consolidated their status as nuclear weapon states since they tested nuclear weapons in

1998. The debate over these 'tough cases' centres around the appropriate balance between engagement and coercion (carrots and sticks): to what extent is it possible to engage with states that are seeking to develop WMD and offer them positive incentives not to do so? To what extent is coercion – diplomatic and economic pressure and sanctions, but ultimately military force – a necessary and effective means of preventing states from developing WMD? Since the early 1990s, various combinations of engagement and coercion have been tried, with varying degrees of success and failure. Up to 2003, an essentially coercive approach was imposed on Iraq, combining UN Security Council-mandated disarmament, diplomatic isolation, economic sanctions and periodic airstrikes by the USA and the UK. In the context of the US decision to intervene in Iraq in 2003 and subsequent developments (in particular the discovery that Iraq's WMD programmes were much less developed than had been widely believed), the extent to which international strategy towards Iraq up to 2003 had succeeded or failed remains deeply controversial. In the North Korean case, international policy – which has been shaped primarily by the USA, but also by South Korea, Japan, China and Russia – has involved a shifting mix of attempts to engage North Korea (in particular through the six-party talks involving Pyongyang and the five aforementioned states) and isolation and sanctions (pursued primarily by the USA, Japan and South Korea). Under a 1994 Agreed Framework negotiated with the Clinton administration, North Korea agreed to halt its nuclear weapons programme in return for the supply of fuel oil and proliferation-resistant light-water nuclear reactors. The 1994 Agreed Framework, however, gradually broke down – the reasons for its collapse remain controversial – and in 2006 and 2009 North Korea tested nuclear devices. North Korea is believed to have sufficient fissile material for a small number of nuclear weapons, but the exact status of its nuclear programme is unclear. In the Iranian case international policy has also involved a shifting mix of engagement and sanctions, although the USA has largely sought to isolate Tehran, whereas European states and the EU have sought to engage with Iran (see below). In a different example, an Anglo-American strategy of engagement – offering the normalization of diplomatic and economic relations – was probably central to Libya's 2003 decision to abandon its WMD programmes (although the stick of economic pressure also played its part alongside the carrot of engagement).

The main coercive options are threefold: diplomatic pressure, economic sanctions, and the use of force. Diplomatic measures (condemnations, demarches or the severing of diplomatic relations) may put political pressure on states, but are unlikely in themselves to persuade them to abandon WMD programmes. Economic sanctions bring significant pressure to bear on states, but are usually only effective in the long term (if at all), are dependent on widespread international support (which often cannot be guaranteed) and may cause significant humanitarian suffering (as in the Iraqi case). The limits of diplomacy and economic sanctions inevitably lead to the discussion of the use of military force as an alternative means of preventing states from developing WMD. The most widely cited precedent is Israel's 1981 airstrike on Iraq's Osirak nuclear reactor, which succeeded in setting back Iraq's nuclear weapons programme by some years. As discussed in Chapter 6, in 2002 the Bush administration made the pre-emptive use of force to prevent WMD proliferation a central part of US national security strategy, and this logic provided the basis for the US intervention in Iraq in 2003. The pre-emptive use of military force to prevent WMD proliferation is, of course, highly controversial, and the instability in Iraq after 2003 reinforced the argument that the negative consequences of pre-emptive military action outweigh whatever good may be achieved in terms of ending or setting back states' WMD ambitions. Nevertheless, the inherent limitations of diplomacy and economic sanctions suggest that the pre-emptive use of force is likely to remain on the non-proliferation agenda, especially for the USA. In particular, there has been ongoing debate about whether the USA and/or Israel may use air and missile strikes to seek to disable or set back Iran's nuclear programme.

In responding to proliferation's tough cases, European states have in general preferred to use diplomacy and the incentive of engagement rather than the more coercive strategies of economic sanctions and military force. It would be misleading, however, to translate this preference into complete Europe-wide opposition to the use of coercive approaches to non-proliferation. European states generally supported the economic sanctions employed against Iraq in the 1990s. The EU has also repeatedly strengthened its economic sanction regimes against Iran and North Korea since the 1990s. European governments and publics have been divided over the possible use of military force to prevent states from developing WMD, but remain on balance wary of the pre-emptive use of force. France, Germany and Russia led international opposition to the 2003 Iraq War, although the UK, Spain, Italy and many other European countries supported the USA, including by deploying military forces. As was noted in Chapter 6, the drafting of the EU's *European Security Strategy* in 2003 prompted debate on the pre-emptive use of force, and the open-ended final document reflected the lack of consensus on the issue within the Union. Similarly, the EU's 2003 *European Strategy Against Proliferation of Weapons of Mass Destruction* said little about the possible use of economic sanctions and nothing about the use of force (European Union, 2003b). The 2008 update of the EU's 2003 *European Security Strategy* stated that Iran's 'development of a nuclear military capability would be a threat to EU security that cannot be accepted', but likewise said little about how this may be prevented if the existing mix of engagement and sanctions fails (European Union, 2008b, p. 7). As the European states with the greatest military power projection capability and strong traditions of the use of force overseas, Britain and/or France might be likely to join the USA in possible air and missile strikes against Iranian nuclear facilities. Press reports in late 2011, for example, indicated that the British government was engaging in contingency planning for airstrikes against Iran and would join the USA if it decided to undertake such action (Hopkins, 2011). Critics of such possible action argued both that a nuclear-armed Iran would be deterrable and that the costs of such action – in terms of likely Iranian retaliation against Israel, other neighbouring states and Western targets, as well as further polarization of Middle Eastern opinion against the West – outweigh the potential benefits in terms of halting or slowing Iran's nuclear programme (*The Economist*, 2012). Whatever the balance of the arguments, the pattern since the early 1990s suggests that there are likely to remain significant European divisions over coercive approaches to non-proliferation and especially over the use of force to prevent proliferation.

European wariness of coercive non-proliferation strategies raises the question of how far Europe, above all the EU, can fashion a credible alternative. In the context of the Bush administration's efforts to promote more coercive non-proliferation policies and the US intervention in Iraq in 2003, Iran became the central test case of the EU's ability to use its 'soft power' to develop an alternative approach to non-proliferation (Charlemagne, 2006) – see Box 7.1. Although the long-term outcome of the crisis surrounding Iran's nuclear ambition remains to be seen, the case illustrates the difficulties the EU faces in translating its general economic and political weight into decisive influence over other states' nuclear policies.

An additional important European dimension to the international non-proliferation debate is the position of Russia – a nuclear weapon state, a permanent member of the UN Security Council, a member of

Box 7.1   The EU, Iran and nuclear proliferation

In the wake of the 2003 Iraq War and concerns about the radicalization of US non-proliferation policy, the EU sought to use diplomacy and a combination of economic incentives and sanctions to persuade Iran to halt its nuclear programme. In October 2003, the foreign ministers of the UK, France and Germany – the E3 (European 3) as they came to be called – negotiated an agreement with Iran under which Tehran agreed to halt its uranium enrichment programme (enriched uranium being the key material necessary for the development of nuclear weapons) in return for European assistance with its civilian nuclear programme and the possibility of improved political and economic ties. Although the USA was initially wary of European attempts to engage Iran on the nuclear issue, it was drawn into the negotiating process and the E3 expanded to become the E3+3 (the three European states, plus the USA, Russia and China – the latter three, along with Britain and France, also being the permanent members of the UN Security Council and thus central to Security Council decisions on Iran, in particular in relation to economic sanctions). In 2004 the EU's High Representative for its Common Foreign and Security Policy (CFSP), Javier Solana, joined the negotiations, becoming the key diplomatic interlocutor between the E3+3 and Iran.

The 2003 agreement brokered by the E3 broke down in 2004 and after this a period of 'on again/off again' negotiations between the E3+3 and Iran continued throughout the 2000s, with periodic hopes of progress but no decisive breakthrough. Meanwhile, Iran was gradually developing its uranium enrichment programme – bringing it closer to the point where it

→

the IAEA Board of Governors, a major supplier of nuclear technology, and a country with political and economic ties with Iran and North Korea. While Russia would prefer to avoid nuclear proliferation in the Middle East and North East Asia, it also has other interests in these regions, in particular limiting the expansion of US influence. Since the early 1990s, while Russia has supported diplomatic efforts to dissuade Iran and North Korea from developing nuclear weapons, it has resisted US-led pressure to take a tough line against these states in the IAEA or the UN Security Council. Russia would probably oppose US military action against Iran or North Korea, and use its permanent seat on the Security Council to veto any resolution authorizing such action. Some observers have argued that Russia also has an interest in maintaining the Iranian and North Korean nuclear situations as ongoing crises, since this gives it influence and bargaining counters *vis-à-vis* the USA and the EU. Given these dynamics, Russia is likely to remain a significant actor in dealing with proliferation's tough cases, and to constrain

→

might have the fissile material necessary to produce nuclear weapons. The exact status of Iran's nuclear programme was, however, unclear, with estimates of the timescale for possible Iranian development of nuclear weapons varying from 1–2 years to a decade or more.

The failure of the E3+3 negotiations to halt Iran's uranium enrichment programme was a major setback for the EU's efforts to use constructive engagement to promote non-proliferation. In diplomatic and economic terms, the EU lacked sufficient 'carrots or sticks' to induce Iran to abandon its efforts to enrich uranium. The 'on again/off again' character of the negotiations between Iran and the E3+3 also suggested that Tehran was using the talks to buy time and avoid pressure from the IAEA and the UN Security Council. Critics also argue that some EU member states (in particular Germany) still have significant economic ties with Iran and have therefore been reluctant to impose the truly tough economic sanctions that might intensify pressure on Iran. Although the EU's efforts to engage Iran have not produced the decisive breakthrough some hoped for, they should not necessarily be considered a complete failure: they may have slowed Iran's nuclear programme, brought the USA, Russia and China into a diplomatic process with Iran and held open the door for a future negotiated settlement of the nuclear issue (for example, in the context of possible domestic political change within Iran). If Iran does, however, go on to develop nuclear weapons, such a development would be a significant defeat for the EU's approach to non-proliferation – as also would an Israeli or US decision to use military force against Iran's nuclear infrastructure.

the ability of the USA and the EU to pursue a tougher line towards Iran and North Korea.

The return of nuclear disarmament?

By the late 2000s growing concern about nuclear proliferation was pushing an old issue – nuclear arms control and disarmament and even the possibility of a nuclear weapon-free world – to the fore of the international agenda. The basic logic was simple: unless the established nuclear weapon states did more to advance nuclear arms control and disarmament by reducing their own nuclear arsenals, it would be difficult to dissuade other states from developing nuclear weapons, and in the long term this might even require a move towards a nuclear weapon-free world. Debates on nuclear arms control and disarmament had been central to the global security agenda during the Cold War, even if the USA and the Soviet Union in practice made little progress in reducing their arsenals. As the Cold War ended in the late 1980s and early 1990s the USA and the Soviet Union/Russia concluded a series of significant nuclear arms control agreements: the 1987 Intermediate Range Nuclear Forces (INF) Treaty (which banned all medium-range nuclear missiles), the 1991 Strategic Arms Reduction Treaty (START) and the 1993 START II agreement (both of which mandated reductions in US and Russian long-range nuclear forces), as well as the 1996 Comprehensive Test Ban Treaty (which banned all nuclear weapon tests and was signed by most states). In the late 1990s and 2000s, however, nuclear arms control and disarmament by the established nuclear weapon states moved away from the centre of the agenda as attention focused on the proliferation of nuclear weapons to other states.

By the late 2000s India's and Pakistan's consolidation of their status as nuclear weapon states, the continuing difficulties of preventing North Korea and Iran from developing nuclear weapons and concern that a wider group of states might develop nuclear weapons in coming decades was creating renewed interest in nuclear disarmament. Debate was triggered by a January 2007 article by George Shultz, William Perry, Henry Kissinger and Sam Nunn – four major figures from the mainstream of the US foreign policy elite – calling for a new 'consensus for reversing reliance on nuclear weapons globally as a vital contribution to preventing their proliferation into potentially dangerous hands', substantial reductions in nuclear forces by the established nuclear weapon states and 'setting the goal of a world free of nuclear weapons and working energetically on the actions required to achieve that goal' (Shultz *et al.*, 2007). Renewed debate on nuclear disarmament and the possibility of a nuclear weapon-free world emerged (Quinlan, 2007–08, Perkovich and Acton, 2008) and a variety of policy and campaigning groups began to call for 'global zero' (i.e., a world free of nuclear weapons). In the USA the new Obama administration supported the logic behind these calls. In a major speech on nuclear policy in Prague in April 2009 President Obama committed the USA to 'seek the peace and security of a world without nuclear weapons' and towards that end to 'reduce the role of nuclear weapons' in US national security strategy and to negotiate further nuclear arms reductions with Russia (Obama, 2009a). The first major result of the new interest in disarmament was the New START Treaty between the USA and Russia, signed in April 2010 and entering into force in February 2011, under which the two states agreed to reduce their deployed strategic nuclear warhead levels to 1,550 each. Table 7.3

TABLE 7.3 *Global nuclear forces*

Country	Deployed nuclear warheads 2010	Total nuclear warheads 2010 (inc. in reserve & awaiting dismantlement)	US–Russian nuclear arms control agreements: treaty-accountable deployed nuclear warheads			
			START I	START II	SORT	New START
United States	2,468	<9,600	6,000	3,000–3,500	1,700–2,200	1,550
Russia	4,630	<12,000	6,000	3,000–3,500	1,700–2,200	1,550
UK	160	225				
France	240	300				
China*		240				
India*		60–80				
Pakistan*		70–90				
Israel*		80				

* China's nuclear warheads are thought to be stored independently of their launchers. India's, Pakistan's and Israel's nuclear warheads are thought to be only partly deployed.

Sources: Data from Stockholm International Peace Research Institute (2010), table 8.1, World nuclear forces, January 2010, and table 9.1, Summary of Russian–US nuclear arms reduction treaties' force limits; US Department of State (nd); and Kristensen (2009).

summarizes the size of existing nuclear arsenals and US–Russian arms control agreements.

The nuclear disarmament agenda laid out by advocates of radical reductions in nuclear weapons, however, faces serious obstacles. Whether the long-term goal of a nuclear weapon-free world is achievable is an open question: the willingness of the established nuclear weapon states to surrender their nuclear arsenals remains to be tested, while a nuclear weapon-free world would presumably require both a highly intrusive verification regime and a robust enforcement mechanism to determine measures against any state trying to break out and develop nuclear weapons. Most observers suggest that these possibilities are at best some decades away. In his 2009 Prague speech President Obama himself noted the goal of a nuclear weapon-free world 'will not be reached quickly – perhaps not in my lifetime' (Obama, 2009a). Even the intermediate step of deep reductions in existing nuclear arsenals faces serious obstacles. The 2010 New START Treaty was the low-hanging fruit of nuclear arms control: a treaty the USA and Russia could agree relatively easily, leaving both states with relatively large total nuclear arsenals (numbering potentially 5,000 warheads or more each). Further reductions in US and Russian nuclear arsenals will be more difficult to agree: for Russia its large nuclear arsenal is an important symbol of great power status and one it may be reluctant to surrender; Russia's remaining arsenal of tactical nuclear weapons (numbering approximately 5,000, of which 2,000 may be deployed or quite rapidly deployable) is much larger than that of the USA, and the USA argues that this must also be included in nuclear force reductions, but Moscow is reluctant to do so because it views tactical nuclear weapons as a counter-balance against NATO's (and China's) larger conventional forces; Russia views US missile defence plans (see below) as a threat to its nuclear deterrent and is reluctant to agree further nuclear reductions without constraints on US missile defences – a measure Washington is unwilling to accept; and in both countries there is domestic opposition from political hawks to further nuclear reductions. Other arms control measures also remain stalled: the entry into force of the CTBT remains stymied by the non-ratification of the treaty by the USA, China, India, Pakistan and other states, while formal negotiations on a possible Fissile Material Cut-off Treaty (FMCT, banning the further production of the fissile material necessary for nuclear weapons) have yet to start because of the opposition of some states (in particular Pakistan). Despite the rhetoric of nuclear disarmament, further, one 2011 study concluded that 'long-term nuclear force modernisation or upgrade programmes are underway in all the currently nuclear armed states ... There is little sign in any of these nuclear armed states that a future without nuclear weapons is seriously being contemplated' (Kearns, 2011, p. 34).

European views on the nuclear disarmament agenda vary significantly. In general, most European publics and governments are sympathetic to further significant reductions in nuclear arsenals and the eventual goal of a nuclear weapon-free world. In response to the nuclear disarmament agenda laid out by Shultz, Perry, Kissinger and Nunn, prominent political leaders in the United Kingdom, Germany, Italy and Poland made statements in support of further nuclear force reductions and the goal of a nuclear weapon-free world (Kulesa, 2010, p. 87). Of the three European nuclear weapon states, the United Kingdom was the most sympathetic to the new nuclear disarmament agenda emerging from the USA (Smith, 2010, pp. 76–80). In contrast, the other two European nuclear weapon states, France and Russia, were at best cautious about and in practice wary of the new nuclear disarmament agenda. In both France and Russia nuclear weapons continue to be viewed as both vital military deterrents and important symbols of great power status (Kulesa, 2010, pp. 88–9 and 93–4). The nuclear disarmament agenda is also a complicated and politically sensitive question within NATO. A small number of US nuclear warheads (numbering in the low hundreds or less) remain forward-deployed in Western Europe. Critics argue that this nuclear posture is a relic of the Cold War that no longer serves a purpose and that these nuclear weapons should be withdrawn as part of efforts to advance nuclear disarmament. Supporters of the retention of these forward-deployed US nuclear weapons argue that they continue to act as an ultimate deterrent of nuclear or conventional attack against NATO's European members and are a vital strategic link between the USA and Europe. When NATO adopted its new Strategic Concept in December 2010 it also initiated a review of the Alliance's overall defence and deterrence posture, including nuclear weapons (NATO, 2010b, para. 30). The review of NATO's defence and deterrence posture was expected to be completed by the next NATO summit in May 2012, but there remain divisions between NATO's member states over the Alliance's nuclear posture and the future of US nuclear weapons in Europe.

The place of Europe in evolving debates on nuclear disarmament is complex. The nuclear arsenals of the USA and Russia are still much larger than those of all the other nuclear weapon powers and these two states will therefore play the central role in determining whether and how the nuclear disarmament agenda advances. Nevertheless, the United Kingdom and France are two of the five established nuclear weapon states and permanent members of the UN Security Council, while NATO is also a nuclear alliance. In this context, some observers argue that Europe needs to play a more proactive and leading role in advancing the nuclear arms control agenda by encouraging the USA and Russia to accelerate force reductions, working within NATO for the removal or reduction of tactical nuclear weapons and exploring how the nuclear arms reduction process can be multilateralized (Browne and Kearns, 2011). How far, and in what ways, Europe will shape the nuclear disarmament agenda remains to be seen.

Living with proliferation?

Given India's and Pakistan's consolidation of their status as nuclear weapon powers, North Korea's 2006 and 2009 nuclear tests and the difficulty of preventing Iran from developing nuclear weapons, it is likely that the world will have to live with at least a limited degree of proliferation. As discussed above, the immediate impact on Europe of proliferation may not be great. Nevertheless, proliferation has already prompted thinking within Europe on two issues: what may be done to deter states from using WMD, and the prospects for defending against WMD attack.

Deterrence, of course, has been the classical rationale for the possession of nuclear weapons. For the USA, the UK, France and NATO as a whole, deterrence of the Soviet Union provided the rationale for nuclear weapons during the Cold War. Since the 1990s, however, there has been a gradual shift in Western thinking on nuclear weapons away from the need to deter Russia and towards the need to maintain nuclear weapons in order to deter WMD attack from elsewhere in the world. The UK's 1998 *Strategic Defence Review* concluded that 'while large nuclear arsenals *and risks of proliferation* remain, our minimum deterrent remains a necessary element of our security' (UK Ministry of Defence, 1998, para. 60, emphasis added). In announcing the conclusions of a major review of French nuclear strategy in 2001, President Jacques Chirac argued that 'Deterrence must also enable us to deal with the threats to our vital interests that regional powers armed with weapons of mass destruction could pose' (quoted in Yost, 2005, p. 118). Deterrence of WMD attack from outside Europe has also become one of the rationales for NATO's continuing strategy of nuclear deterrence based on the USA's strategic nuclear arsenal and US nuclear weapons forward-deployed in Europe (Yost, 1999, pp. 27–33). In the context of the ongoing development of the EU's defence role, it might be thought that the prospect of WMD proliferation would also have increased interest in the possibility of a 'European' deterrent based around the UK's and France's nuclear weapons. However, although the UK and France have engaged in bilateral discussions on nuclear weapons, there has been little support for the development of a 'European' nuclear deterrent.

The prospect of WMD proliferation has also prompted renewed debate and controversy over missile defences – the concept of defensive systems capable of intercepting or shooting down incoming missiles and thereby negating the threat posed by them. Here, one should distinguish between two types of systems: tactical and theatre missile defences, designed to defend military forces or a localized geographic area from short- or medium-range missiles and which are deployed by many countries; and strategic or territorial missile defences, designed to defend a country's territory and population centres from long-range missile attack and which have not yet been deployed on a large scale. Territorial missile defences are controversial for a number of reasons. Technologically, the challenge posed by territorial missile defence is a very difficult one – sometimes described as hitting a bullet in flight with another bullet – and there are serious doubts about the effectiveness of the missile defence systems deployed and under development. Strategically, missile defences have been viewed as destabilizing because they would, especially if combined with a nuclear first strike, threaten to destroy an opposing state's ability to retaliate, thereby creating circumstances in a crisis where one or both states might face pressures to strike first rather than risk having their nuclear deterrent capability removed. As a consequence, during the Cold War the USA and the Soviet Union negotiated an agreement (the 1972 Anti-Ballistic Missile (ABM) Treaty) strictly limiting such missile defences. Although in the 1980s the Reagan administration invested significant resources in research and development on missile defences (the Strategic Defence Initiative (SDI) or 'Star Wars' plan), it did not proceed with the deployment of such defences. When President George W. Bush came to power in 2001, however, territorial missile defences were a central plank of his administration's defence policy. The Bush administration announced plans to deploy missile defences (beginning in 2004) and in 2002 withdrew from the ABM Treaty. Although the USA stated that its planned missile defences were designed only to defend against limited threats from countries such as North Korea and Iran, Russia strongly opposed the US missile defence plans, arguing that they threatened Russia's own nuclear deterrent, would undermine arms control (by making it impossible to negotiate deeper reductions in nuclear forces) and might force Russia to take counter-measures (such as expanding or modernizing its nuclear forces).

The Bush administration's missile defence plans were problematic from a European perspective: most European governments were wary of the US missile defence plans but did not want to explicitly oppose a prominent US policy. In addition, the US missile defence plans involved the actual or planned participation of a number of European allies. In 2003 and 2004 the United Kingdom and Denmark agreed to the upgrading of US radar bases on their territory as part of the US missile defence plans. More controversially, the Bush administration proposed to deploy interceptor missiles in Poland and a new radar base in the Czech Republic, Central European states that had only recently joined NATO and were geographically proximate to Russia. Russia was particularly opposed to the planned Central European missile defence bases and threatened to take retaliatory measures.

The Obama administration was concerned about the risks of undermining relations with Russia and committed to review US missile defence plans. In September 2009 President Obama announced a new missile defence policy, the Phased Adaptive Approach (PAA), which involved halting the planned bases in Poland and the Czech Republic, shifting the focus from ground-based interceptor missiles to the Aegis ship-based interceptor system and adapting the system to the development of missile threats (in particular from Iran) (Obama, 2009b). The Obama administration's Phased Adaptive Approach to missile defence assuaged Russia in the short term, but the possible future expansion of US missile defences (and the potential involvement of European NATO members, including in Central and Eastern Europe) meant that longer-term Russian concerns remained. Since 2009, further, Poland and Romania have agreed to host Aegis Ashore land-based versions of the Aegis naval system, with deployment planned for Romania in 2015 and Poland in 2018.

In addition to the US missile defence system, NATO is also developing missile defences. In 2004 NATO decided to develop an Active Layered Theatre Ballistic Missile Defence (ALTBMD) designed to protect troops deployed overseas against short- and medium-range ballistic missile attack. The ALTBMD involves member states providing sensors and weapon systems, with NATO collectively providing the battle management, command, control, communications and intelligence (BMC3I) to integrate the components into an overall missile defence system. In January 2011 the first stage of the ALTBMD became operational (NATO, 2011b). In terms of territorial missile defences, the technical challenges and potentially destabilizing consequences has made many European NATO members reluctant to develop such systems. Nevertheless, at its Lisbon summit in November 2010 the Alliance agreed to develop a 'NATO missile defence capability ... to provide full coverage and protection for all NATO European populations, territory and forces' and to expand the scope of the ALTBMD towards this end (NATO, 2010b, paras 36–7). The decision reflected growing concern about the threat posed by ballistic missile proliferation, but also US pressure to multinationalize its missile defence plans in the context of NATO. While some European NATO members (in particular some of the Central and Eastern European states) were supportive of the development, other member states (such as France) remained sceptical. The extent to which different NATO member states would contribute to the missile defence plans thus remained to be seen.

In an effort to address Russian concerns, the USA and NATO both sought to engage Moscow in dialogue and co-operation on missile defence. By the early 2010s, however, such efforts had made at best limited progress. Overall, Russia remains significantly concerned about the medium- to long-term potential of US and NATO missile defence plans to negate its nuclear deterrent. US and NATO missile defence plans are therefore likely to remain a significant irritant in Russo-Western relations, with the potential to destabilize the relationship and undermine nuclear arms control (Weitz, 2010).

Even if European states and NATO or the EU strengthen their deterrent capabilities and deploy missile defences, if WMD (especially nuclear) proliferation proceeds, the changed strategic environment is likely to have a significant impact on European and American attitudes to the deployment of military force overseas. To date, the USA and European countries (in particular the UK and France, Europe's leading military powers) have been able to deploy military forces relatively freely in other parts of the world such as the Middle East because the risk of significant direct retaliation against their territory or major attacks on concentrations of forces deployed overseas has been relatively low. The ability of other states to retaliate with nuclear weapons or to use nuclear weapons against concentrations of US or European forces would radically alter this calculus. If Iran develops nuclear weapons, for example, the possibility of using military force against it will effectively be precluded. In the medium term, therefore, proliferation is likely to significantly curtail the ability of the USA or European states to intervene in other parts of the world, at least against those states that develop nuclear weapons.

Conclusion

This chapter has analysed European assessments of and responses to the threat posed by WMD proliferation. European governments generally view multilateral arms control as the primary vehicle for attempting to prevent proliferation, and have sought to strengthen the international non-proliferation regime. In particular, in the context of the EU *Strategy Against Proliferation of Weapons of Mass Destruction*, the EU has sought to strengthen multilateral arms control and non-proliferation regimes through common positions in the main arms control negotiations and a variety of measures of financial and technical assistance. In terms of proliferation's tough cases – those states that appear determined to develop nuclear weapons, in particular Iran and North Korea – the European preference has been to use diplomacy and soft power (backed up by economic sanctions) rather than isolation or military force. The failure of the EU's efforts to persuade Iran to abandon its apparent nuclear weapons ambitions was thus a major setback to the Union's ambitions to show that its soft power approach to proliferation could succeed (although it remains possible that Iran may yet be persuaded to halt its apparent march towards nuclear weapons). While the general European preference is for diplomacy and soft power approaches to non-proliferation, Europeans are also divided over the more contentious issues of economic sanctions and military forces as tools of non-proliferation. Any US or Israeli use of force against Iran would doubtless bring these divisions to the fore once more.

While the 1990s and the 2000s illustrated the limitations of arms control and soft power in preventing proliferation, they also highlighted a deeper problem at the heart of the existing non-proliferation regime: the double standard implicit in the efforts of the five recognized nuclear weapon states to prevent other states from developing WMD while themselves retaining such weapons. So long as the five recognized nuclear weapon states – including three leading European powers, the UK, France and Russia – retain their nuclear arsenals and engage in only modest efforts to reduce those arsenals, it will remain extremely difficult to persuade other states (such as India, Pakistan, Iran or North Korea) not to develop nuclear weapons or to mobilize the sort of international pressure that might compel such states to abandon their nuclear weapons ambitions. Recognition of this logic lay behind the Obama administration's efforts to jump-start nuclear disarmament. As has been seen, although these efforts have produced some steps forwards, such as the 2010 New START Treaty, there remain serious obstacles to much deeper reductions in nuclear arsenals. In these circumstances, India and Pakistan are likely to further consolidate their status as nuclear weapon powers, and North Korea and Iran may well move down this road. The larger, long-term question is probably whether nuclear (and other WMD) proliferation will remain limited to these countries, or whether a significantly wider group of states will develop such weapons, thereby further increasing the risk that they will be used or fall into the hands of terrorists. European states – and the USA – are thus likely to have to live with the reality of at least limited nuclear proliferation and, while they may enhance their own deterrent capabilities and deploy missile defences, this reality is likely to fundamentally constrain their ability to use military force against countries such as Iran and North Korea and reshape the strategic calculus in the Middle East and North East Asia.

Chapter 8

Terrorism and Counter-Terrorism

In the space of two months between September and November 2010 French security services were put on high alert and the Eiffel tower was evacuated because of fears of a planned terrorist attack; a cargo plane bound for the USA was discovered – at Britain's East Midlands airport – to contain a parcel bomb posted in Yemen; a suicide bomb attack in the Turkish capital Istanbul injured at least 32 people; the Greek authorities intercepted parcel bombings sent to diplomatic missions and the Greek parliament by left-wing extremists; and Germany boosted security at airports, railway stations and major tourist attractions in response to 'concrete indications' of a planned terrorist attack by Islamic extremists. Although there may have been particular factors which resulted in an increased threat from globalized Islamic terrorism at this point (International Institute for Strategic Studies, 2010b), these various events indicate the reality of the ongoing threat posed to Europe by terrorism.

Nearly a decade earlier, the 9/11 attacks signalled a new era of globalized Islamic terrorism. The Madrid and London bombings of March 2004 and July 2005, further, made clear that Europe was a major target for Islamic terrorism. European vulnerability to Islamic terrorism is multifaceted and intersects the boundaries of external and internal security. European citizens, embassies, businesses, and military personnel and bases have been the targets of terrorist attacks outside Europe. Terrorists have used European countries as safe havens from which to plan and organize terrorist acts elsewhere in the world (as with the 9/11 attacks on the USA). Terrorist groups from outside Europe have sought to infiltrate Europe in order to undertake terrorist attacks or to foment terrorism. As the London bombings illustrated, elements within Europe's own Islamic populations are also willing to engage in terrorist acts. Coming nearly a decade after 9/11, however, the July 2011 Oslo attacks – committed by a right-wing anti-Islamic extremist and resulting in more deaths than the 2005 London bombings – indicated that Europe continued to face terrorist threats from diverse sources and not simply Islamic extremists.

In response to the 9/11, Madrid and London attacks, European governments – nationally, in the framework of the EU and in conjunction with the USA – instituted a range of new counter-terrorism measures: strengthening legal, police and intelligence institutions designed to detect and prevent terrorist activity, introducing new policies to counter radicalization amongst potential recruits to the cause of terrorism and seeking to address the root causes of terrorism at the global level. This chapter reviews the threat posed to Europe by terrorism post-9/11 and European responses to that threat.

Europe and terrorism: assessing the threat

Terrorism, of course, is hardly new, and Europe has significant experience of the phenomenon. The term 'terrorism' emerged from 'the terror' of the French Revolution (when revolutionaries used violence and brutality against their enemies) and was subsequently used to describe violence by left-wing and anarchist groups and individuals against the established order in 19th- and early 20th-century Europe. In the post-1945 era, European states were subject to terrorist campaigns and acts conducted by ethno-national groups within Europe (Irish republicans in the UK, Basque nationalists in Spain, Corsican separatists in France and Kurdish groups in Turkey); far-left groups (the Baader-Meinhof Gang and the Red Army Faction in Germany, the Red Brigades in Italy, and the Revolutionary Organization 17 November in Greece); and Palestinian groups in the 1960s and 1970s. Indeed, the first hijacking of an Israeli airliner by Palestinian terrorists in 1968, en route from Rome to Tel Aviv, is often seen as the beginning of an 'age of terrorism' (Guelke, 1998, pp. 189–92). By the late 1980s and early 1990s, however, terrorism appeared to be a waning force in Europe: far-left terrorist groups had ceased to be active, many of the main ethno-national terrorist campaigns were winding down (with peace processes beginning to emerge in these conflicts) and the earlier internationalization of Palestinian terrorism had dissipated.

Although 9/11 stands as the symbolic moment in the emergence of the new terrorism, globalized Islamic terrorism had been developing for a decade or more before this and European states and citizens had been targets and victims of this terrorism since the 1990s. France, because of its historic role in Algeria and its support for that country's military government (which had abandoned free elections in 1992 when it became clear that Islamists would win), was subject to a series of terrorist attacks by the Algerian Armed Islamic Group (GIA) in 1995, resulting in the deaths of ten people and the wounding of over 150 (Shapiro and Suzan, 2003, pp. 79–81). European governments prevented other planned terrorist attacks by Islamic groups in Europe before 9/11, including on the 1998 football World Cup in France and on Strasbourg Cathedral in 2000 (Shapiro and Suzan, 2003, p. 68). European citizens were also targets of Islamic terrorism outside Europe: 62 people, mainly European and Japanese tourists, were killed in the November 1997 Luxor massacre in Egypt.

The March 2004 Madrid bombings and the July 2005 London bombings, however, were on a scale not seen previously and indicated that, post-9/11, Europe was a major target of globalized Islamic terrorism alongside the USA. The March 2004 Madrid bombings were committed by the Moroccan Islamic Combat Group, and the individual terrorists were mostly Moroccans, led by a Tunisian (IISS, 2004, p. 101). Although some of the terrorists were Spanish residents, the Madrid bombings nevertheless suggested that the primary threat was still an external one posed by foreign terrorists that had infiltrated Europe. In contrast, the July 2005 London bombings appeared to signal a new, and in many ways more worrying, threat: the emergence of home-grown Islamic terrorism, combined with suicide attacks (a phenomenon not previously seen in Europe). The London bombings were carried out by four British citizens, three of whom had been born in the UK and the fourth of whom had moved to the UK at the age of two and had lived in the country since then (Home Office, n.d.). Two of the London bombers visited Pakistan (and possibly Afghanistan) prior to the bombings, where they may have met and received training from other terrorists, and there is speculation that the London attacks were supported or directed by external terrorist groups (Travis and Norton-Taylor, 2006). Nevertheless, even if the London bombings were supported or masterminded by external Islamic groups, they made it starkly clear that Europe faced the threat not just of external Islamic terrorism but also of a home-grown European version. The extent and nature of the threat posed by indigenous European Islamic terrorism and the challenges of responding to this are discussed below.

A further element of Europe's interrelationship with Islamic terrorism was the way in which the continent became a base for radical Islamic individuals and groups seeking to promote their ideology, gain recruits and, in some cases, plan terrorist attacks. Jonathan Stevenson (2004, p. 27) argues that 'liberal asylum laws and standards of religious and commercial freedom have made Europe an effective safe haven as well as a fundraising hub for aspiring terrorists'. The so-called 'Hamburg cell' – a group of the 9/11 conspirators based in Hamburg, Germany – played a central role in the 9/11 attacks (National Commission on Terrorist Attacks Upon the United States, 2004, pp. 160–9). In the wake of the London bombings, commentators in the USA described the British capital as 'Londonistan': a city that had become a haven for radical Islamic preachers fomenting violence against the West, and a recruiting ground for disciples willing to put that doctrine into practice (Younge, 2005; Bergen, 2005). While the UK may be the most severe case of this phenomenon, other Western European countries face similar problems. Although a liberal approach to both asylum seekers and freedom of speech may be partly to blame for the growth of radical Islam in Western Europe, larger geographical and historical factors are at play. Geography alone means that Europe has been and will remain the primary destination in the West for immigrants from the Middle East and North Africa. The historic ties of former imperial powers with Islamic countries also make them a primary destination for immigration from these states – as in the UK with regard to Pakistan, and France in relation to Algeria. More recently, the Balkan conflicts of the 1990s created a context in which radical Islamists from outside Europe were able to build links with the Muslim communities in Bosnia and Kosovo.

A further interface between Europe and Islamic terrorism lies in southern Russia, the Caucasus and Central Asia. The Central Asian 'stans' (Kazakhstan, Kyrgyzstan, Tajikistan, Turkmenistan and Uzbekistan) and Azerbaijan all have predominantly Muslim populations, as do various parts of the Russian north Caucasus. The authoritarian nature of the Central Asian regimes has made Islam one of the primary outlets for political and socio-economic dissent, and resulted in the emergence of radical Islamic groups that sometimes engage in terrorist acts. This problem is most serious in Uzbekistan, where the Islamic Movement of Uzbekistan (IMU) emerged in the late 1990s, is believed to have links with al-Qaeda, and has engaged in terrorist acts against the ruling regimes and Western targets in Uzbekistan, Kyrgyzstan and Afghanistan (Burgess, 2002). While radical Islam and Islamic terrorism pose a real challenge in Central Asia, the extent of the problem should perhaps not be exaggerated: Central Asian leaders, in particular Uzbek President Islam Karimov use the fear of Islamic radicalism as a means of shoring up their authoritarian regimes; and Kyrgyzstan's 2005 Tulip Revolution indicated that even if these regimes are overthrown they are not necessarily likely to be replaced by fundamentalist Islamic forces.

It is in the Russian north Caucasus, in particular Chechnya, however, that Islamic terrorism has really come to the fore in the former Soviet Union. Starting in the mid-1990s and escalating from the late 1990s, Russia has been subject to a series of major terrorist attacks, primarily in Chechnya and neighbouring parts of the north Caucasus, but also elsewhere in the Russian Federation. These attacks included a hostage crisis in a Moscow cinema in October 2002, in which 120 hostages and 40 terrorists were killed during a rescue attempt, and reached their nadir with the September 2004 school hostage crisis in Beslan, North Ossetia, which resulted in the deaths of over 300 civilians, many of them children. Many Russians thus view themselves as one of the frontlines in the global conflict with Islamic terrorism. The continuing threat posed to Russia by terrorism was confirmed by the January 2011 suicide bomb attack at Moscow's Domodedovo international airport, which resulted in 37 deaths and the injury of over 150 people. The context and nature of the terrorist threat facing Russia are, however, controversial. The Chechen conflict can be viewed in part as a classical example of an ethno-national group using terrorism against a more powerful central government, but Chechen and other north Caucasian radicals have also developed links with and been supported by Islamic terrorists from the Middle East. Chechnya therefore appears to be a situation where 'old'- and 'new'-style terrorism have fused. Russia's brutal interventions in Chechnya in the 1990s, furthermore, can only have contributed to the rise of Chechen terrorism. Western governments have thus been torn between supporting Russia as an ally in the global struggle against Islamic terrorism, and criticism of Moscow for its failed interventions and human rights abuses in Chechnya.

If 9/11 and the Madrid and London bombings suggested that the threat posed by Islamic terrorism was growing, by the late 2000s and early 2010s most observers suggested that this threat was declining. Most obviously, there have been no further major terrorist attacks in Europe by Islamic groups since the 2005 London bombing. In part, the reduced threat may be attributed to counter-terrorism policies: intelligence and police work has resulted in the detection and foiling of a number of planned terrorist attacks, while terrorist groups have faced growing pressure as a result of bans, surveillance and detentions. As was noted in Chapter 2, by the late 2000s and early 2010s al-Qaeda also appeared to be a waning force globally as a result of US military pressure against it in Afghanistan and Pakistan and its failure to gain wider political traction in the Islamic world. The draw-down of US and European military forces in Iraq and Afghanistan may have reduced one of the sources of grievance giving rise to Islamic terrorism. The killing of Osama bin Laden in May 2011, further, was a symbolic defeat for al-Qaeda and created a leadership crisis within the organization. In addition, the 2011 Arab Spring may weaken al-Qaeda, since the group and its affiliates played no role in the uprisings against authoritarian regimes and the broadly democratic Arab Spring movement represents a very different vision of the Islamic world to that advanced by al-Qaeda. Reflecting the reduced threat from Islamic terrorism, in July 2011 British security and intelligence services downgraded their assessment of the threat posed by it from 'severe' to 'substantial' (Norton-Taylor and Travis, 2011). A decade after 9/11, Nigel Inkster, a former senior British security and intelligence official, concluded that Europe and America were more secure because 'the nature of the threat from jihadist extremism is much better understood and the resources and capabilities needed to counter it more effectively are mobilised', and, noting that the overwhelming majority of terrorist attacks were in South Asia and the Middle East, concluded that 'jihadism remains a potent force even if its manifestations ultimately prove more regional than global, as may well prove to be the case' (Inkster, 2011, p. 12).

Europe is also likely to face continuing threats from other types of terrorism. Although traditional ethno-national terrorism has been and may well remain a waning force in Europe, even where terrorist-related conflicts are subsiding radical splinter groups may continue campaigns of violence. This has been the case in Northern Ireland, where the threat from so-called dissident Republican terrorist groups has grown since the late 2000s (*The Economist*, 2010b). Although the Basque terrorist group ETA declared a permanent cease-fire in 2011, such cease-fires had been declared before and there were fears that splinter groups might continue with violence (*The Economist*, 2011a). As was noted at the beginning of this chapter, further, the July 2011 Oslo terrorist attacks were amongst the worst in modern European history – indicating the extent of the threat posed by right-wing anti-Islamic terrorism. Even before the Oslo attacks, Europol concluded that if the Arab Spring 'leads to a major influx of immigrants into Europe, right-wing extremism and terrorism might gain a new lease of life by articulating more widespread public apprehension about immigration from Muslim countries into Europe' (Europol, 2011, p. 30). More generally, the socio-economic conditions created by the global recession since 2008 have created fertile ground for political extremism of various kinds and may exacerbate the risk of terrorism of various kinds. In 2011 therefore Europol's annual terrorism threat assessment concluded that 'the threat from terrorism remains high and is diversifying in scope and impact' (Europol, 2011, p. 5).

Counter-terrorism I: the homeland security agenda

European governments responded to post-1945 terrorism in a variety of different ways, resulting in quite different national policies. Policy responses included intensified intelligence and police action against terrorists; the banning of terrorist groups; the introduction of special judicial courts and procedures to deal with terrorism; political, economic and social measures designed to address the grievances that had given rise to terrorism and undercut support for terrorists; and, in some cases, negotiations (often secret) with terrorists. Some countries emphasized 'tough' policies focusing on legal and security measures directed against terrorists (usually accompanied by a refusal to negotiate with them or to take measures to address their grievances), while others emphasized political, economic and social measures or the possibility of negotiation. Critics, especially in the USA, contended that Europe was soft on terrorism, arguing that negotiation and political, economic and social measures designed to address terrorists' grievances amounted to appeasement and would only show that terrorism worked as a means of advancing one's political goals. The French 'sanctuary doctrine' was particularly controversial: up to the 1980s France tried to avoid becoming a subject of foreign terrorist attacks by making French policy and territory neutral in relation to terrorism, effectively allowing terrorist groups to operate from France in return for a commitment by those groups not to undertake attacks within France (Shapiro and Suzan, 2003, pp. 69–73).

The 9/11 terrorist attacks led to a strengthening of legal, security and intelligence measures against terrorism – or what became referred to in the USA as homeland security. In the USA, the centrepieces of this were the PATRIOT Act, passed by Congress in October 2001, which extended the powers of the US government to counter terrorism, and the creation of the Department of Homeland Security, bringing together US government offices and agencies dealing with borders, immigration, transportation security, and emergency preparedness and response. European governments and the EU introduced similar legal, governmental and operational counter-terrorism measures. These included strengthening internal security policies in relation to terrorism, passing new legislation to deal with terrorism, and increasing the powers of and resources available to police and domestic intelligence services. Many of these steps might traditionally have been labelled internal security measures – that is legal, policing and intelligence policies directed against terrorist threats from within the territory of the state concerned. Governments also, however, took other steps that fell beyond the scope of traditional internal security measures: strengthening immigration and border controls; enhancing airport, airline and port security; devoting more resources to external intelligence services with regard to terrorism; and increasing international counter-terrorism co-operation (in areas such as the financing of terrorism, intelligence and extradition). The new homeland security agenda thus resulted in an increasing blurring of the distinction between internal and external security, and the internationalization of what were traditionally national internal security policies.

At the national level, most European states introduced a variety of new homeland security measures after September 2001 (van de Linde *et al.*, 2002; Foreign and Commonwealth Office, 2005). These included increased resources for intelligence, policing, and immigration and border controls; intensified surveillance of groups or individuals believed to be terrorists, or supporting or encouraging terrorism; and, in some cases, major new legislation. European law enforcement agencies also became 'noticeably more inclined to arrest and detain suspects', with authorities in Belgium, Bosnia-Herzegovina, France, Germany, Italy, the Netherlands, Spain and the UK arresting over 200 suspected al-Qaeda terrorists between 11 September 2001 and February 2003 (Stevenson, 2004, pp. 54 and 27). In the British case, the government introduced two major new pieces of counter-terrorism legislation after 9/11 and the July 2005 London bombings: the Anti-Terrorism, Crime and Security Act 2001, and the Terrorism Act 2006 (Home Office, n.d.). The Anti-Terrorism, Crime and Security Act 2001 introduced new measures to cut off terrorist funding; enable government departments to collect and share information required for countering terrorism; streamline relevant immigration procedures; ensure the security of the nuclear and aviation industries; improve security of dangerous substances that might be targeted or used by terrorists; and

Box 8.1   EU counter-terrorism measures post-9/11

- Action Plan on Combating Terrorism: adopted after the 9/11 attacks in September 2001 to guide EU policy; reviewed and revised on an ongoing basis; reinforced by a formal EU Counter-Terrorism Strategy adopted in November 2005.
- Counter-Terrorism Co-ordinator: the position of EU Counter-Terrorism Co-ordinator was established after the March 2004 Madrid bombings.
- European Arrest Warrant: introduced in 2002; facilitates arrest across the EU of persons indicted in another member state for terrorism (or other serious crimes).
- Mutual recognition of judicial orders to freeze and confiscate assets.
- Common definition of terrorist offences: agreed EU list of terrorist individuals, groups and entities established; minimum sentences for terrorist offences agreed; criminalization of direction of, support of and incitement to terrorism.
- Eurojust: EU judicial agency established to improve co-ordination between member states, magistrates and prosecutors.
- Europol (European Police Office): established to facilitate co-operation in relation to serious crime, including terrorism.
- Frontex (European Agency for the Management of Operational Co-operation at the External Borders of the Member States of the European Union): established to ensure a high and uniform level of control and surveillance on the EU's external frontiers; operational from May 2005.
- Passports: minimum security standards and biometric identifiers introduced for passports and other travel documents issued by member states.

extend police powers. The Terrorism Act 2006 introduced new criminal offences relating to terrorism (acts preparatory to terrorism; encouragement of terrorism, including its glorification; dissemination of terrorist publications; and terrorist training); introduced warrants to enable the police to search any property owned or controlled by a terrorist suspect; extended police powers to detain suspects after arrest for up to 28 days; and increased the powers of the government to proscribe groups (including those which glorify terrorism). A number of the measures introduced by the British government proved controversial, in particular new powers to detain individuals and to proscribe groups (Fenwick, 2002). The House of Lords ruled that so-called Part 4 powers under the Anti-Terrorism, Crime and Security Act 2001 were

$\rightarrow$

- Schengen Information System (SIS): system for exchange of information on persons wanted in relation to cross-border crimes.
- Visa Information System (VIS): system for exchange of data regarding visa applications and applicants among Schengen states.
- Eurodac: European Automated Fingerprints Identification System for asylum applicants and illegal immigrants; operational from 2003.
- Customs controls: new legislation strengthening customs controls.
- Airport/aircraft and harbour/shipping security: new Energy and Transport Security Directorate established within the European Commission – new European Commission inspectorate monitoring security measures across the EU.
- Lost/stolen passports: began delivering information on lost and stolen passports to an International Database managed by Interpol.
- Freezing of terrorist finances: ordered freezing of all funds and assets belonging to those suspected of terrorism or of financing terrorism.
- New anti-money laundering directive: extended existing anti-money laundering defences to cover financing of terrorism; includes structured rules for movement of cash and wired transfers.
- Exchange of information on suspicious financial transactions: intensified exchange of information between member states on suspicious financial transactions.
- Response measures in event of terrorist attacks: mechanism established to facilitate and support civil protection assistance in event of major disasters, including terrorist attacks; rapid alert system established to provide early warning of chemical, biological, radiological and nuclear (CBRN) attacks; enhanced programme for EU preparedness and response to CBRN attack.

Sources: Data from European Union (2001b, 2005a, 2006, 2009a).

incompatible with the UK's civil liberties commitments under the European Convention on Human Rights, and discriminatory because they applied only to foreign nationals, forcing the government to introduce new legislation (the Prevention of Terrorism Act 2005), which established a system of control orders (under which individuals might have their movements restricted or have other prohibitions imposed on them).

In the wake of the 9/11 attacks and the Madrid bombings, the EU also took a series of counter-terrorism measures, including the establishment of a rolling action plan to combat terrorism and the appointment of a Counter-Terrorism Co-ordinator (see Box 8.1). Many of the EU's counter-terrorism policy initiatives after 9/11 built upon the

Justice and Home Affairs (JHA) co-operation established in the 1990s. As discussed in Chapter 4, the EU's policies in this area remain primarily inter-governmental and are characterized by a complex institutional infrastructure, with member states participating to differing degrees in various areas of JHA. The EU's counter-terrorism policies reflect this pattern: although the Union has agreed an extensive and in some ways impressive range of counter-terrorism measures, the implementation of most of these depends on individual member states. Critics point out that member states have been slow to implement some of the key measures that have been agreed, the EU's Counter-Terrorism Co-ordinator has no power to force member states to implement their commitments or to propose EU-wide measures, and states are reluctant to share intelligence information on an EU-wide basis (Keohane, 2005; Wilkinson, 2005, pp. 29–37, 49). In addition to national and EU measures, as is discussed in more detail below, the EU has agreed a number of new counter-terrorism measures in co-operation with the USA.

The debate surrounding these various homeland security measures at the national, EU and transatlantic levels reflects the long-standing tension between security and liberty in responding to terrorism. For liberal democracies, with their basis in the principles of individual rights and limits on the power of the state, striking the appropriate balance between security and liberty in responding to terrorism remains difficult and often deeply contentious (Wilkinson, 2000). Even after the initial post-9/11 measures taken by European governments and the EU, some critics argued that Europe was taking too soft an approach towards terrorism and was overly concerned with protecting individual rights. In the wake of the Madrid and London bombings, however, European governments began to take a tougher approach. The German government, for example, was reported to have initiated 'an aggressive anti-terrorism strategy', including a major counter-terrorism raid in January 2005 involving 700 police and resulting in 22 arrests (Whitlock and Smiley, 2005). The UK's Terrorism Act 2006, with its introduction of a new offence of glorifying terrorism and increased government powers to proscribe groups, was also an implicit recognition that before July 2005 the UK had allowed groups and individuals that might promote terrorism to operate with too great a degree of freedom. Civil liberties and human rights groups have, however, argued that measures taken by European governments and the EU risk undermining basic freedoms (Bunyan, 2005; Human Rights Watch, 2005). While 9/11 and the Madrid and

London bombings have shifted the parameters of this debate, the fundamental tension between security and liberty in counter-terrorism remains, and European governments and the EU are likely to face further controversies over the issue.

The transatlantic dimension of counter-terrorism: co-operation and contestation

In the wake of the 9/11 terrorist attacks, Europe and the United States agreed a range of new common counter-terrorism measures and transatlantic co-operation has become an important part of European counter-terrorism policies. Nevertheless, fairly quickly after 9/11 Europeans became wary, and to varying degrees openly critical, of the Bush administration's 'war on terror'. Gilles Andréani neatly summarized European concerns over the US 'war on terror' as 'good cause, wrong concept' (Andréani, 2004). Similarly, the British academic, Adam Roberts, called for 'a British (or, more ambitiously, a European) perspective on terrorism and counter-terrorism – one that is more historically informed, encompassing certain elements distinctive from the US doctrine' (Roberts, 2005, p. 101). Many Europeans believed that the US 'war' on terror defined the problem too simplistically in terms of good and evil, searched for an impossible total defeat of terrorism and placed too much emphasis on military force (Howard, 2002; Muller, 2003; Andréani, 2004; Roberts, 2005).

For many in Europe, the Iraq War provided the clearest example of the dangers of the broadening of the US 'war on terror' and of conflating terrorism, WMD proliferation and 'rogue states' into a single great threat. European opponents of the Iraq War argued that it would be a major distraction from the more central task of countering al-Qaeda and associated Islamic terrorist groups, polarize opinion in the Middle East against the USA and the West, and thereby act as recruiting sergeant for Islamic terrorism. The logic of this argument was reinforced by developments after 2003. In 2005, the US Central Intelligence Agency (CIA) concluded that Iraq was providing a training ground for terrorists, similar to the role of Afghanistan in the rise of al-Qaeda in the 1980s and 1990s, and that terrorists trained in Iraq might go on to destabilize other countries such as Saudi Arabia and Jordan (Jehl, 2005). British officials and intelligence agencies believed that Iraq had become 'a dominant issue for a range of extremist groups and individuals in the UK and Europe' (Evans, 2005) and was a 'contributory factor' behind the 2005 London bombings (Norton-Taylor, 2006). European states' involvement in Iraq alongside the USA may also have made them prime targets for Islamic terrorism. It was hardly coincidental that two of the countries that were the strongest supporters of the US intervention in Iraq – Spain and the UK – were subsequently subject to major terrorist attacks. Developments after 2003 reinforced the widespread European view of the Iraq War as a dangerous widening of the US 'war on terror'. A June 2005 survey, for example, found that most people in eight European states (the UK, France, Germany, the Netherlands, Poland, Russia, Spain and Turkey) believed that the world was more dangerous rather than safer as a consequence of Saddam Hussein's removal from power (Pew Global Attitudes Project, 2005, p. 27).

Europeans were also concerned about the extent to which the 'war on terror' led the USA to cast aside international human rights commitments. The decision of the USA to define al-Qaeda/Taliban prisoners captured in Afghanistan as 'enemy combatants' rather than 'prisoners of war' (thereby ensuring that they were not legally subject to the protections of the Geneva Conventions), the detention of these prisoners at the US military base at Guantanamo Bay in Cuba, and the decision to try some of them before secret military tribunals left these prisoners in a legal limbo and created the impression of an American government trying to avoid both international and domestic law. Accusations by some of the Guantanamo Bay prisoners of human rights abuses and the 2004 scandal surrounding human rights abuses against prisoners held in the Abu Ghraib prison in Iraq reinforced the perception of the USA being willing to disregard international human rights standards. Reports that Guantanamo Bay and the Bagram airbase in Afghanistan were part of a larger network of secret prisons where the USA and its allies were holding prisoners, and increasing US use of 'extraordinary rendition' – where suspected terrorists are captured covertly in third countries by US intelligence or security agencies and secretly transferred out of those countries – further reinforced perceptions that the USA was operating outside the bounds of international law. For many Europeans, these elements of America's 'war on terror' not only represented a serious challenge to global human rights norms, but were also likely to be counter-productive in addressing terrorism, since they reinforced the perception in the non-Western world of a hypocritical USA (and wider West, including Europe) willing to abuse human rights and flout international law in its anti-terrorist campaign.

These legal and human rights dimensions of the US 'war on terror' also had a number of more specific European dimensions. In a number of cases, European citizens were held at Guantanamo Bay or other similar US facilities and/or were the subject of extraordinary renditions; European governments then faced pressure to secure the release of these prisoners, placing these governments in a political quandary, since whether such citizens were terrorists was often uncertain, the circumstances surrounding their detention were opaque, and governments were reluctant to confront the USA. In some cases, European governments persuaded the USA to release such prisoners, but in others these European citizens remained under US detention. European governments have also been accused of complicity in the Bush administration's use of extraordinary rendition and maintenance of a network of secret prisons for detainees, both by allowing aircraft involved in rendition to stop at airports and by the establishment of prisons in some countries (specifically, Lithuania, Macedonia, Poland and Romania). Both the Council of Europe and the European Parliament undertook investigations of these issues, but the full details remain unclear and are the subject of ongoing controversy.

Despite the various tensions between Europe and America over the Bush administration's 'war on terror', European governments and in particular the EU also agreed a range of new counter-terrorism measures with the USA after 9/11– see Box 8.2 (see also Rees, 2006). The willingness of the EU to agree these various measures of co-operation with the USA reflected the recognition that the two parties face a common terrorist threat, but also the more general political and strategic importance of the USA for Europe.

While European governments and the EU have generally supported counter-terrorism co-operation with the USA, some of the centrepiece measures proposed or agreed have proved to be controversial within Europe. An EU–US agreement on extradition procedures was held up by concerns that persons extradited to and tried in the USA might be subject to the death penalty, and the agreement was only approved by the EU in 2003 on condition that EU member states retained the right to make extradition conditional on US agreement that the death penalty would not be imposed. The issue of the transfer to the USA of passenger name records (PNR) data relating to flights into and out of the USA and held by European airlines has been the subject of ongoing controversy because of concerns over the adequacy of US data protection measures and possible abuse of the data (Archik, 2011, pp. 9–12). The transfer of PNR data was introduced on a provisional basis in

---

Box 8.2   US–EU counter-terrorism co-operation post-9/11

- Cabinet and working level contacts between EU and US officials: includes six-monthly meeting of senior officials to discuss police and judicial co-operation against terrorism, dialogue on terrorist financing, high-level policy dialogue on border and transport security and, since 2010, dialogues on critical infrastructure protection and resilience and on preventing violent extremism.
- EU–US Agreement on Extradition: facilitates extradition between the USA and the EU through an alleviation of legalization and certification requirements and the speeding up of extradition processes; signed at June 2003 EU–US Summit; entered into force in 2010 after relevant parliamentary/legislature approval.
- EU–US Agreement on Mutual Legal Assistance: gives law enforcement agencies access to bank accounts in the EU and the USA for investigations of serious crimes, including terrorism, organized crime and financial crime; allows for Joint Investigative Teams; signed at June 2003 EU–US Summit; entered into force in 2010 after relevant parliamentary/legislature approval.
- Transfer of personal name records (PNR) data: transfer of PNR data held by European airlines to US authorities has taken place on a provisional basis since 2002; the search for a permanent agreement on the issue has, however, been problematic.
- Customs and Border Protection (CBP): co-operation introduced on a provisional basis in 2002; US–EU agreement approved by EU Council of Ministers in May 2004.
- Europol–US co-operation: December 2001 agreement on exchange of strategic and technical information; December 2002 agreement on exchange of personal data; US/European liaison officers based at the headquarters of Europol and of the Federal Bureau of Investigation (FBI).
- Eurojust–US co-operation: contacts established between Eurojust and the USA in relation to investigation and prosecution of terrorists.
- Transport and border security: dialogue on strengthening of aviation and air and maritime cargo security; 2004 customs co-operation agreement includes commitment to extend US Container Security Initiative (CSI – involving pre-screening of all maritime containers travelling to the USA); 2008 agreement on co-ordinating air cargo security measures.

Sources: Data from European Union (2003c, 2005a); and (Archik 2011).

2002. A formal EU–US agreement was concluded in 2004, but the European Parliament lodged a case against the agreement and the EU's European Court of Justice annulled the agreement in 2006 on the basis that it had not been negotiated on the proper legal basis. A new agreement was concluded in 2007, but in 2010 the European Parliament refused to ratify it. A further new agreement was concluded in 2011, but this too was criticized for inadequately protecting EU citizens' rights (Travis, 2011). A further controversial issue has been US access to financial data on international bank transfers via the SWIFT (Society for Worldwide Interbank Financial Telecommunications) system, based in Belgium. In 2006 it was revealed that the US had been granted access to SWIFT data since 2001. Following this, EU–US agreements on continued US access to SWIFT data were agreed in 2007 and 2009. In February 2010 the European Parliament refused to ratify the 2009 SWIFT agreement because of concerns over data protection and privacy, but in July the Parliament approved the agreement after the USA addressed some its concerns (Archik, 2011, pp. 7–8). Underlying these various differences are a US perception that Europe is still sometimes reluctant to take adequate counter-terrorism measures and a European view that the USA is sometimes insufficiently concerned about citizens' rights and in particular is unwilling to extend to EU citizens the guarantees of rights in areas such as data protection that it provides to its own citizens.

The advent of the Obama administration in 2009 reduced much of the transatlantic tension of counter-terrorism that had followed the Bush administration's 'war on terror'. The Obama administration's dropping of the language of the 'war on terror', commitment in principle to close the Guantanamo Bay detention centre, closure of the network of secret US prisons associated with the expanded use of extraordinary rendition and abandonment of Bush-era 'enhanced interrogation techniques' were all broadly welcomed in Europe. Transatlantic co-operation may therefore in future become more part of the normal, everyday operational co-operation of low politics as part of European counter-terrorism policies (Aldritch, 2009). Nevertheless, as the debates over issues such as access to SWIFT and PNR data indicate, US–European differences are also likely to remain. Furthermore, where specific issues of counter-terrorism policy towards key countries arise, more political policy disputes may also be likely – as is discussed below in relation to Afghanistan and Pakistan.

Europe's Islamic population: an internal terrorist threat?

The July 2005 London bombings made clear that Islamic terrorism poses not only an external threat to Europe but also an internal one of terrorist attack by citizens (or other long-term residents) of European states. Combined with a growing European Muslim population and intensifying socio-cultural tensions between Muslims and majority populations in European countries, the emergence of European *jihadi* terrorism prompted growing concerns over an increasingly troubled relationship between Europe and its Islamic minority. Some observers even warned of the possible emergence of a 'Eurabia': an anti-Western Islamic-dominated Europe more like the Middle East than the modern Europe that was hitherto known (*The Economist*, 2006a and 2006b).

Table 8.1 summarizes the number of Muslims in Europe (the exact numbers are disputed because of the limitations of censuses and other sources of data, but the table provides a reasonable estimate). As can be seen, there are about 49 million Muslims in Europe (excluding Turkey, the overwhelming majority of whose population of 73 million are Muslim, as well as the Caucasus and Central Asia, where Azerbaijan, Kazakhstan, Kyrgyzstan, Tajikistan, Turkmenistan and Uzbekistan are predominantly Muslim countries). In percentage terms the Western Balkans has the highest proportion of Muslims (nearly 30 per cent of the region's population), reflecting the fact that Albania and Kosovo are overwhelmingly Muslim and Bosnia-Herzegovina and Macedonia have large Muslim populations. Russia has the largest Muslim minority – 22 million people or nearly 16 per cent of its population. In the Western European EU member states there are over 17 million Muslims or about 4.5 per cent of the population, with France, Germany, the United Kingdom and Spain having the largest Muslim minorities. In percentage terms, France's and Belgium's Muslim minorities are the largest in Western Europe at nearly 10 per cent and 6 per cent respectively.

Europe's Muslim population, especially that in the EU, is predicted to grow in the next few decades, in absolute terms but in particular as a proportion of total EU population. These trends reflect a number of factors: low birth rates and projected population decline among the general European population, a relatively higher population growth rate among the Muslim population and likely future Muslim immigration into Western Europe. Estimates of Europe's future Muslim population are, however, controversial. Some estimates suggest that Muslims could make up a quarter of France's population by 2025, and possibly even a majority in France and elsewhere in Western Europe by 2050 (Savage, 2004, p. 28; Sendagorta, 2005, p. 69). Such estimates are, however, alarmist, based on maximalist assumptions about population decline in the general population, birth rates among the Muslim

TABLE 8.1   *Europe's Muslim population (2010)*

Region/Country	Total population (mn)	Muslims (mn)	Muslims as % of total population
EU 15[1]	388.14	17.56	4.52
CEE 10[2]	102.41	1.05	1.02
EU 27[3]	490.95	18.61	3.79
Western Balkans[4]	24.67	7.28	29.49
Europe[5]	727.17	48.96	6.73
Belgium	10.42	0.63	6.11
France	64.41	6.29	9.77
Germany	82.29	3.49	4.24
Greece	10.75	0.43	4.01
Netherlands	16.78	0.97	5.80
Russia	139.39	22.08	15.84
Spain	40.55	1.14	2.82
Sweden	9.07	0.51	5.57
Switzerland	7.63	0.32	4.26
United Kingdom	61.28	2.45	4.00

Notes: [1] 15 EU members up to 2004
[2] 10 Central and Eastern European states that joined EU in 2004–07 (does not include Cyprus and Malta)
[3] EU post-2004 (figures do not include Cyprus)
[4] Albania, Bosnia-Herzegovina, Croatia, Kosovo, Macedonia, Montenegro and Serbia
[5] Includes Russia, excludes Turkey and the Caucasus and Central Asia

Source: Data from Kettani (2009).

population and immigration (Underhill, 2009). While it seems likely that Muslims will be a growing minority of Europe's population in coming decades, the idea of a Muslim-dominated 'Eurabia', let alone a Europe in which Muslims would be a majority, is deeply misleading.

Nevertheless, socio-economic and political tensions between Europe's majority population and its Islamic minority are real. Relations between Europe's long-standing population and its Islamic minorities are complicated by problems of economic marginalization, ghettoization and socio-cultural conflict. In general, Muslims within the EU are economically worse off than non-Muslims, and concentrated in urban centres, often located within the most disadvantaged neighbourhoods of large cities. Incipient, if not overt, racism in Europe's majority population often results in immigrants, refugees, asylum seekers,

Muslims and non-whites being conflated in the popular consciousness into a threatening 'other'. There are also real tensions between 'European' liberalism and secularism and (some) Islamic attitudes to freedom of speech, individual freedom, gender and sexuality. Whether through exclusion by the majority population, choice by the Islamic population or as a consequence of other socio-economic trends, Muslims have to varying degrees come to form separate, parallel communities within European societies rather than integrating fully into those societies. In recent years, these various dynamics have resulted in, but also been reinforced by, a series of controversial incidents: the French government's 2003 decision to ban Muslim women from wearing headscarves in schools, the murder of the Dutch filmmaker Theo van Gogh by a Muslim extremist in 2004, violent disturbances in predominantly immigrant areas of France in late 2005, and the publication of cartoons depicting the Prophet Muhammad as a terrorist by a Danish newspaper in 2006.

Against this background, it is hardly surprising that many within Europe's Islamic population are alienated from the societies in which they live, nor perhaps that some turn to violence. Analysts argue that conflicts and Western interventions in the Islamic world have played a catalytic role in radicalizing elements within the European Islamic community: French support for the abandonment of democracy in Algeria after the Islamic Salvation Front (FIS) won elections in that country in 1992 played an important role in the Islamic terrorism that France faced in the 1990s; the conflicts in Palestine, Kashmir and Chechnya have become lightning rods for Islamic discontent; and the Spanish and British governments' support for the US intervention in Iraq was arguably an important factor behind the Madrid and London bombings. The extent of support among European Muslims for radical views, and more specifically for terrorism, is difficult to gauge. A 2004 survey of British Muslims found that, while the overwhelming majority (73 per cent) strongly opposed terrorist attacks by al-Qaeda and other organizations, a significant minority (13 per cent) believed further such attacks on the USA would be justified (Travis, 2004). Studies in Germany and the Netherlands have suggested that 5–10 per cent of the Muslim population sympathize with radical Islamic views (Sendagorta, 2005, p. 65). European counter-terrorism officials estimate that 1–2 per cent of the continent's Muslims – 250,000 to 500,000 people – are involved in some type of extremist activity (Savage, 2004, pp. 31–3). Even if only a very small proportion of Europe's Muslims might actually participate in or operationally support terrorism, the scale of the continent's Islamic population is nevertheless such that this provides a significant pool of potential terrorists.

The recognition that Europe faced a significant internal terrorist threat from within its own Islamic communities led European governments to re-orient counter-terrorism, intelligence and policing efforts away from longer-standing ethno-national terrorist groups (such as the IRA and ETA) and towards the new threat from Islamic terrorism within Europe. In the longer term, however, addressing the terrorist threat from within European Islam will depend not only on counter-terrorism, intelligence and police responses but also, and arguably more, on the degree to which Europe succeeds in integrating its growing Muslim population into its societies. Since 1945, European states have been divided between two broad approaches to integrating immigrant communities. The integrationist or assimilationist approach, of which France is viewed as the archetype, encourages and to some degree requires immigrants to adopt and adapt to their new society's existing values, culture and identity. The multicultural approach, symbolized by the UK, accepts and to some extent supports the development of multiple cultural identities. The increasing alienation of Europe's Islamic communities and the emergence of *jihadi* terrorism from within those communities, however, suggest that both approaches have failed in important ways. British-style multiculturalism has resulted in the emergence of separate, parallel societies and allowed extremism ('Londonistan') to flourish within parts of those societies. In the early 2010s, both German Chancellor Angela Merkel and British Prime Minister David Cameron made prominent speeches arguing that multiculturalism had failed and that their countries need to place a greater emphasis on integration and the affirmation of liberal values (Connolly, 2010; BBC News, 2011a). French-style integrationism has, however, also failed to truly integrate Islamic minorities, instead resulting in the marginalization and resentment that produced the violent riots of late 2005. The failure of both the integrationist and multicultural models suggests that a new approach to integration is needed, perhaps one that combines acceptance of certain core values (such as democracy and freedom of speech) with a recognition of distinctive cultures. More also arguably needs to be done to address the economic marginalization of Europe's Muslim populations.

Growing concern about indigenous Islamic terrorism also produced a new debate on what became referred to as radicalization, with research efforts to identify what factors lead people to adopt extremist views and governments initiating policies to counter such extremism (Neumann, 2008). In 2005 the European Union adopted a *Strategy for Combating Radicalization and Recruitment to Terrorism* (European Union, 2005b). The EU's strategy called for limiting the activities of those promoting radicalization in places of education and worship, greater efforts to prevent people receiving terrorist training, empowering moderate voices within European Islam, and addressing structural factors that support radicalization by targeting inequalities and discrimination.

If the 9/11, Madrid and London terrorist attacks prompted growing concern (and sometimes alarmist warnings) about the potential terrorist threat posed by Europe's Muslim population in the early and mid-2000s, by the late 2000s and early 2010s such fears were beginning to fade (Burke and Traynor, 2009). The absence of further major terrorist attacks and the failure of terrorists to gain mass support amongst Europe's Muslim population reinforced the point that supporters of terrorism were a very small minority amongst Europe's Muslim population. The July 2011 Oslo terrorist attacks, further, starkly illustrated that Europe faced a terrorist threat not only from Islamic extremism but also from right-wing anti-Islamic extremism.

Tensions between Europe and its Islamic population, and the threat of European Islamic terrorism, are nevertheless real problems. Alienation and discontent within Europe's Muslim communities and the sense of threat felt by Europe's majority populations create the risk of a vicious circle of escalating conflict that might be difficult to break. In the worst case, this could result in a deeply polarized division between the old ethnically 'white' Europe and Europe's newer Islamic population, endemic civil strife and increasingly widespread terrorism. Intensifying conflict between Europe and its Islamic communities should not, however, be viewed as inevitable. European Islam is a far from homogeneous entity: it is divided between different branches of the Islamic faith (Sunnis, Shias and others), immigrants and their descendants from many different countries, and people in diverse socio-economic situations. While there may be growing discontent within Europe's Islamic communities, the majority of European Muslims have not rejected the core European values of individual freedom and democracy, nor do they support terrorism. The current debates over terrorism, security and identity, further, are leading at least some within European Islam to engage not in terrorism but in more traditional forms of political activity and social dialogue – exactly the kind of integration that may be necessary if a new modus vivendi is to be found between Europe and its Muslim communities (*The Economist*, 2006b, p. 34). Equally, although xenophobia may be on the rise in Europe, many people in old, 'white' Europe reject such views and are searching for new means of engaging with their Islamic fellow citizens. In short, there is a struggle within Europe between forces pushing Europe and its Islamic communities towards conflict and forces that might integrate Muslims successfully into mainstream European society. This struggle involves large questions of national and European identity, and its outcome will have a significant bearing on Europe's future. It may also have a significant impact on the relationship between Islam and the West at the global level. Intensifying conflict between Europe and its Islamic communities will reinforce the view elsewhere in the Islamic world that the West is irredeemably anti-Islamic and that Muslims have little alternative but to use violent means to defend themselves. In contrast, the successful integration of Europe's Muslim minority will provide a powerful illustration of the possibility of a peaceful relationship between Islam and the West. The emergence of a new European Islam that combines the Muslim faith with the values of liberalism and democracy might also be an influential exemplar of how these two sets of values can coexist elsewhere in the Islamic world.

Counter-terrorism II: foreign policy and the root causes of terrorism

The rise of global Islamic terrorism prompted debate on the underlying causes of terrorism and how these may be addressed. The EU's 2005 counter-terrorism strategy document lists prevention as one of four key strands of counter-terrorism policy, alongside protection, pursuit of terrorists and responding in the event of terrorist attacks. According to the EU strategy the aim is '(T)o prevent people turning to terrorism by tackling the factors or root causes which can lead to radicalisation and recruitment, in Europe *and internationally*' (European Union, 2005c, p. 3, emphasis added). In practice, however, most European thinking and policy in this area has focused on countering radicalization within Europe rather than addressing the root causes of terrorism globally.

EU policies towards the Mediterranean and the Middle East since the 1990s may be viewed as part of efforts to counter terrorism by encouraging reform within these countries and co-operation between them and Europe. As was noted in Chapter 4, however, the EU had at best limited success in promoting these objectives in the 1990s and

2000s and the EU response to the Arab Spring has been a modest one. The long-term outcome of the Arab Spring may have a very significant impact on underlying patterns of terrorism: successful transitions which allow the forces of political Islam to become a peaceful part of democratic societies may help to undermine terrorism; in contrast, failed transitions involving either the seizure of sole power by radical Islamic forces or the repression of political Islamic by military or other authoritarian forces may breed further terrorism. While European states and the EU may be able to quietly support democratic transitions in North Africa and the Middle East, it is unlikely that they will have a decisive impact on the success or failure of these transitions.

At the global level also, many aspects of European foreign policy may be viewed as part of overall efforts to address the root causes of terrorism. For some decades, Europe (in terms of the EU member states plus the separate aid programmes of the EU) has been the leading provider of economic aid to the developing world. To the extent that poverty and economic underdevelopment are viewed as important underlying causes of terrorism, Europe thus plays a leading role in international efforts to tackle these problems. European development policies and their relationship with security are examined in more detail in the next chapter. It should be noted here, however, that while Europe is relatively generous as an aid provider, it has been much more reluctant to open its markets to goods from the developing world, and subsidies to European agriculture and industry mean that the developing world does not compete with European agriculture and industry on a level playing field. If Europe is serious about using development policy as a strategic means of addressing poverty as a root cause of terrorism, there is a powerful case that it should do much more to address the difficult economic issues of market access for goods from the developing world *vis-à-vis* European agricultural and industrial subsidies.

European states and the EU also play a prominent role in international efforts to address another challenge that some analysts view as a key part of the context for globalized Islamic terrorism: civil wars and failed states. Since the 1990s, the EU has developed a growing interest and role in the area of conflict prevention. In 2001, the Union adopted an *EU Programme for the Prevention of Violent Conflicts* (European Union, 2001a). Within this context, the EU has sought both to pay greater attention to conflict prevention (for example, through the development of detailed conflict prevention Country Strategy Papers focusing on countries that have experienced, or may be particularly

---

Box 8.3   Europe and the 'AfPak' problem

When it came to power in 2009 the Obama administration used the term 'AfPak' to describe Afghanistan and Pakistan, reflecting its view that the two countries were at the centre of the problem of global terrorism and constituted a single inter-linked problem (not suprisingly, Pakistan's government disliked being lumped in with Afghanistan and strongly opposed the term). In this context, the Obama administration significantly increased the US military presence in Afghanistan and escalated drone (unmanned aerial vehicle) attacks on reported terrorist targets in Pakistan. Some analysts, further, argued that Pakistan – with its own extremist Islamic groups and intelligence and military services who have been accused of supporting these Islamic extremists – rather than Afghanistan was really at the heart of the problem of globalized Islamic extremism.

European governments supported the USA in Afghanistan by providing forces for the NATO-led International Security Assistance Force (ISAF). In some cases, such as the UK, this reflected genuine support for the US-dominated operation. Other states, such as France and Germany, were sceptical of the operation and contributed forces largely to avoid a serious rupture within NATO.

Although European governments were to varying degrees critical of the US approach, they failed to articulate or advance an alternative European 'AfPak' strategy. In Afghanistan, European governments placed a greater emphasis than the USA on nation-building and on the possibility of negotiation with the Taliban, but were unable to substantively advance either agenda. On Pakistan, European governments were wary of the Obama administration's drone war – fearing that it risked alienating and radicalizing Pakistan's population and government – but did not advanced an alternative strategy. As was noted in Chapter 6, by 2011–12 both the USA and its European allies were looking for the exit door in Afghanistan, with most NATO combat forces due to be withdrawn by 2014.

---

vulnerable to, violent conflict), and on mainstreaming conflict prevention in its wider relations with third countries (by trying to ensure that political, trade, aid, environmental and other aspects of these relations take into account their impact on potential conflicts). A number of European governments, such as those of Sweden and the UK, have also sought to promote conflict prevention (Swedish Ministry for Foreign Affairs, 1999; Foreign and Commonwealth Office, 2003; Department for International Development, 2004). The case of Afghanistan and Pakistan, however, illustrates the difficulty of implementing a distinctively European approach to conflict prevention – see Box 8.3.

Addressing the root causes of terrorism is inherently problemati-cal. Our understanding of the causes of terrorism is limited and the question of what factors lie behind the emergence of globalized Islamic terrorism is deeply contentious. Even if it is correct that conflicts in the Islamic world, failed states and economic underdevelopment are the underlying causes of globalized Islamic terrorism, these are very large, long-term problems that will not be addressed easily. Europe's ability to influence, let alone resolve, these problems is limited, and whether European leaders and publics are willing to provide the resources and take the difficult political decisions necessary to address these prob-lems is open to serious doubt. While European governments may be correct to argue that the international community should do more to tackle the long-term causes of terrorism, translating that desire into effective action is likely to remain extremely challenging.

Conclusion

After the 9/11 terrorist attacks, some, especially in the USA, viewed terrorism as *the* primary security challenge of the 21st century and the 'war on terror' as likely to be the defining global conflict for decades to come. In this context, Europe, with its large Islamic minority popula-tions, might *in extremis* have become something like a large version of Israel: an entire region facing a semi-permanent and all-pervasive high level of terrorist threat. From the perspective of a decade later, this view seems exaggerated: terrorism is only one of a range of security chal-lenges facing Western societies and, as discussed in Chapter 2, the longer-term defining feature of 21st century global politics is likely to be the rise of the non-West. Although European states face a continu-ing threat from terrorists of various kinds, that threat is closer to terrorist threats that European states have faced in the past: a serious and ongoing threat requiring a significant intelligence and security response, but also a threat that is limited in scale, cannot be definitively defeated and societies have little choice but to live with it.

European states and the EU, nevertheless, face major dilemmas in responding to the threat posed by globalized Islamic terrorism. The various internal and external security measures that European states have undertaken – nationally, collectively through the EU, and together with the USA – have reopened the long-standing debate on the balance between security and liberty, and calibrating that balance will be an ongoing challenge for governments and publics alike. Europe also faces major challenges in integrating its growing Muslim population: the limitations of both the assimilationist and the multicultural models suggest that a new approach is needed, but the debate on this question will involve fundamental issues of national and European identity.

The external, foreign policy dimension of counter-terrorism also poses major challenges for Europe. While addressing the root causes of terrorism, both in general and in specific contexts such as Afghanistan and Pakistan, is a laudable goal, determining what this requires and how it may be achieved is far more problematic. Although European states and the EU can perhaps claim to contribute to addressing some of the root causes of terrorism through their development aid and peacekeeping policies, they have yet to articulate a truly strategic approach to countering the causes of terrorism at the global level.

Chapter 9

Non-Military Security

As discussed in Chapter 2, there has since the 1980s been a growing recognition that non-military threats should be viewed as part of the security agenda. This redefinition of the concept of security has two elements. First, it is increasingly recognized that while military means are central to war, the underlying causes of war and large-scale violent conflict are largely non-military, relating to political conflicts, economics and the environment. Second, non-military problems such as economic instability, environmental degradation and organized crime are increasingly viewed, in themselves, as major threats to the security of states and societies. The primary European security organizations have accepted the logic behind this new, wider security agenda and have to varying degrees been at the forefront of efforts to respond to the challenges it poses. Since it was established in the 1970s, the then Conference on (now Organization for) Security and Co-operation in Europe (C/OSCE) has pioneered the concept of a comprehensive security agenda, including issues such as human rights, democracy, economics and the environment. The EU's unique combination of political foreign policy co-operation, an emerging military role, justice and home affairs co-operation, and economic, social and environmental competences means that it operates across the entire spectrum of issues that constitute the wider security agenda. NATO's 2010 *Strategic Concept* also stated that:

> Instability or conflict beyond NATO borders can directly threaten Alliance security, including by fostering extremism, terrorism, and transnational illegal activities such as trafficking in arms, narcotics and people ... Key environmental and resource constraints, including health risks, climate change, water scarcity and increasing energy needs will further shape the future security environment in areas of concern to NATO and have the potential to significantly affect NATO planning and operations. (NATO, 2010a, paras 11 and 15)

There is also increasing acceptance that the best long-term means of preventing violent conflict both between and within states are through political and economic co-operation and the promotion of democracy and good governance. In this context, the EU may be viewed as an unprecedented – and remarkably successful – exercise in long-term conflict prevention, having helped to transform much of Europe into the largely peaceful security community of the early 21st century. The EU is thus the leader and archetype of this new approach to security building, and it is no coincidence that other regional organizations – the Association of South East Asian Nations (ASEAN), the Southern Common Market (MERCOSUR) and the African Union (AU), for example – have to varying degrees sought to model themselves on the EU.

Although increasingly accepted by governments and international organizations, the concept of a wider, non-military security agenda is not unproblematical. The nature of the wider security agenda is amorphous: what does or does not constitute a security issue is unclear, as is the point at which a problem becomes (or should be viewed as) a security threat rather than simply a part of normal politics. Defining a particular challenge – climate change, say, or organized crime – as a security threat or challenge, does not necessarily make any difference to the nature of that challenge, nor even perhaps to the way societies respond to it. The definition of an issue as a security threat or challenge – the process of securitization (Buzan *et al.*, 1998) – may also have negative consequences, importing undesirable security dynamics into previously non-security areas by encouraging a defensive fortress-type response.

From a European perspective, a number of non-military security challenges have gained particular prominence since the end of the Cold War:

- *Economics and development policy*: over the last two to three decades there has been a growing recognition that development policy (efforts to help the world's poorest countries to develop economically and to address global poverty) cannot be separated from security. Many of the world's poorest countries are also amongst the most conflict-prone states in the world: economic problems make countries more likely to succumb to violent conflict; violent conflict severely retards the prospects for successful economic development; the result is a 'conflict trap' where countries are caught in a mutually reinforcing cycle of conflict and underdevelopment (Collier *et al.*, 2003). As a result, addressing violent conflict has become a growing component of European and global development policy.

- *Environment*: the 1986 Chernobyl nuclear accident highlighted the vulnerability of European states to environmental threats such as radioactive pollution from nuclear accidents. Since then, the environment has become a major political issue across Europe. Most prominent on this new environmental security agenda is climate change, with increasing recognition both that the consequences of climate change may pose major security threats in themselves and that climate change may increase the likelihood of violent conflict in a number of countries and regions.
- *Population movements*: since the 1980s there has been growing concern in much of Europe about immigration. The issue has become increasingly 'securitized', with various politicians, elements of the media and political/social movements, particularly on the right of the political spectrum, viewing immigration as a security problem or threat that requires radical remedial action.
- *Energy security*: energy security first emerged as a major concern for the West in the wake of the 1973 Arab–Israeli war, when the major Middle Eastern oil suppliers cut off oil exports to the West, triggering a major global economic crisis. Over time, although the problem of dependence on Middle Eastern oil remained, concern over energy security subsided. In the 2000s, however, increasing dependence on gas and oil imports from Russia, combined with high global gas and oil prices, moved energy security to the fore once again. EU member states are particularly vulnerable to the consequences of energy (in)security because they have very few indigenous oil or gas reserves. Disruptions of Russian gas supplies to Ukraine and Belarus in the late 2000s highlighted the issue, especially because of knock-on effects on a number of Central and Eastern European EU member states who depend on gas supplied via the pipelines in Ukraine and Belarus.
- *Organized crime*: some European states have longed faced particular problems with organized crime, such as Italy with regard to the mafia. In the wake of the collapse of communism, however, organized criminality emerged as a major feature of economy, society and politics in the eastern half of the European continent. The problem, further, has a significant transnational dimension, with criminal activity flowing across state borders – in various forms such as drugs, arms and human trafficking – and thereby impinging not just on the eastern half of Europe but also on Western Europe.

• *Cyber security*: the widespread use of information technology (computers and the internet) in almost all aspects of modern, (post-) industrial societies has created a new security problem: vulnerability to cyber attacks. The reality of this threat was made clear in 2007 when Estonia suffered a large-scale cyber attack that brought down the websites and information infrastructure of many of its state institutions and major businesses – the attack was widely suspected (but never proven) as having been orchestrated by the Russian authorities. Since then, European states, NATO and the EU have undertaken major initiatives to strengthen their cyber defences.

Even if the widening of the security agenda to include a range of non-military challenges is sensible, the policy challenges of responding to the wider security agenda are very large indeed. Problems such as global poverty, economic instability, environmental degradation, weak states, mass migration and organized crime have deep roots and are not easily addressed. Addressing the wider security agenda is thus a massive, long-term challenge: a decades-long task requiring the mobilization of global political will and large-scale material resources. This chapter focuses on three key non-military security issues – economic development policy, climate change and migration – and explores European engagement with these challenges.

Economic development policy

Economic underdevelopment and poverty are arguably at the heart of the new, wider security agenda. Economic underdevelopment and poverty contribute to the internal weakness of many states, civil wars and larger North–South tensions. As the EU's 2003 *European Security Strategy* put it:

> In much of the developing world, poverty and disease cause untold suffering and give rise to pressing security concerns. Almost 3 billion people, half the world's population, live on less than 2 Euros a day. 45 million die every year of hunger and malnutrition ... In many cases, economic failure is linked to political problems and violent conflict ... A number of countries and regions are caught in a cycle of conflict, insecurity and poverty. (European Union, 2003a)

Similarly, the Union's *European Consensus on Development*, adopted in 2005 as the framework for EU development policy, argued that:

The context within which poverty eradication is pursued is an increasingly globalized world; this situation has created new opportunities but also new challenges. Combating global poverty is not only a moral obligation; it will also help to build a more stable, peaceful, prosperous and equitable world, reflecting the interdependency of its richer and poorer countries ... without development and poverty eradication no sustainable peace will occur. (European Union, 2005d, pp. 3 and 12)

Europe, in particular the EU, is a key player in international economic development policy. The EU – considered as its member states plus the European Commission, which runs a separate EU development aid programme – is the largest donor of economic development to aid poor countries, providing over half of all development aid. Table 9.1 indicates levels of overseas development aid (ODA – the most widely used official definition of aid) provided by the main developed countries (the members of the Organisation for Economic Co-operation and Development (OECD) Development Assistance Committee (DAC)) since the 1990s. As can be seen from the table, the EU-15 states (the 'old' member states of the EU, not including the countries which joined in 2004 and are not DAC members) have provided about half (or more) of total ODA since the 1990s (the total EU figure is higher if the 'new' EU members are added and because the figures do not include the separate aid programme run by the European Commission). In terms of ODA as a percentage of donors' gross national income (GNI) – one of the main ways of comparing aid – the average for the EU-15 was 0.45 per cent of GNI in 2009–10, compared to 0.21 per cent for the USA and 0.19 per cent for Japan. This reflects a long-term trend, with Europe having supplied about 40 per cent of development aid since the 1970s and the previously higher US share having declined (Organisation for Economic Co-operation and Development, 2011a, Figure B.3, 222).

While the EU may be more generous as an aid provider than the USA and Japan, the EU's generosity should not be exaggerated. Since 1969–70, developed countries have, in theory, been committed to achieving a target of 0.7 per cent of GNI for aid – a target they have consistently failed to meet. While a small number of European states (Denmark, Luxembourg, the Netherlands, Norway and Sweden) have

TABLE 9.1 European, Japanese and US contributions to development aid

	Volume of net ODA (mn US$ at 2009 prices and exchange rates)			Share of total DAC ODA (% at current prices and exchange rate)			ODA as percentage of GNI (two-year averages, net disbursements)		
	1989–90	1999–2000	2009–10	1989–90	1999–2000	2009–10	1989–90	1999–2000	2009–10
EU-15	44,189	41,653	69,236	52.5	48.4	55.1	0.38	0.32	0.45
Japan	12,604	13,635	10,020	18.0	23.9	8.3	0.28	0.27	0.19
USA	14,702	11,931	29,440	19.1	17.8	23.8	0.14	0.10	0.21
Total DAC	80,291	76,412	123,539	100.0	100.0	100.0	0.27	0.22	0.32

Notes:
ODA = overseas development aid; DAC = (members of) OECD Development Assistance Committee; DAC also includes other states.
EU-15 = Austria, Belgium, Denmark, Finland, France, Germany, Greece, Ireland, Italy, Luxembourg, Netherlands, Portugal, Spain, Sweden and United Kingdom.

Source: Data from Organisation for Economic Co-operation and Development (2011a) Statistical Annex (table 9, Long-term Trends in DAC ODA).

met this target, the majority of EU member states have not come close to it, nor has the EU as a whole. Furthermore, according to EURODAD (European Network on Debt and Development, a coalition of European non-governmental development organizations):

> The figures they are officially reporting are misleading because they are inflated by imputed non-aid items such as debt relief, or costs for refugees and students from developing countries in Europe. Moreover, the majority of all contracts in EU-funded development projects go to European firms and consultants. Consequently, much European aid never flows to developing countries in the first place, and an additional share quickly flows back to Europe rather than promoting development and fighting poverty in the South. Most worryingly, while the European treaties clearly state that poverty eradication is the goal of European aid, aid allocation is in fact largely distorted by other foreign policy interests, in particular security and foreign trade. (EURODAD, nd)

Since the late 1990s there has been increasing debate on international development policy and economic aid. In 2000, the UN adopted the Millennium Development Goals (MDGs), a set of core development targets – including, for example, reducing by half the proportion of people living on less than one dollar a day, reducing by half the proportion of people who suffer hunger, and reducing by two-thirds the mortality rate for children under five – to be achieved by 2015. In the context of the MDGs, the EU significantly increased its development aid. In 2005 the EU committed to a major increase in ODA to 0.7 per cent of GNI for the fifteen 'old' EU member states by 2015, and 0.33 per cent of GNI for the ten states that joined the EU in 2004. By the late 2000s/early 2010s significant progress had been made in meeting some of the MDGs, but it was clear that the overall objectives would not be met. Although EU-15 aid as a percentage of GNI had increased from 0.32 per cent in 1999–2000 to 0.45 per cent in 2009–10 (see Table 9.1), it was clear that the EU-15 were unlikely to meet the 0.7 per cent target by 2015.

Parallel to the debate on aid since the 1990s has been a new debate about the relationship between trade and economic (under)development in poor countries. Most economists agree that trade liberalization – the reciprocal removal of barriers to free trade between states – promotes economic growth and development. In this context, the developed states of the world – the EU, but also the USA, Japan,

Canada and Australia – have been subject to growing criticism regarding their protectionist trade practices towards developing countries, and in particular their use of subsidies to support agriculture (which means that developing countries do not compete on a level playing field) and trade barriers (which undermine the ability of poor countries to export goods to the developed world). It is estimated that the protectionist trade policies of developed countries cost poor countries over US$100bn a year – twice what they receive in aid. Although all developing countries practise such protectionist policies, Oxfam estimates that of the 'quad' of major industrialized countries – the USA, the EU, Japan and Canada – the EU is marginally the most protectionist (Oxfam International, 2002, pp. 8–9, 96–101). In short, while the EU may be comparatively generous as a donor of development aid, there is a powerful argument that whatever good is done by European aid is undermined by European trade protectionism on an even larger scale.

The international response to growing criticism of developed countries' protectionism was the Doha development round of World Trade Organization (WTO) negotiations, launched in Doha, Qatar, in 2001. One of the central aims of the Doha round is to extend trade liberalization into the areas of greatest benefit to poor countries, in particular by removing tariffs and reducing subsidies in agriculture and textiles. The Doha round of WTO negotiations was thus a key test of multilateral trade liberalization as a means of benefiting the poorer countries of the world. More than a decade after the Doha round was launched, however, no agreement has been concluded – nor does such an agreement appear likely in the short to medium term at least. The Doha round of WTO negotiations is extremely complex and the reasons for the lack of progress are contentious; nevertheless, one underlying factor has been the reluctance of the developing world, in particular the EU and the USA, to agree to reduce trade barriers and make far-reaching cuts in subsidies in relation to agriculture and textiles (Elliott, 2006).

The EU has, however, undertaken a number of other initiatives designed to support developing countries by removing or reducing EU protectionist measures and to increase the ability of these states to benefit from the international trade system. In 2001 the EU agreed an Everything But Arms (EBA) policy, designed to eliminate all tariffs on imports from the world's least developed countries (LDCs). In 2006 the EU introduced a GSP+ scheme providing reduced import tariffs for those developing countries implementing core international conventions on human rights, labour rights, environmental protection and good governance (the Generalized System of Tariff Preferences or GSP is the system, within the WTO, under which states are permitted to offer lower import tariffs to developing states than they do to other countries). In 2007 the EU also introduced an Aid for Trade (AfT) strategy, providing financial and technical assistance to developing countries to enable them to participate in and benefit from international trade. Although the specific impact of these individual policies may be limited, they nevertheless appear to be helping to create the circumstances under which LDCs can expand their exports and begin to develop by integrating themselves into the world economy (Faber and Orbie, 2009).

These debates on development and trade have in turn prompted growing discussion about the EU's Common Agricultural Policy (CAP). The CAP supports European agriculture, through a variety of subsidies, to the tune of €55bn annually (about 40 per cent of the EU's total budget) (European Commission, nd, 18). Critics argue that the CAP contributes to poverty in the Third World because it makes it impossible for developing-world farmers to compete with subsidized European agriculture, while the slow pace of CAP reform within the EU has been a significant obstacle to progress in the Doha WTO negotiations. Although assessing the impact of the CAP on developing countries is inherently difficult because it involves modelling exports and agricultural development if CAP did not exist, according to a 2011 paper from the UK Overseas Development Institute '(T)he main message from these models is that in many cases CAP instruments are distorting and can damage developing country economies' (Overseas Development Institute, 2011, p. 3). Since the late 1990s there has been a series of reforms to the CAP, but these have been limited in nature, not altering the underlying reality that the EU continues to subsidize European agriculture on a large scale. Some critics argue that agricultural subsidies should be phased out completely (*Guardian*, 2003). There remains strong support for the CAP, however, within some EU member states, in particular France and Germany. Reform of the CAP faces the challenge of overcoming a powerful farming lobby, as well as an emotional attachment to the countryside. Jacques Delors, French politician and president of the European Commission in the 1980s and 1990s, for example, argued that he would not sacrifice the French countryside on the altar of world trade (Charlemagne, 2003, p. 31). Given ongoing budgetary pressures, the CAP is likely to be the subject of further reforms. The extent and speed of CAP reform, however, will be a significant test of the EU's willingness to give further substance to its commitment to supporting development in poorer parts of the world.

The EU has long played a central role in international development policy, as a donor of aid, through its bilateral and multilateral relationships with the developing world and in global trade negotiations. As this brief overview has indicated, however, the EU's role and record on development is a complex and contradictory one: the EU is the world's largest donor of economic aid and can legitimately claim to have made a significant contribution to alleviating poverty and promoting development through such aid; at the same time, large parts of European aid are tied, thereby limiting their benefit to developing countries, while European protectionist barriers and subsidies (in particular the CAP) act as major obstacles to economic development in the developing world.

The changing global environment – the rise of the non-West, the global economic crisis since 2008 and the Arab Spring of 2011 – is also likely to have a major impact on European development policies. The economic development of China, India, Brazil and other non-Western states is resulting not only in these countries increasingly no longer needing European aid, but also in their becoming significant economic actors and aid/investment providers in their own right. In some cases, such as China's growing involvement in Africa, this is resulting in clashes with European policies, with China offering aid/investment without conditions in contrast to European (and US) conditionality linking aid to human rights and democracy. The post-2008 economic crisis, further, resulted in most (although not all) EU countries reducing their aid budgets, with development groups fearing that aid spending could fall by as much as a fifth (*Economist*, 2010a). The shifting agenda on development was reflected in European Commission policy papers on development and on trade published in 2011 and 2012. Key messages in these papers included: the need to recognize that the term 'developing countries' was increasingly irrelevant since it now embraced a large group of countries in very different circumstances; the need for the EU to focus its development policy more clearly on the poorest countries (the LDCs); the need, in the wake of the Arab Spring, for the EU to provide more support for human rights, democracy and good governance; and the need for the large emerging economies to themselves show greater reciprocity in relation to trade, including with poorer developing countries (European Commission, 2011b, 2012).

Climate change

As was noted in Chapter 2, the most important global environmental security challenge is climate change (also known as global warming or the greenhouse effect). Climate change is the net increase in the earth's temperature resulting from the increased presence of greenhouse gases (GHGs), such as carbon dioxide, methane and nitrous oxide, in the earth's atmosphere. Like a greenhouse, these gases trap heat in the atmosphere, resulting in an increase in the earth's temperature. There is a broad scientific consensus that very significant climate change is occurring, and that human activity is largely responsible. Scientists estimate that concentrations of carbon dioxide (the main greenhouse gas) in the atmosphere are now at their highest level for the last half a million years, and that the earth is warming more rapidly than at any time in at least the last thousand years. The Intergovernmental Panel on Climate Change (IPCC) – the global body co-ordinating scientific research on climate change – estimates that global temperatures rose by 0.6°C in the 20th century and may rise by between 1.4°C and 5.8°C in the 21st century (Maslin, 2004, p. 1). The agricultural and industrial bases of modern human society have caused very large-scale GHG emissions, and there is a broad scientific consensus that anthropogenic GHG emissions – emissions resulting from human activity – are largely responsible for climate change. In particular, the use of fossil fuels (oil, gas and coal) for energy production, industrial processes and transport are the primary sources of anthropogenic GHG emissions.

Climate change is likely to have – indeed, is already having – a number of major effects, most of which may either be viewed as security threats in their own right or will exacerbate other major security problems (such as new wars, mass migration and diseases). Assessing the likely impact of climate change is inherently problematic because it involves estimating (i) future GHG concentration levels in the atmosphere (which will depend on global population growth, economic growth rates and the extent to which a transition to a low/zero-carbon economic model is achieved); (ii) resultant global temperature increases; and (iii) the likely consequences of these temperature increases. Most analyses therefore consider a range of scenarios, ranging from a relatively low global temperature increase of 1.5–2°C above pre-industrial temperatures, with very significant but nonetheless limited consequences, to 5–6°C above pre-industrial temperatures, with severe and potentially catastrophic consequences for the natural environment and the human race. The likelihood of different scenarios

---

Box 9.1   The consequences of climate change

The emerging and likely future consequences of climate change include:

- Rising sea levels, which will threaten river delta-based regions and small island nations.
- Altered weather patterns, including more frequent and severe storms, hurricanes and tornadoes (resulting in a consequent increase in flooding), and more frequent and severe droughts and heatwaves.
- The spread of diseases into areas previously free from them; for example, as increased temperatures allow disease-carrying mosquitoes to move into these areas.
- Eco-system disruption and loss of species diversity as a result of climatic change.
- Disruption of agriculture as the climatic conditions and weather patterns on which it has rested alter.
- Mass migration, in particular as a result of rising sea levels but also as a consequence of other effects of climate change (such as the disruption of eco-systems and agriculture).
- Increased likelihood of environmental and resource conflicts as the effects of climate change increase competition for limited environmental and economic resources.

Sources: Data from Mark Maslin, *Global Warming: A Very Short Introduction* (Oxford: Oxford University Press, 2004), pp. 83–101; Natural Resources Defense Council (n.d.) *Consequences of Global Warming*, Natural Resources Defense Council website: http://www.nrdc.org/ globalWarming/fcons.asp (accessed 16 August 2006).

---

is a matter of debate and depends on the extent to which actions to reduce GHG emissions are taken in the next couple of decades, but most analysts suggest that a temperature increase of 1.5–2°C is already unavoidable and that a temperature increase of 3–4°C is likely unless radical reductions in GHG emissions are achieved quite soon. Box 9.1 summarizes the likely consequences of climate change.

Europe, in particular the EU region, is less vulnerable to the consequences of climate change than much of the developing world, in particular Africa and parts of Asia and South America. A 2009 study by the European Commission's scientific Joint Research Centre, for example, found that the impact of climate change on EU member states might be relatively limited (Ciscar, 2009). Nevertheless, Europe will not be immune to the impact of climate change. A European heatwave in summer 2003, which may be attributed to climate change, caused more than 20,000 deaths. A 2010 study for the OSCE found that

Box 9.2   Potential impact of climate change in the OSCE area and its periphery

- *The Arctic*: emergence/exacerbation of territorial claims and maritime border disputes; degradation of livelihoods and threats to ecosystems, impacting local indigenous communities in particular.
- *The Southern Mediterranean*: severe reduction in available food and water resources, potentially leading to economic stagnation, social dissatisfaction and grievances, and weakened authorities.
- *South-East and Eastern Europe*: threats to food and energy security; this may negatively impact on the economic and political situation.
- *South Caucasus and Central Asia*: negative impact on water resources, affecting food and electricity production, as well as economic development.

Sources: Data from *Shifting Bases, Shifting Perils: A Scoping Study on Security Implications of Climate Change in the OSCE Region and Beyond*, commissioned by the Office of the Co-ordinator of OSCE Economic and Environmental Activities (Berlin: Adelphi Research, 2010), http://www.osce.org/eea/ 78356 (accessed 23 February 2012).

climate change was likely to have significant security implications for a number of sub-regions within or bordering Europe, in particular those on the geographical periphery of the continent (see Box 9.2).

European governments and the EU have become increasingly concerned about the consequences of climate change, including for security. In 2007 EU heads of state and government tasked the EU's foreign policy High Representative and the European Commission with preparing a joint report on the impact of climate change on international security. That report, published in March 2008, described climate change as 'a threat multiplier which exacerbates existing trends, tensions and instability' and 'threatens to overburden states and regions which are already fragile and conflict prone'. The report identified a number of threats likely to arise from or be exacerbated by climate change: conflicts over natural resources; economic damage (which could cost up to 20 per cent of global GDP per year in a business-as-usual scenario of continued growth in GHG emissions); loss of territory (as a result of sea level increases) and border disputes; environmentally induced migration; increased instability in weak or failing states and increased potential for political radicalization; tensions over energy resources; and increased pressure on the institutions of global governance (European Union, 2008a). This was followed up by further recommendations on climate change and security from the High

Representative in December 2008 and a progress report from the High Representative and the Commission in November 2009. These reports have resulted in increased work within the EU in terms of identifying potential security consequences of climate change in specific regions and action to prevent the emergence of climate change related security threats (European Union, 2008c and 2009b).

Europe has played a central role in relation to climate change – historically as a major producer of GHGs and since the 1990s as a leading force in international efforts to limit these emissions. The industrialized developed world, including Europe, has been responsible for the majority of anthropogenic (human-generated) GHG emissions to date. Table 9.2 summarizes past, recent and projected future GHG emissions for the EU and a number of other major developed and developing states. As can be seen, as of 2000 the EU was responsible for 14 per cent of anthropogenic GHG emissions, China about 15 per cent and the USA about 20 per cent. Since then, continued high economic growth rates in China, India and other major developing countries has meant that their GHG emissions have grown significantly (both in total and as a proportion of anthropogenic GHG emissions), with China estimated to have overtaken the USA as the world's largest emitter of GHGs.

The EU has played a central role in efforts to establish an international regime to limit GHG emissions since negotiations began in the late 1980s (Bretherton and Vogler, 2006, pp. 105–9). A UN Framework Convention on Climate Change (UNFCCC) was agreed at the Rio Earth Summit in 1992, establishing the goal of reducing GHG emissions. Negotiations proceeded throughout the 1990s, with the EU leading the case for legally binding emission reduction targets. The Kyoto Protocol was signed in 1997, committing developed states to reduce their GHG emissions by 5.2 per cent, compared to 1990 levels, by 2012 (within this the EU was to reduce its GHG emissions by 8 per cent and the USA by 7 per cent). Developing states were excluded from legally binding emission reduction targets under the Kyoto agreement, based on the argument that it was developed states which were historically responsible for the majority of anthropogenic GHG emissions (see table 9.2). The USA, under the Clinton administration, signed the Kyoto Protocol in 1997, but in the same year the Senate passed a resolution refusing to commit the USA to any reduction agreement that did not include binding targets for developing countries, making it clear that it would not ratify Kyoto. From this point in particular, the EU became the driving force behind the Kyoto Protocol. In 2001, the Bush

TABLE 9.2 Changes in GHG emissions over time

Country/Group	Percentage of world GHG emissions 2000	Percentage of world population 2000	GHG emissions per capita 2000 (tons C equiv.)	Percentage of cumulative world GHG emissions 1850–2000	Emissions growth 1990–2000 (%)	Projected GHC emissions 2000–25 (% growth) – low and high growth estimates	
						Low	High
USA	20.6	4.7	6.6	29.8	18	20	52
China	14.8	20.9	1.1	7.3	39	50	181
EU-25	14.0	7.5	2.8	27.2	–3	–1*	39*
Russia	5.7	2.4	3.6	8.3	–22	37**	109**
India	5.5	16.8	0.5	2.0	64	73	225
Japan	4.0	2.1	2.9	4.1	12	4	46
Brazil	2.5	2.8	1.3	0.8	53	84	165
Mexico	1.5	1.6	1.4	1.0	25	68	215

Notes: * = EU-15; ** = Former Soviet Union.

Source: Data from Baumert and Pershing (2004).

administration stated its unwillingness to ratify or implement the Kyoto Protocol, with US National Security Advisor Condoleezza Rice describing the agreement as 'dead' (Borger, 2001). The EU, however, continued to pursue the ratification and implementation of Kyoto. The EU was central to persuading other states, in particular Japan and Russia, to ratify the Kyoto Protocol – a key hurdle, since Kyoto could only come into force if fifty-five states accounting for at least 55 per cent of developed-world GHG emissions ratified the agreement. Russia agreed to ratify the agreement at a May 2004 EU–Russia summit and the Kyoto Protocol came into force in February 2005. Without the EU's leadership, there would have been no agreement with legally binding GHG emission reduction targets, and the Kyoto Protocol would not have been ratified or come into force.

The Kyoto Protocol was, however, at best a small initial step in reducing global GHG emissions. The Kyoto emission reduction target of 5.2 per cent for developed states was far below the 50 per cent or more GHG emission reductions that scientists suggest will be necessary to seriously curb climate change. The exclusion of developing states from emission reduction targets and the eventual refusal of the USA to join the agreement, furthermore, meant that many of the world's main emitters of GHGs were not covered by the agreement. Nevertheless, Kyoto was significant because it established the principles of global emission reduction targets and legally binding national targets within this.

With growing recognition that addressing climate change required much deeper reductions in GHG emissions and the Kyoto Protocol's period of application ending in 2012, from the mid-2000s attention turned to a possible successor agreement. In 2007–08 the EU adopted a climate change policy known as '20-20-20', with three targets to be achieved by 2020: a 20 per cent reduction in EU GHG emissions (from 1990 levels), 20 per cent of EU energy consumption to come from renewable sources and a 20 per cent reduction in primary energy use compared with projected levels, to be achieved by improving energy efficiency (European Commission, 2007). Globally, the EU set the objective of seeking a post-Kyoto agreement that would be legally binding, would involve deep reductions in GHG emissions and would involve all countries in accepting emission reduction targets (if other countries were willing to sign up to such an agreement, the EU would also increase its own emission reduction target from twenty per cent to thirty per cent). It was initially hoped that a post-Kyoto climate change agreement would be reached at the Copenhagen climate change summit in December 2009. In the event, the Copenhagen summit was a near-disaster, with bitter diplomatic wrangling between states and only a last-minute agreement to continue negotiations on a possible eventual accord. None of the EU's core objectives – a legally binding agreement, a clear commitment to deep GHG emission reductions or acceptance of GHG emission reduction targets by all states – were met. The last-minute agreement which came out of the summit, further, was hammered out between the USA and major developing countries (in particular, China, India, Brazil and South Africa), all of whom opposed a strong legally binding agreement, with the EU marginalized. European Commission president José Manuel Barroso acknowledged that the agreement fell 'far short' of EU expectations: 'I will not hide my disappointment, the level of ambition is honestly not what we were hoping for' (European Commission, 2009).

The setback at Copenhagen led to a recognition that the EU needed to strengthen its global climate change diplomacy if it was to advance its objectives. In July 2011 the recently established European External Action Service (EEAS) and the European Commission published a joint reflection paper entitled *Towards a Renewed and Strengthened EU Climate Diplomacy*, stating that the time had come to 'step up efforts on climate diplomacy to address climate change at political levels and to strengthen the EU voice internationally' (European External Action Service/European Commission, 2011). The first result of the EU's efforts to enhance its climate diplomacy came at the next round of global climate change negotiations in Durban, South Africa, in November/December 2011. At the Durban meeting the EU agreed to sign up to a 'second commitment period' under the Kyoto agreement, involving a commitment to further legally binding GHG emission reduction targets for EU member states up to 2020 (with the exact targets to be agreed during 2012–13). In return, all other states, but most significantly the USA and major developing countries such as China and India, agreed to pursue a new legally binding climate change agreement involving GHG emission reduction targets for all states, with that agreement to be concluded by 2015 and to enter into force in 2020 (C2ES Center for Climate and Energy Solutions, 2011). The latter commitments were a significant step towards the EU's position on the part of the USA and the major developing countries, resulting in part from a new alliance between the EU and the smaller and poorer developing states (both of which supported more radical action on climate) which had put political pressure on the USA and the major developing countries (Mabey, 2012). Nevertheless, while the

Durban meeting was a significant diplomatic victory for the EU in its struggle to build a global climate change regime, whether the new agreement would indeed be agreed by 2015 and enter into force in 2020 remained to be seen, as did the all-important detail of any such agreement.

The EU can reasonably claim to have shown significant leadership in responding to climate change: by moving ahead with the Kyoto Protocol, pressuring other states to recognize the seriousness of the likely implications of climate change and pressing for a global agreement committing all states to GHG emission reduction targets, the EU has played an important role in focusing global political attention on the issue and creating a context in which deep reductions in GHG emissions may at least be possible. Whether deep reductions in GHG emissions will be achieved and the worst potential consequences of climate change averted, however, remains deeply uncertain. In this context, the EU faces two major challenges. First, can the EU's members actually achieve deep reductions in their own GHG emissions? The EU was able to reach its 2012 Kyoto emission reduction targets largely because those targets were not very demanding, but also because the accession of the Central and Eastern European states to the EU in 2004 brought into the Union a group of countries whose economies, and hence also GHG emissions, had contracted very significantly after the collapse of communism, reducing what would otherwise have been higher GHG emission levels of the enlarged EU. Deeper reductions in GHG emissions will require a more radical and demanding transition to a low-carbon economy. The EU's 20-20-20 package was designed, in part, to initiate that transition. Nevertheless, deep reductions in GHG emissions will require very major changes in power production, transport, industry, agriculture and building construction – and the extent to which the EU and its members will be willing and able to make these changes remains to be seen. Second, can the EU persuade other states, especially the USA and the world's largest developing countries, to buy into a similar transition to a low-carbon economy? As discussed above, the experience of the Kyoto and post-Kyoto climate change negotiations showed that, despite growing awareness of the reality and likely extremely serious implications of climate change, both the USA and the major developing countries were reluctant to sign up to any global agreement committing them to specific GHG emission reduction targets. The EU will likely therefore face continuing challenges in persuading other major powers to support its global climate change agenda. Climate change and its security implications will without doubt remain major items on both the internal and the international agenda of the EU.

Population movements

The movement of people has become an increasingly prominent and controversial issue in European politics since the 1980s: questions relating to migration, refugees, asylum seekers, the free movement of labour, and border controls are now a central part of political debate in most European countries. These issues, furthermore, are increasingly discussed in security terms: as actual or potential threats to the security, welfare and identity of states and societies.

A number of trends in migration within and into Europe can be identified. Since the Second World War, Europe has 'experienced a historical shift from emigration to immigration' (International Organization for Migration, 2005, p. 141). Historically, European states were a major global source of emigrants, as they populated their colonies and empires as well as the new states of the USA, Canada, Australia and New Zealand. From the 1950s and 1960s, however, growing demand for labour made Western Europe a major destination for immigration (Weiner, 1995, pp. 21–5). Since then, immigration into Europe, primarily Western Europe, has increased significantly. The number of immigrants in Western Europe increased from 10 million in 1970 to 29 million in 2000, and for Europe as a whole – including Central and Eastern Europe and the former Soviet Union – from 19 million to 33 million (although a significant part of the latter increase was accounted for by the break-up of the Soviet Union, which overnight turned previously internal migrants into international migrants) (International Organization for Migration, 2005, p. 381). In 2010 the migrant population in Europe as a whole (the EU, plus the Balkans, including Turkey, and the former Soviet Union) was estimated to be 72.6 million, constituting 8.7 per cent of total European population and about one-third of all global migrants (International Organization for Migration, 2010, p. 183). In general, immigration into Europe increased throughout the 1990s and 2000s, with Western European countries being the primary destination countries (International Organization for Migration, 2005, pp. 141–7, 385; International Organization for Migration, 2010, pp. 183–4). In 2010 the total number of migrants in the EU, plus other Western Europe states (Iceland, Lichtenstein, Norway and Switzerland) and EU candidates (Croatia and Turkey) was 51 million, with the

TABLE 9.3   *Migration: inflows of foreign population into EU and selected OECD countries (000s)*

Country/Group	1992	2000	2009
EU*	1,727.6	2,115.6	2,310.5
Australia **	107.4	331.1	697.4
Canada	313.3	481.7	634.5
Japan	267.0	345.8	297.1
Switzerland	112.1	87.4	132.4
USA **	974.0	2,090.4	2,550.0

Notes: * EU: 1992 = 11 member states (excludes Austria, Greece, Ireland and Italy); 2000 and 2009 = 20 member states (excludes Bulgaria, Cyprus, Greece, Latvia, Lithuania, Malta and Romania).
** Australia and United States: 1992 figures exclude temporary inflows.

Sources: Data from Organisation for Economic Co-operation and Development (2003), table A.1.1, Inflows of foreign population into selected OECD countries, and Organisation for Economic Co-operation and Development (2011b), table A.1.1, Inflows of foreign population into selected OECD countries.

largest migrant populations in Germany (10.8 million), France (6.7 million), the United Kingdom (6.5 million), Spain (6.4 million) and Italy (4.5 million) (International Organization for Migration, 2010, p. 185).

Table 9.3 provides details of annual migration into the EU and a number of other major developed countries since the early 1990s. As can be seen, the number of migrants entering EU countries annually rose from over 1.7 million people in 1992 to over 2.3 million people in 2009. As a consequence, since the early 1990s, many European countries have experienced major increases in migrant populations, with numbers of migrants more than doubling in Finland, Ireland, Italy, Portugal and Spain, and increasing by 50 per cent or more in Austria, Denmark, Luxembourg and the UK (International Organization for Migration, 2005, p. 385). In 2003, the European countries with the net largest immigration were Spain (+594,000), Italy (+511,000), Germany (+166,000), the UK (+103,000), Turkey (+98,000), Portugal (+64,000) and France (+55,000) (International Organization for Migration, 2005, p. 141). While a significant part of migration into EU countries is from other EU states, the majority of migrants are nevertheless third-country nationals: in 2000–01, for example, of 20 million migrants in EU-15 states, 14 million were third-country nationals (International Organization for Migration, 2005, p. 142). Southern

Europe has the fastest growing immigrant population in the early 21st century. In 2003, Spain had an estimated 2.66 million immigrants, and the large numbers of irregular immigrants in Spain, Italy, Portugal and Greece has led these countries to undertake periodic regularization programmes under which irregular immigrants are granted residence and work permits (International Organization for Migration, 2005, p. 147).

These trends in population movements into Europe reflect a long-term pattern discernible since the 1970s, the defining feature of which is the global migration of people from the poorer southern part of the world to the richer northern areas. The end of the Cold War, however, added a new dimension to population movements within Europe. The opening of the old Iron Curtain border allowed people to move between Eastern and Western Europe in significant numbers for the first time in four decades. The massive and uncontrolled movements of people from East to West which some observers feared might follow the end of the Cold War, however, did not happen. Western European states maintained relatively tight immigration policies and border controls, and the scale of both legal and illegal immigration from Eastern to Western Europe was thus limited. Germany was a partial exception to this trend, receiving between 280,000 and 500,000 migrants annually from post-communist Europe, not only ethnic Germans entitled to German citizenship but also other Eastern Europeans, from the mid-1980s onwards (International Organization for Migration, 2005, p. 384).

Although alarmist predictions of very massive migration have proven exaggerated, the scale of migration has grown over the last few decades and it has become a high-profile political issue in much of Europe. To varying degrees, further, migration has been 'securitized', with migration and migrants viewed as posing a threat to the security or stability of states, the economic position and welfare of citizens and/or national identity and cohesion. The degree to which such perceptions of threat are warranted is contentious: it may be argued that they are based on exaggerated assessments of both the scale and impact of migration. Nevertheless, these perceptions are real and consequently have a significant impact on politics and policy. Three types of migration – conflict-driven migration, migration within the context of the enlarged EU and the interrelated issues of refugees, asylum seekers and illegal immigration – have been particularly prominent and are discussed in more detail below.

Conflict-driven migration

The most direct link between population movements and security is conflict-driven migration. In the 1990s conflicts in post-communist Europe, in particular the Yugoslav wars, created major conflict-driven population movements within Europe for the first time since the Second World War. Between 1991 and 1999, the Yugoslav wars generated over 3.7 million refugees and internally displaced persons (IDPs – people displaced from their homes but remaining in their country of origin) (Radovic, 2005, pp. 12–13). The first phases of the Yugoslav wars in Slovenia, Croatia and especially Bosnia between 1991 and 1995 created nearly 1.7 million refugees and 1.3 million IDPs. In the 1999 Kosovo war, nearly one million of Kosovo's two million population fled (primarily to neighbouring Macedonia, Albania and Montenegro) and another half a million were internally displaced within Kosovo. The majority of Kosovo's population, however, returned in the second half of 1999, following the deployment of a NATO peacekeeping force. The Kosovo war also illustrated the way in which population movements can exacerbate conflict situations in neighbouring states: the temporary influx of large numbers of Kosovar Albanians into Macedonia increased tensions between that country's majority Macedonian population and its own ethnic Albanian minority, while the porous Kosovo–Macedonia border allowed Albanian guerrillas in Kosovo and Macedonia to make common cause, resulting in low-level warfare between Albanian guerrillas and Macedonian government forces in 2001. The Yugoslav wars also left a significant long-term refugee/IDP problem: in 2010, Bosnia still had over 113,365 IDPs and 62,910 Bosnian refugees outside the country, while Serbia and Kosovo had 228,442 IDPs and 73,608 refugees within their borders and 182,955 refugees overseas (United Nations High Commissioner for Refugees, 2011). It should be noted that the majority of refugees from the Yugoslav conflict moved into neighbouring states in the Balkans rather than Western Europe: with the exception of Germany which had accepted 345,000 Yugoslav refugees by 1995, other Western European states received much smaller numbers of refugees (Radovic, 2005, p. 12).

Similar patterns of conflict-driven migration also occurred in the former Soviet Union – in particular, the Caucasus – primarily in the early 1990s. The conflict between Armenia and Azerbaijan over Nagorno-Karabakh created refugee populations in both countries of over 200,000, and 600,000 IDPs within Azerbaijan; conflicts in

Georgia generated more than 200,000 IDPs (further exacerbated by the country's 2008 war with Russia); and the conflict in Chechnya displaced about 500,000 people (United Nations High Commissioner for Refugees, 2004). The Nagorno-Karabakh conflict in particular created one of the largest protracted IDP situations, with Azerbaijan still having 592,860 IDPs twenty years later in 2010. Georgia also has a very large IDP population, numbering 359,716 in 2010 (United Nations High Commissioner for Refugees, 2011). Migration resulting from conflicts in the former Soviet region has, however, essentially remained limited to the states/regions involved in the conflicts and their immediate neighbours, reflecting the reality that it is often difficult for refugees or IDPs to move further afield.

The Arab Spring of 2011 triggered a further wave of refugee movement into Europe, in particular from political instability in Tunisia in early 2011, the war in Libya in spring/summer 2011 and escalating violence in Syria from autumn 2011. As the most proximate European state to Tunisia and Libya, Italy was the primary European destination for those fleeing Libya and Tunisia: in spring 2011 nearly 50,000 migrants arrived in Italy from these two countries (Brady, 2012, p. 1), triggering a crisis in relation to the EU's Schengen travel free zone (see below). Italian Foreign Minister Franco Frattini warned of the danger of a much larger wave of refugees from the Libyan war, potentially up to 200,000 or 300,000 (Squires, 2011). In the event, such massive refugee movements to Europe did not occur: Italy received about 26,000 refugees from the Libyan war, whereas the majority of the total of 721,000 refugees from the conflict fled to neighbouring African countries (with Tunisia and Egypt receiving the largest numbers, 313,000 and 230,000 respectively) (International Organization for Migration, 2011b). In late 2011–early 2012, escalating violence in Syria triggered a growing refugee movement, with over 19,000 Syrians fleeing to Turkey, 10,000 to Lebanon and 1,500 to Jordan (Stack, 2011).

Conflict-driven migration has thus been a not insignificant force in post-Cold War Europe. Nevertheless, the scale of such migration has not been as great as some feared, while its greatest impact has been on those countries immediately neighbouring conflict zones in the Balkans, the Caucasus and North Africa/the Middle East rather than on the European Union or Europe as a whole. The experience in the Libyan and Syrian crises, further, suggests that the Mediterranean Sea presents a formidable barrier to more large-scale conflict-driven migration from North Africa or the Middle East to Europe. If, as was argued at the beginning of this book, large-scale war is increasingly unlikely within Europe, then conflict-driven migration is likely to pose greater challenges for conflict-prone regions themselves, such as Africa and the Middle East, than for Europe.

Migration within the enlarged EU

The eastward enlargement of the EU in the 2000s opened a new era in migration *within* Europe, giving citizens of the new Central and Eastern European member states the right to live and work in the Western European member states. The free movement of workers – the right of citizens to work and reside in any member state of the EU – is a core principle of the Union, enshrined since the 1957 European Community Treaty. Given the relative poverty of the Central and Eastern European states compared to their Western European neighbours, it was always likely that there would be significant migration from the 'new' EU member states to the 'old' member states. The likely scale of such migration was, however, contentious. Prior to enlargement, the European Commission (and many economists) predicted that East–West labour migration would be limited in scale, with the Commission estimating that it would initially be between 70,000 and 80,000 a year, declining thereafter (Kay, 2006). Western European governments, however, feared being swamped by much larger-scale migration, resulting in the negotiation of transitional arrangements allowing member states to apply national restrictions on the free movement of labour. When the eight Central and Eastern European states (EU-8), plus Cyprus and Malta, joined the Union in 2004, EU-15 member states were allowed to apply national restrictions on the free movement of labour from EU-8 states up to 2011. When Bulgaria and Romania joined the EU in 2007, similar transitional arrangements were negotiated allowing the other 25 EU member states to apply national restrictions on the free movement of labour up to 2013.

In the event, the initial scale of East–West labour migration was much larger than expected. Of the EU-15 states only the UK, Ireland and Sweden chose to allow free movement of labour for EU-8 citizens from the point when these states joined the EU in 2004. By 2006 the UK had received 450,000–600,000 workers from the EU-8 states and Ireland more than 100,000 (Kay, 2006). The number of migrants from the EU-8 states in the EU-15 states increased from 942,000 in 2003 to 2.29 million in 2009. The number of migrants from Bulgaria and Romania in the EU-15 states increased from 1.48 million in 2003 to 2.56 million in 2009. The countries which Central and Eastern

European citizens move to varied: for the EU-8 states the United Kingdom and Germany hosted the largest numbers by 2009 (814,000 and 615,000 respectively); for Bulgaria and Romania, Spain and Italy hosted the largest numbers by 2009 (991,000 and 934,000 respectively) (Holland *et al.*, 2011, pp. 46–7). The scale of this migration created some disquiet in Western Europe, especially in those countries receiving the largest numbers of workers. The European Commission and supporters of enlargement argue, however, that the extension of free movement of labour to the enlarged EU benefits both new and old member states (for example, the influx of workers from the EU-8 states into the UK and Ireland helped to fill labour market shortages in these countries and did not result in increased unemployment amongst indigenous workers) (Commission of the European Communities, 2006; Traser, 2006).

The longer-term extent and impact of such East–West migration within the EU remains to be seen. The scale of the migration after 2004 suggests that the presence of significant numbers of workers from the 'new' EU member states in the 'old' member states is likely to become a long-term feature of economies and societies. At the same time, after the initial post-enlargement influx, the pace of such migration has slowed, with overall migrant numbers likely to stabilize. In the longer term, assuming economies in the Central and Eastern European states gradually catch up with those in Western Europe, economic incentives for migration may decline. The likelihood of significant destabilizing consequences as a result of East–West migration within the EU is therefore probably quite low.

The experience of the significant inflows of migrants from the 'new' member states to the 'old' member states has probably also contributed to the EU's enlargement fatigue (see Chapter 1), making the Union more reluctant to take in more relatively poor states from the Balkans or the former Soviet Union. Nevertheless, as discussed in Chapter 1, the EU is likely to gradually accept the Western Balkan states as full members over the next decade or so (in part because the relatively small size of most of these states makes them easier to integrate). The possibility of large-scale migration from Turkey has also been a factor – although only one among a number – contributing to the declining likelihood since the mid-2000s of Turkey joining the EU. Turkey's large and growing population (over 70 million, predicted to grow to 80 million) and relative poverty would likely make it a major source of westward migration were it to join the Union. If Turkey ever comes truly close to EU membership, the issue of free movement of labour will presumably be a major issue in accession negotiations. At present, however, concerns about migration are one factor amongst a number making it unlikely that the EU will extend its membership to Turkey or the former Soviet states.

Refugees, asylum seekers and illegal immigrants

Although the majority of migration is legal migration for labour purposes, the interrelated issues of asylum seekers, refugees and illegal immigrants have also become increasingly controversial in Europe since the 1980s and are thus central to the larger debate on migration. It is estimated that the number of refugees in Europe (including the former Soviet Union) rose from 600,000 in 1970 to 2.4 million in 2000 (International Organization for Migration, 2005, p. 399). More significant, however, are the numbers of asylum seekers – that is, those claiming political asylum and seeking recognized refugee status. Table 9.4 provides details of the numbers of asylum seekers entering the EU and other major developed countries since the early 1990s. The number of asylum seekers entering the EU annually peaked in the 1990s at more than half a million and has subsequently declined. The EU receives approximately two-thirds of the total number of asylum seekers entering major developed countries. The majority of applications for refugee

TABLE 9.4   *Inflows of asylum seekers into EU and selected OECD countries (000s)*

Country/Group	1993	2000	2010
EU*	517.5	423.1	230.6
Australia	4.9	13.1	8.3
Canada	21.1	34.3	23.2
Japan	0.1	0.2	1.2
Switzerland	24.7	17.6	13.5
USA	144.2	40.9	41.0

Note: * EU: 1992 = 15 member states; 2000 and 2009 = 20 member states (excludes Bulgaria, Cyprus, Ireland, Latvia, Lithuania, Malta and Romania).

Sources: Data from Organisation for Economic Co-operation and Development (2003), table A.1.3. Inflows of asylum seekers into selected OECD countries; and Organisation for Economic Co-operation and Development (2011a), table A.1.3, Inflows of asylum seekers into selected OECD countries.

status are rejected and while some asylum seekers are returned to their countries of origin, many remain, with such 'disappeared asylum seekers' becoming illegal immigrants.

Estimates of the numbers of illegal immigrants in Europe are inherently problematical. Illegal immigrants include those entering countries illegally, 'disappeared asylum-seekers' and those who overstay their legal visas. In the early 2000s Jandl (2003) estimated that there were between 2.6 and 6.4 million illegal immigrants in Western Europe, with a medium estimate of 4 million, and that each year approximately 650,000 illegal immigrants were entering the EU-15 and 150,000 the ten states that joined the EU in 2004. An EU-funded research project estimated illegal immigrant populations in 2008 at between 1.8 and 3.3 million in the EU-15 and 1.9 and 3.4 million in the EU 27 (CLANDESTINO, 2009, p. 4). According to some reports, however, the European Commission estimates the EU's illegal immigrant population to be as high as 8 million (Reuters, 2008).

As discussed in Chapter 4, under the Schengen regime, the majority of EU member states (with the exception of the UK and Ireland) have agreed to abolish internal border controls and establish common external border controls and visa policies. In this context, attention in relation to asylum seekers and illegal immigrants has turned to the potential weak spots on the Schengen zone's external borders. Although Greece joined the Schengen zone, it was widely recognized that Greece had inadequate border controls and no real system for dealing with asylum seekers. In the 2000s, a crisis grew as Greece's border with Turkey became the primary route for asylum seekers and illegal immigrants entering the EU: by the late 2000s to early 2010s almost 9,000 illegal entries were occurring in busy months across the Greek–Turkish border and in November 2010 Greece lost control of a 12-kilometre section of its border with Turkey, leading to an emergency mission by the EU's new Frontex border security force to secure the border. Up to this point, other EU member states had been willing to live with the Greek exception in part because Greece shared no land border with other EU member states. With Bulgaria and Romania joining the EU in 2007 and in particular scheduled to join the Schengen zone in 2012, however, the prospect of a 'land bridge' between Greece and the rest of the Schengen zone emerged. In addition, highly prevalent corruption in Bulgaria and Romania suggested that their own border controls and asylum systems were likely to remain weak. Bulgaria's border with Turkey and the Romanian Black Sea port city of Constanta were viewed as likely weak spots in the Schengen zone's external borders similar to the Greek–Turkish border (Brady, 2012, pp. 18–24).

Whatever the specifics of migration routes and border control weak spots, the larger picture is clear: the EU is likely to remain a major destination for asylum seekers and illegal immigrants. Dealing with this issue will remain a serious challenge for European governments and the EU.

Policy responses

European governments and the EU have adopted a number of policy responses to changing patterns of migration into and within Europe. Since the 1970s, most Western European states have had relatively restrictive immigration policies, allowing limited numbers of workers from outside Western Europe to enter either as permanent immigrants or on temporary work visas. Western European states also sought to strengthen border controls through enhanced screening at entry points and intensified policing of land and sea borders. With the establishment of the Schengen regime, however, the external border of the Schengen zone became the key border for controlling migration into Europe, marking the boundary between the EU, in which there is free movement of persons, and third countries, whose citizens face strict limitations on their ability to enter the Schengen zone. When the ten Central and Eastern European states joined the EU in 2004, they were required to significantly strengthen controls on their non-EU borders before they joined the Schengen zone in December 2007. In the late 2000s and early 2010s, however, the Greek border issue noted above and the Arab Spring combined to raise questions about the future of the Schengen regime. In particular, the influx of Tunisian and Libyan refugees into Italy led the Italian government, in April 2011, to grant these refugees temporary residence permits giving them the right to move freely within the Schengen zone; the French government responded by restoring border checks at its border with Italy, turning back some immigrants and blocking trains. The incident implied that countries might suspend the operation of Schengen or even seek a complete return to national border controls. The immediate Franco-Italian diplomatic crisis was overcome, but one outcome was an agreement amongst EU leaders in June 2011 to review the Schengen regime, including the circumstances in which countries may temporarily re-introduce national border controls, improving the monitoring of border standards and the possibility of suspending countries that fail to maintain adequate border controls (Brady, 2012, pp. 1–2). Whatever combination of revised Schengen and/or national border controls emerges, however, the outcome is likely to be continued or strengthened immigration policies and border controls, or what critics have sometimes described as a 'fortress Europe': a defensive security response, closing Europe's borders in reaction to the perceived threat posed by migration. In addition, in response to continuing concern about migration, in the late 2000s and early 2010s a number of European countries, such as the UK, Switzerland, Denmark, Spain and Italy, introduced national measures designed to limit migration. These measures included caps on the number of work visas available for non-EU/non-European Economic Area migrants, points systems for assessing work visa applications and co-operation agreements with migrant-sending countries making work visas dependent on these countries' efforts to control illegal immigration (International Organization for Migration, 2011a, pp. 73–4).

The desire to contain immigration, in particular to limit the numbers of asylum seekers and illegal immigrants entering the EU, has led European political leaders and the EU to look for measures that might limit migration 'at source'. The EU has thus sought to develop co-operation with third countries in managing migration:

> EU policy should aim at assisting third countries ... in their efforts to improve their capacity for migration management and refugee protection, prevent and combat illegal immigration, inform on legal channels for migration, resolve refugee situations by providing better access to durable solutions, build border-control capacity, enhance document security and tackle the problem of return. (European Union, 2004b, p. 11)

In 2005 the EU adopted a 'Global Approach to Migration and Mobility' based on strengthened co-operation with third countries to limit illegal immigration while at the same time facilitating legal migration for work purposes (European Commission, 2011d). The EU provides various forms of financial and technical assistance to support states in addressing these issues, focusing in particular on neighbouring states in Africa, the Balkans and the former Soviet Union. Given the overwhelming economic imperatives behind migration, the problems of violent conflict and human rights abuses, and the fact that many of these countries are weak states with severe governance problems, EU co-operation and assistance programmes are likely to have a limited impact in reducing migration. The EU has also pursued the conclusion of Readmission Agreements with third countries, under which countries agree to re-admit nationals who have entered the EU illegally and (in some cases) third-country nationals who have entered the Union illegally via the country concerned. By 2011, the EU had concluded Readmission Agreements with Hong Kong, Macao, Sri Lanka, Albania, Russia, Ukraine, Macedonia, Bosnia and Herzegovina, Montenegro, Serbia, Pakistan and Georgia and was negotiating such agreements with Morocco, Turkey, Cape Verde, China and Algeria (European Commission, 2011a).

The difficulty of limiting the numbers of asylum seekers and illegal immigrants entering EU countries has led political leaders, such as British prime minister Tony Blair and Spanish prime minister José Maria Aznar in the early 2000s, to explore more radical measures, including cutting development aid to countries that fail to limit migration flows, establishing transit centres outside the EU where asylum seekers can be held while their applications for refugee status are assessed, and withdrawing from the 1951 Refugee Convention (under which signatories are bound to accept genuine refugees and consider the applications of asylum seekers for refugee status). Critics argue that such measures would be both morally objectionable and ineffective, and they have not to date been adopted, but the fact that European political leaders have been willing to propose them indicates levels of public and elite concern over the issue.

Given the overwhelming economic imperatives driving migration into Europe, European states and the EU are likely to face continuing large-scale immigration, both legal and illegal. European responses to migration, furthermore, are underpinned by a central contradiction: the public and politicians to some extent view migration as a threat, yet European states are likely to need increasing numbers of migrants to meet labour market needs as Europe's indigenous population declines. Europe will therefore face major challenges in balancing its need for immigration with continuing concern about the impact of that immigration.

Conclusion

As this chapter has shown, European governments and the EU are increasingly engaging with the non-military security agenda. The extent and nature of non-military security threats is, however, more problematical to assess. In many ways, Europe is much less vulnerable than most other regions of the world to non-military security threats. The relatively internally strong character of most European states means that they are better able to respond to, or to resist, non-military security threats than are weaker states in Africa, the Middle East, parts of Asia and Latin America. There are, however, significant variations in vulnerability to non-military security threats within Europe: the weak states of the Balkans and the former Soviet Union have proved to be particularly vulnerable to some non-military security threats (such as economic instability and crime), a vulnerability reinforced by their relatively weak border controls.

In terms of responses to non-military security threats, the examples of development policy and climate change examined here illustrate that Europe, and especially the EU, has played a significant global leadership role in recent years. Development policy, climate change and migration, however, also show that the EU faces major difficulties in responding to non-military security challenges on two levels. First, EU members and the EU face significant domestic obstacles to the development of more effective policies in these areas. Support for protectionist trade policies remains strong within many EU states, and such policies are a major obstacle to the achievement of the Union's development goals. Similarly, although the EU has shown international leadership on the issue of climate change, most member states have failed to confront the major domestic challenges involved in seriously reducing greenhouse gas emissions. European leaders have also allowed an increasingly securitized debate on migration to develop, if not having actively encouraged that debate, while failing to recognize or to explain to the public the reality that Europe will increasingly need migration to counter-balance the problem of an ageing and declining population. Second, at the international level, the problems of economic development and climate change illustrate that, while the EU may be able to play a leadershop role, it cannot address such problems alone. The EU thus faces a major foreign policy challenge in terms of persuading other states to join with it in order to take effective action in areas such as economic development and climate change. Non-military security will continue to pose major domestic and international challenges for European states and the EU.

Chapter 10

Conclusion

The new European security order

This book has examined security in Europe since the end of the Cold War and European responses to the new global security agenda. Its central thesis is that the nature of security within Europe has been transformed fundamentally by the development of a security community – a zone of peace where war is inconceivable and states no longer prepare for war against one another – that now covers all of Western, and much of Central and Eastern, Europe. The emergence of this security community has dramatically reduced the likelihood of great power war in Europe and moved much of the continent beyond its historic pattern of great power security competition, balance of power politics and rival alliances. Although there were significant international disputes within the European security community in the 1990s and the 2000s – over the future direction of the EU, over the Yugoslav conflict in the 1990s and in relation to the 2003 Iraq War – these did not give rise to the type of old-fashioned, action–reaction competitive security dynamics between states that might fundamentally undermine the security community.

The European security community and its key institutions – the European Union and NATO – form the core of the new Europe: collectively they have been the dominant political and economic force in the new Europe and they provide the framing context in which states outside the EU and NATO operate. Through the EU and NATO, the members of the European security community have increasingly adopted common policies towards the rest of Europe. Contemporary Europe has thus been defined, to a significant degree, by a core–periphery relationship between the European security community and those states that remain outside that community. This relationship is, however, complicated by two further features. First, the core – the European security community – is not a hard entity like a traditional state, with clearly defined boundaries and a single centralized government, but is rather a soft, multi-level entity, with

259

blurred and overlapping boundaries and decentralized governance. Jan Zielonka thus describes the EU as a neo-medieval empire (Zielonka, 2006). The multi-level, decentralized nature of the European security community significantly shapes its policies towards the rest of Europe, which tend to be complex, multi-layered and long-term in impact rather than the type of decisive application of hard power normally associated with great powers. Second, two states outside the European security community, Russia and Turkey, are major powers in their own right: the security community's relations with Russia and Turkey are thus a distinctive mix of core–periphery relationships between dominant and weaker powers on the one hand and more traditional relations between powerful international actors on the other.

Many of the greatest strategic uncertainties and central security policy challenges in contemporary Europe have related to the regions and countries on the periphery of the European security community. In the Western Balkans, the end of the Yugoslav wars has left a group of weak states under a form of Western suzerainty, and a situation where a return to violent conflict and warfare cannot be ruled out. Gradually, however, the countries of the Western Balkans are being integrated into NATO and the EU, suggesting that the region will – over time – become part of the European security community. In Turkey's case, while Turkey is a member of NATO, it is not a full part of the European security community and is torn between integration with that community and pursuing an independent policy as a power in its own right. In the 1990s and early 2000s, it appeared that Turkey was on a possible path to EU membership; since then, however, both Turkey and the EU have become more wary of possible Turkish membership of the Union. Turkey's anomalous status – inside NATO, outside the EU and a significant power in its own right – may thus remain. As was seen in Chapter 5, Russia is not a member of the European security community and its relations with the West are characterized by an uneasy mix of co-operation and competition. In contrast to Turkey, however, Russia has little interest in or prospect of membership of NATO or the EU (except perhaps in the long term), and the ability of both institutions to influence Russia's direction is thus limited. Russia's drift into authoritarianism in the 2000s reinforced its status as an 'outsider' in relation to the Western security community, although a return to an all-out Russo-Western Cold War also seems unlikely. In the case of the other former Soviet states, by the late 2000s it was increasingly clear that they were unlikely to join

NATO or the EU for the foreseeable future. The combination of the internal weakness of the former Soviet states, the potential for violent conflict within or between them and their situation in a strategic no man's land is likely to continue to pose security problems for these states, their neighbours and the wider Europe.

The euro crisis and European security

Up to the late 2000s, the European security community, the EU and NATO were the underlying bedrock of post-Cold War European security: debates on European security revolved around how these institutions should develop and what policies they should adopt towards the wider Europe and other regions and powers – not whether or not they might survive. By the early 2010s, however, the European financial and economic crisis discussed at the end of Chapter 4 was leading observers to question the future not only of the euro, but also of the entire EU and even of the post-1945 European security community. Europe appeared to have entered a period of radical uncertainty: a point at which previously established features of Europe's international political order were suddenly being called into question and the range of politically conceivable scenarios over the next few years was potentially very broad. The ongoing crisis, and in particular the possibility that the eurozone might break up, was generating concern about the possible consequences for European security. In October 2011, in a speech urging the German parliament to support measures designed to rescue the euro, German Chancellor, Angela Merkel, argued that:

> No one should think that a further half century of peace and prosperity is assured. It isn't. And that's why I say if the euro fails, Europe will fall, and that mustn't happen ... We have an historic obligation to defend and protect the unification of Europe that our ancestors brought out of the war more than 50 years ago after centuries of hate and bloodshed. None of us can foresee the consequences if that weren't to succeed. (Spiegel, 2010)

Similarly, in a September 2011 speech to the European Parliament, Polish finance minister Jan Vincent-Rostowski warned of the possibility of war in Europe: war in Europe was not likely 'within a four-year legislative timeframe. Not in the months ahead, but maybe over a 10-year time frame, this could place us in a context that is almost

Box 10.1 The euro crisis: possible scenarios

At the beginning of 2012, a wide range of potential future scenarios for the evolution of the European debt and eurozone crisis were conceivable (BBC News, 2011b). While the likelihood or otherwise of different scenarios could be debated, the fact that such a wide range of outcomes were being seriously discussed indicated the scale of the crisis and the significance of its outcome for the future of Europe. The range of possible scenarios could be summarized as follows:

- *Federal Europe*: pressure to save the euro results in the eurozone countries agreeing to much greater central EU control of national budgets, managed by a European economic government; this trend is replicated in other areas of policy, such as defence; the outcome is a much more integrated federal Europe – at least among the eurozone countries. The January 2012 Fiscal Stability Treaty could be viewed as the first step in this direction.
- *The euro and the EU pull-through*: European governments and the EU take sufficient measures to stabilize the debt crisis, reassure financial markets and begin to restore economic stability and growth. The recovery is based on an underlying bargain: greater support for struggling economies from more successful ones (above all Germany) in return for closer economic and fiscal union and stronger EU oversight of national economic policies, but not a fully federal Europe. The EU can claim it has successfully overcome the most severe crisis in its history.
- *A smaller eurozone*: facing unmanageable debt problems, Greece and some other peripheral eurozone economies (such as Portugal and Ireland), default on their debts and choose (or are forced) to leave the euro in order to pursue policies of national currency devaluation designed to reflate their economies. A key question in this scenario is whether the larger southern eurozone economies (Italy, Spain and even France) also leave the euro. Politically, a eurozone encompassing most of its current members, including the larger southern states, would be very different from a largely northern European eurozone with Germany at its core.
- *Britain leaves the EU*: following the December 2011 EU summit, where British Prime Minister David Cameron alone opposed

→

unimaginable at the moment' (Phillips, 2011). Debate around such issues was triggered by a report from the Swiss Bank UBS warning that historically the break-up of currency unions has not usually occurred 'without some form of authoritarian or military government, or civil war' (Trumpet.com, 2011). In the USA, in December 2011 General Martin Dempsey, the Chairman of the Joint Chiefs of Staff, expressed concerns about negative implications for the USA arising from the

→

proposals for closer fiscal union agreed by the other 26 EU member states, the United Kingdom is increasingly isolated within the EU. The other EU member states press ahead with closer economic union. With EU policy increasingly determined by the other EU member states and British influence marginalized, Britain chooses to leave the EU. An important question in this scenario would be whether other non-eurozone EU members – such as Sweden, Denmark and most of the Central and Eastern European members – remain in the EU or follow the United Kingdom in leaving.

- *The euro breaks up*: with debt problems and austerity measures creating a spiral of economic decline and wealthier EU states unwilling to provide large funds to stabilize poorer members, eurozone countries begin to leave the currency, resulting in all member states returning to national currencies. Economically and politically, it is a major setback for the EU, but other core elements of the EU – the single market and perhaps also the Schengen zone – are maintained.

- *The EU breaks up too*: the break-up of the euro results in an increasing emphasis on national economic and political interests, triggering the break-up of the entire EU. The return to national currencies causes competitive currency devaluations; countries demand constraints on imports from neighbours with cheaper currencies and the European single market is abandoned; national border controls are restored within the Schengen zone; and the EU common budget and legal system are abandoned.

- *Everything falls apart*: in the context of the break-up of the euro and the EU and a global depression, European politics becomes increasingly nationalist and populist; with the USA also facing a severe recession, the US president announces America's withdrawal from all overseas military commitments and alliances, including NATO; European security and defence policies are fully re-nationalized; with growing concern about Germany's position as Europe's strongest economy, other states seek to mobilize a coalition to contain German influence; an arms race between a German-centred alliance and its opponents breaks out. In 2023, after a prolonged period of tension, France strikes pre-emptively against the German alliance and the Third World War breaks out.

'potential for civil unrest and the break-up of the Union' (BBC News, 2011c). Box 10.1 summarizes the main alternative potential international political scenarios arising from the euro crisis.

Although it has thus far been impossible to predict the outcome of the euro crisis, a number of arguments may be made, in particular as relates to the possible break-up of the European security community. First, although the withdrawal or expulsion of one or more states from the euro, the emergence of a smaller German-centred northern euro-zone or the complete break-up of the euro, are all possibilities, whether this would inevitably lead to the larger disintegration of the EU is another question. The institutions and policies of the EU are deeply embedded: core elements of the EU – such as its basic institutional structure, the single market and the Schengen zone – might well there-fore survive the break-up of the euro. Even if the EU were to disinte-grate completely, this, in itself, is unlikely to trigger a parallel collapse of NATO. Whereas EU policies and institutions impose significant constraints and burdens on member states and EU-related Euroscepticism has consequently become a significant political force within Europe, there is little similar NATO-scepticism (few, if any, significant politicians, for example, in NATO member states call for their countries' withdrawal from the Alliance). Indeed, were the EU to break up, countries would likely attach greater importance to NATO as a force for political stability and integration – and a bulwark against the re-nationalization of foreign, security and defence policy – within Europe. The European security community is also underpinned by other factors, in particular democracy and economic interdependence. Democracy is now much more deeply entrenched in Western European states, especially the major powers, than was the case before the Second World War, suggesting that the collapse of democracy in one or more states and the emergence of an aggressive authoritarian-nationalist regime is unlikely. Economic interdependence is also quite deeply entrenched: although the ongoing economic crisis and the possible break-up of the eurozone could produce a more general unravelling of economic interdependence and a return to protectionism, the likeli-hood of such a development should at least be questioned. In addition, the European security community may also be underpinned by a signif-icant long-term change in general attitudes to war (Mueller, 1990): whereas in 1914 and 1939 European publics were relatively willing to be dragged into war, in the early 21st century the publics of Europe may be more aware of the costs and risks of war and less willing to follow leaders likely to take them down that path. Overall, the European security community is underpinned by a range of different factors and the breakdown of that security community would probably only result from a very particular combination of worst-case scenarios in a number of areas. While that possibility cannot be entirely ruled out and its likelihood may have increased (perhaps even significantly so) as a result of the financial and economic crisis since 2008, this author's assessment is that a breakdown of the European security community is still unlikely and that this community will remain the defining feature of the contemporary European security order.

Nevertheless, the euro crisis is obviously likely to have significant implications over the next decade or so. First, given the severity and nature of the economic problems facing many European countries, the crisis is likely to be a protracted one. Second, given the scale and complexity of the economic, political and institutional questions facing the eurozone and the EU, it will likely take some years before a more stable new order may emerge. Even if the EU succeeds in putting in place new institutional arrangements that save the euro, the development and bedding-in of those arrangements will presumably take some years. Equally, if the euro breaks up, such a break-up is more likely to occur over a number of years, with a series of consecutive crises, rather than in a single cataclysmic event. Even in a best-case scenario – from an EU perspective – of the euro and the EU being rescued, Europe is likely to experience only a slow economic recovery, characterized by some years of low economic growth. Overall, there would appear to be a strong possibility of Europe experiencing something akin to Japan's 'lost decade' (a term initially used to describe Japan's experience in the 1990s, but reframed as the 'lost years' when Japan's economic problems extended into the 2000s): a period characterized by poor economic performance and preoccupation with the continent's internal economic and political problems. In terms of foreign and security policy, this may result in strategic insularity: a Europe, and especially an EU, with a declining ability to shape the international environment and address security challenges beyond its borders.

Europe and America, NATO and the EU

As discussed in the first chapters of this book, the end of the Cold War triggered a major debate on Europe's institutional security architecture, in particular the transatlantic relationship and the roles of NATO and the EU. In the 1990s and 2000s a number of clear trends emerged. America remained strongly engaged in European security (most obviously in the management of the Yugoslav conflict and the eastward enlargement of NATO) and NATO was radically overhauled, taking on new roles, in particular in the field of peacekeeping. NATO, however, also became less central to Western security than it had been during the Cold War, becoming only one of a range of institutional frameworks available to Western states for addressing security problems. Parallel to this, the EU developed its common foreign and security policy, internal security – Justice and Home Affairs – co-operation and a role in peace-keeping and crisis management. By the 2000s, the EU was becoming an increasingly important foreign and security policy actor, although still constrained by its primarily inter-governmental consensus-based decision-making and the limits to the Union's hard power.

The eurozone crisis of the early 2010s called these trends into question, particularly in relation to the EU. In one scenario – federal Europe – closer fiscal union amongst the eurozone states (and perhaps most other EU members) might create political and economic dynamics favouring close co-operation in foreign, security and defence policy (for example, through modifying consensus decision-making and through greater pooling of defence resources). Such a development might significantly enhance the cohesiveness and effectiveness of the EU as a foreign policy actor. In most other scenarios, however, the EU's foreign policy ambitions are likely to be undermined. A smaller eurozone would produce new political fractures within the EU, perhaps a two-tier Union, making it ever more difficult to maintain foreign policy unity amongst the full EU membership. Were Britain to withdraw from the EU, the Union would lose one of its more outward-looking and militarily capable members, and there would be a new risk of political divisions between the EU-minus-Britain on the one hand and the USA and the UK on the other. Although a complete break-up of the euro would not necessarily have direct implications for EU foreign policy-making, the more general political momentum behind the Union would surely be undermined, including in the sphere of foreign and security policy.

As was noted above, NATO is likely to be affected less severely than the EU by the economic crisis, and problems within the EU may reinforce states' support for NATO. Nevertheless, although the European security debate is sometimes cast as 'NATO versus the EU', the EU's problems are not likely to be to NATO's advantage. In Europe, the EU's and NATO's members are essentially the same group of states. An economically weak and politically fragmented group of states within the EU are hardly likely to find dramatically greater political unity or will in the context of NATO. Falling military budgets will undermine the defence ambitions of both the EU and NATO. For NATO, the outcome is likely to be a more constrained alliance: one more cautious about military intervention beyond its borders and less likely to advance grand ambitions (whether in terms of further enlargement, engagement with other regions or addressing new challenges such as proliferation, terrorism or piracy).

New threats?

The declining likelihood of war within much of Europe has focused attention on other types of security threat, in particular other forms of violent threat and non-military security challenges. In both cases, the nature, scale and implications of emerging threats, and the appropriate policy responses, are deeply contentious.

In terms of new forms of violent threat, 9/11 pushed the twin issues of terrorism and proliferation to the centre of the security agenda. In both cases, there is an argument that alarmist public debate produced exaggerated threat perceptions and that the dangers posed by terrorism and proliferation are both limited and ones that European states will have to (and indeed can) learn to live with. The London and Madrid bombings made clear that Europe is a major target of globalized Islamic terrorism, and that the threat is both external (coming from Islamic groups outside Europe) and internal (coming from sections of Europe's growing Islamic population). While the threat posed to Europe by terrorism is real and significant, it is, however, limited in important ways: it does not pose a risk of complete political subjugation, as past dangers of military invasion and occupation have; nor does it risk the wholesale destabilization of European societies. As was noted in Chapter 8, further, by the early 2010s observers were suggesting that the threat from globalized Islamic terrorism was declining. Although there remain concerns about the possibility of large-scale terrorists attacks ('spectaculars' equivalent to 9/11 and in the worst case using nuclear weapons), the more likely scenario is that Europe will have to live with a long-term, persistent but limited level of terrorist threat: while protective security measures and longer-term preventive policies may contain that threat, the difficulty of preventing all attacks suggests that the threat – and periodic reality – of terrorist attacks will remain.

India's and Pakistan's consolidation of their status as nuclear weapon states, North Korea's 2006 and 2009 nuclear tests and the possibility that Iran may develop nuclear weapons suggest that Europe is also likely to face a continuing threat from the proliferation of weapons of mass destruction (WMD), especially nuclear weapons. The nature of that threat may, however, be limited, at least in the short to medium term. The threat posed by chemical and biological weapons, though real, is limited in scale because of the difficulties of dispersing chemical agents or biological pathogens over large areas. A direct nuclear attack on Europe is probably unlikely, given the political and economic costs and the likely military retaliation any state undertaking such an attack would incur. The real impact of nuclear proliferation will probably be in constraining the freedom of the USA and European states to intervene militarily against states that have nuclear weapons. In the longer term, however, the greatest danger may be of more widespread nuclear proliferation and the possible erosion of the international taboo against the use of nuclear weapons. The difficulty of preventing determined states from developing nuclear weapons suggests that, as with terrorism, Europe is likely to have to live with at least limited nuclear proliferation.

Since the 1980s there has also been a growing debate on the issue of non-military threats to security. While it is clear that a range of non-military problems – economic instability and poverty, climate change, migration, organized crime and diseases such as HIV/AIDS – pose significant challenges for Europe, either directly or in terms of a spillover from other parts of the world, whether these pose dangers to Europe's *security* is more contentious. Non-military problems may pose direct threats to people's lives, or major threats to the stability of states and societies, but the extent to which this is the case in much of Europe is debatable. The degree of vulnerability to non-military security threats also depends to a significant degree on the internal strength of states: the weak states of the Balkans and the former Soviet Union are particularly vulnerable to many non-military security challenges, whereas the capacity of Western European states and the EU as a whole to withstand or respond to such challenges is much greater. There is also a case that some issues have been unnecessarily or dangerously securitized: as was discussed in Chapter 9, European states have since the 1980s implemented increasingly defensive, securitized responses to migration, despite persuasive evidence that migration produces net economic gains and the fact that Europe increasingly needs migrants for its workforce. In other cases, however, there may be a strong argument that the scale of emerging non-military problems is such that they should be viewed as major threats to global security – as with climate change. The diverse range of issues usually bracketed together as part of the non-military security agenda make it difficult to draw conclusions that apply equally to different areas. Nevertheless, although the wider, non-military security agenda may be rather amorphous, European states and institutions have increasingly accepted its logic, and non-military issues are likely to remain an important part of the European security agenda.

Europe and global security

The declining likelihood of war within Europe and the emergence of a new global security agenda have raised the question of what role Europe can and should play in addressing global security challenges beyond Europe. As was seen in Chapters 6 to 9, in the 1990s and 2000s European states and in particular the EU played an increasing role in responding to new global security challenges. As these chapters also illustrated, European states and the EU developed a distinctive European approach with an emphasis on multilateralism, the application of soft power and long-term conflict prevention and peacebuilding – or what can be characterized as an emerging European 'strategic culture' (Cornish and Edwards, 2005).

Europe's role in responding to global security challenges relates to larger questions of world order, debate over which emerged with renewed vigour post-1989 and post-9/11. Kishore Mahbubani has described these debates on world order as a choice between four competing visions: the Truman world order (an essentially liberal vision based on co-operation among sovereign states, underpinned after 1945 by American power); the Jiang Zemin world order (a multipolar world in which China will eventually rise to become the world's leading power); the neo-conservative world order (based on the unilateral assertion of American power); and the Osama bin Laden world order (based on the overthrow of Western power in the Islamic world and the eventual establishment of an Islamic caliphate as the world's dominant force) (Mahbubani, 2005–06). During the Cold War, (Western) Europe largely supported the US-led vision of a liberal international order. After the end of the Cold War, while some in Europe viewed the EU as a counterweight to the USA (partly reflecting a balance of power *realpolitik* view), European support for a liberal international order largely continued. With the USA shifting towards a policy based on the unilateral assertion of American power after 9/11, Europe became the primary supporter of a liberal global order based on international norms, multilateralism, constraints on power and the primacy of political and economic (rather than military) instruments – as illustrated by its support, in the face of US opposition, for the United Nations, multilateral arms control agreements, the Kyoto agreement and the International Criminal Court. Although the USA shifted back towards a more liberal vision of international order under the Obama administration, there remain tensions between Europe and America over this underlying issue.

The 'rise of the rest' – the shift in the balance of global power from the Western to the non-Western world – will also have major implications for these debates on world order. The world of the 21st century will be one of multiple centres of power, including the USA, China, India, Japan and Russia, as well as other emerging powers such as Brazil and South Africa. The extent to which Europe, primarily in the form of the EU (assuming it remains intact), will be a significant centre of power remains to be seen. Some observers warn of further European decline or a European retreat into insularity – Europe becoming like a larger version of Switzerland. Others suggest that predictions of European decline are exaggerated and that Europe will remain a significant centre of global economic and political power. Even if Europe remains a significant centre of global power, however, it will be only one such centre in a world of many. The viability of the European vision of a liberal international order will depend, in part, on Europe's ability to persuade other states to buy into and support that vision. One of the central challenges for Europe, and especially the EU, in the 21st century will therefore be to engage with other states and regions, including the USA, but also with other major powers (and in particular, perhaps, democracies such as India, Brazil and South Africa), in supporting the maintenance of a liberal international order.

Bibliography

Adler, Emmanuel and Barnett, Michael (eds) (1998) *Security Communities.* Cambridge, Cambridge University Press.

Aldritch, Richard J. (2009) 'US-European Intelligence Cooperation on Counter-Terrorism: Low Politics and Compulsion', *British Journal of Politics and International Relations*, vol. 11, no. 1, pp. 122–39.

Allin, Dana, H. (1995) 'Can Containment Work Again?', *Survival*, vol. 37, no. 1, pp. 53–65.

Allison, Graham (2006) 'The Nightmare This Time', *The Boston Globe*, 12 March. http://www.boston.com/news/globe/ideas/articles/2006/03/12/the_nightmare_this_time/? page=full (accessed 11 May 2006).

Anderson, Perry (2007) 'Russia's Managed Democracy', *London Review of Books*, vol. 29, no. 2, 25 January.

Andréani, Gilles (1999–2000) 'The Disarray of US Non-Proliferation Policy', *Survival*, vol. 41, no. 4, pp. 42–61.

Andréani, Gilles (2004) 'The "War on Terror": Good Cause, Wrong Concept', *Survival*, vol. 46, no. 4, pp. 31–50.

Antonenko, Oksana (2001) 'Putin's Gamble', *Survival*, vol. 43, no. 4, pp. 49–59.

Arbatov, Alexei G. (1993) 'Russia's Foreign Policy Alternatives', *International Security*, vol. 18, no. 2, pp. 5–43.

Archik, Kristin (2011) *US-EU Cooperation Against Terrorism*, CRS Report for Congress, 18 July. Washington, DC, Congressional Research Service, Federation of American Scientists website www.fas.org/sgp/crs/row/RS22030.pdf (accessed 18 December 2011).

Arms Control Association (2007) *Worldwide Ballistic Missile Inventories.* Washington, DC, Arms Control Association. http://www.armscontrol.org/factsheets/missiles (accessed 22 May 2012).

Aron, Raymond (1954) *The Century of Total War.* New York, Doubleday.

Asmus, Ronald D. (2004) *Opening NATO's Door: How the Alliance Remade Itself for a New Era.* New York, Columbia University Press.

Asmus, Ronald D. (2010) *A Little War That Shook the World: Georgia, Russia and the Future of the West.* New York, Palgrave Macmillan.

Asmus, Ronald D., Kugler, Richard L. and Larrabee, F. Stephen (1995) 'NATO Expansion: The Next Steps', *Survival*, vol. 37, no. 1, pp. 7–33.

Associated Press (2006) 'German, Polish Leaders Seek Friendlier Relations but Remain Apart on Key Issues', *International Herald Tribune*, 30 October. http://www.iht.com/articles/ap/2006/10/30/europe/EU_GEN_Germany_Poland.php (accessed 23 November 2006).

Aznar, Jose María, Durão Barroso, José Manuel, Berlusconi, Silvio, Blair, Tony, Havel, Vaclav, Medgyessy, Peter, Miller, Leszek and Rasmussen, Anders Fogh (2003) 'United We Stand', *The Wall Street Journal*, 30 January. http://www.opinionjournal.com/extra/?id=110002994 (accessed 29 November 2006).

Baev, Pavel K. (1999) 'External Intervention in Secessionist Conflicts in Europe in the 1990s', *European Security*, vol. 8, no. 2, pp. 22–51.

Bailes, Alyson J. K. and Cottey, Andrew (2010) 'Euro-Atlantic Security and Institutions: Rebalancing in the midst of Global Change', in Stockholm International Peace Research Institute (SIPRI), *SIPRI Yearbook 2010: Armaments, Disarmament and International Security*. Oxford, Oxford University Press, pp. 149–74.

Baker, James A., III (2002) 'Russia in NATO?', *The Washington Quarterly*, vol. 25, no. 1, pp. 95–103.

Bakri, Nada (2011) 'UN Says Action Needed to Prevent Civil War in Syria', *New York Times*, 2 December. http://www.nytimes.com/2011/12/03/world/middleeast/un-says-action-needed-to-prevent-civil-war-in-syria.html (accessed 4 December 2011).

Barber, Benjamin R. (2003) *Jihad vs. McWorld: Terrorism's Challenge to Democracy*. London, Corgi Books.

Barber, Tony (2010) 'The Appointments of Herman van Rompuy and Catherine Ashton', *Journal of Common Market Studies*, Annual Review, vol. 48, s. 1, pp. 55–67.

Barnes, Julian E. (2012) 'US to Cut Forces in Europe', *The Wall Street Journal*, 13 January. http://online.wsj.com/article/SB10001424052970203721704577158873628227852.html (accessed 24 January 2012).

Baumert, Kevin and Pershing, Jonathan (2004) *Climate Data: Insights and Observations*. Arlington, VA, Pew Center on Global Climate Change. http://www.c2es.org/docUploads/Climate%20Data%20new.pdf (accessed 6 July 2012).

BBC News (2011a) 'State Multiculturalism has Failed, Says David Cameron', BBC News, 5 February. http://www.bbc.co.uk/news/uk-politics-12371994 (accessed 14 December 2011).

BBC News (2011b) 'How will the euro crisis end?', 9 December. BBC News website: http://www.bbc.co.uk/news/business-16098582 (accessed 15 March 2012).

BBC News (2011c) 'Euro Crisis: General Martin Dempsey Warns of Unrest', BBC News, 10 December. http://www.bbc.co.uk/news/world-us-canada-16122887 (accessed 11 January 2012).

Beer, Daniel (2009) 'Russia's Managed Democracy', *History Today*, vol. 59, issue 5.

Begg, Iain (2011) *Fiscal Union for the Euro Area: An Overdue and Necessary Scenario?* Guttersloh, Bertelsmann Stiftung.

Belke, Ansgar (2011) *Doomsday for the Euro Area: Causes, Variants and Consequences of Breakup*. Guttersloh, Bertelsmann Stiftung.

Bellamy, Alex J. (2010) 'The Responsibility to Protect – Five Years On', *Ethics & International Affairs*, vol. 24, no. 2, pp. 143–69.

Bergen, Peter (2005) 'Our Ally, Our Problem', *The New York Times*, 8 July. http://www.newamerica.net/publications/articles/2005/our_ally_our_problem (accessed 26 February 2007).

Biscop, Sven and Coelmont, Jo (2011) *Europe, Strategy and Armed Forces: The making of a distinctive power: Security Strategy and Defence Integration in Europe*. London and New York, Routledge.

Black, Ian (2003) 'Powell Calls on NATO to Send Troops to Iraq', *Guardian*, 5 December. http://www.guardian.co.uk/Iraq/Story/0,2763,1100481,00.html (accessed 6 December 2003).

Bobinski, Krzysztof (2011) 'Europe's Eastern Question', Open Democracy, 29 September. http://www.opendemocracy.net/krzysztof-bobinski/europes-eastern-question (accessed 9 November 2011).

Borger, Julian (2001) 'Bush Kills Global Warming Treaty', *Guardian*, 29 March. http://www.guardian.co.uk/international/story/0,3604,464902,00.html (accessed 4 September 2006).

Bovt, George (2009) 'EU–Russia Relations: Reset or Stagnation?', 24 November. Brussels, EU–Russia Centre. http://www.eu-russiacentre.org/our-publications/column/eurussia-relations-reset-stagnation.html (accessed 5 January 2012).

Brady, Hugo (2012) *Saving Schengen: How to Protect Passport-free Travel in Europe*. London, Center for European Reform. http://www.cer.org.uk/publications/archive/report/2012/saving-schengen-how-protect-passport-free-travel-europe (accessed 7 March 2012).

Bremmer, Ian and Charap, Samuel (2006–07) 'The Siloviki in Putin's Russia: Who They Are and What They Want', *The Washington Quarterly*, vol. 30, no. 1, pp. 83–92.

Bretherton, Charlotte and Vogler, John (2006) *The European Union as a Global Actor*, 2nd edn. London/New York, Routledge.

Brown, Derek (2001) 'The European Rapid Reaction Force', *The Guardian*, 11 April, http://www.guardian.co.uk/world/2001/apr/11/qanda.derek-brown (accessed 17 May 2012).

Brown, Michael E. (1995) 'The Flawed Logic of NATO Expansion', *Survival*, vol. 37, no. 1, pp. 34–52.

Brown, Michael E. (1999) 'A Minimalist NATO', *Foreign Affairs*, vol. 78, no. 3, pp. 205–18.

Brown, Michael E. (ed.) (2000) *The Rise of China*. Cambridge, MA, The MIT Press.

Brown, Michael E. (ed.) (2003) *Grave New World: Security Challenges in the 21st Century*. Washington, DC, Georgetown University Press.

Brown, Michael E., Lynn-Jones, Sean M. and Miller, Steven E. (eds) (1999) *Debating the Democratic Peace*. Cambridge, MA, MIT Press.

Browne, Des and Kearns, Ian (2011) 'Europe Needs to Shoulder More

Responsibility for Addressing Nuclear Dangers', *Strategic Europe*, 25 October. Brussels, Carnegie Endowment for International Peace, http://carnegieeurope.eu/publications/?fa=45797 (accessed 3 November 2011).

Buhler, Pierre (2011) 'Putin's Brezhnev Syndrome Means End of an Era', *The Moscow Times*, 7 December. http://www.themoscowtimes.com/print/article/putins-brezhnev-syndrome-means-end-of-an-era/449393.html (accessed 7 January 2011).

Bunyan, Tony (2005) *While Europe Sleeps ...*, ECLN Essays No. 11 (European Civil Liberties Network), reproduced on the Statewatch website. http://www.statewatch.org/news/2005/oct/ecln/essay-11.pdf (accessed 14 June 2006).

Burgess, Mark (2002) *In the Spotlight: Islamic Movement of Uzbekistan (IMU)*, CDI Terrorism Project, 25 March. Washington, DC: Centre for Defense Information. http://www.cdi.org/terrorism/imu.cfm (accessed 18 May 2006).

Burke, Jason (2004) *Al-Qaeda: The True Story of Radical Islam*. London, Penguin Books.

Burke, Jason and Traynor, Ian (2009) 'Fears of an Islamic Revolt in Europe Begin to Fade', *The Observer*, 26 July.

Bush, George W. (2002) *State of the Union Address*, 29 January. Washington, DC, The White House, Office of the Press Secretary. http://www.whitehouse.gov/news/releases/2002/01/20020129-11.html (accessed 24 November 2006).

Butler Committee (2004) *Review of Intelligence on Weapons of Mass Destruction: Report of a Committee of Privy Counsellors*, HC 898. London, The Stationery Office. http://www.butlerreview.org.uk/report/report.pdf (accessed 18 November 2006).

Buzan, Barry (1991a) *People, States and Fear: An Agenda for International Security Studies in the Post-Cold War Era*, 2nd edn. Hemel Hempstead, Harvester Wheatsheaf.

Buzan, Barry (1991b) 'New Patterns of Global Security in the Twenty-First Century', *International Affairs*, vol. 67, no. 3, pp. 431–51.

Buzan, Barry, Waever, Ole and de Wilde, Japp (1998) *Security: A New Framework for Analysis*. Boulder, CO/London, Lynne Rienner.

C2ES Center for Climate and Energy Solutions (2011) *Outcomes of the UN Climate Change Conference in Durban, South Africa*, December. Arlington, VA, C2ES Center for Climate and Energy Solutions. http://www.c2es.org/international/negotiations/durban/cop17 (accessed 29 February 2012).

Carnegie Endowment for International Peace (2009) *The Global Proliferation Status Map 2009*. Washington, DC, Carnegie Endowment for International Peace. http://carnegieendowment.org/2009/02/26/global-proliferation-status-map/ss7 (accessed 22 May 2012).

Carrera, Sergio, Guild, Espeth, Merlino, Massimo and Parkin, Joanna (2011) *A Race Against Solidarity: The Schengen Regime and the Franco-Italian Affair*. Brussels, Centre for European Policy Studies. http://www.ceps.eu/book/race-against-solidarity-schengen-regime-and-franco-italian-affair (accessed 1 December 2011).

Carter, Ashton B. and Perry, William J. (1999) *Preventive Defense: A New Security Strategy for America*. Washington, DC, Brookings Institution.

Carter, Ashton B., Perry, William J. and Steinbruner, John D. (1992) *A New Concept of Cooperative Security*, Brookings Occasional Papers. Washington, DC, Brookings Institution.

Charlemagne (2003) 'Let Them Eat Foie Gras', *The Economist*, 21 June, p. 31.

Charlemagne (2006) 'Playing Soft or Hard Cop', *The Economist*, 21 January, p. 33.

Chyba, Christopher F. and Greninger, Alex L. (2004) 'Biotechnology and Bioterrorism: An Unprecedented World', *Survival*, vol. 46, no. 2, pp. 143–62.

Ciscar, Juan-Carlos (ed.) (2009) *Climate Change Impacts in Europe: Final Report of the PESETA Research Project*. Brussels, European Commission Joint Research Centre, http://ftp.jrc.es/EURdoc/JRC55391.pdf (accessed 23 February 2011).

CLANDESTINO (2009) Comparative Policy Brief – Size of Irregular Migration. Athens, CLANDESTINO Research Project, http://irregular-migration.net//typo3_upload/groups/31/4.Background_Information/4.2.Policy_Briefs_EN/ComparativePolicyBrief_SizeOfIrregularMigration_Clandestino_Nov09_2.pdf (accessed 4 March 2012).

Clover, Charles and Gorst, Isabel (2011) 'Putin calls for new "Eurasian Union"', *Financial Times*, 4 October, http://www.ft.com/intl/cms/s/0/3901988c-eea2-11e0-9a9a-00144feab49a.html#axzz1id6OW1vA (accessed 5 January 2012).

Cole, David (2011) 'After September 11: What We Still Don't Know', *The New York Review of Books*, 29 September.

Collier, Paul, Elliott, Lani, Hegre, Havard, Hoeffler, Anke, Reynal-Querol, Marta and Sambanis, Nicholas (2003) *Breaking the Conflict Trap: Civil War and Development Policy*. Washington, DC, World Bank and Oxford University Press.

Colombani, Jean-Marie (2001) 'We Are All Americans', *Le Monde*, 12 September, reproduced in *World Press Review*, vol. 48, no. 11, November. http://www.worldpress.org/1101we_are_all_americans.htm (accessed 22 May 2006).

Commission of the European Communities (2006) *Communication from the Commission to the Council, the European Parliament, the European Economic and Social Council and the Committee of the Regions: Report on the Functioning of the Transitional Arrangements set out in the 2003 Accession Treaty (Period 1 May 2004–30 April 3006)*, COM (2006) 38 final, 8 February. Brussels, Commission of the European Communities). http://eur-lex.europa.eu/LexUriServ/site/en/com/2006/com2006_0048en 01.pdf (accessed 19 September 2006).

Commission on Human Security (2003) *Human Security Now*. New York, Commission on Human Security.

Commission on the Intelligence Capabilities of the United States Regarding Weapons of Mass Destruction (2005) *Commission on the Intelligence Capabilities of the United States Regarding Weapons of Mass Destruction: Report to the President of the United States*. Washington, DC, Commission on the Intelligence Capabilities of the United States Regarding Weapons of Mass Destruction. http://www.wmd.gov/report/wmd_report.pdf (accessed 18 November 2006).

Commission to Assess the Ballistic Missile Threat to the United States (1998) *Report of the Commission to Assess the Ballistic Missile Threat to the United States: Executive Summary*. http://www.fas.org/irp/threat/missile/rumsfeld (accessed 26 February 2007).

Congressional Budget Office (2011) *Budget and Economic Outlook: Fiscal Years 2011 to 2021*. Washington, DC, Congressional Budget Office. http://www.cbo.gov/doc.cfm?index=12039 (accessed 12 October 2011).

Connolly, Kate (2010) 'Multiculturalism is a Failure, says Merkel', *The Guardian*, 18 October.

Cornish, Paul and Edwards, Geoffrey (2005) 'The Strategic Culture of the European Union: A Progress Report', *International Affairs*, vol. 81, no. 4, pp. 801–20.

Cottey, Andrew (1995) *East–Central Europe after the Cold War: Poland, the Czech Republic, Slovakia and Hungary in Search of Security*. London, Macmillan.

Cottey, Andrew (ed.) (1999a) *Subregional Cooperation in the New Europe: Building Security, Prosperity and Solidarity from the Barents to the Black Sea*. London, Macmillan.

Cottey, Andrew (1999b) 'Central Europe Transformed: Security and Cooperation on NATO's New Frontier', *Contemporary Security Policy*, vol. 20, no 2, pp. 1–30.

Council of the European Union (2008a), *The European Union Strategy Against the Proliferation of Weapons of Mass Destruction: Effective Multilateralism, Prevention and International Cooperation*. Brussels, Council of the European Union. http://www.consilium.europa.eu/uedocs/cmsUpload/EN%20prolif_int%202008.pdf (accessed 22 May 2012).

Council of the European Union (2008b) *New Lines for Action by the European Union in Combating the Proliferation of Weapons of Mass Destruction and Their Delivery Systems*, 17172/08, 17 December. Brussels, Council of the European Union. http://www.consilium.europa.eu/eeas/foreign-policy/non-proliferation,-disarmament-and-export-control-/wmd.aspx?lang=en (accessed 14 October 2011).

Council of the European Union (2009) *Joint Declaration of the Prague Eastern Partnership Summit*, Prague, 7 May, 8435/09 (Presse 78), Brussels, European Union. http://www.consilium.europa.eu/uedocs/cms_data/docs/pressdata/en/er/107589.pdf (accessed 9 November 2011).

Council of the European Union (2010) *Internal Security Strategy for the European Union*, 5843/2/10, REV 2, JAI 90, 23 February. Brussels: Council of the European Union. http://register.consilium.europa.eu/pdf/en/10/st05/st05842-re02.en10.pdf (accessed 13 November 2011).

Cox, Michael (1995) *US Foreign Policy After the Cold War: Superpower Without a Mission?* London, Pinter.

Cox, Michael (2005) 'Beyond the West: Terrors in Transatlantia', *European Journal of International Relations*, vol. 11, no. 2, pp. 203–33.

Croft, Stuart, Redmond, John, Rees, G. Wyn and Webber, Mark (1999) *The Enlargement of Europe*. Manchester, Manchester University Press.

Daalder, Ivo H. (1999) *Getting to Dayton: The Making of America's Bosnia Policy*. Washington, DC, Brookings Institution Press.

Daalder, Ivo H. and Lindsay, James M. (2003) *America Unbound: The Bush Revolution in Foreign Policy*. Washington, DC, Brookings Institution.

Daalder, Ivo H. and O'Hanlon, Michael E. (2000) *Winning Ugly: NATO's War to Save Kosovo*. Washington, DC, Brookings Institution Press.

Dando, Malcolm (2005) 'The Bioterrorist Cookbook', *Bulletin of the Atomic Scientists*, vol. 61, no. 1, pp. 34–9, http://www.thebulletin.org/article.php?art_ofn=nd05dando (accessed 21 November 2006).

Dannreuther, Roland (ed.) (2004) *European Union Foreign and Security Policy: Towards a Neighbourhood Strategy*. London/New York, Routledge.

de Haas, Marcel and Schroder, Henning (2009) 'Russia's National Security Strategy', *Russian Analytical Digest*, No. 62, 18 June. http://www.clingendael.nl/publications/2009/20090618_cscp_medvedev_homan.pdf (accessed 4 January 2012).

Department for International Development (2004) *The Africa Conflict Prevention Pool: A Joint UK Government Approach to Preventing and Reducing Conflict in Sub-Saharan Africa*. London, Department for International Development. Foreign and Commonwealth Office website: http://www.fco.gov.uk/Files/kfile/ACPP%20Information%20Doc%20-%20final.pd (accessed 9 July 2006).

Department of Defense (2002) *Secretary Rumsfeld Speaks on '21st Century Transformation' of U.S. Armed Forces (transcript of remarks and question and answer period) Remarks as Delivered by Secretary of Defense Donald Rumsfeld, National Defense University, Fort McNair, Washington, D.C., Thursday, January 31, 2002*. http://www.defenselink.mil/speeches/2002/s20020131-secdef.html (accessed 24 November 2006).

Department of Defense (2012) *Sustaining US Global Leadership: Priorities for*

21ˢᵗ Century Defense. Washington, DC, Department of Defense. http://www.defense.gov/news/Defense_Strategic_Guidance.pdf (accessed 23 January 2012).

de Nevers, Renée (1994) *Russia's Strategic Renovation*, Adelphi Paper 289. London, Brassey's for International Institute for Strategic Studies.

Deutsch, Karl W., Burrell, Sidney A., Kann, Robert A., Lee, Maurice, Jr., Lichterman, Martin, Lindgren, Raymond E., Loewenheim, Francis L. and Van Wagenen, Richard W. (1969) *Political Community in the North Atlantic Area: International Organization in the Light of Historical Experience*. New York, Greenwood Press.

de Vasconcelos, Álvaro and Zaborowski, Marcin (eds) (2009) *The Obama Moment: European and American perspectives*. Paris, European Union Institute for Security Studies.

Duchêne, François (1972) 'Europe's Role in World Peace', in Mayne, Richard (ed.), *Europe Tomorrow: Sixteen Europeans Look Ahead*. London, Fontana, pp. 32–47.

Duffield, Mark (2001) *Global Governance and the New Wars*. London, Zed Books.

Duke, Simon (2000) *The Elusive Quest for European Security: From EDC to CFSP*. Basingstoke, Palgrave Macmillan.

Dunlop, John B. and Menon, Rajan (2006) 'Chaos in the North Caucasus and Russia's Future', *Survival*, vol. 48, no. 2, pp. 97–114.

Eberstadt, Nicholas (1999) 'Russia: Too Sick to Matter?', *Policy Review*, vol. 95. http://www.policyreview.com/jun99/eberstadt.html (accessed 5 December 2006).

Eberstadt, Nicholas (2011) 'The Dying Bear: Russia's Demographic Disaster', *Foreign Affairs*, vol. 90, no. 6, pp. 95–108.

Economist, The (2006a) 'Tales from Eurabia', *The Economist*, 24 June, p. 11.

Economist, The (2006b) 'Special Report: Islam, America and Europe – Look Out, Europe, They Say', *The Economist*, 24 June, pp. 29–34.

Economist, The (2008) 'Dr Keynes's Chinese patient', *The Economist*, 13 November. http://www.economist.com/node/12601956 (accessed 12 October 2011).

Economist, The (2010a) 'Europe and Development Aid: Waylaid', *The Economist*, 4 December, p. 38.

Economist, The (2010b) 'The Curse of the Conflict Junkies', *The Economist*, 4 December, pp. 41–2.

Economist, The (2011a) 'The End of ETA?', *The Economist*, 21 October. http://www.economist.com/blogs/newsbook/2011/10/terrorism-spain (accessed 7 December 2011).

Economist, The (2011b) 'Voting, Russian-style', *The Economist*, 10 December, pp. 31–2.

Economist, The (2011c) 'First We Take Sakharov Avenue', *The Economist*, 31 December, p. 20.

Economist, The (2012) 'Bombing Iran', *The Economist*, 25 February. http://www.economist.com/node/21548233 (accessed 18 May 2012).

Elbe, Stefan (2003) *Strategic Implications of HIV/AIDS*, Adelphi Paper 357. Oxford, Oxford University Press for International Institute of Strategic Studies.

Elegant, Simon (2009) 'Is China's Economy Strong Enough To Save the World?', Time, 10 April. http://www.time.com/time/world/article/0,8599, 1890568,00.html (accessed 12 October 2011).

Elliott, Larry (2006) 'It Will Take Years to Revive Trade Talks', *The Guardian*, 31 July. http://business.guardian.co.uk/story/0,,1833708,00.html (accessed 14 August 2006).

EU-Russia Centre (2010) 'The EU-Russia Modernisation Partnership', *The EU-Russia Centre Review* (Brussels: EU-Russia Centre), Issue 15. http://www.eu-russiacentre.org/reviews (accessed 5 January 2012).

EURODAD (nd) *Aid*, European Network on Debt and Development (Brussels, EURODAD). http://eurodad.org/?page_id=10243 (accessed 23 February 2012).

European Commission (nd) *The Common Agricultural Policy Explained*. Brussels, Directorate-General for Agriculture and Rural Development, http://ec.europa.eu/agriculture/publi/capexplained/cap_en.pdf (accessed 23 February 2012).

European Commission (2001) *Country Strategy Paper 2002–2006, National Indicative Programme 2002–2003: Russian Federation*. Brussels, European Commission. EU website: http://ec.europa.eu/comm/external_relations/russia/csp/02-06_en.pdf (accessed 5 December 2006).

European Commission (2004) *Communication from the Commission: European Neighbourhood Policy Strategy Paper*, COM(2004) 373 Final. Brussels, European Commission. EU website: http://ec.europa.eu/world/enp/pdf/strategy/strategy_paper_en.pdf (accessed 30 November 2006).

European Commission (2007) *Communication from The Commission to The Council, The European Parliament, The European Economic and Social Committee and The Committee of the Regions: Limiting Global Climate Change to 2 Degrees Celsius: The way ahead for 2020 and beyond*, COM(2007) 2 final, 10 January. Brussels, European Commission. http://eur-lex.europa.eu/LexUriServ/LexUriServ.do?uri=COM:2007:0002: FIN:EN:PDF (accessed 27 February 2012).

European Commission (2009) *After Copenhagen*, 21 December. Brussels, European Commission. http://ec.europa.eu/news/environment/091221_ en.htm (accessed 28 February 2012).

European Commission (2010) *Communication from the Commission to the European Parliament and the Council: The EU Internal Security Strategy in Action: Five Steps Towards a More Secure Europe*, COM(2010) 673 final, 22 November. Brussels: European Commission. http://eur-lex.europa.eu/LexUriServ/LexUriServ.do?uri=COM:2010:0673:FIN:EN:PDF (accessed 13 November 2011).

European Commission (2011a) *Commission Staff Working Document: EU Readmission Agreements: Brief Overview Of State Of Play (February 2011)*, SEC (2011) 209, 23 February. Brussels, European Commission. http://ec.europa.eu/transparency/regdoc/rep/eims/HOME/136966/SEC (2011)209.pdf (accessed 11 March 2012).

European Commission (2011b) *EU Response to the Arab Spring: New Package of Support for North Africa and Middle East*, Press Release, 27 September. Brussels, European Commission. http://europa.eu/rapid/ pressReleasesAction.do?reference=MEMO/11/636&format=HTML&age d=0&language=EN&guiLanguage=en (accessed 10 November 2011).

European Commission (2011c) *Increasing the impact of EU Development Policy: an Agenda for Change: Communication from the Commission to the European Parliament, the Council, the European Economic and Social Committee and the Committee of the Regions*, COM(2011) 637 final, 13 October. Brussels, European Commission. http://ec.europa.eu/ europeaid/infopoint/publications/europeaid/documents/257a_en.pdf (accessed 23 February 2012).

European Commission (2011d) *Communication From The Commission To The European Parliament, The Council, The European Economic And Social Committee And The Committee Of The Regions: The Global Approach to Migration and Mobility*, 18 November, COM(2011) 743 final. Brussels, European Commission. http://ec.europa.eu/home-affairs/ news/intro/docs/1_EN_ACT_part1_v9.pdf (accessed 9 March 2012).

European Commission (2012) *Trade, Growth and Development: Tailoring Trade and Investment Policy for those Countries Most in Need: Communication from the Commission to the European Parliament, the Council and the European Economic and Social Committee*, COM(2012) 22 final, 27 January. Brussels, European Commission. http://trade.ec. europa.eu/doclib/docs/2012/january/tradoc_148992.EN.pdf (accessed 23 February 2012).

European Commission/High Representative of the Union for Foreign Affairs and Security Policy (2011a) *Joint Communication to the European Council, the European Parliament, the Council, The European Economic and Social Committee and the Committee of the Regions: A Partnership for Democracy and Shared Prosperity with the South Mediterranean*, COM(2011) 200 final, 8 March. Brussels, European Commission. http://eeas.europa.eu/euromed/docs/com2011_200_en.pdf (accessed 10 November 2011).

European Commission/High Representative of the Union for Foreign Affairs and Security Policy (2011b) *Joint Communication to the European Parliament, the Council, the European Economic and Social Committee and the Committee of the Regions: A New Response to a Changing Neighbourhood: A Review of European Neighbourhood Policy*, COM(2011) 303, 25 May.Brussels, European Commission. http://ec.

europa.eu/world/enp/pdf/com_11_303_en.pdf (accessed 10 November 2011).

European External Action Service (nd) *Russia*. European External Action Service website http://www.eeas.europa.eu/russia/index_en.htm (accessed 5 January 2012).

European External Action Service/European Commission (2011) *Joint Reflection Paper: Towards a Renewed and Strengthened EU Climate Diplomacy*, 9 July. Brussels, European External Action Service/European Commission. http://eeas.europa.eu/environment/docs/2011_joint_paper_euclimate_diplomacy_en.pdf (accessed 23 February 2012).

European Policy Centre/Egmont/Centre for European Policy Studies (2010) *The Treaty of Lisbon: A Second Look at the Institutional Innovations*. Brussels, European Policy Centre/Egmont-The Royal Institute for International Relations/Centre for European Policy Studies. http://www.epc.eu/pub_details.php?cat_id=1&pub_id=1150 (accessed 7 November 2011).

European Union (1992) *The Maastricht Treaty: Treaty on European Union*, Maastricht, 7 February. http://www.eurotreaties.com/maastrichtext.html (accessed 1 March 2007).

European Union (1993) European Council in Copenhagen, 21–22 June 1993, Conclusions of the Presidency, SN 180/1/93 REV 1., http://www.consilium. europa.eu/ueDocs/cms_Data/docs/pressData/en/ec/72921.pdf (accessed 29 September 2006).

European Union (1997) *The Amsterdam Treaty – Amending the Treaty on European Union, The Treaties Establishing the European Communities and Certain Related Acts*, Amsterdam, 2 October 1997. http://eurotreaties. com/amsterdamtreay.pdf (accessed 1 December 2006).

European Union (1999) 'European Council, Cologne, 3–4 June 1999, Declaration of the European Council on Strengthening the Common European Policy on Security and Defence', in Maartje Rutten, *From St-Malo to Nice – European Defence: Core Documents*, Chaillot Paper 47. Paris, Institute for Security Studies, Western European Union, May 2001, pp. 41–5.

European Union (2001a) *EU Programme for the Prevention of Violent Conflicts, adopted by the General Affairs Council on 11–12 June 2001 and endorsed by the European Council at Gotborg 15–16 June 2001*. EU website: http://www.eu2001.se/static/eng/pdf/violent.PDF (accessed 30 November 2006).

European Union (2001b) 'Meeting of the Heads of State or Government of the European Union and the President of the European Commission, Ghent, 19 October 2001, "Road Map" of All the Measures and Initiatives to be Implemented Under the Action Plan Decided on by the European Council on 21 September 2001', in Maartje Rutten (2002) *From Nice to Laeken – European Defence: Core Documents, Vol. II*. Paris, Institute for Security Studies European Union, pp. 164–85.

European Union (2003a) *European Security Strategy: A More Secure Europe in a Better World.* http://ue.eu.int/uedocs/cmsUpload/78367.pdf (accessed 6 October 2011).

European Union (2003b) *European Strategy Against Proliferation of Weapons of Mass Destruction,* Brussels, 12 December. EU website: http://register.consilium.europa.eu/pdf/en/03/st15/st15708.en03.pdf (accessed 1 March 2007).

European Union (2003c) *European Union Factsheet: Extradition and Mutual Legal Assistance.* Brussels, General Secretariat of the Council of the European Union. http://www.consilium.europa.eu/uedocs/cms_data/docs/pressdata/en/er/76324.pdf (accessed 23 May 2012).

European Union (2004a) *Headline Goal 2010: Approved by General Affairs and External Relations Council on 17 May 2004 and Endorsed by the European Council of 17 and 18 June 2004.* http://ue/eu.int/eudocs/cmsUpload/2010%20Headline%20Goal.pdf.

European Union (2004b) *The Hague Programme: Strengthening Freedom, Security and Justice in the European Union,* 16054/50. Brussels, European Union, 13 December. EU website: http://ec.europa.eu/justice_home/doc_centre/doc/hague_programme_en.pdf (accessed 14 January 2007).

European Union (2005a) *European Union Factsheet: The Fight Against Terrorism.* Brussels, EuropeanUnion. http://www.consilium.europa.eu/uedocs/cmsUpload/3Counterterrorfinal170605.pdf (accessed 28 May 2006).

European Union (2005b) *The European Union Strategy for Combating Radicalisation and Terrorism.* Brussels, European Union, 24 November. http://register.consilium.eu.int/pdf/en/05/st14/st14781-re01.en05.pdf (accessed 29 June 2006).

European Union (2005c) *The European Union Counter-Terrorism Strategy,* 14469/4/05 REV 4. Brussels, European Union, 30 November.

European Union (2005d) *The European Consensus on Development: Joint statement by the Council and the Representatives of the Governments of the Member States meeting within the Council, the European Parliament and the Commission on the European Union Development Policy.* 20 December. EU website: http://ec.europa.eu/comm/development/body/development_policy_statement/docs/edp_declaration_signed_20_12_2005_en.pdf#zoom=125 (accessed 14 August 2006).

European Union (2006) *EU Action Plan on Combating Terrorism,* 5771/1/06 REV 1. Brussels, Council of the European Union. http://register.consilium.eu.int/pdf/en/06/st05/st05771-re01.en06.pdf (accessed 3 May 2006).

European Union (2008a) *Climate Change and International Security: Paper from the High Representative and the European Commission to the European Council,* S113/08, 14 March. Brussels, European Union. http://www.consilium.europa.eu/uedocs/cms_data/docs/pressdata/en/reports/99387.pdf (accessed 26 February 2012).

European Union (2008b) *Report on the Implementation of the European Security Strategy: Providing Security in a Changing World*, S407/08, 11 December. Brussels, European Union. http://www.consilium.europa.eu/ eeas/security-defence/european-security-strategy.aspx?lang=en (accessed 19 October 2011).

European Union (2008c) *Climate Change and Security: Recommendations of Javier Solana, the High Representative, on follow-up to the High Representative and Commission report on Climate Change and International Security*, 18 December. Brussels, European Union. http://www.eu-un.europa.eu/articles/fr/article_8382_fr.htm (accessed 26 February 2012).

European Union (2009a) *The European Union and the Fight Against Terrorism: Factsheet*. Brussels, EU Council Secretariat. http://www. consilium.europa.eu/uedocs/cmsUpload/Factsheet-fight%20against%20 terrorism%20091002.EN.revised.PDF (accessed 12 December 2011).

European Union (2009b) *Joint Progress Report and Follow-up Recommendations on Climate Change and International Security (CCIS) to the Council*, 16645/09, 25 November. Brussels, European Union. http://register.consilium.europa.eu/pdf/en/09/st16/st16645.en09.pdf (accessed 26 February 2012).

Europol (2011) *TE-SAT 2011: EU Terrorism Situation and Trend Report*. The Hague, European Police Office (Europol). https://www.europol.europa.eu/ sites/default/files/publications/te-sat2011.pdf (accessed 7 December 2011).

Evans, Michael (2005) 'MI5 Analysts Admit Link between Iraq War and Bombings', *The Times*, 28 July. http://www.timesonline.co.uk/ article/0,,22989-1711093,00.html (accessed 23 May 2006).

Faber, Gerrit and Orbie, Jan (2009) 'Everything But Arms: Much More than Appears at First Sight', *Journal of Common Market Studies*, vol. 47, no. 4, pp. 767–87.

Fenwick, Helen (2002) 'Responding to 11 September: Detention without Trial under the Anti-Terrorism, Crime and Security Act 2001', in Lawrence Freedman (ed.), *Superterrorism: Policy Responses*. Oxford, Blackwell, pp. 80–104.

Ferguson, Niall (2010) *Fiscal Crises and Imperial Collapse: Historical Perspective on Current Predicaments*, Ninth Annual Niarchos Lecture, 13 May. Washington, DC, Peterson Institute for International Economics. http://www.petersoninstitute.org/publications/papers/niarchos-ferguson-2010.pdf (accessed 27 October 2010).

Fishman, Boris (2003) *Wild East: Stories from the Last Frontier*. Boston, Mass., Justin, Charles & Co.

Fogh Rasmussen, Anders (2011) 'NATO After Libya', *Foreign Affairs*, vol. 90, no. 4, July–Aug, pp. 2-6.

Foreign and Commonwealth Office (2003) *The Global Conflict Prevention Pool: A Joint UK Government Approach to Reducing Conflict*. London,

Foreign and Commonwealth Office. http://www.fco.gov.uk/Files/kfile/ 43896_Conflict%20Broc,0.pdf (accessed 9 July 2006).

Foreign and Commonwealth Office (2005) *Counter-Terrorism Legislation and Practice: A Survey of Selected Countries*, FCO Research Paper. London, Foreign and Commonwealth Office. http://www.fco.gov.uk/Files/kfile/ QS%20Draft%2010%20FINAL1.pdf (accessed 14 June 2006).

Forster, Anthony (2006) *Armed Forces and Society in Europe*. Basingstoke, Palgrave Macmillan.

Freedland, Jonathan (2002) 'Rome, AD … Rome, DC?', *The Guardian*, 18 September. http://www.guardian.co.uk/world/2002/sep/18/usa.comment (accessed 7 October 2011).

French Ministry of Foreign Affairs (2003) *Iraq: Declaration Russia–Germany–France, 5 March 2003*, Permanent Mission of France to the United Nations. http://www.un.int/france/documents_anglais/030305_mae_france_irak.htm (accessed 24 November 2006).

Frost, Robin M. (2005) *Nuclear Terrorism After 9/11*, Adelphi Paper 378. London, Routledge for International Institute for Strategic Studies.

Gaddis, John Lewis (1986) 'The Long Peace: Elements of Stability in the Postwar International System', *International Security*, vol. 10, no. 4, pp. 99–142.

Gaddis, John Lewis (1998) 'History, Grand Strategy and NATO Enlargement', *Survival*, vol. 40, no. 1, pp. 145–51.

Gambles, Ian (ed.) (1995) *A Lasting Peace in Central Europe?*, Chaillot Paper 20. Paris, Institute for Security Studies, Western European Union.

Gardner Feldman, Lily (1999) 'The Principle and Practice of "Reconciliation" in German Foreign Policy: Relations with France, Israel, Poland and the Czech Republic', *International Affairs*, vol. 75, no. 2, pp. 333–56.

Garton Ash, Timothy (2005) *Free World: Why a Crisis of the West Reveals the Opportunity of Our Time*. London, Penguin.

Gates, Robert M. (2011a) 'United States Military Academy', West Point, New York, 25 February. US Department of Defense website: http://www.defense.gov/speeches/speech.aspx?speechid=1539 (accessed 4 December 2011).

Gates, Robert M. (2011b) 'Future of NATO', Speech at Security and Defense Agenda, Brussels, Belgium, 10 June. US Department of Defense website: http://www.defense.gov/speeches/speech.aspx?speechid=1581 (accessed 27 September 2011).

Giegerich, Bastian (2008) *European Military Crisis Management: Connecting Ambition and Reality*, Adelphi Paper 397. Abingdon, Routledge for The International Institute for Strategic Studies.

Giles, Keir (2010) *The Military Doctrine of the Russian Federation 2010*. Rome, NATO Defense College, http://www.ndc.nato.int/research/series.php?icode=9 (accessed 4 January 2012).

Gleick, Peter H. (1993) 'Water and Conflict: Fresh Water Resources and International Security', *International Security*, vol. 18, no. 1, pp. 79–112.

Goble, Paul (2008) 'Crime out of Control in Putin's Russia', La Russophobe website, 30 June, http://larussophobe.wordpress.com/2008/06/30/crime-out-of-control-in-putins-russia/ (accessed 6 January).

Goldgeier, James M. and McFaul, Michael (1992) 'A Tale of Two Worlds: Core and Periphery in the Post-Cold War Era', *International Organization*, vol. 46, no. 2, pp. 467–91.

Gomart, Thomas (2008) *EU-Russia Relations: Towards a Way Out of Depression*. Washington DC/Paris, Center for Strategic and International Studies and Institut Francais des Relations Internationales. http://www.ifri.org/files/Russie/Gomart_EU_Russia.pdf (accessed 5 January 2012).

Goodson, Roy (2003) 'Transnational Crime, Corruption, and Security', in Michael E. Brown (ed.), *Grave New World: Security Challenges in the 21st Century*. Washington, DC, Georgetown University Press, pp. 259–78.

Gordon, Philip H. (1997–8) 'Europe's Uncommon Foreign Policy', *International Security*, vol. 22, no. 3, pp. 74–100.

Gordon, Philip H. (2002) *Iraq: The Transatlantic Debate*, Occasional Paper 39. Paris, European Union Institute for Security Studies.

Gordon, Philip H. (2008) *Winning the Right War: The Path to Security for America and the World*. New York: Henry Holt & Co.

Gormley, Denis M. (2004) 'The Limits of Intelligence: Iraq's Lessons', *Survival*, vol. 46, no. 3, pp. 7–28.

Grabbe, Heather (2006) *The EU's Transformative Power: Europeanization through Conditionality in Central and Eastern Europe*. Basingstoke, Palgrave Macmillan.

Graham, Thomas, Jr. (1999) *World without Russia?*, Jamestown Foundation Conference. Washington, DC, Carnegie Endowment for International Peace. http://www.carngieendowment.org/publications/index.cfm?fa=view&id=285 (accessed 17 January 2006).

Grand, Camille (2000) *The European Union and the Non-Proliferation of Nuclear Weapons*, Chaillot Papers 37. Paris, Western European Union Institute for Security Studies.

Gray, Colin S. (1999) *The Second Nuclear Age*. Boulder, CO, Lynne Rienner.

Grevi, Giovanni and de Vasconcelos, Alvaro (eds) (2008) *Partnerships for Effective Multilateralism: EU Relations with Brazil, China, India and Russia*, Chaillot Paper No. 109. Paris, European Union Institute for Security Studies.

Grgic, Borut (2004) 'There Are Worse Things than a Nuclear Iran', *International Herald Tribune*, 2 December. Global Policy Forum website: http://www.globalpolicy.org/security/sanction/iran.1202worsethings.htm (accessed 6 December 2004).

Gross, Eva and Juncos, Ana E. (eds) (2010) *EU Conflict Prevention and Crisis Management: Roles, Institutions, and Policies*. Abingdon, Routledge.

Guardian, The (2003) 'Kicking the Subsidies: Third World Farmers Need a Fair Deal', *The Guardian*, 18 August. http://www.guardian.co.uk/wto/article/0,2763,1020721,00.html (accessed 14 August 2006).

Guelke, Adrian (1998) *The Age of Terrorism and the International System.* London, I. B. Tauris.

Habermas, Jürgen (2006) *The Divided West.* Cambridge, Polity Press.

Harbom, Lotta and Wallensteen, Peter (2006) 'Patterns of Major Armed Conflicts, 1990–2005', Appendix 2A in Stockholm International Peace Research Institute, *SIPRI Yearbook 2006: Armaments, Disarmament and International Security.* Oxford, SIPRI/Oxford University Press, pp. 108–19.

Harbom, Lotta and Wallensteen, Peter (2010) 'Patterns of Major Armed Conflicts, 2000–2009', Appendix 2A in Stockholm International Peace Research Institute, *SIPRI Yearbook 2010: Armaments, Disarmament and International Security.* Oxford, SIPRI/Oxford University Press, pp. 61–71.

Harris, Martha (2003) 'Energy and Security', in Brown, Michael E. (ed.), *Grave New World: Security Challenges in the 21st Century.* Washington, DC, Georgetown University Press, pp. 157–77.

Hart, Douglas and Simon, Steven (2006) 'Thinking Straight and Talking Straight: Problems of Intelligence Analysis', *Survival*, vol. 48, no. 1, pp. 35–60.

Hassner, Pierre (2010) 'All Shock Up?', Survival, vol. 52, no. 4, 2010, pp. 183–90.

Heisbourg, François (1992) 'The Future of the Atlantic Alliance: Whither NATO, Whether NATO?', *The Washington Quarterly*, vol. 15, no. 2, pp. 127–39.

Herspring, Dale R. (2002) 'Deprofessionalising the Russian Armed Forces', in Anthony Forster, Timothy Edmunds and Andrew Cottey (eds), *The Challenge of Military Reform in Postcommunist Europe: Building Professional Armed Forces.* Basingstoke, Palgrave Macmillan, pp. 197–210.

Herz, John H. (1950) 'Idealist Internationalism and the Security Dilemma', *World Politics*, vol. 2, pp. 157–80.

Hill, Fiona (2002) 'Russia: The 21st Century's Energy Superpower', *The Brookings Review*, vol. 20, no. 2, pp. 28–31. http://www,brookings.edu/press/review/spring2002/hill.htm (accessed 3 December 2006).

Hill, Fiona (2004) *Energy Empire: Oil, Gas and Russia's Revival.* London, Foreign Policy Centre. http://fpc.org.uk/fsblob/307.pdf (accessed 3 December 2006).

Hoge, James F., Jr. (2004) 'A Global Power Shift in the Making', *Foreign Affairs*, vol. 83, no. 4, pp. 2–7.

Holbrooke, Richard (1995) 'America: A European Power', *Foreign Affairs*, vol. 74, no. 2, pp. 38–51.

Holland, Dawn, Fic, Tatiana, Rincon-Aznar, Ana, Stokes, Lucy and Paluchowski, Pawel (2011) *Labour Mobility Within the EU: The Impact of Enlargement and the Functioning of the Transitional Arrangements – Final Report.* London, National Institute of Economic and Social Research.

http://ec.europa.eu/social/main.jsp?langId=en&catId=89&newsId=1108& furtherNews=yes (accessed 5 March 2012).

Home Office (nd) 'Terrorism and the Law'. Home Office website: http://www.homeoffice.gov.uk/security/terrorism-and-the-law/?version=1 (accessed 14 June 2006).

Homer-Dixon, Thomas F. (1991) 'On the Threshold: Environmental Changes as Causes of Acute Conflict', *International Security*, vol. 16, no. 2, pp. 76–116.

Homer-Dixon, Thomas F. (1994) 'Environmental Scarcities and Violent Conflict', *International Security*, vol. 19, no. 1, pp. 5–40.

Hopkins, Nick (2011) 'MoD prepares to take part in US strikes against Iran', *The Guardian*, 3 November.

Houghton, John (2003) 'Global Warming Is Now a Weapon of Mass Destruction', *The Guardian*, 28 July. http://www.guardian.co.uk/politics/2003/jul/28/environment.greenpolitics (accessed 6 October 2011).

Howard, Michael (2002) 'What's In a Name? How to Fight Terrorism', *Foreign Affairs*, vol. 81, no. 1, pp. 8–13.

Howorth, Jolyon (2003–4) 'France, Britain and the Euro-Atlantic Crisis', *Survival*, vol. 45, no. 4, pp. 173–92.

Howorth, Jolyon (2007) *Security and Defence Policy in the European Union*. Basingstoke, Palgrave Macmillan.

Human Rights Watch (2005) *Proposed Anti-Terrorism Measures Threaten Fundamental Rights*, 10 August, reproduced on Global Policy Forum website: http://www.globalpolicy.org/empire/terrorwar/liberties/2005/0810ukterrormeasures.htm (accessed 17 January 2005).

Human Security Centre (2005) *Human Security Report 2005: War and Peace in the 21st Century*. Oxford, Oxford University Press. http://www.hsrgroup.org/human-security-reports/2005/text.aspx (accessed 6 July 2012).

Hunter, Robert E. (1999) 'Maximizing NATO', *Foreign Affairs*, vol. 78, no. 3. pp. 190–203.

Huntington, Samuel P. (1993) 'The Clash of Civilizations?', *Foreign Affairs*, vol. 72, no. 3, pp. 22–49.

Hutton, Will (2007) *The Writing on the Wall: China and the West in the 21st Century*. London, Abacus.

Ikenberry, G. John (2001) *After Victory: Institutions, Strategic Restraint and the Rebuilding of Order After Major Wars*. Princeton, NJ/Oxford, Princeton University Press.

Ikenberry, G. John (2008) 'The Rise of China and the Future of the West: Can the Liberal System Survive?', *Foreign Affairs*, vol. 87, no. 1, pp. 23–37.

Inkster, Nigel (2011) '9/11/11: A Decade of Intelligence', *Survival*, vol. 53, No. 6, pp. 5–13.

International Commission on Intervention and State Sovereignty (2001) *The Responsibility to Protect: Report of the International Commission on Intervention and State Sovereignty*. Ottawa, ICISS/International Development Research Centre.

International Institute for Strategic Studies (1991) *The Military Balance 1991–92*. London, Brassey's for the IISS.

International Institute for Strategic Studies (1995) 'Transnational Crime: A New Security Threat?', in *Strategic Survey 1994–95*. Oxford, Oxford University Press for the IISS, pp. 25–33.

International Institute for Strategic Studies (2000) *The Military Balance 2000–2001*. Oxford, Oxford University Press for the IISS.

International Institute for Strategic Studies (2004) *Strategic Survey 2003–4*. Oxford, Oxford University Press for the IISS.

International Institute for Strategic Studies (2006) *The Military Balance 2006*. London, Routledge for the IISS.

International Institute for Strategic Studies (2010a) *The Military Balance 2011*. London, Routledge for the IISS.

International Institute for Strategic Studies (2010b) 'Terrorist Threats in Europe: Hype or Reality?', *Strategic Comments*, vol. 16, comment 18, October.

International Institute for Strategic Studies (2011a) 'War in Libya: Europe's Confused Response', *Strategic Comments*, vol. 17, comment 18, April.

International Institute for Strategic Studies (2011b) 'Medvedev momentum falters in Nagorno-Karabakh', *Strategic Comments*, vol. 17, comment 27, August.

International Organization for Migration (2005) *World Migration 2005: Costs and Benefits of International Migration*, vol. 3 – IOM World Migration Report Series. Geneva, International Organization for Migration. http://www.iom.int/jahia/Jahia/cache/bypass/pid/8?entryId= 932 (accessed 21 September 2006).

International Organization for Migration (2010) *World Migration Report 2010: The Future of Migration: Building Capacities for Change*. Geneva, International Organization for Migration. http://publications.iom.int/ bookstore/index.php?main_page=product_info&cPath=37&products_id= 653 (accessed 4 March 2012).

International Organization for Migration (2011a) *World Migration Report 2011: Communicating Effectively about Migration*, 10 October. Geneva, International Organization for Migration. http://publications.iom.int/ book-store/index.php?main_page=product_info&cPath=37&products_id=752& zenid=8b30228d097fb2140906d603579ab949 (accessed 11 March 2012).

International Organization for Migration (2011b) IOM Response to the Libyan Crisis: External Situation Report, 10 October. Geneva, International Organization for Migration. http://www.iom.int/jahia/ webdav/shared/shared/mainsite/media/docs/reports/IOM-sitrep-MENA. pdf (accessed 7 March 2012).

Jacques, Martin (2009) *When China Rules the World: The Rise of the Middle Kingdom and the End of the Western World*. London, Allen Lane.

Jandl, Michael (2003) *Estimates on the Numbers of Illegal and Smuggled*

Immigrants in Europe: Presentation at Workshop 1.6, 8th International Metropolis Conference, 17 September 2003, PowerPoint presentation. Vienna, International Centre for Migration Policy Development. http://www.icmpd.org/uploading/Metropolis%20Presentation%2D2003 %2DMJ%2D1.pdf (accessed 21 September 2006).

Jehl, Douglas (2005) 'Iraq May Be Prime Place for Training of Militants, C.I.A. Report Concludes', *The New York Times*, 22 June. http://www. nytimes.com/2005/06/22/international/middleeast/22intel.html?ex=12770 92800&en=cca56f7374b2b81a&ei=5090&partner=rssuserland&emc=rss (accessed 23 May 2006).

Jenkins, Brian Michael (2006) 'The New Age of Terrorism', in David Kamien, *The McGraw-Hill Homeland Security Handbook: The Definitive Guide for Law Enforcement, EMT, and All Other Security Professionals*. McGraw-Hill Professional, pp. 117–30. http://www.rand.org/content/dam/rand/ pubs/reprints/2006/RAND_RP1215.pdf (accessed 4 October 2011).

Jervis, Robert (1976) *Perception and Misperception in International Politics*. Princeton, NJ, Princeton University Press.

Jervis, Robert (1978) 'Cooperation Under the Security Dilemma', *World Politics*, vol. 30, no. 2, pp. 167–214.

Jervis, Robert (1982) 'Security Regimes', *International Organization*, vol. 36, no. 2, pp. 357–78.

Jervis, Robert (1985) 'From Balance to Concert: A Study of International Security Cooperation', *World Politics*, vol. XXXVIII, no. 1, pp. 58–79.

Jervis, Robert (1991–2) 'The Future of World Politics: Will It Resemble the Past', *International Security*, vol. 16, no. 3, pp. 39–73.

Jervis, Robert (1997) *System Effects: Complexity in Political and Social Life*. Princeton, NJ, Princeton University Press.

Jervis, Robert (2002) 'Theories of War in an Era of Leading-Power Peace: Presidential Address, American Political Science Association, 2001', *American Political Science Review*, vol. 96, no. 1, pp. 1–14.

Joffe, Josef (2009) 'The Default Power: The False Prophecy of America's Decline', *Foreign Affairs*, vol. 88, no. 5, pp. 21–35.

Johnson, Chalmers (2000) *Blowback: The Costs and Consequences of American Empire*. New York, Metropolitan Books.

Jones, Bruce D. (2011) 'Libya and the Responsibilities of Power', *Survival*, vol. 53, no. 3, pp. 51–60.

Joyner, James (2009) 'Europe's Obama Fatigue: Bush was better for Europe. No, seriously', *Foreign Policy*, 29 October. http://www.foreignpolicy. com/articles/2009/10/29/europes_obama_fatigue?page=full (accessed 19 January 2012).

Judah, Tim (2000) *Kosovo: War and Revenge*. New Haven, Conn./ London, Yale University Press.

Kagan, Robert (2002) 'Power and Weakness', *Policy Review*, vol. 113. http://www.hoover.org/publications/policy-review/article/7107 (accessed 6 July 2012).

Kagan, Robert (2003) *Paradise and Power: America and Europe in the New World Order*. London, Atlantic Books.

Kaldor, Mary (2001) *New and Old Wars: Organized Violence in a Global Era*. Cambridge, Polity Press.

Kalicki, Jan H. and Goldwyn, David L. (eds) (2005) *Energy and Security: Toward a New Foreign Policy Strategy*. Baltimore, MD, Johns Hopkins University Press.

Kaplan, Robert D. (1994) 'The Coming Anarchy', *The Atlantic Monthly*, vol. 273, no. 2, pp. 44–76.

Kay, John (2006) 'How the Migration Estimates Turned Out Wrong', *Financial Times*, 6 September. Reproduced at http://www.johnkay.com/print/459.html (accessed 19 September 2006).

Kaysen, Carl (1990) 'Is War Obsolete? A Review Essay', *International Security*, vol. 14, no. 4, pp. 42–64.

Kearns, Ian (2011) *Beyond the United Kingdom: Trends in the Other Nuclear Armed States*, Discussion Paper 1 of the BASIC Trident Commission. London/Washington, DC, British American Security Information Council (BASIC). http://www.basicint.org/publications/dr-ian-kearns-trident-commission-consultant/2011/beyond-uk-trends-other-nuclear-armed-s (accessed 3 November 2011).

Kegley, Charles W., Jr. (1991) *The Long Postwar Peace: Contending Explanations and Projections*. New York, HarperCollins.

Kennedy, Paul (1988) *The Rise and Fall of the Great Powers: Economic Change and Military Conflict from 1500 to 2000*. London, Fontana.

Keohane, Daniel (2005) 'One Step Forward, Two Steps Back', *E!Sharp*, November–December, pp. 37–8. Centre for European Reform website: http://www.cer.org.uk/pdf/article_keohane_esharp_nov05.pdf.

Keohane, Robert O. and Martin, Lisa L. (1995) 'The Promise of Institutionalist Theory', *International Security*, vol. 20, no. 1, pp. 39–51.

Keohane, Robert O. and Nye, Joseph S. (2001) *Power and Interdependence*, 3rd edn. New York, Longman.

Keohane, Robert O., Nye, Joseph S. and Hoffman, Stanley (1993) *After the Cold War: International Institutions and State Strategies in Europe, 1989–1991*. Cambridge, Mass., Harvard University Press.

Kettani, Houssain (2009) 'Muslim Population in Europe', Proceedings of the 2009 International Conference on Social Sciences and Humanities, Singapore, 9–11 October 2009, www.pupr.edu/hkettani/papers/ICSSH2009Europe.pdf (accessed 14 December 2011).

Keukeleire, Stephan and MacNaughtan, Jennifer (2008) *The Foreign Policy of the European Union*. Basingstoke, Palgrave Macmillan.

Krastev, Ivan (2011) 'The Balkans and the EU after Mladic', Survival, vol. 53, no. 4, pp. 13–18.

Krause, Joachim (1996) 'The Proliferation of Weapons of Mass Destruction: The Risks for Europe', in Yves Boyer, Paul Cornish, Peter van Ham and Joachim

Krause (eds), *Europe and the Challenge of Proliferation*, Chaillot Papers 24. Paris, Western European Union Institute for Security Studies, pp. 5–21.

Krause, Keith and Williams, Michael C. (eds) (1997) *Critical Security Studies: Concepts and Cases*. London, UCL Press.

Krauthammer, Charles (1990–1) 'The Unipolar Moment', *Foreign Affairs*, vol. 70, no. 1, pp. 23–3.

Kremenyuk, Viktor (2002) 'Russia's Defence Diplomacy in Europe: Containing Threat Without Confronation', in Andrew Cottey and Derek Averre (eds), *New Security Challenges in Postcommunist Europe: Securing Europe's East*. Manchester/New York, Manchester University Press, pp. 98–111.

Kristensen, Hans (2009) 'French Aircraft Carrier Sails Without Nukes', FAS Strategic Security Blog, 4 August. http://www.fas.org/blog/ssp/2009/08/degaulle.php.

Kulesa, Lukasz (2010) 'Global Zero: Implications for Europe', in Zanders, Jean Pascal (ed.), *Nuclear Weapons After the 2010 NPT Review Conference*, Chaillot Papers 120. Paris, European Union Institute for Security Studies, pp. 87–102.

Layne, Christopher (1993) 'The Unipolar Illusion', *International Security*, vol. 17, no. 4, pp. 5–51.

Lehne, Stefan (2004) 'Has the "Hour of Europe" Come at Last? The EU's Strategy for the Balkans', in Judy Batt (ed.), *The Western Balkans: Moving On*, Chaillot Papers 70. Paris, European Union Institute for Security Studies, pp. 111–24.

Leonard, Mark and Popescu, Nicu (2007) *A Power Audit of EU-Russia Relations*. London, European Council on Foreign Relations. http://ecfr.eu/page/-/documents/ECFR-EU-Russia-power-audit.pdf (accessed 5 January 2012).

Levy, Jack (1989) 'Domestic Politics and War', in Robert I. Rotberg and Theodore K. Rabb (eds), *The Origin and Prevention of Major Wars*. Cambridge, Cambridge University Press, pp. 79–99.

Levy, Marc A. (1995) 'Is the Environment a National Security Issue?', *International Security*, vol. 20, no. 2, pp. 35–62.

Lindstrom, Gustav (2004) 'On the Ground: ESDP Operations', in Nicole Gnesotto (ed.), *EU Security and Defence Policy: The First Five Years (1999–2004)*. Paris, European Union Institute for Security Studies, pp.111–29.

Lipset, Seymour Martin (1990) *Continental Divide: The Values and Institutions of the United States and Canada*. London, Routledge & Kegan Paul.

Loescher, Gil and Milner, James (2005) *Protracted Refugee Situations: Domestic and International Security Implications*, Adelphi Paper 375. Abingdon, Routledge for International Institute for Strategic Studies.

Lucas, Edward (2008) *The New Cold War: Putin's Russia and the Threat to the West*. New York, Palgrave Macmillan.

Lugar, Richard G. (1993) *NATO: Out of Area or Out of Business – A Call for US Leadership to Revive and Redefine the Alliance*, Presentation to the Open Forum of the US Department of State, 2 August.

Lugar, Richard G. (2005) *The Lugar Survey on Proliferation Threats and Responses*. Washington, DC, US Senate. http://lugar.senate.gov/reports/NPSurvey.pdf (accessed 1 March 2007).

Lukasik, Stephen J., Goodman, Seymour E. and Longhurst, David W. (2003) *Protecting Critical Infrastructure Against Cyber-Attack*, Adelphi Paper 359. Oxford, Oxford University Press for International Institute for Strategic Studies.

Lungescu, Oana (2003) 'Chirac Blasts EU Candidates', BBC News website, 18 February. http://news.bbc.co.uk/1/hi/world/europe/2774139.stm (accessed 2 December 2006).

Lynch, Marc (2010) *Rhetoric and Reality: Countering Terrorism in the Age of Obama*. Washington, DC, Center for a New American Security. http://www.cnas.org/files/documents/publications/CNAS_Rhetoric%20and%20Reality_Lynch.pdf (accessed 5 October 2011).

Mabey, Nick (2012) 'Understanding Europe's unexpected Durban success', *E!Sharp*, January. http://esharp.eu/big-debates/the-green-economy/16-understanding-europe-s-unexpected-durban-success/ (accessed 29 February 2012).

MacFarlane, S. Neil, Thielking, Carl J. and Weiss, Thomas G. (2004) 'The Responsibility to Protect: Is Anyone Interested in Humanitarian Intervention?', *Third World Quarterly*, vol. 25, no. 5, pp. 997–92.

Mahbubani, Kishore (2005–06) 'The Impending Demise of the Postwar System', *Survival*, vol. 47, no. 4, pp. 7–18.

Mandelbaum, Michael (1998–9) 'Is Major War Obsolete?', *Survival*, vol. 40, no. 4, pp. 20–38.

Manners, Ian (2002) 'Normative Power Europe: A Contradiction in Terms?', *Journal of Common Market Studies*, vol. 40, no. 2, pp. 235–58.

Manners, Ian and Whitman, Richard (eds) (2000) *The Foreign Policies of European Union Member States*. Manchester, Manchester University Press.

Mannion, Jim (2012) 'Britain warns US not to forget Russia', *NineMSN*, 6 January. http://news.ninemsn.com.au/world/8399109/britain-warns-us-not-to-forget-russia (accessed 23 January 2012).

Mansfield, Edward D. and Snyder, Jack (1995) 'Democratization and the Danger of War', *International Security*, vol. 20, no. 1, pp. 5–38.

Maslin, Mark (2004) *Global Warming: A Very Short Introduction*. Oxford, Oxford University Press.

Mayhew, Alan (1998) *Recreating Europe: The European Union's Policy Towards Central and Eastern Europe*. Cambridge, Cambridge University Press.

McCrisken, Trevor (2011) 'Ten years on: Obama's war on terrorism in rhetoric and practice', *International Affairs*, vol. 87, no. 4, pp. 781–801.

Mearsheimer, John J. (1990) 'Back to the Future: Instability in Europe After the Cold War', *International Security*, vol. 15, no. 1, pp. 5–56.

Melvin, Neil (1995) *Russians Beyond Russia: The Politics of National Identity*, Chatham House Papers. London, Cassell/Royal Institute of International Affairs.

Melvin, Neil (2010) 'Eurasian Security Arrangements Face Reality Check After Kyrgyzstan Crisis', *SIPRI Newsletter*, July/Aug. Stockholm, Stockholm International Peace Research Institute (SIPRI). http://www.sipri.org/media/newsletter/essay/julyaugust10 (accessed 3 December 2011).

Menon, Anand (2011) 'European Defence Policy from Lisbon to Libya', *Survival*, vol. 53, no. 3, pp. 75–90.

Micklethwait, John and Wooldridge, Adrian (2004) *The Right Nation: Why America Is Different*. London, Allen Lane.

Minogue, Kenneth (2000) *Politics: A Very Short Introduction*. Oxford, Oxford University Press.

Mohan, C. Raja (2006) 'India and the Balance of Power', *Foreign Affairs*, vol. 85, no. 4, pp. 17–32.

Monar, Jorg (ed) (2010) *The Institutional Dimension of the European Union's Area of Freedom, Security and Justice*. Brussels, Peter Lang.

Moore, Rebecca R. (2007) *NATO's New Mission: Projecting Stability in a Post-Cold War World*. Westport/London. Praegar Security International.

Morgenthau, Hans J. (1985) *Politics Among Nations: The Struggle for Power and Peace*, 6th edn. New York, McGraw-Hill.

Moshes, Arkady (2009) 'EU–Russia Relations: Unfortunate Continuity', *European Issues* (Paris/Brussels: Fondation Robert Schuman), No. 129, 24 February. http://www.robert-schuman.eu/doc/questions_europe/qe-129-en.pdf (accessed 5 January 2012).

Mueller, John (1990) *Retreat from Doomsday: The Obsolescence of Major War*. New York, Basic Books.

Mueller, John, (2005) 'The Iraq Syndrome', *Foreign Affairs*, vol. 84, no. 6, pp. 44–54.

Muller, Harald (2003) *Terrorism, Proliferation: A European Threat Assessment*, Chaillot Papers No. 58. Paris, European Union Institute for Security Studies.

National Commission on Terrorist Attacks Upon the United States (2004) *The 9/11 Commission Report: Final Report of the National Commission on Terrorist Attacks Upon the United States*. New York/London, W. W. Norton.

National Intelligence Council (2008) *Global Trends 2025: A Transformed World*. Washington, DC, National Intelligence Council. http://www.dni.gov/nic/PDF_2025/2025_Global_Trends_Final_Report.pdf (accessed 12 October 2011).

NATO (1991) *The Alliance's New Strategic Concept, Agreed by the Heads of State and Government participating in the meeting of the North Atlantic Council in Rome, on 7th–8th November 1991*. http://www.nato.int/docu/comm/49-95/c911107a.htm (accessed 24 November 2006).

NATO (2001) Statement by the North Atlantic Council, Press Release (2001)124, 12 September. http://www.nato.int/docu/pr/2001/p01-124e.htm (accessed 22 May 2006).

NATO (2010a) *Strategic Concept for the Defence and Security of the Members of the North Atlantic Treaty Organisation*, Adopted by Heads of State and Government in Lisbon, 19 November. Brussels, NATO._http://www.nato.int/cps/en/natolive/news_68172.htm (accessed 1 February 2012).

NATO (2010b) *Lisbon Summit Declaration: Issued by the Heads of State and Government participating in the meeting of the North Atlantic Council in Lisbon*, 20 November, Press Release (2010) 155. Brussels, NATO. http://www.nato.int/cps/en/natolive/official_texts_68828.htm?mode=press release (accessed 3 November 2011).

NATO (2011a) ISAF Placemat (as of 20 October 2011), NATO International Security Assistance Force (ISAF) website, http://www.isaf.nato.int/troop-numbers-and-contributions/index.php (accessed 4 December 2011).

NATO (2011b) *NATO achieves first step on theatre ballistic missile defence capability*, 27 January. Brussels, NATO. http://www.nato.int/cps/en/natolive/news_70114.htm (accessed 3 November 2011).

Natural Resources Defense Council (2002) *Table of Global Nuclear Weapons Stockpiles, 1945-2002*. New York: Natural Resources Defense Council. http://www.nrdc.org/nuclear/nudb/datab19.asp (accessed 23 May 2012).

Nelson, Daniel N. (1991) 'Europe's Unstable East', *Foreign Policy*, vol. 82, pp. 137–58.

Neumann, Peter R. (2008) *Joining Al-Qaeda: Jihadist Recruitment in Europe*, Adelphi Paper 399. Abingdon, Routledge for The International Institute for Strategic Studies.

Nicoll, Alexander (2011) 'Fiscal Union by Force', *Survival*, vol. 53, no. 6, pp. 17–36.

Norton-Taylor, Richard (2006) 'Iraq War "Motivated London Bombers"', *The Guardian*, 3 April.

Norton-Taylor, Richard and Travis, Alan (2011) 'Terror Attack in UK Now Less Likely, say Experts', *The Guardian*, 12 July.

Nottebaum, Dennis (2011) *Till Debt Do Us Part? European Integration after the Financial Crisis?*, UIbrief. Stockholm, Swedish Institute of International Affairs. www.ui.se/Files.aspx?f_id=58791 (accessed 1 December 2011).

Nye, Joseph S., Jr. (2000) 'The US and Europe: Continental Drift?', *International Affairs*, vol. 76, no. 1, pp. 51–9.

Nye, Joseph S., Jr. (2002) *The Paradox of American Power: Why the World's Only Superpower Can't Go It Alone*. Oxford, Oxford University Press.

Obama, Barack (2009a) *Remarks by President Barack Obama, Hradcany Square, Prague, Czech Republic*, 5 April. Washington, DC, The White House, Office of the Press Secretary. http://www.whitehouse.gov/the_press_office/Remarks-By-President-Barack-Obama-In-Prague-As-Delivered/ (accessed 27 October 2011).

Obama, Barack (2009b) *Remarks By The President On Strengthening Missile Defense In Europe*, 17 September. Washington, DC, The White House, Office of the Press Secretary. http://www.whitehouse.gov/the-press-office/remarks-president-strengthening-missile-defense-europe (accessed 3 November 2011).

Obama, Barack (2009c) *Remarks by President Barack Obama at Suntory Hall*, Tokyo, Japan, 14 November. Washington, DC, The White House, Office of the Press Secretary. http://www.whitehouse.gov/the-press-office/remarks-president-barack-obama-suntory-hall (accessed 26 January 2012).

Obama, Barack (2009d) *Remarks by the President at the Acceptance of the Nobel Peace Prize, Oslo City Hall, Oslo, Norway*, 10 December. Washington, DC, The White House, Office of the Press Secretary. http://www.whitehouse.gov/the-press-office/remarks-president-acceptance-nobel-peace-prize (accessed 2 December 2011).

Obama, Barack (2011) *Remarks by the President on the Way Forward in Afghanistan*, 22 June. Washington, DC, The White House, Office of the Press Secretary. http://www.whitehouse.gov/the-press-office/2011/06/22/remarks-president-way-forward-afghanistan (accessed 2 December 2011).

O'Hanlon, Michael and Singer, P. W. (2004) 'The Humanitarian Transformation: Expanding Global Intervention Capacity', *Survival*, vol. 46, no. 1, pp. 77–100.

O'Neil, Jim (2001) *Building Better Global Economic BRICS*, Global Economics Paper No. 66. New York, Goldman Sachs. http://www2.goldmansachs.com/our-thinking/brics/building-better.html (accessed 7 October 2011).

Organisation for Economic Co-operation and Development (2003) Trends in International Migration 2003. Paris, OECD. http://www.oecd.org/document/37/0,3746,en_2649_33931_28703185_1_1_1_1,00.html (accessed 22 May 2012).

Organisation for Economic Co-operation and Development (2011a) *Development Co-operation Report 2011*. Paris, Organisation for Economic Co-operation and Development. www.oecd.org/dac/dcr (accessed 21 February 2012).

Organisation for Economic Co-operation and Development (2011b), *International Migration Outlook 2011*. Paris, OECD. http://www.oecd.org/document/40/0,3746,en_2649_37415_48303528_1_1_1_37415,00.html (accessed 22 May 2012).

Ortega, Martin (2002) *Iraq: A European Point of View*, Occasional Paper 40. Paris, European Union Institute for Security Studies.

Overseas Development Institute (2011) *Making the EU's Common Agricultural Policy Coherent with Development Goals*, Briefing Paper 69. London, Overseas Development Institute. http://www.odi.org.uk/resources/docs/7279.pdf (accessed 23 February 2012).

Oxfam International (2002) *Rigged Rules and Double Standards: Trade, Globalisation and The Fight Against Poverty*. Oxford, Oxfam.

Oxford Dictionaries (2011) *Security*. Oxford Dictionaries website: http://oxforddictionaries.com/definition/security (accessed 22 September 2011).

Palme Commission (1982) *Common Security: A Programme for Disarmament*. London, Pan.

Perkovich, George (2003) 'Bush's Nuclear Revolution: A Regime Change in Non-proliferation', *Foreign Affairs*, vol. 82, no. 2, pp. 2–8.

Perkovich, George (2004) *Deconflating 'WMD'*, Published Study No. 17. Stockholm, Weapons of Mass Destruction Commission. http://www.wmdcommission.org/ (accessed 24 November 2006).

Perkovich, George and Acton, James M. (2008) *Abolishing Nuclear Weapons*, Adelphi Paper 396. Abingdon, Routledge for the International Institute for Strategic Studies.

Perlo-Freeman, Sam, Ismail, Olawale, Kelly, Noel and Solmirano, Carina (2010) 'Military Expenditure Date 2000–2009', Appendix 5A in Stockholm International Peace Research Institute, *SIPRI Yearbook 2010: Armaments, Disarmament and International Security*. Oxford, SIPRI/Oxford University Press, pp. 201–42.

Peters, Katharina, Schlamp, Hans-Jurgen and Schmitz, Gregor Peter (2010) 'A Crisis in Trans-Atlantic Relations: Why Obama is Ignoring Europe', *Spiegel Online*, 9 Febuary. http://www.spiegel.de/international/europe/0,1518,676799,00.html (accessed 19 January 2012).

Peterson, John (2004) 'Europe, America, Iraq: Worst Ever, Ever Worsening?', *Journal of Common Market Studies*, vol. 42, Issue s1 (The JCMS Annual Review of the European Union in 2005), pp. 9–26.

Pew Global Attitudes Project (2005) *American Character Gets Mixed Reviews: US Image up Slightly but Still Negative – 16-Nation Pew Global Attitudes Survey*. Washington, DC, Pew Research Center, 23 June. http://pewglobal.org/reports/pdf/247.pdf (accessed 23 May 2006).

Phillips, Leigh (2011) 'Poland warns of war "in 10 years" as EU leaders scramble to contain panic', *euobserver.com*, 14 September. http://euobserver.com/18/113625 (accessed 11 January 2012).

Pirozzi, Nicoletta (2006) *UN Peacekeeping in Lebanon: Europe's Contribution*, European Security Review, No. 30. Brussels, International Security Information Service (ISIS) Europe. http://www.isis-europe.org/ftp/Download/ESR30.Lebanon.pdf (accessed 8 December 2006).

Pomeranz, Kenneth (2001) *The Great Divergence: China, Europe, and the Making of the Modern World Economy*. Princeton, NJ, Princeton University Press.

President of Russia (2008) *The Foreign Policy Concept of the Russian Federation*, 12 July. President of Russia Official Web Portal: http://archive.kremlin.ru/eng/text/docs/2008/07/204750.shtml (accessed 4 January 2012).

President of Russia (2009) *Russia's National Security Strategy to 2020*, 12 May (unofficial English Translation). Rustrans website: http://rustrans.wikidot.com/russia-s-national-security-strategy-to-2020 (accessed 4 January 2012).

Quinlan, Michael (2007–08) 'Abolishing Nuclear Armouries: Policy or Pipedream?', *Survival*, vol. 49, no. 4, pp. 7–16.

Rachman, Gideon (2011) 'Foreign Intervention in Syria?', 24 November, The World – Financial Times blog: http://blogs.ft.com/the-world/2011/11/foreign-intervention-in-syria/#axzz1faeMCLRb (accessed 4 December 2011).

Radovic, Borislav (2005) 'A Brief Retrospective on the Problem of Refugees in the Yugoslav Wars 1991–99', in Goran Opa?ić, Ivana Vidaković and Branko Vujadinovi?, *Living in Post-War Communities*. Belgrade, IAN – International Aid Network, pp. 11–26. http://www.ian.org.yu/publikacije/posleratnezajednice/book/book.pdf (accessed 19 October 2006).

Record, Jeffrey (2003) *Bounding the Global War on Terrorism*. Carlisle, PA, Strategic Studies Institute of the US Army War College. http://www.strategicstudiesinstitute.army.mil/pdffiles/PUB207.pdf (accessed 21 November 2006).

Rees, Wyn (2006) *Transatlantic Counter-Terrorism Cooperation: The New Imperative*. London, Routledge.

Renard, Thomas (2011) *The Treachery of Strategies: A Call for True EU Strategic Partnerships*, Egmont Paper 45. Brussels, Egmont – The Royal Institute for International Relations. http://www.egmontinstitute.be/paperegm/sum/ep45.html (accessed 11 November 2011).

Reuters (2008) 'EU Illegal Immigration Law Faces Knife-edge Vote', Reuters, 17 June. http://uk.reuters.com/article/2008/06/17/uk-eu-immigration-detention-idUKL1772587520080617 (accessed 4 March 2012).

Risse-Kappen, Thomas (1996) 'Identity in a Democratic Security Community: The Case of NATO', in Peter Katzenstein (ed.), *The Culture of National Security*. New York, Columbia University Press, pp. 359–99.

Roberts, Adam (2005) 'The "War on Terror" in Historical Perspective', *Survival*, vol. 47, no. 2, pp. 101–30.

Robertson, Lord George (2003) *NATO's Transformation: Remarks by NATO Secretary-General Lord Roberston at the Geneva Centre for Security Policy*, 13 October. http://www.nato.int/docu/speech/2003/s031013a.htm (accessed 9 December 2006).

Rodham Clinton, Hillary (2011) *America's Pacific Century*, Remarks by the Secretary of State, East-West Center, Honolulu, HI, 10 November 2011. US Department of State website: http://www.state.gov/secretary/rm/2011/11/176999.htm (accessed 23 January 2012).

Rumer, Eugene B. (2007) *Russian Foreign Policy Beyond Putin*, Adelphi Paper 390. Oxford, Routledge for The International Institute for Strategic Studies.

Ruppe, David (2005) 'Biological Terrorism Dangers Overstated, Expert Says', *Global Security Newswire*. Nuclear Threat Initiative website: http://www.nti.org/d_newswire/issues/2005_12_7.html#C03902CA (accessed 1 March 2007).

Russett, Bruce (1982) 'Defense Expenditures and National Well Being', *American Political Science Review*, vol. 76, pp. 767–77.

Russett, Bruce (1993) *Grasping the Democratic Peace: Principles for a Post-Cold War Era*. Princeton, NJ, Princeton University Press.

Russett, Bruce and Oneal, John R. (2001) *Triangulating Peace: Democracy, Interdependence, and International Organizations*. New York, W. W. Norton.

Salmon, Trevor C. (1992) 'Testing Times for European Political Cooperation: The Gulf and Yugoslavia, 1990–1992', *International Affairs*, vol. 68, no. 2, pp 233–53.

Sample, Ian (2003) 'You Ain't Seen Nothing Yet', *The Guardian*, 19 June. http://www.guardian.co.uk/science/2003/jun/19/society.research (accessed 6 October 2011).

Savage, Timothy M. (2004) 'Europe and Islam: Crescent Waxing, Cultures Clashing', *The Washington Quarterly*, vol. 27, no. 3, pp. 25–50.

Schmitt, Burkhard (2003) 'Conclusions', in Mark Smith, Gustav Lindstrom and Burkhard Schmitt (eds), *Fighting Proliferation: European Perspectives*, Chaillot Papers No. 66. Paris, European Union Institute for Security Studies, pp. 89–92.

Schmitt, Burkhard (2005) *Information Security: A New Challenge for the EU*, Chaillot Paper No. 76. Paris, European Union Institute for Security Studies.

Sendagorta, Fidel (2005) 'Jihad in Europe: The Wider Context', *Survival*, vol. 47, no. 3, pp. 63–71.

Shapiro, Jeremy and Suzan, Benedicte (2003) 'The French Experience of Counter-terrorism', *Survival*, vol. 45, no. 1, pp. 67–98.

Shultz, George P., Perry, William J., Kissinger, Henry A. and Nunn, Sam (2007) 'A World Free of Nuclear Weapons', *Wall Street Journal*, 4 January. Hoover Institution, Stanford University. http://www.hoover.org/publications/hoover-digest/article/6109 (accessed 27 October 2011).

Silber, Laura and Little, Allen (1995) *The Death of Yugoslavia*. London, Penguin/BBC Books.

Simms, Brendan (2002) *Unfinest Hour: Britain and the Destruction of Bosnia*. London, Penguin.

Simon, Steven and Benjamin, Daniel (2001–2) 'The Terror', *Survival*, vol. 43, no. 4, pp. 5–18.

Singer, Max and Wildavsky, Aaron (1993) *The Real World Order: Zones of Peace/Zones of Turmoil*. Chatham, NJ, Chatham House.

Sjursen, Helene (2004) 'On the Identity of NATO', *International Affairs*, vol. 80, no. 4, pp. 687–703.

Smith, Mark (1991) *The Soviet Fault Line: Ethnic Insecurity and Territorial*

Dispute in the Former USSR, Whitehall Paper Series. London, Royal United Services Institute for Defence Studies.

Smith, Mark (2010) 'Disarmament in the Anglo-American Context', in Zanders, Jean Pascal, (ed.), *Nuclear Weapons After the 2010 NPT Review Conference*, Chaillot Papers 120. Paris, European Union Institute for Security Studies, pp. 71–86.

Smyth, Jamie (2006) 'EU Faces Challenge to Secure Energy Supplies', *The Irish Times*, 6 January.

Spiegel (2010) 'Merkel Says Future Peace and Prosperity at Stake in Crisis Talks', Spiegel Online, 26 October, http://www.spiegel.de/international/europe/0,1518,794141,00.html (accessed 11 January 2012).

Squires, Nick (2011) 'Libya: Italy Fears 300,000 Refugees', *The Daily Telegraph*, 23 February.

Stack, Liam (2011) 'For Refugees from Syria, a Visit With No Expiration Date', *New York Times*, 14 November. http://www.nytimes.com/2011/11/15/world/middleeast/refugees-from-syria-settle-in-for-long-wait-in-turkey.html?pagewanted=all (accessed 8 March 2012).

Steinberg, James B. (2003) 'An Elective Partnership: Salvaging Transatlantic Relations', *Survival*, vol. 45, no. 2, pp. 113–46.

Stevenson, Jonathan (2004) *Counter-terrorism: Containment and Beyond*, Adelphi Paper 367. Oxford, Oxford University Press for International Institute for Strategic Studies.

Stiglitz, Joseph (2002) *Globalization and its Discontents*. London, Penguin Books.

Stockholm International Peace Research Institute (2010) *SIPRI Yearbook 2010: Armaments, Disarmament and International Security*. Oxford, Oxford University Press.

Strange, Susan (1987) 'The Persistent Myth of Lost Hegemony', *International Organization*, vol. 41, no. 4, pp. 551–74.

Swedish Ministry for Foreign Affairs (1999) *Preventing Violent Conflict: A Swedish Action Plan*. Stockholm, Ministry for Foreign Affairs. http://www.sweden.gov.se/content/1/c6/02/01/61/aad1f9e6.pdf (accessed 9 July 2006).

Swift, Richard (2004) 'The Wild East', *New Internationalist*, April, Issue 366.

Thies, Wallace J. (2009) *Why NATO Endures*. Cambridge, Cambridge University Press.

Tisdall, Simon (2012) 'You've been Romney-ed! Obama must beware GOP foreign policy vortex', *The Guardian*, 15 January. http://www.guardian.co.uk/commentisfree/2012/jan/15/romney-obama-republican-foreign-policy (accessed 19 January 2012).

Tonra, Ben (2001) *The Europeanisation of National Foreign Policy: Dutch, Danish and Irish Foreign Policy in the European Union*. Aldershot, Ashgate.

Townsend, Mark and Harris, Paul (2004) 'Now the Pentagon Tells Bush: Climate Change Will Destroy Us', *The Observer*, 22 February. http://www.

guardian.co.uk/environment/2004/feb/22/usnews.theobserver (accessed 6 October 2011).

Tran, Mark (1999) '"I'm Not Going to Start Third World War for You," Jackson told Clark', *Guardian Unlimited*, 2 August. http://www. guardian. co.uk/Kosovo/Story/0,2763,208120,00.html (accessed 4 December 2006).

Traser, Julianna (2006) *Who's Still Afraid of EU Enlargement?*, 5 September. Brussels, European Citizen Action Service. http://ecas.org/file_uploads/ 1182.pdf (accessed 19 September 2006).

Travis, Alan (2004) 'Muslims Abandon Labour over Iraq War', *The Guardian*, 15 March. http://politics.guardian.co.uk/iraq/story/0,12956,1169486, 00.html (accessed 28 June 2006).

Travis, Alan (2011) 'Air Passenger Data Plans Illegal, Say EU Lawyers', *The Guardian*, 21 June.

Travis, Alan and Norton-Taylor, Richard (2006) 'Evidence Points to al-Qaida Link to 7/7 Bombs', The *Guardian*, 12 May. http://www.guardian.co.uk/ uk/2006/may/12/july7.uksecurity3 (accessed 6 July 2012).

Traynor, Ian, Astill, James and Aglionby, John (2004) 'Secret network passed on nuclear design', *The Guardian*, 6 February.

Trumpet.com (2011) 'Bank warns Eurozone Breakup Could Lead to War or Military Government', TheTrumpet.com, 12 September, http://www. thetrumpet.com/print.php?q=8636.7370.0.0 (accessed 11 January 2012).

Tuchman Mathews, Jessica (1989) 'Redefining Security', *Foreign Affairs*, vol. 68, no. 2, pp. 162–77.

UK Ministry of Defence (1998) *Strategic Defence Review: Modern Forces for a Modern World*. London, Ministry of Defence.

Ulgen, Sinan ((2010) *Turkey's Shifting Foreign Policy: What Next?*, Carnegie Europe, Carnegie Endowment for International Peace, July 14. http:// carnegieeurope.eu/publications/?fa=41198 (accessed 23 September 2011).

UNAIDS (2004) 2004 *Report on the Global AIDS Epidemic: Executive Summary*. Geneva, UNAIDS – Joint United Nations Programme on HIV/AIDS. http://data.unaids.org/Global-Reports/Bangkok-2004/unaids bangkokpress/gar2004html/execsummaryen/ExecSumm_en.htm#TopOf Page (accessed 22 May 2012).

Underhill, William (2009) 'Why Fears of a Muslim Takeover are All Wrong', *The Daily Beast (Newsweek)*, 10 July. http://www.thedailybeast.com/ newsweek/2009/07/10/why-fears-of-a-muslim-takeover-are-all- wrong.print.html (accessed 14 December 2011).

United Nations (1945) *Charter of the United Nations*. http://www.un.org/ aboutun/charter/ index.html (accessed 28 March 2006).

United Nations (2003) *Report of the Secretary-General: Implementation of the United Nations Millennium Declaration*, 2 September, UN General Assembly, Fifty-Eighth Session, A/58/323. New York, United Nations. UN website:http://www.un.org/millenniumgoals/sgreport2003.pdf? OpenElement (accessed 1 March 2007).

United Nations (2004) *A More Secure World: Our Shared Responsibility: Report of the Secretary-General's High-Level Panel on Threats, Challenges and Change*, 2 December, UN General Assembly, A/59/565. New York, United Nations. http://www.un.org/secureworld/report.pdf (accessed 21 November 2006).

United Nations (2005) *2005 World Summit Outcome*, United Nations General Assembly A/60/L.1, 15 September. New York, United Nations. http://daccessdds.un.org/doc/UNDOC/GEN/N05/487/60/PDF/N0548760.pdf?OpenElement (accessed 1 March 2007).

United Nations (2010) *World Population Prospects the 2010 Revision.* New York: United Nations Department of Economic and Social Affairs, Population Division. http://esa.un.org/unpd/wpp/ (accessed 23 May 2012).

United Nations High Commissioner for Refugees (2004) *2004 UNHCR Statistical Yearbook: Country Data Sheets.* Geneva, UNHCR. http://www.unhcr.org/statistics (accessed 19 October 2006).

United Nations High Commissioner for Refugees (2011) *UNHCR Statistical Yearbook 2010 – Statistical Annex.* Geneva, United Nations High Commissioner for Refugees. http://www.unhcr.org/4ef9c7269.html (accessed 4 March 2012).

United Nations Security Council (2011) *Resolution 1973 (2011) Adopted by the Security Council at its 6498th meeting, on 17 March 2011.* New York: United Nations. http://daccess-dds-ny.un.org/doc/UNDOC/GEN/N11/268/39/PDF/N1126839.pdf?OpenElement (accessed 2 December 2011).

United States (2002) *The National Security Strategy of the United States of America.* http://georgewbush-whitehouse.archives.gov/nsc/nss/2002/ (accessed 6 October 2011).

United States (2006) *The National Security Strategy of the United States of America.* http://georgewbush-whitehouse.archives.gov/nsc/nss/2006/ (accessed 6 October 2011).

United States (2010) *The National Security Strategy of the United States of America.* http://www.whitehouse.gov/sites/default/files/rss_viewer/national_security_strategy.pdf (accessed 6 October 2011).

US Commission on National Security in the 21st Century (1999) *New World Coming: American Security in the 21st Century – The Phase I Report on the Emerging Global Security Environment for the First Quarter of the 21st Century.* http://govinfo.library.unt.edu/nssg/Reports/NWC.pdf (accessed 22 May 2012).

US Department of Defense (2006) *Quadrennial Defense Review Report.* Washington, DC, Department of Defense. http://www.defense.gov/qdr/report/report20060203.pdf (accessed 5 October 2011).

US Department of State (nd) *Article-by-Article Analysis of the New START Treaty Documents*, http://www.state.gov/documents/organization/142041.pdf.

van de Linde, Erik, O'Brien, Kevin, Lindstrom, Gustav, De Spiegeleire, Stephan and Vayrynen, Mikko (2002) *Quick Scan of Post-9/11 National Counter-terrorism Policymaking and Implementation in Selected European Countries*, Research Project for the Netherlands Ministry of Justice, MR-1590. Leiden, RAND Europe. http://www.rand.org/pubs/monograph_reports/2005/MR1590.pdf (accessed 29 May 2006).

Van Evera, Stephen (1990–1) 'Primed for Peace: Europe After the Cold War', *International Security*, vol. 15, no. 3, pp. 7–57.

Vilnius Group (2003) 'Statement of the Vilnius Group Countries in Response to the Presentation by the United States Secretary of State to the United Nations Security Council Concerning Iraq, 5 February 2003', in Antonio Missiroli, (ed.), *From Copenhagen to Brussels: European Defence: Core Documents*, Chaillot Papers 67. Paris, European Union Institute for Security Studies, p. 345.

Volker, Kurt (2010) 'The "Obama effect" has been to lay bare deep transatlantic tensions', *Europe's World*, Spring. http://www.europesworld.org/NewEnglish/Home_old/Article/tabid/191/ArticleType/articleview/ArticleID/21568/Default.aspx (accessed 8 November 2011).

Waever, Ole, Buzan, Barry, Kelstrup, Morten, and Lemaitre, Pierre (1993) *Identity, Migration and the New Security Agenda*. London, Pinter.

Wallensteen, Peter and Axell, Karin (1993) 'Armed Conflict at the End of the Cold War, 1989–92', *Journal of Peace Research*, vol. 30, no. 3, pp. 331–46.

Walt, Stephen M. (1991) 'The Renaissance of Security Studies', *International Studies Quarterly*, vol. 35, no. 2, pp. 211–39.

Walt, Stephen M. (1997) 'Why Alliances Endure or Collapse', *Survival*, vol. 39, no. 1, pp. 156–79.

Waltz, Kenneth N. (1979) *Theory of International Politics*. New York, McGraw-Hill.

Waltz, Kenneth N. (1993) 'The Emerging Structure of International Politics', *International Security*, vol. 18, no. 2.

Weiner, Myron (1995) *The Global Migration Crisis: Challenge to States and to Human Rights*. New York, HarperCollins College Publishers.

Weisbrode, Kenneth (2001) *Central Eurasia: Prize or Quicksand? Contending Views of Instability in Karabakh, Ferghana and Afghanistan*, Adelphi Paper No. 338. Oxford, Oxford University Press for The International Institute for Strategic Studies.

Weiss, Thomas G. (2004) 'The Sunset of Humanitarian Intervention? The Responsibility to protect in a Unipolar Era', *Security Dialogue*, vol. 35, no. 2, pp. 135–53.

Weiss, Thomas G. (2005) *Military–Civilian Interactions: Humanitarian Crises and the Responsibility to Protect*, 2nd edn. Lanham, Rowman & Littlefield.

Weitz, Richard (2005) *Revitalising US–Russian Security Cooperation*, Adelphi Paper 377. Abingdon, Routledge for International Institute for Strategic Studies.

Weitz, Richard (2010) 'Illusive Visions and Practical Realities: Russia, NATO and Missile Defence', *Survival*, vol. 52, no. 4, pp. 99–120.

Wheeler, N. J. (2000) *Saving Strangers: Humanitarian Intervention in International Society*. Oxford, Oxford University Press.

Whitlock, Craig and Smiley, Shannon (2005) 'Germans Arrest 22 in Anti-Terror Raids', *The Washington Post*, 13 January. Reproduced on Global Policy Forum website: http://www.globalpolicy.org/empire/terrorwar/analysis/2005/1013german.htm (accessed 17 January 2005).

Whitman, Richard G. and Juncos, Ana E. (2011) 'Relations with the Wider Europe', *Journal of Common Market Studies*, 49, S1(Annual Review), pp. 187–208.

Wilkinson, Paul (2000) *Terrorism versus Democracy: The Liberal State Response*. London, Frank Cass.

Wilkinson, Paul (2005) *International Terrorism: The Changing Threat and the EU's Response*, Chaillot Paper No. 84. Paris, European Union Institute for Security Studies.

Willerton, John P. and Cokerham, Geoffrey (2003) 'Russia, the CIS and Eurasian Interconnections', in James Sperling, Sean Kay and S. Victor Papacosma, *Limiting Institutions? The Challenge of Eurasian Security Governance*. Manchester/New York, Manchester University Press, pp. 185–207.

Wilson, Dominic and Purushothaman, Roopa (2003) *Dreaming With BRICs: The Path to 2050*, Global Economics Paper No. 99. New York: Goldman Sachs. http://www2.goldmansachs.com/our-thinking/brics/brics-dream.html (accessed 7 October 2011).

Wimmer, Andreas (2003–4) 'Democracy and Ethno-religious Conflict in Iraq', *Survival*, vol. 45, no. 4, pp. 111–34.

Wolf, Martin (2011) 'In the grip of a great convergence', *The Financial Times*, 4 January.

Wohlfeld, Monika (1997) *The Effects of Enlargement on Bilateral Relations in Central and Eastern Europe*, Chaillot Papers 26. Paris, Institute for Security Studies of Western European Union.

Wolfers, Arnold (1962) *Discord and Collaboration: Essays on International Politics*. Baltimore, MD, Johns Hopkins University Press.

Wolff, Stefan (2011) 'The regional dimensions of state failure', *Review of International Studies*, vol. 37, no. 3, pp. 951–72.

Woodall, Pam (2006) 'The New Titans: A Survey of the World Economy', *The Economist*, 16 September.

Woodward, Bob (2010) *Obama's Wars*. New York: Simon & Schuster.

Woollacott, Martin (2005) 'A Bigger Threat Than the Bomb', *The Guardian*, 13 May.

World Bank (2005) *Dying Too Young: Addressing Premature Mortality and Ill Health Due to Non-Communicable Diseases in the Russian Federation*. World Bank, Human Development Department, Europe and Central Asia. http://www_wds.worldbank.org/servlet/WDSContentServer?WDSP/IB/20

06/02/10/000160016_20060210125603/Rendered/PDF/323770v10RU0
Wh1ung1Summary01PUBLIC1.pdf (accessed 15 February 2006).

World Health Organization (WHO) (2005) *Climate and Health Fact Sheet*.
Geneva, World Health Organization. http://www.who.int/globalchange/
news/fsclimandhealth/en/print.html (accessed 22 May 2006).

Yost, David S. (1998) *NATO Transformed: The Alliance's New Roles in
International Security*. Washington, DC, United States Institute of Peace
Press.

Yost, David S. (1999) *The US and Nuclear Deterrence in Europe*, Adelphi
Paper 326. Oxford, Oxford University Press for International Institute for
Strategic Studies.

Yost, David S. (2005) 'France's Evolving Nuclear Strategy', *Survival*, vol. 47,
no. 3, pp. 117–46.

Younge, Gary (2005) 'US Reaction: Newspapers Warn of Threat to America
from "Londonistan"', *The Guardian*, 12 July.

Zakaria, Fareed (1997) 'The Rise of Illiberal Democracy', *Foreign Affairs*,
vol. 76, no. 6, pp. 22–43.

Zakaria, Fareed (2003) *The Future of Freedom: Illiberal Democracy at Home
and Abroad*. New York, W. W. Norton.

Zakaria, Fareed (2009) *The Post-American World and the Rise of the Rest*.
London, Penguin.

Zartman, I. William and Kremenyuk, Victor A. (eds) (1995) *Cooperative
Security: Reducing Third World Wars*. Syracuse, NY, Syracuse University
Press.

Zelikow, Philip D. and Rice, Condoleezza (1995) *Germany Unified and
Europe Transformed: A Study in Statecraft*. Cambridge, MA, Harvard
University Press.

Zielonka, Jan (2006) *Europe as Empire: The Nature of the Enlarged European
Union*. Oxford, Oxford University Press.

Index